Arms for Spain

ALSO BY GERALD HOWSON

The Flamencos of Cádiz Bay

Thief-Taker General—The Rise and Fall of Jonathan Wild
(republished as *It Takes a Thief*)

*The Macaroni Parson—The Life of the
Unfortunate Doctor Dodd*

Burgoyne of Saratoga

Aircraft of the Spanish Civil War, 1936–1939

Arms for Spain

The Untold Story of the
Spanish Civil War

GERALD HOWSON

St. Martin's Press
New York

ISBN 0-312-24177-1

First published in Great Britain by John Murray (Publishers) Ltd.

First U.S. Edition: November 1999

10 9 8 7 6 5 4 3 2 1

For my grandchildren,
Thomas and
Eva Rosalind Titherington

Contents

Acknowledgements

To:

The Cañada Blanch Foundation for the senior fellowship (1991–2), which enabled me to carry out research in Amsterdam and Madrid, and for subsequent assistance in obtaining essential documents from Spain and France.

TV-3 de Catalunya SA, Barcelona, and Sra. María-Dolors Genovès, their Head of Special Programmes, for supplying me with some 200 photocopies of documents in the Russian State Military Archives and for their permission to use them. Sra. Genovès obtained them, with many hundreds of other papers relating to the Spanish gold reserve sent to the USSR in 1936, for the purpose of making her documentary film *L'or de Moscou* ('The Gold of Moscow'), which was transmitted by TV-3 de Catalunya in 1994. The documents concerning arms supplies have made a contribution of central importance to this book. My special thanks to Sra. Genovès in person for the many hours she spent in helping me to select the documents I needed.

Mr Andrzej Suchcitz, Keeper of Archives at the Polish Institute and Sikorski Museum, London, for his advice and help in searching out the SEPEWE file and the reports of Major Kedzior, the Polish military attaché in Lisbon during the Spanish Civil War period, and to the Polish Institute for permission to use the documents obtained.

Professor Marian Zgorniak, of Kraków University, for permission to use his published article 'Wojna Domowa w Hispanii w Oswietlienu Polskiego . . .' in *Studia Historyczne*, vol. XXV (1983), on which Appendix II is based.

Elena Burnett and my son Robert, for translating the Russian documents; Pawel Swieboda, for translating the Polish documents.

James Carmody, for assistance too constant and multifarious to itemize, but especially for his help in searching through Lloyd's lists and sorting out shipping voyages during the Spanish Civil War period, a task of fear-some complexity and tediousness.

Ian V. Hogg and Rafael Varo Estacio for their tireless patience in giving me information and advice relating to the history and technicalities of armaments. To Sr. Varo too for his generous hospitality during my visits to Madrid.

Carlos Lázaro Avila for his invaluable help in facilitating access to the Archivo del Ministerio del Aire at Villavicioso de Odón, and for other assistance.

Richard Sanders Allen and Dr Richard K. Smith for supplying copies and digests of State Department records and other papers and related material in the USA, as well as for their valuable comments and advice.

Mme Bernadette Suau, Director of the Archives Départementales de la Haute-Garonne, Toulouse, for supplying photocopies of documents in the Archives, Sr. José Falco San Martín for his help in this matter, and to Julia Farrer and Françoise Vernotte for translating my application and letters into acceptable French.

Sofía and Tom Entwistle for their generous hospitality during my stay in Madrid in October 1992.

Eric Taylor, for easing the difficulties of my trip to Amsterdam, and Margriet and Bram van Mills for their generous hospitality throughout my stay there.

William Green, for constant help and advice on aeronautical matters, and Dr Michael Alpert for supplying numerous items of information.

Dr Thanasis D. Sfikas for information on Greek arms shipments.

Dr Enrique Moradiellos, for information and advice.

Professor Paul Preston, for frequent practical help and advice.

Dr Angel Viñas, for help which has been of vital importance to my research.

Sir Raymond Carr and Lord Hugh Thomas of Swynnerton, for their support and encouragement.

The following, in alphabetical order, for providing information, advice or assistance, or all three: Neal Ascherson, Juan Avilés Farré, Sebastian Balfour, Patrick Burke, Herschel B. Chipp, Major J. Chmielewski, Stuart Christie, Sam Cummings of Interarms, Jerzy Cynk, Len Deighton, Luis Ferrao, Dr Helen Graham, Bill Gunston, Dr Francisco Xavier Hidalgo, Augusto Lecha Vilasuso, Joaquín Maluquer Wahl, Justo Miranda and Paula Mercado, Vincent Piatti, Dr Anita Prasmovska, General Jesús Salas Larrazábal, Tom Sarbaugh, Frank Schauff, Peter Selz, Nigel Townson, Colonel José Warleta.

A Note on Money

Because the arms trade in the 1930s was no less international than it is now, the number of currencies that appear in this book is large. I have therefore put in brackets behind each sum mentioned its equivalents in US dollars and of British pounds, shillings and pence as they stood at the particular date. For convenience, I have used $5 to £1 throughout, as the exchange rate hovered around that figure during the period of 1936–9. Younger British, and all non-British, readers should remember that there were 20 shillings (s.) in £1 and twelve pence (d.) in 1 shilling. On 26 September 1936 the French franc (Ffr.) was devalued from 76 to £1 to 104, and by December it dropped to 105. The conversions are only a rough guide, however, for in their dealings arms traders seem often to have set their own exchange rates. Moreover, government ministers or military chiefs-of-staff and the like, when accepting bribes or 'commissions' in return for approving illegal arms exports to Republican Spain, could, and usually did, extort exchange rates more favourable to themselves and then demand payment in another foreign currency, usually in American dollars or sterling.

I have made no attempt to translate the prices into those of the 1990s, since the increases would vary enormously, some by a factor of between ten and thirty, others by more than a thousand.

The exchange rates are those quoted in the British newspapers, usually *The Times*, of 1936–9 and in such books as *Keesing's Contemporary Archives* and *Whitaker's Almanack*.

The Division of Spain, 1 August 1936

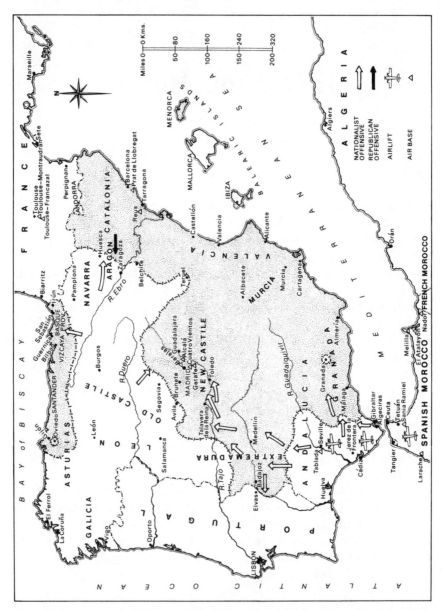

Note: Franco's Army of Africa, airlifted from Spanish Morocco, advanced rapidly northwards and linked up with Mola's forces in Extremadura. The combined Nationalist armies converged on Madrid, whose outskirts they reached on 4 November.

The Division of Spain, 1937–8

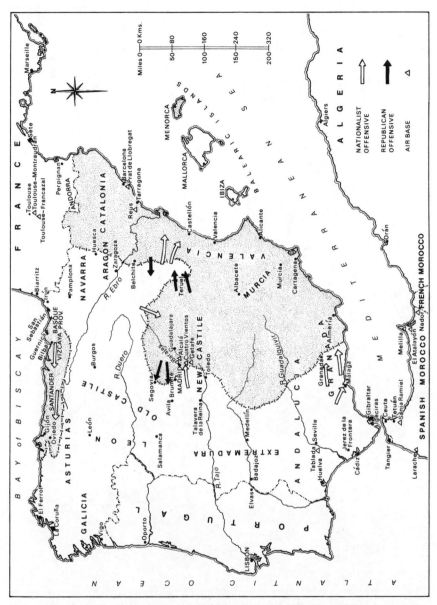

Note: The Nationalists' unsuccessful attempts to capture Madrid ended with the defeat of the Italian motorized divisions north of Guadalajara in March 1937. The Nationalists then concentrated their attacks on the Basque–Asturian enclave in the north, overrunning it completely by the end of October. The Republicans tried, in vain, to relieve pressure on the northern zone by offensives at Segovia, Brunete (Madrid), Belchite (Zaragoza) and Huesca. In December they attacked and captured Teruel, only to lose it again in February 1938.

The Division of Spain, 1938–9

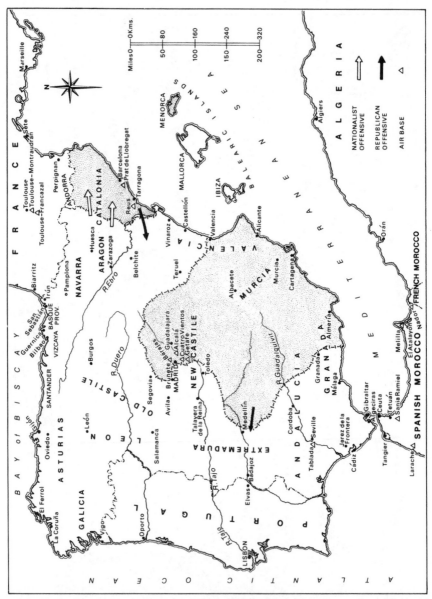

Note: On 9 March 1938, the Nationalists opened a major offensive in Aragón. They reached the Mediterranean coast on 16 April and separated Catalonia from the main Republican zone. The Republicans attacked across the Ebro river on 25 July. The battle continued until 15 November, when the last Republican troops withdrew back across the river. On 23 December, the Nationalists began their attack on Catalonia, reaching the French frontier on 9 February 1939. The Republicans mounted an offensive in Extremadura. The war, however, ended with the surrender of the Republic on 31 March 1939.

I

Contrasts

O N 17 AND 18 July 1936 several thousand Spanish army officers and their regiments proclaimed rebellion and a state of war against the Popular Front government of the Spanish Republic. They were assisted by a large section of the police and by various organizations of the political right, including a Monarchist and a Fascist party, and they had the support of the aristocracy, the wealthy classes and the Catholic Church, as well as of many of the peasants in those regions of Spain which were ardently royalist.

In their broadcast manifesto they accused the government of incompetence and treason. 'The situation in Spain is becoming more critical with every day that passes; anarchy reigns in most of her villages and fields, and government-appointed authorities preside over the tumults, when they are not actually fomenting them.' It went on to depict a Motherland torn apart by revolutionary chaos, unceasing strikes, bombings, gunfights and assassinations, where churches and their artistic treasures were burnt, the clergy persecuted, the armed services calumniated, the independence of the judiciary subverted and the masses 'hoaxed by Soviet agents who veil the bloody reality of a regime that has already sacrificed twenty-five million lives in order to exist'. All Spaniards must therefore gird themselves to 'wage war without quarter on the exploiters of politics, on the deceivers of the honest worker, and on the foreigners and foreignly inclined people who are openly or deceitfully attempting to destroy Spain'.

There was no mention of a return of the monarchy or call for the creation of a corporate Fascist state; indeed, apart from the reordered slogan 'Fraternity, Liberty, Equality!' there was no political programme mentioned at all. Nor, for that matter, were enemies other than Soviet agents clearly identified. In their later pronouncements, however, the rebels were more specific. Spain was in the front line of a titanic struggle between Christian civilization and an unholy alliance of Bolsheviks, Freemasons,

Jews and international financiers, who had already conquered one sixth of the surface of the globe. Since the rebellion was a crusade to defend the true Spanish Nation against this conspiracy and all the alien, un-Spanish heresies of atheism, materialism and the like that it brought with it, the rebels called themselves 'Nationalists' and all who opposed or were luke-warm towards them, for whatever reasons, 'Reds'.

In 1931 King Alfonso XIII had gone into exile and Spain had become a Republic. The difficulties facing the new government, which contained a high proportion of distinguished academics, writers and liberal intellectu-als, were enormous. Every travel book described Spain as 'a land of con-trasts', the only assertion about Spain and Spaniards upon which there was universal agreement. Madrid contained more buildings in the ultra-modern style than London, and when its new airport at Barajas was opened Croydon airport would resemble the air terminal of a second-class Balkan state by comparison.* Yet an hour away were villages which had hardly changed since the fall of the Roman empire; indeed, their hovels were perhaps more wretched in 1931 than they had been in AD 431. During sowing and harvest times, the estates of a duke or a marquis who might own a castle, a palace, three country houses, a house in Madrid, a flat in Monte Carlo, two private aeroplanes and six Rolls-Royces, and enjoy an income of about 25,000 pesetas (£1,000 in 1931) a day all the year round, were worked by *braceros*, or landless peasants, who owned nothing, earned 2.5 pesetas a day for five months of the year and had no employment or wages during the rest.

Spanish artists, writers and musicians – Picasso, Grís, Miró, Dalí, Lorca, Buñuel, Gómez de la Serna (a surrealist before Surrealism had been invented), the Machado brothers, de Falla, Casals – were at the head of the European cultural avant-garde but came from a country where more than half the population was completely illiterate. Not far from the biggest complex of textile factories in Europe, penitents in the Easter processions flagellated themselves with barbed thongs; yet, sixty miles from the University of Salamanca, one of the great institutions of Christendom,

---

* Unfavourable comparisons of Croydon to modern European and American airports can be found, in this exact wording, in several articles in *The Aeroplane* and *Flight*, the leading aeronautical journals in Britain between the wars. Barajas was never completed according to its original plan, for by July 1936 only one large modern hangar and one or two steel-and-glass control buildings had been finished. They were heavily damaged in the civil war. Barajas was the base for the state airline LAPE (Líneas Aéreas Postales Españoles), created in 1931. In order for LAPE to establish a monopoly over air services between the capital and foreign destinations, in 1932 work began on an international airport, to be used by foreign airlines only, at Villafría, 6 km north of Burgos. It was used by the Condor Legion bomber group K88 during the Basque–Asturian campaign in 1937, and after the war the project for an international airport at Burgos was cancelled.

were mountain villages whose inhabitants had not been converted from paganism to Christianity until the beginning of the 20th century. Spaniards, in many ways the kindest of people, regarded bullfighting as a performance art akin to acting or ballet, in a western Europe where bear-baiting and dog-fighting had been outlawed for nearly a century. Spain was a byword for creaking autocracy in government, yet its political life was a seething cauldron of ideas and in that respect more vigorous than that of Britain or any other Western nation. To the new parliament, the Cortes, were elected deputies from no fewer than twenty-six political parties and, if one took in as well the ideologies not represented in parliament, Spanish political life could be seen to cover the whole spectrum of concepts then in existence, from the most backward-looking to the most future-oriented.

Beginning at the extreme right with the Carlists, who believed in an absolute monarchy deriving its legitimacy from God, the spectrum passed through constitutional monarchists, Catholics, militarists, Fascists (after 1933), conservatives, moderate conservatives, right, centre and left Republicans, Radicals and Radical Socialists, moderate Socialists, Social Democrats, left-wing Socialists, two small and mutually hostile parties of Stalinist and anti-Stalinist Communists, and ended with Anarcho-Syndicalists and pure Anarchists on the extreme left, who believed in no government at all and claimed more than a million enthusiastic followers.

The Republican government embarked on a programme of reforms intended to change Spain into a modern and progressive democracy. Its enlightened constitution, written under the supervision of a world-famous penologist, don Luis Jiménez de Asúa, even contained a clause in which Spain renounced war as an instrument of foreign policy. Except in a tiny number of free institutes, education had hitherto been the privilege of the rich and been controlled by the Church, which received a sizeable annual grant from the state. The grant was cancelled and the money used to build secular schools in every province, 7,000 being completed in the first year. Divorce was to be allowed and freedom of expression and opinion guaranteed for the first time in Spanish history. The army, with its 800 generals on full pay, had to be pruned. Some system of providing fair wages and of alleviating the poverty of the millions of agricultural workers and peasants had to be established.

Not surprisingly, these measures outraged the Church, the military and the possessing classes, who opposed them by every means they could devise, fair or foul. The government, lacking the financial resources and political muscle to enforce its will, hesitated, whereupon militants of the left, especially the Socialists and the Anarchists, tried to goad it back into activity by means of strikes, riots and burning down churches – an anti-clerical gesture which had been popular among revolutionaries in Spain for a century. The government, goaded, introduced measures, including a minimum wage, intended to give the *braceros* some means of sustenance during their months of unemployment. The landowners refused to carry them out and, when the agricultural unions called strikes, summoned the Civil Guard. There were shootings, people were killed, mutual aggression intensified, there were more shootings and more people were killed. Then at a political meeting in Bilbao two Socialist and two Republican deputies of the Cortes were murdered by right-wing gunmen. In August 1932 General Sanjurjo, a hero of the Moroccan war of 1909–27 and a monarchist leader, attempted a military coup. It failed, and he and his associates went to prison. In January 1933 the CNT (Confederación Nacional del Trabajo), the Anarchist trade union, called for revolution. The revolts were repressed quickly, but in the village of Casas Viejas, near Cádiz, an elderly anarchist, with his family and a group of *braceros*, barricaded himself into a building and refused to surrender. The police set the building on fire and those *braceros* who were not shot as they ran out were burnt alive inside. Twenty-five villagers were killed.

As the disturbances increased, a right-wing government under Alejandro Lerroux, an old Radical turned opportunist, was elected in September 1933 to restore order and dismantle the reforms. General Sanjurjo was released and went to live in Portugal. Wage cuts, the introduction of laws to reduce the legal rights of the labour organizations, a moratorium on school-building, the admission into the cabinet of the powerful new Catholic-right party the CEDA (Confederación Española de Derechas Autónomas), which had been created to defend the 'persecuted Church', and the creation of the Falange, a Fascist party, provoked an armed uprising by Asturian miners in the north and an attempt at secession by Catalonia; for, to add to Spain's many troubles, the Basques and Catalans had long been agitating for independence. Both were quelled, but at the cost of 4,000 lives and 30,000 imprisoned, including members of the previous government, the leaders of the trade unions, the Catalan regional government and those army and air force officers and men who had refused to take part in the Asturian repression. With the left in disarray, the landowners hammered home their advantage. Wages were cut still further, thousands of agricultural workers were sacked and evicted from their homes for being unable to pay their rents, all workers known to have been affiliated to the CNT were forbidden employment, plans were drawn up to introduce compulsory identity cards showing the holders' work records, and in Berlin the Spanish ambassador was instructed to seek formal co-operation between the Gestapo and the Spanish police in combating 'Communist subversion'. Even the leader of the Falange, José Antonio Primo de Rivera, was shocked by this 'unChristian' behaviour, and in July 1935 told parliament that life in the countryside had become 'absolutely intolerable':

> Yesterday I was in the province of Seville. In that province there is a village called Vadolatosa, where the women leave their homes at three in the morning to gather chickpeas. They end this work at noon, after a nine-hour day, which cannot be prolonged for technical reasons. And for this labour these women receive one peseta.[1]

By the winter of 1935 financial scandals, as so often happens with governments of this character, had discredited Lerroux and his colleagues, and a general election was called for 16 February 1936. To defeat the right, the parties of the left and centre formed a 'Popular Front'. This name had been coined in Moscow at the 7th World Congress of the Third International, or Comintern, in 1935. Stalin, alarmed by the growing power and aggressiveness of Nazi Germany, wanted a rapprochement with the Western democracies. In future elections in democratic countries, Communists should therefore support at the polls any parties, no matter how 'bourgeois', that were willing to make common cause against Fascism. 'World Revolution' and 'Dictatorship of the Proletariat' were to be removed from the agenda indefinitely, since the Communists were now supporting the parliamentary democracy system they had been denouncing as a fraud since the days of Marx. Indeed, they went further: any Popular Front seeking election need not even include Socialism in its programme.

The Popular Front coalition of centre and left parties won the election by a majority so narrow that the right, which had itself been guilty of much electoral chicanery and intimidation, denounced it as invalid. Nevertheless, it formed a government, containing no Socialists or Communists (who were one of the smallest political parties in Spain at that time), and one of its first actions was to send the army generals most likely to attempt a military coup to faraway garrisons where, it was hoped, they could do least harm. General Franco, the chief-of-staff who had put down the Asturian rising with chilling brutality, was appointed military governor of the Canary Islands, General Goded was sent to the Balearic Islands and General Mola to Pamplona in Navarra, but their distance from the capital merely enabled them to plan their coup in greater secrecy.

Meanwhile, violence flared up again. Demanding the immediate restoration of higher pay, industrial and agricultural workers began a wave of strikes. Landowners clubbed together, refused to increase pay by a single *real* (farthing) and threatened to kill any landowner who did so. A few bravely defied the threat. Convinced that they would never obtain justice from a bourgeois government, bands of peasants moved on to great estates and declared themselves 'free collectives'. Militants of the left fought running battles with militants of the right, attacking one another's party and trade union headquarters and newspaper offices. Young hotheads from the Falange tried to assassinate Jiménez de Asúa, author of the Republican constitution, and the leaders of the Falange were imprisoned to prevent a repetition. Hundreds of churches were set on fire, 160 of them burnt to the ground. According to the CEDA leader, Gil Robles, between 16 February and 15 June alone there were no fewer than 269 murders (about 16 every week), most of them political.

Especially damaging to the Popular Front was the open breach between the two wings of the Socialist Party (PSOE), who, if unified, would have been the strongest political body in Spain, with more than 2 million members. The moderate, or right, wing, led by Indalecio Prieto, believed in achieving socialism by legal and parliamentary methods. The left wing, led by Francisco Largo Caballero, who had been chief of the General Workers' Union (UGT), argued that the power of vested interest in Spain made this impossible and that revolution by the organized masses was the only way forward. Quarrels raised passions to such an extent that at one meeting at Ecija, near Seville, in May 1936, Prieto and two of the leaders of the Asturian miners, who had been released from prison by the Popular Front, were fired on by 'Caballeristas'. Largo Caballero, who was being hailed as 'the Spanish Lenin' on account of his revolutionary speeches, was suddenly discomfited from the rear, however, when, without warning, the Socialist Youth movement united itself with the Communist Youth, a development which the right saw as ominous to the point of provocation.

The effect of all this was to paralyse the government. Unable to judge whether the greater threat was coming at it from the right or the left, it dared not take strong action against the extreme left for fear of unleashing a general but disorganized revolt that would bring everything down in a chaos of bloodshed and ruin, yet ignored warnings that a military coup was imminent. Thus, when it was found that two previously unarmed Fokker F.VII trimotor trainers at Alcalá de Henares military flying school had been surreptitiously fitted with bomb-racks and machine-guns, and that other weapons were hidden in the hangar, in obvious preparation for a military coup, the two large aircraft and the weapons were simply transferred to the safer airfield at Getafe, and no action was taken against the officers at the school.[2]

Reciprocal killing reached a shameful climax when Lieutenant Castillo of the Assault Guards (a corps created to defend the Republic) was murdered by Falangists on 11 July and the monarchist leader Calvo Sotelo, who had already been threatened in the Cortes, was murdered no less brutally in reprisal the following night. The murder of Calvo Sotelo was often cited in later years as the conclusive justification for the Nationalist uprising. In fact, the plans were already complete by then and all that remained to be fixed was the date. What the murder did do was to remove the last differences between the main groups of rebels and the monarchists, whose leaders, weeping and kissing the royal flag, swore that they would never rest until this crime had been avenged and Spain saved. It also removed the last hope of conciliation between the rebels and the government.

2

'The Time of Chaos'

THE REVOLT BEGAN in Spanish Morocco, which the colonial 'Army of Africa' subdued during the night of 17–18 July. The Canary Islands were seized next day and their military governor, General Francisco Franco, flew, in a de Havilland Dragon Rapide which had been hired for the purpose at Croydon airport, London, to Spanish Morocco to take command, arriving at Tetuán early on 19 July. Similarly, General Goded took control of the Balearic Islands, except Menorca, and flew off with a squadron of flying boats to lead the uprising in Barcelona.

In Spain itself, the rebellion did not go so well. For one thing, the garrisons acted with little co-ordination or sense of urgency, some rising at dawn on 18 July, others in the afternoon, others not until the 19th, a Sunday, and others not until the 20th. It was therefore fortunate for the rebels, or Nationalists, that the government acted with even less decisiveness. President Manuel Azaña, who had dealt with all warnings of a military uprising by refusing to believe them, succumbed to despair at the very moment resolute leadership was most needed. Prime Minister Casares Quiroga suffered bouts of near hysteria, screaming and shouting orders which he countermanded minutes later. One of his follies was to send the director-general of aeronautics, General Nuñez de Prado, to Zaragoza to persuade General Cabanellas, a Republican who had nonetheless joined the rebellion, to change his mind. As soon as they landed, Nuñez de Prado, his aide and his pilot were arrested for 'treason' and later they were shot. This loss deprived the Republican air force of one of its ablest commanders and, in addition, presented the Nationalists with a militarized Dragon Rapide, one of three recently delivered to the Aviación Militar.

The most agonizing dilemma facing the government was whether or not to distribute arms to the thousands of trade union militants who were clamouring for them. With most of the army and police on the side of the rebels, who would defend the Republic? Yet the apprehension, amounting to terror, of the cabinet was that once given arms the masses would become uncontrollable and go on a rampage of indiscriminate massacres. Casares Quiroga resigned, and a second government was appointed under Martínez Barrio; but since he had been right-hand man to the disgraced Lerroux, threatening crowds gathered outside the ministerial buildings roaring 'Traitor!' This government resigned after failing to come to terms with General Mola, who had risen at the head of 6,000 Carlists in Pamplona, and a third, under Giral, a former lawyer and journalist, took office late on 19 July. Arms were distributed to the people and what had been most feared happened. The surrender of the regiments in the Montaña barracks in Madrid next morning was followed by a slaughter of the officers and many of the men. The government lost its authority and power passed to self-appointed 'Anti-Fascist Militia Committees', who set up road-blocks and began house-to-house searches through the better residential districts in search of 'class enemies'. In Barcelona, General Goded arrived shortly before the revolt was overwhelmed by the combined forces of the loyal Civil Guards, Assault Guards and thousands of armed men and women of the CNT, the Communist Party, the POUM (Partido Obrero de Unificación Marxista – i.e., anti-Stalinist Marxists similar, but not connected, to the Trotskyists) and the Esquerra (Catalan separatists). The garrisons surrendered, and Goded and his fellow rebels were later tried and executed. As in Madrid, power fell from the hands of the constituted authorities and was picked up in the street by the militias, who began to round up and shoot everyone known or suspected to have been sympathetic to the coup.

These scenes of spontaneous revolution were repeated in Valencia, Alicante, Albacete, Cartagena, Almería, Málaga and hundreds of towns and villages all over southern and eastern Spain, where the poor wreaked a terrible vengeance on those whom they saw as their former oppressors – the aristocrats and their *señorito* sons, the landowners (at least those who had not already escaped), the *caciques* (landowners' agents and political bosses), the clergy, captured army officers and Civil Guards and anybody else who was thought to deserve death. Republican Spain began to disintegrate, each area falling under the rule of the militia of whichever political organization happened to be dominant. The politicians in Madrid, often supported by the militia leaders themselves, appealed in vain for the killings to stop, and Azaña predicted that these barbarities would so alienate world opinion as to lead to the eventual defeat of the Republic.

In the north, the two largest Basque provinces of Vizcaya and Guipuzcoa declared for the Republic in exchange for a promise of independence. The neighbouring provinces of Santander and Asturias were loyal to the Republic too, though Oviedo, the capital of Asturias, was held by a besieged Nationalist garrison. By 23 July General Mola was in fairly secure control of a large area of northern Spain containing Navarra, Alava,

León, Galicia, most of Old Castile as far south as Segovia and Avila, the northern parts of Extremadura and about half of Aragón, including Zaragoza and Huesca and a part of the province of Teruel, including the town itself. Like Oviedo, Granada and the surrounding countryside were in Nationalist hands, and small garrisons were holding out here and there, most notably in the Alcázar fortress in Toledo and in a shrine east of Córdoba.

The crucial drama, however, was taking place in the south-west, either side of the Straits of Gibraltar. The Army of Africa, consisting mainly of Moorish regular troops (*regulares*) and Foreign Legionaries, the majority of whom were Spanish convicts whose sentences had been commuted to military service, was the most effective fighting force Spain possessed and was now under the command of General Francisco Franco. This officer had led it courageously and well during the latter part of the Moroccan Rif Wars of 1909–27 and as a result had become the youngest general in the Spanish army. As acting chief-of-staff under the two-year Lerroux government of 1933–5 he, it will be remembered, had put down the Asturian revolt with efficiency but a singular lack of humanity. It was in his name that the army officers' manifesto had been broadcast and so, when he arrived at Tetuán, the officers welcomed him as a conquering hero and saviour of Spain. To save Spain, however, he would have to transfer his army across the water without delay.

The officers of the Spanish navy had not been entrusted with the details of the conspiracy, with the result that on 18 July they had no clear notion of what to do. Ordered by the government to set course for the Straits to prevent any attempt at a crossing by the Army of Africa, most of the ships' officers decided to join the uprising and began delaying, temporizing and changing course. Tumbling to what was afoot, the government ordered the ships' chief engineers to depose the officers. Accordingly, the engineers, petty officers and ratings mutinied, killed the officers who resisted, clapped the rest in irons and, managing the warships themselves, set course again for the Pillars of Hercules.

In Seville the rebel General Queipo de Llano was in precarious control. Although suspected of secret Republican sympathies, to the surprise of everyone and with only three officers to help him, he succeeded in arresting the garrison commander and all the other officers and officials who refused to join him or could not decide quickly enough which way to jump. The vital thing now was to capture the nearby airport at Tablada, which was also the largest and most important military airfield, complete with depot and aircraft factory, in southern Spain.

The airbase was already in turmoil, with tension rising between those who wanted to join and those who wanted to resist the rebellion, while the commander was unwilling to take sides. During the course of the morning, two Douglas DC-2s belonging to the state airline LAPE and two Fokker F.VIIb3ms, probably the same pair that the rebel conspirators had converted into bombers two weeks before with the intention of using them in the coup, arrived from Madrid, their crews under orders to load with bombs and attack the rebels in Spanish Morocco. The first Douglas to land was promptly immobilized when a royalist officer fired his shotgun into its port engine. After much argument, the airmen from Madrid extracted solemn promises from the officers at Tablada to observe their oath of loyalty to the Republic and defend the airbase against the rebels in Seville. There arrived too from Madrid, in a beautiful little de Havilland Leopard Moth belonging to the director-general of aeronautics, Capitán Antonio Rexach, a military pilot and left-wing activist. Claiming an authority he did not have, but supported by some mechanics armed with rifles, Rexach dismissed the commander for indecisiveness and replaced him by an old acquaintance whom he felt he could trust.[1] By that time the three converted airliners had been 'bombed up', the bombs in the remaining Douglas being laid on the passenger seats for crew members to pass along by hand and throw out of the passenger door when over the target. Rexach climbed aboard the Douglas to have the honour of joining the first aerial combat mission of the Spanish Civil War.

Since the crews had no experience of bombing and the bomb-sights were primitive and had been hastily fitted, the raid was a disaster. The bombs thrown out of the Douglas over Sania Ramel airfield, Tetuán, were scattered across the surrounding countryside. Those at Larache did no damage. At Tetuán itself, the bombs fell not on the high commission building as intended but on the Moorish quarter, killing a number of civilians and enraging the populace against the Spanish government. The Moorish Grand Vizier immediately agreed to support the rebellion and that night the first 220 Moorish troops, or *regulares*, were sent by ship to Cádiz and, next day, a further 170 were sent to Algeciras. Worse, it transpired that the officer newly appointed to command Tablada had, unknown to them, lately become a leader of the local Falange, and by dawn on 19 July the aerodrome and all the aircraft on it were in Nationalist possession.

These small and almost forgotten incidents were to have a decisive effect on the Spanish Civil War. With an airfield on the mainland, three Fokker military trimotors from West Africa, two Dornier flying boats and the soon-to-be-repaired Douglas at his disposal, Franco was able to fly platoons of Moorish and Foreign Legionary troops to Spain and tighten General Queipo de Llano's uncertain grip on Seville. By 23 July resistance in the city was crushed and Queipo able to proclaim that if any strike continued all trade union leaders would be arrested 'and immediately shot, together with an equal number of union members selected discretionally'.[2] Within a few days, as more reinforcements arrived by air, he had linked up with the Nationalists in Córdoba to the north and Cádiz to the south and begun the elimination of 'Marxist, Masonic and left-wing elements' in south-western Spain.

While the terror in the Republican zones was disorganized, often spontaneous and motivated by a desire for revenge, and always carried out against the will of the government, the terror in the Nationalist zones was carried out systematically on the orders of the military commanders. When the Nationalists occupied a town or village, they began by executing anyone who had fired a rifle, a bruise on the shoulder being all that was needed as proof. Consulting town hall records, newspapers and informers, they then compiled lists of members of left-wing political parties, trade unionists, Freemasons, doctors and other educated people known or alleged to harbour liberal sympathies. These were rounded up and, depending on the humanity or bigotry of their interrogators, released, sentenced to twenty years in prison or shot.

The collective madness of political obsession swept across Nationalist and Republican country alike. For example, Gonzalo Aguilera, the Conde de Alba (not to be confused with the Duque de Alba), told an important English visitor that on the first day of the uprising he had assembled the agricultural workers on one of his estates and had six of them shot in front of the rest, *'pour encourager les autres,* you understand!' I myself knew a girl in Cádiz, one of the first cities to fall to the Nationalists, whose father had been shot for 'suspected atheism'. In León, which likewise fell to the Nationalists in the first few days, the brother-in-law of an airman of my acquaintance was denounced for, a year previously, having attended a public lecture on Darwin's theory of evolution and for having asked questions that exhibited a more than casual knowledge of the subject. He was arrested, condemned and shot. In some Republican areas it was notorious that, if stopped in the street by the wrong people, a man might be shot for wearing that token of bourgeois complacency, a tie. I had a friend from the province of Málaga whose uncle, a minor landowner, had defied the threats from his neighbouring landowners that they would have him killed if he raised the wages he paid his workers. He never evicted a family from his estate, but took care of the doctor's bill for anyone who fell sick and arranged for the cleverer children of his tenants to go to school at his expense. When the 'Time of Chaos' came, none of this availed him. He was arrested, by the Communists, interrogated, condemned to death and shot for 'blunting the class struggle'.

Whereas the Republican government did manage to bring most of these brutalities to a stop after about eight months, terror thenceforth being usually attributable to the Stalinist-controlled secret police (Servicio de Investigación Militar, or SIM) in their compulsive hunting-down of the

POUM and other left-wing heretics, in the Nationalist zones and in the whole of Spain after the end of the civil war multiple executions did not begin to slacken until 1943. Thus a recent estimate puts the number of Republican executions during the civil war at between 20,000 and 30,000, and of Nationalist executions up to 1943 in the region of 200,000.[3] However, the killings and atrocities in the Nationalist zones during the first weeks of the fighting received little coverage in the Western press and, when reported, were usually dismissed by the right-wing newspapers as leftist propaganda. Republican atrocities and executions were not only reported but frequently given headline treatment and, moreover, received vivid confirmation in the confidential dispatches of diplomatic officials in the Republican zones. Consular reports from the Nationalist zones, on the other hand, told of law and order restored, business as usual and life nearly back to normal. The effect of such dispatches from British officials in Spain was to harden the already adverse opinion that the British government, a Conservative administration led by Prime Minister Stanley Baldwin, already had of the Spanish Republic in general and of the Popular Front in particular.

In April a similar Popular Front coalition led by a Socialist prime minister, Léon Blum, had won the elections in France, Britain's foremost ally in Europe. The workers had immediately staged waves of strikes to demonstrate their determination that the new government would fulfil its promises of reform, an action which the right had derided as proof, if any were needed, of the folly of working-class behaviour the world over. The wealthy, for their part, had bought as much gold as they could and sent it abroad in the hope that when the new government took office, there being in France a two-month interval between the election and inauguration of a government, it would quickly fall through lack of money to carry out its programme and be replaced by men of sense. When the Popular Front had come to power in June, it had begun to introduce socialistic legislation, such as a 40-hour working week, annual paid holidays and the right to join a trade union and bargain collectively, which the Foreign Office in London viewed with deep misgiving. Such a course had already provoked a reaction in the form of armed rebellion in Spain, where incidents reported from those areas still loyal to the Popular Front resembled the worst excesses of the Russian Revolution. How long would it be before the same catastrophe befell France?

3

'Air-mindedness'

THE 1930s WERE the golden decade of air races, record-breaking and the expansion of airlines. During these years too the technical development of aircraft advanced more rapidly and in a manner more varied than at any time before or since. Through the whole of the period between the world wars statesmen, press barons and other eminent people extolled the virtues of 'air-mindedness'. Monarchs, duchesses and industrialists sponsored rallies, transcontinental races and endurance flights across half the globe and even round it. Some daily newspapers ran a column of aviation news once or twice a week, and no illustrated magazine appeared without at least one photograph of a new prototype gleaming against a panorama of towering clouds, or a smiling aviator receiving a trophy. Record-breaking flyers were national heroes, and heroines, for many were women. Their fame combined the glamour surrounding sportsmen and film stars with the grave respect once shown to great explorers.

Yet however much the public might applaud these achievements, enthusiasm was always tainted by a sense of unease. Since the early 1920s Brigadier Mitchell in the USA, General Douhet in Italy and Lord Trenchard in Britain, among many like-minded pundits, had been propagating theories that air forces would win the next war almost single-handed. Thousands of giant 'aerial cruisers' would sink the fleets and destroy the industrial heartland of an enemy nation and bring its demoralized people to sue for peace before any costly ground operations were necessary. Generals and admirals, supposing their usefulness in question, dismissed such a proposition as rubbish and in some countries, including France, the USA and Japan, successfully obstructed the creation of independent air forces. In Britain a preponderance of Blimpish men in the Air Ministry and Air Staff vitiated many of the advantages an independent air force, as the RAF was, should have brought. Nevertheless, fear of the unknown worked its effect and in 1932 Stanley Baldwin, the British prime minister, told the House of Commons, 'I think it is well for the man in the street to realize that there is no power on earth that can protect him from being bombed. Whatever people may tell him, the bomber will always get through.'[1] He went on to task the younger generation to consider whether the aeroplane was not a weapon so terrible that mankind must resolve not to use it, in order to avoid self-destruction.

In March 1935 Hitler told Sir John Simon, the British Home Secretary, that the German League of Sportsflyers had become the German Air Force, or Luftwaffe, with a first-line strength as great as that of the RAF. At that time, the largest air force in the world was believed to be the Russian, though this was pure conjecture, and after it the French. The best-equipped was perhaps the Italian. The Regia Aeronautica had already gained world renown through two spectacular Atlantic crossings carried out by mass formations of flying boats under the command of General Balbo, one of the founders of Italian Fascism. During the Italian invasion of Ethiopia, then usually called Abyssinia, Mussolini's son-in-law and foreign minister, Count Ciano, had personally taken part in air attacks on defenceless villages.

Thus there were those who regarded the aeroplane as a marvellous new weapon with which to overpower neighbouring countries, or at least as the best guarantee of national sovereignty, and there were those who saw it as the Angel of Death in material form. The apprehensions of this last group were graphically expressed in the film *Things to Come*, which alarmed audiences in the summer of 1936 with scenes depicting the collapse of civilization beneath aerial bombardment. The script was written by H. G. Wells.

All these notions were greatly exaggerated, for, despite the publicity on behalf of 'air-mindedness', no one who was not intimately familiar with aircraft knew the first thing about them, or what they could or could not do. In Spain, where aircraft were comparatively rare, ignorance of them was correspondingly greater and every achievement was welcomed with an outburst of national pride. For this reason, when civil war broke out, not only the leaders but many people at all levels on both sides believed that aircraft would provide the key to success.

Franco landed at Sania Ramel airfield, Tetuán, at 7 a.m. on 19 July, accompanied by several aides and Luis Bolín, the journalist who had hired the Dragon Rapide at Croydon twelve days before.[2] The general wanted Captain Bebb, the pilot of the Rapide, to return to the Canaries and fetch his fellow conspirator General Orgaz, for 'we need him here!' Since this exceeded the hire terms, Bebb declined. All the aircraft on the field had been sabotaged during the uprising by men loyal to the Republic. This was on the orders of Major Ricardo de la Puente Bahamonde, who was in fact General Franco's cousin and had been a close friend since childhood. He was nevertheless arrested and shot. Bolín observed, 'it seems we're short of aeroplanes.' Franco thereupon scribbled a note authorizing Bolín to buy aircraft in Britain, Germany or Italy and ordered him to leave immediately in the Rapide for Portugal, where General Sanjurjo, the nominal leader of the rebellion and designated future head of state, would endorse the letter. After further discussion, Franco agreed that Bolín should then go only to Rome, since he could speak no German but a little Italian, while in Britain there were already others to handle the business. When Bolín asked what kind of machines were needed, Franco added in pencil at the bottom of the page, '12 bombers, 3 fighters with bombs (and bombing equipment) of 50 to 100 kilos – 1,000 of 50 kilos and 100 more of 500 kilos.'[3] Bolín left at 9 a.m., only two hours after he had arrived. The letter was endorsed in Lisbon by General Sanjurjo, who was killed next morning when the little Puss Moth monoplane that was to take him to Spain crashed on take-off. Bolín flew in the Rapide as far as Marseille and went on by train to Rome, which he reached on 21 July.

Contrary to so much that has been written, General Franco's first thought was to ask not for transport aircraft in which to fly his army across to Seville, but for bombers and fighters. His request for one hundred 500 kg bombs shows too that he had an unclear notion of what was required or even possible. These were then the heaviest bombs in service anywhere and their purpose was to destroy strong fortifications, of which there were none between Seville and Madrid. It is true that the only bombers in any friendly European air force able to carry them without complicated and time-consuming adaptation were the Italian Savoia-Marchetti S.81, which could carry two, and the German Junkers Ju 52/3mge, which could carry three.* However, to have dropped two or three on any of the closely packed *pueblos* (small towns or large villages – there are few small villages in the southern half of Spain) on the roads to

---

* Most heavy bombers in service in 1936 (e.g. Handley Page Heyford, Amiot 143, Potez 54) carried their bombs externally in racks beneath the fuselages or wings, which restricted the size and weight of each bomb to about 250 kg or less. The deep fuselages of the S.81 and the Ju 52 allowed room for internal bays which could be adjusted to take bombs of different sizes up to 500 kg. The only aircraft known to have employed 500 kg bombs in Spain, however, were the Heinkel He 59 float-planes of the sea reconnaissance group (AS/88) of the Condor Legion, which arrived in the autumn of 1936 and, from May 1937 on, used them to attack shipping, and possibly the five Junkers Ju 87B 'Stukas', which arrived in October 1938 and might have used them during the Catalan campaign of January–February 1939. Contrary to many reports, none was dropped on Guernica (Klaus Maier, *Guernica 26.4.1937*, appendix 12). During the air raids on Barcelona in March 1938, one exceptionally large explosion gave rise to reports in the press that 1,000 kg bombs were being used against the city. It was probably a 500 kg bomb dropped by an He 59, for not until 1939 was any country able to develop a system strong enough to hold, and release safely and precisely at the instant required, a bomb of such weight and size.

Madrid would have flattened the *pueblo*, killed most of the people in it and destroyed its artistic treasures, a result inconsistent with his proclaimed objective of 'saving Spain'. Moreover, three fighters, given that accidents and the need for maintainance would have prevented the three from flying together for much of the time, were insufficient to protect twelve bombers.

The story of how Hitler and Mussolini were persuaded to intervene in the Spanish war on behalf of General Franco has been dramatically related in many books and articles and need only be summarized here. When it became evident, as more and more Republican warships appeared in the Straits of Gibraltar, that sea crossings would be hazardous, if not impossible, Franco commissioned the manager of the Ibarrola Oil Company at Ceuta, Sr. Delgado, to purchase some 'passenger-carrying aeroplanes' in England[4] and, commandeering a Deutsche-Lufthansa Junkers Ju 52 which was in the region, sent three emissaries to Germany with a request for ten transport aircraft complete with their pilots and crews.* The deputation saw Hitler, late at night on Saturday 25 July, at Bayreuth, where the Führer was attending the Wagner festival and in a state of exaltation after hearing a performance of *Siegfried*. The decision was made at about 1 a.m. In fact, the Germans sent more military assistance than had been asked for: twenty Junkers Ju 52/3mges, which had just been built for the Luftwaffe and were adaptable as bombers or transports; six Heinkel He 51s, the standard fighters of the Luftwaffe; maintainance facilities; twenty 20 mm anti-aircraft cannons;** munitions; and other equipment, with a full complement of airmen, mechanics, engineers, gunners, a medical unit and instructors. Eleven of the Junkers flew to Seville or Tetuán from 28 July onwards, one losing its way and landing in Republican territory. The rest of the expeditionary force, its personnel disguised as a party of tourists,

---

* The emissaries were: Johannes Bernhardt, a German businessman in Morocco; Adolf Langenheim, Nazi Party 'group leader' in Morocco; and Capitán Francisco Arranz Monasterio, whom Franco had appointed chief-of-staff, under General Kindelán, of his small air force. The Ju 52 was D-APOK *Max von Müller*, piloted by Flugkapitän Alfred Henke.
** The word 'cannon' (*cañón, canon, kanone*) can be a cause of confusion, for in the 1930s Spanish, French, German and even American diplomats and intelligence agents used it indiscriminately in their dispatches to denote field-guns, howitzers or any other artillery pieces. However, during the inter-war years 'cannon' also came to mean any ultra-heavy machine-gun, or 'pom-pom', of 20 mm to 37 mm calibre firing explosive or armour-piercing shells. Solothurn, a German-owned Swiss company, and Becker-Semag produced early models, of which examples turned up in the Spanish Civil War, but by the 1930s the best-known type was the Oerlikon, likewise of Swiss make. They were chiefly used as anti-tank or anti-aircraft guns. Aircraft-mounted cannons, which had first appeared experimentally in 1917, were first used operationally in the Spanish war. The German 20 mm anti-aircraft cannon, an excellent weapon produced by Rheinmetall, was the 'Flak 30'.

sailed from Hamburg abroad the *Usaramo* on 29 July and docked at Cádiz on 6 August. The organizing of this astonishingly rapid operation was the responsibility of Sonderstab (Special Staff) 'W', a unit hastily created within the German air ministry. The operation itself was code-named *Unternehmen Feuerzauber* ('Operation Magic Fire'), since Wagner's Siegfried had had to pass through the Magic Fire to free Brünnhilde. To camouflage the adventure as a commercial undertaking, a 'Spanish' company was formed, HISMA (La Compañía Hispano-Marroquí de Transportes SA), with offices in Ceuta and Seville to handle the importation of 'goods' from, and the exportation of certain raw materials such as iron ore and copper to, Germany. Later, a second holding company, ROWAK (Rohstoffe und Waren Einkaufsgesellschaft), was created to act as a cover for the German end.[5]

Meanwhile, Franco had supplemented the letter he had given Bolín by appealing to the Italian minister in Tangier, which at that time was controlled by an international commission of ministers and consuls-general, and it was the telegrams to Rome from this minister, De Rossi del Nero Lion, as well as erroneous reports from the Italian ambassador in Madrid that French military aircraft were already landing at Barcelona,[6] that finally convinced Mussolini, on 26 and 27 July, to send military aircraft to the Spanish rebels. Mola in Burgos and Queipo de Llano in Seville sent their own deputations to Germany and Italy with requests for arms and aircraft, but the German and Italian governments mutually agreed to send all material aid only to General Franco, a decision which, since General Sanjurjo was now dead, greatly assisted the election by the Nationalist leaders two months later, on 1 October, of General Franco as both Generalísimo of the armed forces and political head of state in Nationalist Spain.

By 26 July Franco's original request for 12 bombers and 3 fighters had changed to one for 8 transports, and then to one for 12 bombers, 12 reconnaissance aircraft, 10 fighters, 5,000 bombs, 40 anti-aircraft machine-guns of 13 mm or 25 mm and a cargo ship of about 4,000 or 5,000 tons.[7]

Twelve Savoia-Marchetti S.81s, drawn from various squadrons of the Regia Aeronautica, armed and carrying an extra complement of mechanics and technicians as well as 173,000 rounds of ammunition, took off from Elmas, Sardinia, on 30 July. Strong headwinds separated the formation and three of the aircraft were lost, one going down in the sea and the other two crash-landing in French Morocco, where the French authorities immediately broadcast the news to the world. The remaining nine reached Nador at the eastern end of Spanish Morocco but, as the high-octane petrol required for their Alfa-Romeo engines was unavailable in the colony, they were immobilized until a tanker arrived from Italy five days later. Meanwhile, the crews were enrolled into the Spanish Foreign Legion (El Tercio de Extranjeros, i.e. 'the third, foreign, part of the army') to enable them to engage in military operations with an appearance of legality. From then until the end of the year the Italian component of the Nationalist air force was designated La Aviación de El Tercio, as though it were the Foreign Legion's own air arm. The twelve (not ten) fighters, Fiat C.R.32s, reached Spanish Morocco by ship on 13–14 August. More aircraft and crews followed, until by 30 September the Nationalists had received between 132 and 140 military aircraft (64–72 from Germany and 68 from Italy), of which 80 or so, plus some 70 captured Spanish air force machines, gave Franco decisive air superiority during his advance on Madrid.* All this and all subsequent aid were supplied on credit, the terms agreed by the Italians being particularly favourable.

When Hitler revealed the existence of the Luftwaffe in March 1935, his boast that it had a first-line strength equal to that of the RAF, about a thousand aircraft, was pure bluff. Even by the autumn of 1936, with production at full output, the first-line strength of the Luftwaffe had reached only 650. In 1937 it grew to 1,233, in 1938 to 3,104 (an increase of 152% in one year) and in 1939 to 3,694. To Spain the Germans sent between 621 and 732 military aircraft and 110 trainers,[8] which is an indication of how seriously they took their Spanish 'adventure' and of their real intentions towards Europe and the world. Corroboration of this can be seen in the directives and technical specifications for new types of warplanes issued by the German authorities (the army ordnance department under the Weimar Republic and the state air ministry after Hitler's accession to power) to aircraft manufacturers between July 1932 and the time of Munich. Regardless of what Hitler or other Nazi or German chiefs, statesmen and politicians may or may not have said, whether on or off the record, and of the various interpretations that different historians have

---

* Italian (on mainland): 9 S.81 bombers, 24 Fiat C.R.32 fighters up to 3 September; 12 Fiat C.R.32s, 10 IMAM Ro 37 reconnaissance biplanes and 1 Cant Z.501 flying boat, which crashed on its first mission, by 30 September. Also Italian (on Mallorca): 3 Savoia-Marchetti S. 55Xs, which flew only one mission, 3 Fiat C.R.32s, 3 Savoia-Marchetti S.81s and 3 Macchi M.41 flying-boat fighters.

German (all on mainland): 28 Junkers Ju 52s, 24 Heinkel He 51 fighters, 20 Heinkel He 46 reconnaissance monoplanes. These figures (from Manfred Merkes, *Die deutsche Politik im spanischen Bürgerkrieg*, p. 178 of 1969 edn) differ from mine in *Aircraft of the Spanish Civil War*, pp. 26 and 170: 20 Ju 52s, 24 He 51s and 29 He 46s. The eight extra Ju 52s given by Merkes may have arrived at the beginning of October. Most Spanish sources refer to the arrival of 20 He 46s in mid-September, followed by nine at the end of September, which Merkes does not mention. Moreover, on p. 387 of his book it is stated that only 21 He 46s were delivered by 5 November 1937, which contradicts the Spanish total of 29. The He 46s were flown by Spanish crews, who found them little better, and less pleasant to fly, than their old Breguet Bre 19s.

since put upon their utterances, the intent behind these technical specifications is plain and points directly towards aggression and conquest.

The belief that aircraft, any aircraft, would bring victory was as firm among Republican as among Nationalist leaders; indeed, one might say that the principal factor in bringing about foreign intervention was the parlous state of the Spanish air forces. When André Malraux flew to Madrid on 25 July to enquire what the most urgent needs of the embattled government might be, the people he met replied almost with one voice, 'warplanes, and the men to fly them!' Early that same day the Marquis of Donegall, then a reporter for the *Daily Mail*, had been on Burgos airfield interviewing General Mola, who had told him that aircraft would decide whether he would lead his 'Northern Revolutionary Army' to triumph in Madrid or to defeat in the Sierra de Guadarrama. Landing that afternoon at Bordeaux airport, Donegall spoke with the crew of the Republican Douglas DC-2 that was carrying the first consignment of gold bullion from Madrid to Paris. The Spaniards confessed that the gold was to pay for aircraft, for, they said, 'this war will be won from the air.'[9]

Three weeks afterwards, President Azaña, who as a peacetime war minister had so ruthlessly cut back on defence expenditure, gloomily looked out of a window of the presidential palace towards the south-west, from where Franco's army was hurrying nearer every day, and told the French journalist Jean Cassou of his bitterness at the refusal of Britain and France – the latter being a nation he had loved and admired all his life – to allow the Spanish government to buy the arms with which to defend itself. Then he turned and said, 'With fifty aircraft I could have crushed the rebellion!'[10] At about this time, Luis Araquistaín, Largo Caballero's 'spiritual guide' in matters of socialist theory, was appointed as the new ambassador in Paris, where one of his most important and difficult duties would be to organize the purchase of armaments for the Republic. Before leaving Madrid he met the American journalist Louis Fischer and told him 'With a hundred aeroplanes we could win the war!'[11] It was the habitual reply too of Indalecio Prieto, Republican minister of marine and air and later of defence, to those who asked how victory might be achieved against mounting adversities, 'La guerra le ganará quien domine con sus aparatos el aire!' ('Whoever dominates the air with his machines will win the war!').[12] Hence the perceived necessity of obtaining them by whatever means and at whatever cost; for when the Popular Front government of Spain had turned to the Popular Front government of France for help, the response had been very different from that of the dictators to General Franco.

4

Paris

AFTER THE CIVIL war many Spanish Republicans directed their bitterest recriminations not at Hitler, Mussolini, the British or even the Soviets but at the French premier, Léon Blum. He, they said, was more to blame than anyone for their defeat. What made the matter worse was that he was a socialist, a democrat and a man of culture who shared the same values as themselves. Like many of the academics and intellectuals in the Spanish government and members of the British Labour Party, he was a pacifist and had long campaigned for unilateral disarmament, in the belief that a moral example set by France would induce others to follow.

Since coming to office six weeks before, he had been the target of a relentless hate campaign by the newspapers of the extreme right, such as *L'Action Française*, who reviled him as a Bolshevik stooge, a traitor and a Jew. On the other side, the Communists, who had helped him to power, now sneered that, for all his vaunted socialism, he was still a bourgeois dilettante at heart, more interested in frequenting the theatre and smart salons than in fighting for the workers. Therefore, what he needed above all, with the strikes settled and the street battles dying down, was a time of stability in which his reforms could begin to work their effect.

The telegram from Madrid was sent not through the Spanish embassy but personally to Blum by Giral and arrived in the small hours of 20 July: 'We are surprised by a dangerous military coup stop beg you arrange assistance with arms and planes stop fraternally Giral.' It was not even in code.[1]

Blum's immediate impulse was to comply at once. The arguments in favour seemed overwhelming. The Popular Front existed to oppose Fascism. Here was the only other such government in Europe already threatened by a Fascist-supported coup. If the rebellion succeeded, it would not only give tremendous encouragement to Fascists in France, but France herself would be threatened by Fascist neighbours on three frontiers. Nevertheless, sensing that some of the more conservative-minded Radicals in his cabinet might prove troublesome, he consulted first with the two ministers most directly concerned. As it happened, they were among those who, though Radicals, were more likely to be sympathetic: Edouard Daladier, the defence minister, who gave his cautious approval, and Pierre Cot, the air minister, who gave his whole-hearted approval.

Cot was a gifted ex-lawyer who, although only forty-one, had already held office, including that of air minister, in three previous governments. Since 1934, however, he had been visibly moving further and further to the left, publicly upbraiding his colleagues for their failure to face the danger of Fascism and advocating a military alliance with the Soviet Union, the very idea of which was anathema to all conservatives. No sooner had he returned to the air ministry on 4 June than he had revealed his intention to nationalize the French aircraft industry and disperse its factories from their dangerously vulnerable concentration round Paris.* In the midst of the furore over this, an indignant official in the air ministry leaked to the press the news that Cot had authorized the sale of a Dewoitine D.510 fighter, armed with a 'moteur-canon', to the Soviet government. In parliament on 17 July, the day before the Nationalist uprising in Spain, he was attacked as a crypto-Communist who was delivering 'the most precious secrets of our national defence' to the Bolshevik enemy'.[2] The accusation pursued him for the rest of his career. For example, in his book *Spycatcher* (1987) Peter Wright states that in 1964–5 the CIA provided the British secret service with intelligence proving that Cot had been not merely a Communist fellow-traveller but an active Soviet spy. Wright does not say, however, what the proof was, and until it is published the allegation is better treated with reserve.[3]

Having instructed Daladier and Cot to begin preparations and informed the foreign minister, Yvon Delbos, whose response to the news was cool, Blum received the Spanish ambassador, Juan de Cárdenas Rodríguez de Rivas, for consultation. However, one of the most damaging blows to the Spanish government in its present precarious position was the defection of the greater part of the diplomatic corps to the rebels. A

---

* Another problem was that there were no fewer than twenty-eight aircraft and aero-engine companies in France, most making little profit and suffering continual financial crises. (See, for instance, the article by Emmanuel Chadeau, 'Government, Industry and the Nation: The Growth of Aeronautical Technology in France, 1900–1940' in *Aerospace Historian*, March 1988, p. 32.) So dire was the situation and so urgent the strategic need to disperse the factories across France that to Cot nationalization seemed the only answer, but this made him a target of relentless personal abuse from the newspapers of the political right, especially the seven owned or controlled by the arms industry. This is not to deny that the programme, which began in the autumn of 1936, caused the disorganization that still prevailed when the Second World War broke out three years later.

few of the ambassadors, ministers and consuls openly declared their support of the uprising and resigned within hours. The majority, including the ambassadors in the key posts at London and Washington, decided that they could serve the Nationalist cause better by remaining in place, pretending loyalty to the government and doing what they could to undermine its standing abroad and sabotage its attempts to buy arms. At the Paris embassy most of the officials loathed the Popular Front and prayed fervently for its downfall. Indeed, several weeks before the uprising the Spanish government had decided to replace Cárdenas, an aristocratic monarchist, by Alvaro de Albornoz, a left-wing deputy and author whom it regarded as more in tune with its policies, the change-over being scheduled for 15 August.

At his meeting with Blum, therefore, Cárdenas contrived to play for time by advising the French premier to do nothing until Madrid sent more specific details of the arms and planes required. He took care besides not to send the telegram asking for these details until late that evening.[4] Nevertheless, two Spanish air force *comandantes* (majors), Ismael Warleta and Juan Aboal, arrived by plane early next morning, bringing the list with them. It was modest: 20 Potez aircraft, complete with air crews and material on board; 1,000 Lebel 8 mm rifles and 1 million cartridges; 50 Hotchkiss machine-guns with 12 million cartridges; and 8 Schneider 75 mm field-guns with accessories and ammunition.[5]

'Potez aircraft' referred to the Potez 54, a large twin-engined bomber in service with, and still in production for, the Armée de l'Air. Since only four were currently available at such short notice, Cot offered to make up the balance with seventeen old Potez 25 two-seat biplanes withdrawn from service several years before and now in storage.[6] Yvon Delbos, the French foreign minister, warned that to allow French pilots to ferry them to Spain might have international repercussions. Besides, where was the money to pay for the aircraft or even the pilots? Delbos left for London on Wednesday 22 July for a tripartite conference over Hitler's violation of the Treaty of Locarno and occupation of the Rhineland in March.

On 23 July Cárdenas resigned, followed by Castillo (embassy counsellor) and Barroso (military attaché). The latter two held a press conference at which they declared that they had resigned rather than approve an order for arms that would be used to kill their fellow Spaniards. Castillo then departed for Germany, where he became very busy in the procurement of arms for the Nationalists and Barroso left for Spain, where he served in General Franco's headquarters. That afternoon Cárdenas met the press attaché at the British embassy, Sir Charles Mendl, and, while they drove round and round the Bois de Boulogne in order not to be overheard, told him everything he knew. The information was passed to London.

During the same day Cot informed the French foreign ministry that he now had more than twenty aircraft standing by and, in view of Delbos's absence and the fact that the Spanish rebels were not going to wait upon formalities, he intended to order their departure for Spain immediately. The foreign ministry could surely waive the rules and deal with the export permits and other documentation later. This so infuriated Delbos's deputy, Coulondre, that everything was now at a standstill. Moreover, somebody in Blum's cabinet, or perhaps in the foreign ministry, informed the German ambassador of what was going on and the information was passed to Berlin, where, however, it was not considered important enough to send up to the Führer.

Meanwhile, Blum had flown to London to take part in the last session of the conference. No decision was reached on what to do about Hitler, and Spain was not mentioned. However, the French journalist 'Pertinax' (André Géraud) interviewed him in his room at Claridges and asked if it was true that he was furnishing arms to Spain to enable it to defend itself against Franco's military coup. When Blum said it was, Pertinax commented 'You must know that it won't go down very well here.'

'Possibly, but I know nothing about that and in any case we're going to do it.'

Later, in the same room, the British Foreign Secretary, Anthony Eden, with whom Blum got on very well as they both admired Marcel Proust, came to say goodbye and before leaving asked him if he intended to give arms to the Spanish Republicans. When Blum said 'Yes', Eden replied, 'That's your business, but I ask one thing of you: I beg you, be careful.'[7]

Blum returned to Paris, on Thursday 24 July, to face strong opposition in the cabinet organized by Camille Chautemps, the minister of state, uproar in both chambers of parliament, Président Lebrun in tears as usual and a furious campaign by the right-wing press supported by leading Catholic writers, including François Mauriac. *L'Action Française* was raising a storm over the presence in Paris of the two Spanish air officers. 'What do they want? Money? Guns? Planes? Whatever it is, the French people forbids the Jew Blum to give it!'[8]

Professor Fernando de los Rios, a benign and bearded academic legal historian, a moderate Socialist and the minister in the 1931–3 government who had been mainly responsible for building the 7,000 schools in Spain, had been on holiday in Geneva, visiting his fellow legal historian Professor Pablo de Azcárate, deputy secretary-general at the League of Nations, when the Madrid government asked him to go to Paris and take charge of the Spanish embassy until the new ambassador, Alvaro de Albornoz, arrived. His immediate task would be to review and sign the contracts for the arms and aircraft now ready and organize their delivery to Barcelona. When he reached Paris on the 23rd, however, he found that he was unable to sign the contracts since he had no diplomatic status; as for checking the contracts, he was utterly ignorant of armaments of any kind and had no experience of business, let alone of the sharp practices of the international arms trade. When, for example, an official from the air ministry mentioned that the Potez 54s would require some 100 kg bombs, Rios exclaimed in horror, 'A hundred kilos! But that's barbaric! Surely fifteen kilos would be quite sufficient?'[9]

During these two days, the writer André Malraux and Carlo Rosselli, leader of the Giustizia e Libertà group of Italian anti-Fascists in Paris, had discussed with Leo Lagrange, minister of sport and leisure, and so of sports flying in France, a scheme for recruiting volunteers to ferry French military aircraft to Spain, and on 24th Pierre Cot agreed, in view of the confusing information coming from Republican Spain, to send Malraux to Madrid on a fact-finding mission. Meanwhile, Rios had telegraphed Madrid for money to pay for the arms, aircraft and volunteers. That night Blum conferred with Rios, Cot, Daladier and Delbos. Rios pointed out that a Commercial Accord between France and Spain of December 1935, of which a secret clause bound Spain to buy 20 million francs' worth of French armaments, might serve as a legal justification for sending aid. Blum agreed.[10] Cot explained that a contract for fourteen Dewoitine D.372 fighters ordered by Lithuania had been cancelled on 5 June[11] and that these aircraft, now looking for a customer, could be sold to Spain, as well as the four Potez 54s and seventeen obsolete Potez 25s. To calm the opposition and right-wing press, the orders might be channelled through an amenable government such as that of Mexico, so far the only government in the world to have openly declared its sympathy for the Spanish Republic. Blum's original intention to *give* arms to the Spanish Republic had been quietly dropped. It would create too many obstacles and besides the Spanish government, with the entire gold reserve still safely in the Bank of Spain, was not only able but would prefer to pay for any aid received. At the end of the discussion Blum decided to call a cabinet meeting for next afternoon at 4 p.m., Saturday 25 July.

Next morning, while Malraux and his wife, Clara, were on their way to Madrid, Rios encountered 'insuperable difficulties', whatever they were, at the office of the Potez aircraft company.[12] That afternoon Rios spent an hour or two with Blum, who was now in an agony of mind and spoke of resigning. During the night Delbos had added to their difficulties by absolutely refusing to grant permission to French pilots to fly the aircraft to Spain, despite Rios's explaining that the few Spanish pilots who had sufficient experience to be able to handle these modern machines and were still loyal to the government were already fully engaged at the front.

At 4 p.m., about the same time as the LAPE Douglas DC-2 was landing at Le Bourget with the first cargo of gold (£144,000 in British sovereigns) to pay for the arms and aircraft, the cabinet began its meeting. There is no record of what was said, beyond the fact that the debate was heated. If the Commercial Accord was mentioned as a justification for selling arms, the argument carried no weight, for at the end a vote was taken and the majority went against Blum.

Afterwards Delbos issued a statement to the press declaring that the cabinet had 'unanimously' decided not to intervene in the internal conflict in Spain. Regarding the supply of war material that the Spanish government was 'said to have requested', it was untrue that the French government was 'determined to follow a policy of intervention'. He was able to pretend that the Spanish government was only 'said' to have requested aid, rather than admit that it had actually done so, owing to the fact that the requests had been made first from premier to premier and then directly to the ministries of war and air, instead of through the proper channel of foreign ministries. For although, after the resignation of Cárdenas, the Spanish consul-general in Paris, Antonio Cruz Marín, who had remained loyal to the Republic and been asked by Madrid to act as chargé d'affaires at the embassy until the arrival of a new ambassador, *had* presented the orders to the Quai d'Orsay (the French foreign ministry) on 24 July precisely for the purpose of formalizing them,[13] Delbos could still argue that an order for arms required the signature of an accredited ambassador and that as this order had no such signature it could not officially be said to exist. Thus began the torments of the Republicans in their quest for arms.

Delbos then sent a circular to the French embassies abroad making it known that the delivery of war material to Spain was prohibited. 'Nevertheless, following certain precedents, the exportation of unarmed aircraft, which may be supplied to the Spanish government by private industry, is authorized.'[14]

Late that night, at about the time that Hitler was receiving Franco's deputation at Bayreuth, Rios wrote to Giral to say that, although no material would be delivered government to government, he had been assured that it could be obtained from private industry and that the first aircraft would be in Spain by Monday or Tuesday. With the help of Cruz Marín and other Spaniards, and some 'excellent French friends', he was trying to organize 'the safe passage of the bombs, a difficult matter, especially for one who, like myself, is not an astute old fox, but we shall see what necessity makes us capable of'. So far as the ground arms were concerned, it seemed that the only company they could deal with would be Hotchkiss. Secrecy was almost impossible. It seemed that every conversation of his was overheard and, with slight alterations to make it appear more damaging, was published in the newspapers next day. For security reasons he had taken residence in the embassy, for which he hoped Giral would forgive him; this made it all the more imperative that the new ambassador arrive as soon as possible.[15] Next morning, knowing that the

Doublas DC-2 that had brought the gold to Paris was about to return to Madrid, Rios asked Major Warleta, one of the two officers who had come to Paris the previous Tuesday, to return with it and deliver the letter personally to Giral. At the door he took Warleta by the arm and, 'staring through his glasses fixedly with affection and sincerity', said, 'Warleta, there are those who think that duty no longer obligates them when they don't happen to like it.'[16]

It was a pointed compliment. Ismael Warleta, who had been director-general of aeronautics in 1934–5, was one of the monarchist officers in the air forces who refused to join the uprising because it would have meant breaking their oath of loyalty to the Spanish constitution. He had been sent to Paris, as were others in his position, to avoid assassination by revolutionaries who did not trust any officers, let alone monarchist ones. At the end of the civil war, those who had not fled abroad were arrested by the Franco regime, sentenced to ten or twenty years in prison with hard labour for 'treason' and, when they had completed their terms, proscribed from taking any but menial employment.

5

Men and Armaments

THE PRE-CIVIL WAR Spanish army on the mainland, the Balearics and the Canary Islands had numbered about 90,000 men and been divided into eight administrative regions, or *divisiones orgánicas*. Of these, three (Madrid, Barcelona and Valencia) and some units in the Basque country and Asturias remained loyal to the government. The other five (Seville, Zaragoza, Burgos, Valladolid and La Coruña), together with the garrisons on the Balearics (except Menorca) and the Canary Islands, joined the rebellion. Thus, after desertions and the like, the army appeared, on paper, to be split roughly in half, with some 27,000 troops on the Republican and 30,000 on the Nationalist side, the 3,000 Nationalist majority consisting mostly of infantry. The paramilitary forces – the Civil Guards, Carabineros (frontier guards) and Assault Guards – totalling about another 100,000 men were likewise divided fairly equally.[1]

However, while the Nationalist regiments continued under their familiar officers and NCOs and so retained their cohesion, in the Republican zones 90% of the officers and NCOs had either tried to join the rebellion and been arrested and shot, or had vanished, many to reappear in the Nationalist army a few weeks later. As a result, most units virtually disintegrated. None of this, however, takes account of the Army of Africa, whose 35,000 men, including many hardened veterans of the Moroccan war of 1909–27, when brought across the Straits of Gibraltar would not only raise the number of Nationalist troops to more than twice that of the Republican but would also bring into the fighting the most effective military force Spain possessed.[2]

Of the 500,000 or so rifles in Spain, some 200,000 are said to have been retained by the government. However, of 65,000 issued to the Madrid populace on 19 and 20 July, only 7,000 had bolts and were usable. Moreover, a very large number, perhaps as many as 70,000, were lost during the Nationalist advances in August and September 1936.

One feature of the Spanish Civil War which continues to intrigue military and aeronautical historians is the astounding variety of weapons and aircraft used in it as a direct, though unintended, consequence of the international Non-Intervention embargoes. It has been a common complaint among veterans of the war, especially International Brigaders, that they were obliged to use antiquated weapons, including rifles and artillery pieces dating from the Boer War and earlier. Although many of the weapons sold to the Republicans were indeed old and worn out, the complaints, especially when taken up by journalists and propagandists, can sometimes be seen to be based on misunderstanding. Nearly all the rifles, for example, used by armies at that time, and until the end of the Second World War, dated from, that is to say had been designed during, the last decades of the nineteenth century. The rifle that I was issued with when I joined the British Army in 1944 was a standard Lee-Enfield 'No. 1 Rifle Model 1903', which was a modification of a design of 1895. The standard rifle of the German army of both world wars was the Mauser 98 (i.e., of 1898). The Mauser repeating rifle, of which the first version was produced in 1884, was indeed the most widely used military rifle in the world and appeared in well over thirty versions. The Spanish regulation rifle was the Mauser 93, made in Spain and using Spanish ammunition. It is remembered as one of the best Mausers produced anywhere and Spaniards have assured me that it was superior to the Mauser 98 in several respects, chiefly in that its slightly lower muzzle velocity gave it a greater 'stopping power' against enemy infantry.[3]

The Spanish regulation calibre for small arms was 7 mm, which was used only by Mexico and a few Latin American countries. Thus the variety of calibres of weapons and ammunition obtained from abroad became a major problem for the Republicans during the coming months as they found themselves obliged to buy rifles and machine-guns using cartridges of no fewer than ten different calibres: 6.5, 7, 7.62, 7.65, 7.7, 7.707, 7.92, 8, 8.03 and 11 mm.

The Spanish heavy machine-gun was the French-designed Hotchkiss Model 1903, 7 mm, made at Oviedo. It was an old but tough and reliable weapon, and some were still being used in the Communist conquest of China in 1948 and in the wars in Korea and Vietnam. The light machine-gun was the Hotchkiss Model 1922 O.C. (Oviedo-La Coruña), 7 mm. Of the 2,000 or so heavy machine-guns, the government retained only 628 and of the 3,000 light machine-guns about 1,000.[4]

The Republicans were markedly outnumbered in artillery. Of the 1,007 field pieces, the government retained only 387, 620 being in Nationalist areas. There were two types of medium gun, both Schneider, and two of howitzer, the Schneider short-barrelled 105/11 and the Vickers long-barrelled 105/22, both relatively modern. The heaviest mobile piece was the Schneider 155 Model 1917, a medium-heavy gun used by more than half a dozen different armies. There were also 241 ancient pieces, some of bronze, used for decorating barracks and castles or lying in store. Of these, the government had 171 and the Nationalist 70. On the government side, some of these continued in service until the end of the civil war.

The Spanish army had eighteen tiny Renault FT-17 tanks, of which the government retained ten. The Renault FT-17 had been the first 'modern' tank (i.e. with a turret) and in Spain was armed either with a single Hotchkiss machine-gun or with a 37 mm light cannon. It was too small to negotiate a trench and had a top speed of only 5 m.p.h. (7.7 km/h).[5]

The Republicans started the war with twenty-seven warships, the Nationalists seventeen. However, the Nationalist ships included the *Canarias* and *Baleares*, two recently built modern cruisers which were still being fitted out on 18 July at El Ferrol, Galicia.[6] When the *Canarias* entered service in August and the *Baleares* in December, they more than compensated for the Nationalist inferiority in numbers. Besides, the Nationalists enjoyed active and substantial assistance from the Italian and German navies, who not only enforced the Non-Intervention blockade to the letter but on occasion sank ships taking supplies to the Republicans. The Republican fleet, on the other hand, was in the same predicament as the army in that most naval officers had tried to join the rebellion and, on the ships whose crews had mutinied, had died as a result. Many too had been executed after the rebellion had been crushed at the naval base at Cartagena and the nearby naval airfield at San Xavier.

There were two air forces: the Aviación Militar, controlled by the army, and the Aeronáutica Naval, controlled by the navy. The Fuerzas Aéreas de Africa consisted of a few patrols detached from each of the services. In 1933 a Dirección General de Aeronáutica had been established as an embryonic air ministry responsible for all technical, administrative, supply and training aspects of military, naval and civil aviation, though the director-general was always an army officer.

On 18 July 1936 there were between 536 and 553 aircraft of all types in Spain, the islands and Spanish Africa, plus about thirty military machines under repair, and during June and early July the Director General de Aeronáutica, General Nuñez de Prado (arrested and shot in Zaragoza shortly after the uprising), had gradually been concentrating all the best serviceable aircraft on the airfields round Madrid as a precaution against the coup that he, for one, expected, with the result that the government was able to retain two-thirds of the military and naval, as well as most of the civil, aircraft. Even so, all the military and naval aircraft, except three de Havilland D.H.89M militarized Dragon Rapides, were obsolete. The CASA-Breguet 19 light bomber, the workhorse of the Aviación Militar, was a stately two-seat biplane dating from 1921 and the fighter, the Hispano-Nieuport 52, dated from 1924.[7] With a top speed of only 140 m.p.h. (225 km/h) the cumbrous Nieuport was slower than not only the slow Junkers Ju 52 (172 m.p.h. or 276.7 km/h) but also the ancient Breguet Bre 19 (142 m.p.h. or 230 km/h). In those days the top speed of even an obsolescent fighter in the air force of any of the major powers was between 205 and 240 m.p.h. and airliners with cruising speeds of *c.* 200 m.p.h. had been in regular service for two or more years, the Douglas DC-2 being the outstanding example.

Of the 120 or so Breguets in service, the Nationalists captured 63 in the first two weeks, but of the 56 Nieuports the Nationalists captured only seven under repair at Seville and three which landed at Granada on the day the airfield fell into their hands. With the crushing of the revolt at San Xavier (Cartagena), seventeen CASA-Vickers Vildebeests were saved for the government. Two were seaplanes but the rest were intended as torpedo-bombers. Since they could carry 725 kg of bombs, a heavier load than that of any other aircraft in Spain at that time, they were rushed into action as ordinary day bombers, some being sent to Catalonia, others to Madrid and two to the Basque zone in the north. No less vulnerable and even slower than the Breguets, seven were shot down during the first phases of the war. Of twenty-six Dornier Wal flying boats (designed in 1922), each side had thirteen, but five of the Republican machines had no engines and only two on the Nationalist side were airworthy.

Since the majority of the staff, pilots, crews and mechanics of the state airline LAPE voted to stay loyal to the government, all the aircraft remained in Republican hands except the Douglas DC-2 captured at Tablada, Seville, on 18 July and an antique Junkers F.13 which happened to be on an airfield captured by the Nationalists on that day.[8] Indeed, the Douglas DC-2s, of which the government retained three, were the only truly modern aircraft in Spain.

In 1934 Gil Robles, the minister of defence in the Lerroux government, had initiated a programme of re-equipment and modernization of the air forces, including the creation of a multi-engined bomber group which would be the nucleus of an independent air force. The bomber eventually chosen, after much lobbying and debate, had been the Martin 139W, an export version of the Martin B-10 of the USAC. When the Director General de Aeronáutica, General Goded (who became one of the four leaders of the Nationalist uprising), announced this decision in January 1936, the Germans, who had been energetically bidding for the contract, were furious. Count von Welczeck, the German ambassador in Madrid, sent a dispatch to Berlin saying that according to a confidential source the Glenn Martin Company of Baltimore had won this contract by means of 'presents' to certain Spanish officials worth 1 million Reichsmarks (£79,239, or $396,196). 'This is a practice', he added, 'to which the German aviation industry neither can, nor will, stoop.'[9]

This may have been intended to excuse the failure of the Germans to secure the orders, all the types on offer having been inferior to the Martin 139, but the fact that the Martin was, although already somewhat outdated in concept, probably the best bomber available on the world market in December 1935 does not exclude the possibility that the Martin company was, or felt, obliged to resort to 'sweeteners'. The recipients would have been General Goded himself and/or Major Ramón Franco, General Franco's younger brother, who was still famous in Spain for having made the first flight across the South Atlantic in the Dornier Wal *Plus Ultra* in January 1926 and who, as air attaché in Washington in 1935–6, had sent a glowing report on the Martin bomber to Goded. There was already in circulation a rumour that Ramón had been offered, and had accepted, 2 million pesetas (£80,000, or $400,000) from the Dornier company as a reward for some chicanery in connection with his round-the-world flight attempt in 1929, which had ended in failure and nearly in disaster.[10]

Two hundred and forty-nine new aircraft had been ordered under the programme.[11] None was notably modern and the only machines delivered by 18 July 1936 had been a Hawker Osprey, three Hawker Spanish Furies, as yet unarmed, and three de Havilland D.H.89M militarized Dragon Rapides intended for colonial policing, of which the aircraft that had taken General Nuñez de Prado to Zaragoza on 18 July had already been captured by the Nationalists, as had three of the four Fokker F.VIIb3mM trimotor bombers used by the Army of Africa.

Any Republican numerical superiority in aircraft, however, was offset by a lack of experienced pilots and aircrews. One of the more serious effects of Azaña's applauded cut-backs in defence spending had been an extreme shortage of petrol, which had prevented pilots from putting in sufficient flying hours to keep themselves in practice. For example, the log-book of Andrés García Lacalle, who had been trained in the class of 1925–6 and during the civil war became an 'ace', rising from sergeant to command the entire Republican fighter force (the Escuadra de Caza), showed a mere eighty hours' flying by 18 July 1936. In the US Navy at that time, a trainee pilot had to show 250 flying hours even to get his wings and, having joined a squadron, to put in 30 hours a month merely to qualify for pay.[12] In the Spanish air forces, the only pilots who were able to put in a reasonable quantity of flying hours per month were those wealthy enough to join flying clubs and, not surprisingly, nearly all of these either took part in the rebellion or joined the Nationalists at the first opportunity, often bringing their aircraft with them.

6

'Non-Intervention'

SINCE SATURDAY 25 July Yvon Delbos, the French foreign minister, had been reassuring everybody who would listen that to have sent arms to the Spanish government would have constituted an interference in the internal affairs of a foreign country and so a violation of international law. When objectors pointed out that this could hardly be true since it was the Spanish government itself that had requested the arms, he tried, in vain, to clarify the position by telling the Chamber of Deputies, during the evening session of Thursday 30 July, that to have sent the arms would not have violated international law after all, since that law allowed every legitimate government to buy arms for self-defence. Moreover, he admitted, the Spanish government was not only legitimate in law and in fact, but a friendly government whose interests coincided with those of the French government. No, he went on, 'we acted as we did for reasons of principle and humanity. We did not wish *to give any pretext* to those who might be tempted to furnish war material to the insurgents and thus enlarge the scope of the conflict.'[1]

The bottom fell out of this argument minutes later, when news arrived that two Italian bombers had crashed in French Morocco on their way to the insurgents and had thus enlarged the scope of the conflict. At first, Blum hoped that the news would arouse such public indignation as to remove all obstacles to his helping the Republicans. Instead, however, even the moderate newspapers next morning tended to blame Blum himself rather than Mussolini, arguing that it was only Blum's ill-considered promise to the Spanish government that had panicked Mussolini into rushing bombers to the rebels, while the newspapers of the right claimed that Blum and Cot, in cynical disregard of their own proclaimed policy, had already sent the first military aircraft to Barcelona.

It may be remembered that it was just such a report as this, sent from the Italian embassy in Madrid three days before, which had finally persuaded Mussolini to order the dispatch of aircraft to Franco. In fact, as is explained in the next chapters and Appendix I, no military aircraft, French or otherwise, reached the Republicans before 7–8 August. All foreign airline services to Spain were suspended at dawn on 18 July[2] and the only aircraft that crossed the frontier between then and 8 August were the LAPE Douglas DC-2 carrying gold to Paris on 25, 26 and 30 July and returning, the solitary French mailplanes, which had been permitted to keep up the twice-daily service between Toulouse and Barcelona, and four or five old Latécoère 28 passenger planes taken from reserve and sent to Barcelona and Alicante to evacuate French citizens, starting on 28 July.[3] No one pointed this out at the time, official denials were derided as cover-ups and the story that between twenty and fifty French 'military aircraft' were delivered to the Republicans prior to 8 August 1936 took hold. It continued to appear in histories and critiques of the Spanish Civil War for the next half-century.

The three titular heads of France – Président Lebrun, the president of the Senate, Jeanneney, and the president of the Chamber of Deputies, Herriot – volubly declared their opposition to the sending of arms to the Spanish Republic, while Blum's cabinet was split between those who threatened to resign if arms were sent and those who threatened to resign if they were not. One side warned that the rebellion would soon triumph and that it would be folly to offend the victors, the other that a rebel victory would tempt right-wing army officers to stage a coup in France. To Blum, the advent of the Popular Front had seemed the most significant step so far achieved towards the realization of a lifelong dream, the creation of a welfare state that would gradually erode the extremes of wealth and poverty and lay the foundations of the first society in history to combine individual freedom with social justice. If the coalition were to collapse barely four months after its election, the right-wing zealots of the government that succeeded it would not only do everything in their capacity to help the Spanish rebels but at home would reverse Blum's programme of reforms and thereby cause tumults and violence too appalling to contemplate.

It was at this moment that the general secretary, that is to say permanent chief, of the French foreign ministry, Alexis Léger, offered a way through the dilemma. Léger, perhaps better remembered today, at least in France, as the Nobel-Prize-winning poet Saint John Perse, was an Anglophile who had been alarmed by hearing from his friends in London that there were senior men in the British government, notably Sir Maurice Hankey, the chairman of the Imperial Defence Committee, who were thinking that if France continued to drift leftwards in this rudderless fashion, Britain could do worse than disengage herself from her alliance and throw in her lot with Germany and Italy.[4] He therefore proposed that France, Britain, Italy and Portugal – whose dictator, Antonio Oliveiro Salazar, had already begun to assist the rebels – should agree by signed pact to prevent the delivery of war materials and the passage of troops or the like to either side in Spain. A draft was sent to the four governments on 2 August. The British 'welcomed' it but recommended that it include as many countries as possible and, when the text was recast as 'An International Agreement of Non-Intervention in the Present Spanish Crisis', energetically canvassed the governments of Europe, especially those of Germany, Italy and the Soviet Union, for its support.

Prime Minister Stanley Baldwin's national government had started life in 1931 as a coalition of Conservative, Labour and Liberal ministers brought together to cope with the 'national emergency' resulting from the Great Depression, but by 1936 it had become dominated by the right wing of the Conservative Party. Its primary duties, as it saw them, were to maintain the empire and restore prosperity by means of what we would now call 'monetarist' policies controlled by Neville Chamberlain, the Chancellor of the Exchequer, and Montagu Norman, the Governor of the Bank of England. Baldwin himself disliked 'abroad' and had no interest in foreign affairs. Nazi Germany was seen as a potential enemy in the future with whom, since Hitler was an obsessive anti-Communist, conflict might nonetheless be avoided. Some in the government even hoped that the Nazis and Bolsheviks would one day exhaust themselves in a mutually destructive war. A programme of rearmament, denounced and opposed by the numerous pacifists in the Labour Party, had been approved but little so far had been achieved. The whole country indeed dreaded another war, after the horrors of the last, and, while the fleet was still the most powerful in the world and people exclaimed 'Thank God we've got a navy!', the army was small and ill equipped and the aircraft of the RAF, even those entering or about to enter service, such as the Hawker Fury II, Gloster Gladiator, Fairey Hendon and Handley Page Harrow, were few in number and outdated in concept. The Hawker Hurricane, which first flew in November 1935, and the Supermarine Spitfire, which first flew on 5 March 1936, two days before Hitler occupied the Rhineland, were as yet prototypes in early stages of testing, and there was disagreement besides over whether they were the kind of fighters really needed.*

---

* The appearance, beginning in America with the Lockheed Orion, during the early 1930s, of passenger planes that could fly faster than any fighters then in service faced air staffs everywhere with a dilemma. The new aircraft were streamlined cantilever monoplanes with retractable undercarriages and enclosed accommodation for the passengers and crew, and were usually of monocoque stressed-skin construction, and it would be a matter of only a year or two before bombers of equally modern design and performance were developed. Fighters fast enough to intercept them would have to be designed on similar principles. However, many, especially fighter pilots, argued vehemently that the manoeuvrability and ruggedness of the traditional biplane fighter, with

Mussolini's invasion of Abyssinia had obliged a reluctant administration to impose economic sanctions, whose only effect had been a worsening of relations with Italy. The Foreign Office planned, therefore, to re-establish friendship with Mussolini in the hope of using him as a counterbalance to Hitler. This, however, would come to nothing if Blum and his friends sent arms to Spain, a backward and unstable nation whose government, to judge by reports, would soon be brushed aside by Communists controlled from Moscow as easily as the Kerensky government of Russia had been brushed aside by Lenin and the Bolsheviks in 1917. Hence, on 26 July, when there were no Russians and fewer than 30,000 Communists in Spain, Baldwin confided to his friend Thomas Jones, 'I told Eden [the Foreign Secretary] yesterday that on no account, French or other, must he bring us into the fight on the side of the Russians.'[5] There was more to it than that, however. Helping, or allowing others to help, the Spanish Republic might awaken expectations among the Labour movement at a time when, despite the apparently irreducible army of 1½ million unemployed and a recent reduction of unemployment relief, prosperity for the rest of the people was increasing and the government regaining popularity. Such expectations could well bring on the same kind of troubles as had led to the General Strike of 1926. Nevertheless, the government of Spain had been duly elected, whatever the rebels might be saying, and was internationally recognized; and diplomatic etiquette, which meant neutrality, had to be observed. As the Conservative chief whip, David Margesson, explained to the counsellor at the Italian embassy in London, Signor Vitetti, on 29 July, 'It is our interest, indeed our wish, to see the rebellion (of the Spanish army officers) triumph. At the same time, we do not want to abandon our neutrality, for there is no other way of controlling Labour agitation.'[6]

Five days later, Sir Samuel Hoare, First Lord of the Admiralty, extended this line of argument to encompass the whole of the British empire. On 3 August Blum sent two senior French naval officers to explain to their counterparts in London the dangers that would arise if Mussolini gained a foothold on the Balearic Islands. The British admirals were unimpressed, assuring the Frenchmen that Franco was a stout patriot who would never concede a square inch of Spanish soil to any foreigner. The French admi-

---

reliable fixed undercarriage and open cockpit, would continue to be decisive in air combat and thus in gaining air superiority. Attempts to reach a compromise between these alternatives resulted in the astonishing variety of permutations in fighter designs during the 1930s. The Germans decided on speed and the Messerschmitt Bf 109. Fortunately for Britain, Air Marshal Dowding pushed through the acceptance of the Hurricane and the Spitfire against strong opposition. Had he not done so, the RAF would have been destroyed in 1940, with unimaginable consequences to the future of the world.

rals then asked to see Sir Maurice Hankey (the same who, unknown to them, had recently suggested that Britain should lean away from France and towards Germany and Italy) in the belief that he might be more sympathetic. Hoare obstructed this with a note to Hankey, one paragraph of which read:

> When I speak of 'neutrality' I mean strict neutrality, that is to say, a situation in which the Russians neither officially nor unofficially give help to the Communists. On no account must we do anything to bolster up Communism in Spain, particularly when it is remembered that Communism in Portugal, to which it would probably spread, and particularly Lisbon, would be a grave danger to the British empire.[7]

His interpretation of 'neutrality' was idiosyncratic in the light of what was happening at Gibraltar. On 20 July the Republican warships in the Straits, which had left their bases without waiting to take on supplies, put into Tangier with a request to buy fuel, food and water. Franco threatened to bomb the docks if the request was granted, and the oil companies, with the approval of the international commission that governed the port, refused to sell. The ships crossed to Gibraltar and again asked to be allowed to buy oil and supplies. The senior officials and naval and military officers on the Rock, who had been friendly with local Spanish landowners for years and had often been invited to hunting parties and fiestas on their estates, were horrified at the sight of warships manned by unkempt ratings exchanging clenched-fist salutes and by rumours that below decks were officers in chains awaiting torture and death. There were no legal grounds for prohibiting the private oil companies to sell oil to the navy of a government still recognized as friendly, but the problem of how to avoid such sales was solved when a few of Franco's aircraft tried to bomb the warships, which were lying in the Bay of Algeciras. The oil companies then decided that the risks of selling their product were too great and the Republican ships were obliged to sail to Málaga, leaving the Straits temporarily unguarded. Asked in the House of Commons why oil had been refused by the government to the navy of a friendly nation, Eden replied that the government had not refused. Spanish ships, and a British tanker in the bay, had been attacked from the air. 'In these circumstances His Majesty's Government felt that they could not put pressure on commercial firms which might involve their running abnormal risks.'[8]

Shortly after this incident, the battlecruiser HMS *Queen Elizabeth* was stationed across the mouth of the bay to discourage further intrusions. When the Republican battleship *Jaime I* returned from Málaga to bombard Algeciras, it was turned back and the Nationalist troops in the town, no longer needed for its defence, were freed to join the Nationalist force advancing from Jerez de la Frontera towards Ronda and Granada.

On 5 August, however, a Nationalist convoy of small vessels sailed past the *Queen Elizabeth* and disembarked 2,000 troops and a battery of 105 mm howitzers at Algeciras.[9] Meanwhile, after Hitler's decision to send aid became known to Franco, General Kindelán, the Nationalist air chief, was permitted to use the telephone exchange at Gibraltar to put long-distance calls through to Lisbon, Berlin and Rome for the purpose of co-ordinating the operation.[10] Since Gibraltar was the most important British communications centre on the European continent and presumably under appropriate security-control regulations, it is hard to see how this could have been managed without the fact becoming known to the Admiralty in London and thus to the First Lord himself, Sir Samuel Hoare.

There is no mystery as to why the British government welcomed 'Non-Intervention'. The English are less a 'nation of shopkeepers', as Napoleon called them, than a nation of schoolmasters, whose chief satisfaction is to put other people ever so slightly, or better still very much, in the wrong. In this respect, 'Non-Intervention' fitted the bill perfectly. As it was a French initiative, the British could disclaim responsibility for it when it attracted criticism. Above all, it showed that British motives in adopting it were not selfish but disinterested: by preventing the division of the European powers into two blocks lined up behind one or the other side in Spain, it would reduce the risk of a general war. There were, naturally, other strategic considerations, such as the vulnerability of Gibraltar, the vital necessity of keeping open the chain of communication between the United Kingdom, Suez, India and the Far East, and the menace of Nazi expansionism, but these were not brought into the discussion until weeks, in some instances years, later.

Anthony Eden and his successor, Lord Halifax, always denied that the British government put any pressure on the French in this affair. Blum told contradictory stories. To Hugh Dalton, several times a Labour minister and one of the few on that side to support rearmament, Blum said that it was untrue that Britain had imposed Non-Intervention upon him against his will. It had, on the contrary, all been his idea, for he believed that if everyone honoured the agreement it would benefit the Republicans more than the Nationalists, whereas the free sale of arms to both sides would have the opposite effect.[11] To his Socialist colleagues, however, he always said that he had been forced to give in to intolerable British pressure. Jiménez de Asúa, in a statement written for a conference of historians on the subject in 1965, relates that Blum, 'his eyes full of tears', explained that Baldwin had gone over his head and contacted Président Lebrun, warning him 'in the most formal terms' that if the sale of arms to Spain provoked a confrontation with Germany, Britain would no longer feel herself bound by her treaties to stand by France.[12]

Blum dealt with the threats of Pierre Cot to resign if arms and aircraft were not sent by telling the Chamber of Deputies that until the agreement was ratified by all the powers concerned, France would reserve the right to act as she saw fit, should other powers continue to aid the Spanish rebels. He then privately told Cot to proceed with the dispatch to Barcelona of the military aircraft, which, with the help of André Malraux and his friends, could be sold through commercial agencies. However, in compliance with the declaration of 25 July, they must, of course, be delivered *unarmed*.

7

Malraux and his Men

B Y THE SUMMER of 1936 André Malraux was thirty-five years old and already a celebrity as the winner of the Prix Goncourt for his novel *La condition humaine* and as one of the most brilliant defenders of the Communists. He was not, however, a Party member. His life seemed to have been crowded with adventures, he seemed to know an astonishing array of famous people, from Trotsky and T. E. Lawrence to Picasso and André Gide, and he seemed to be everywhere at once. In conversation he tended to drown his listeners in a torrent of words, always eloquent and occasionally dazzling. As even André Gide noted in his diary, 'he makes one feel so unintelligent!'

He belonged to innumerable committees, some of them the brain-children of the ever-inventive Willi Meunzenberg, who was then chief of the propaganda bureau of the Communist International in Paris. In May 1936, as the delegate of one such committee, Malraux had visited Spain, where he had met most of the leading politicians and writers of the left, and it was presumably on the strength of this that yet another body, La Comité Mondiale des Intellectuels contre la Guerre et le Fascisme, of which he was chairman at a meeting on Tuesday 21 July, decided to send him to Madrid with a message expressing its solidarity with the Spanish people in their world struggle against Fascist aggression.[1] The journey would have to be made by air and, not being a pilot, Malraux turned to his friend Edouard Corniglion-Molinier, a soldier, airman and adventurer who had been pilot when he and Malraux had flown to the Yemen in 1934 to search for the lost city of the Queen of Sheba. Through Leo Lagrange they applied to Pierre Cot. Cot explained that, since the Spanish request for arms had seemed more appropriate to quelling a small colonial disturbance than to defeating a full-scale military rebellion, it would be valuable if they brought back information as to what assistance the Madrid government really needed. When they agreed, he put at their disposal a beautiful American-built Lockheed Orion passenger monoplane, painted silver-grey with a red flash down each side of its fuselage. It had been bought by the racing pilot Michel Detroyat for the great 'McRobertson' England-Australia air race of 1934 but, when the engine with which he had refitted it had yielded a lower performance than expected, had been scratched and sold to the CEMA (Centre d'Essais des Materiels Aériens), the air ministry testing centre at Villacoublay, south of Paris.[3]

André Malraux, his wife, Clara, and Corniglion-Molinier left Villacoublay late on Friday evening 24 July.* As dawn broke next morning at Biarritz, the airport controller told them, with unconcealed satisfaction, that there was no point in going on since Madrid had just fallen to the rebels. They took off nonetheless, climbed above the Pyrenees and dropped down to follow the road across Navarra and Old Castile towards Madrid. The only traffic they saw was an occasional ox cart or military lorry and, indeed, they detected no signs of life anywhere until, passing over a castle that towered above a hillside village, they noticed soldiers firing up at them from its battlements. Once, looking down into a village square, they saw some men and women huddled by a wall and, facing them, a semi-circle of men holding rifles. As they climbed again to cross the Sierra de Guadarrama, north of Madrid, a curl of smoke, motionless against the clearing mist, betokened a burning building. They reached Barajas airport at about 8 a.m., to see two large Douglas DC-2 transports, a Fokker trimotor and a small Nieuport fighter, with Republican red bands on its wings, lined up on the tarmac in front of the hangars. But who was in possession? They circled anxiously for some five minutes before they saw red sheets being spread on the grass as an invitation to land. A party of government officials was waiting to greet them.[4]

During the morning Malraux was taken to see President Azaña and then the editors of the larger newspapers. In the office of the Communist daily *Mundo Obrero* he talked for half an hour with the Communist

---

* In *André Malraux*, the film director Denis Marion stated that Malraux and he flew to Madrid early on Monday 20 July, aboard the last regular passenger service before the route was closed. When questioned about this by Professor Thornberry in 1970, Marion confirmed the date and insisted he was not mistaken (Robert S. Thornberry, *André Malraux et l'Espagne*, p. 28), and the story reappears in several histories of the Spanish Civil War. Since all passenger flights were cancelled at dawn on 18 July (see above, Chapter 6, n. 2), they cannot have been on one. The only aeroplane to fly from Paris to Madrid on 18 July, leaving in the small hours, was a LAPE Douglas DC-2 which, on the strict orders of the operations manager, Capitań Joaquín Mellado, carried no passengers (Andrés García Lacalle, *Mitos y verdades*, p. 71). Had Malraux and Marion flown not to Madrid but to Barcelona in a mailplane, sitting uncomfortably on the floor amidst postbags, Marion would have mentioned it. He did not, and must have been mistaken. Curiously, Clara Malraux-Goldschmidt also mistakes the date of their flight on 25 July, giving it as the 20th (*Le bruit de nos pas*, vol. 5, *La fin et le commencement*, pp. 13–14).

deputy and orator Dolores Ibárurri, known as La Pasionaría. After a quick sightseeing tour round Madrid, they flew to Barcelona to interview the leaders of the Generalitat, the Catalan regional government.

Malraux had planned to stay in Spain a week. On Sunday afternoon, however, the Madrid government, having received Rios's information about the change of policy of the French government, telephoned Corniglion to ask if he could fly Albornoz, the newly appointed ambassador, to Paris without delay. Malraux decided to go with them, for everything he had heard had by now convinced him that his best service to the Republic would be to raise a squadron of aircraft and volunteer airmen. Shortly after landing at Villacoublay on Monday evening (27 July), Malraux told a correspondent for the Basle weekly *Rundschau über Politik* that Fascist troops, who were carrying out wholesale executions as they advanced, were within 80 kilometres of the capital:

> The freedom fighters (*Freiheitstruppen*) defending Madrid lack arms, planes, pilots and military technicians . . . and it is in the interest of France and Britain to make good these deficiencies . . . or do we stand idly by while Hitler and Mussolini close up the Mediterranean and overrun all Europe? There is not a day, not an hour, to lose! The Fascist powers are already shipping military equipment to the rebels![5]

This was as yet untrue and, moreover, the Madrid government was not to learn of Italian intervention for another three days or of German intervention for another fortnight. However, when Malraux spoke at a huge rally in support of the Spanish Republic at the Salle Wagram on Thursday evening, 30 July, he backtracked slightly, warned of the dangers of irresponsible intervention by armed powers and appealed for humanitarian aid only. Blum, the last to speak, was nevertheless heckled throughout by the rhythmic chanting of 'des AVIONS pour l'Espagne! Des CANONS pour l'Espagne!' which, as a British embassy official who was present noted with approval, he pretended to ignore.

Because it was essential that there should be no visible contact with the Spanish embassy in connection with the provision of arms, aircraft or volunteers, Malraux's function was that of a go-between whose existence, since he had no official standing, could be denied. Similarly, it was because they needed someone with the intelligence, contacts and sufficiently senior rank to act as a confidential liaison with the French that Rios and Albornoz asked Malraux to be the nominal commander of the squadron that was to be formed. Perhaps too it occurred to them that to have a famous novelist as the leader of a squadron of airmen who had volunteered to defend freedom might later acquire considerable propaganda value. Malraux's ignorance of aircraft and military aviation was to some extent remedied by the arrival of Andrés García de la Barga y Gómez de la

Serna, better known as the journalist and author Corpus Barga, whose novels have in recent years come to be admired in Spain. Indeed, his last book, *Los galgos verdugos* ('The Executioner Greyhounds') won the Premio de la Crítica Española ('Spanish Critics' Prize') in 1974, a year before his death at the age of eighty-eight. He had adopted the pen-name Corpus simply because the day of his birth (9 June 1887) had coincided with the feast of Corpus Christi.

In 1936 Corpus Barga was well known in Madrid cultured society and a close friend of President Azaña. Although he never joined a political party, he had always supported liberal causes and had twice been forced into exile under the monarchy. He was by all accounts a civilized and entertaining companion with a vast repertoire of picaresque tales abut life at the Madrid court, which he had heard from his father, who had been a confidant of King Alfonso XIII. On 18 July he had been in Moscow as a correspondent for the Argentine newspaper *La Nación* and had immediately left for Spain. However, since he had some knowledge of flying, having covered aviation stories since before the Great War, Rios asked him, when he reached Paris, to stay and assist in the buying of aircraft.[6]

Since the aircraft were to be delivered unarmed, they came under the aegis of Cot's chef de cabinet for civil aviation, Jean Moulin, who during the Second World War was to become the co-ordinator of the Resistance until he was murdered in Lyon by Klaus Barbie in 1943. Moulin was obliged to work with a small number of trusted colleagues in order to outwit the obstruction of all those officials and officers around him who were opposed to any form of aid to the Spanish Republicans. He was able to keep a great deal secret, and the first reasonably accurate list of the French aircraft sent to the Republicans during the civil war was not published until 1990.[7] His principal collaborators who can be identified were Joseph Sadi-Lecointe, Edouard Serre of Air France and Lucien Bossoutrot, all of whom belonged to that remarkable generation of French airmen who, during the 1920s and early 1930s, had pioneered air mail services and airlines over every hazardous and hitherto inaccessible quarter of the globe. By 1936 these three held influential positions in the French aviation world. Sadi-Lecointe had been the first person to fly at over 200 m.p.h. (in 1920) and had broken six world speed records and two world high-altitude records. Until 1934 he had also been the chief test pilot of the Nieuport and Loire-Nieuport companies and in 1936 was the director of the French civil airmen's association APNA (Association Professionale des Navigants Aériens), supervisor of training to the FPSA (Fédération Populaire des Sports Aéronautiques), which possessed a number of flying schools created to provide a pool of trained airmen who could be called up in the event of war, and in June had been made director of the new Aviation Populaire, which had been established by Cot as a

state-funded organization for exactly the same purpose. Finally, he held a
senior position in the Constructions Aériennes department of the air ministry.

Edouard Serre was a man of strong character and strong left-wing views
who had been employed as a pilot and radio engineer by the Aéropostale
company, the perilous lives of whose airmen have been described in the
books of Antoine de Saint-Exupéry. After many adventures in Africa,
including a long spell as a prisoner of the fierce R'Guibat tribesmen of the
western Sahara, Serre had been chief of radio communications for the
airline in South America. Aéropostale, however, had gone bankrupt in
1932 after labour troubles in which Serre had played a well-meaning but
disastrous part by forcing a pay rise, at an inopportune moment, out of the
embattled management for his radio technicians but for nobody else. In
the dispute that followed Saint-Exupéry accused him of having 'destroyed
the spirit of sacrifice' that since the beginning had kept the line (known to
the airmen who flew for it as simply 'La Ligne,' as though there were no
other in the world) solvent; as a result the two had become estranged.[8]
Serre's reputation as a radio engineer, nevertheless, had ensured his being
kept on when Aéropostale was absorbed by Air France in 1933 and the
patronage of the politically sympathetic Pierre Cot had ensured his rapid
promotion. He was now the technical director.

Lucien Bossoutrot had been a minor ace in the Great War and, as a civil
pilot since then, had won no fewer than twenty-nine world records,
mostly for long-distance flying. In 1934 he had gone into politics and been
elected as a Radical Socialist deputy for Seine (Paris). Since then he had
become the Président de la Commission Aéronautique de la Chambre des
Députés, with the result that he spent much of his time in parliament field-
ing furious verbal attacks from the right against the air minister. He
was also director of the FPSA and technical adviser to CAMAT (La
Compagnie des Assurances Maritimes, Aériennes et Terrestres), an insur-
ance company used by airmen and the aviation industry.

In her autobiography Clara Malraux implies that most of the recruiting
was done by André and herself, using their apartment in the Rue Lafayette
as an office. In fact, most of it was done through Giustizia e Libertà,
APNA or the FPSA, while Armée de l'Air pilots on the reserve list were
enrolled by Capitaine Roznet, chief of the reservists' training centre at
Orly.[9] During the morning after his return from Madrid, Malraux visited
Carlo Rosselli and others of the Giustizia e Libertà group to discuss
recruitment for the proposed squadron. Giustizia e Libertà, led by the
brothers Carlo and Nello Rosselli, was a remarkable association of exiles
from Fascist Italy who published books, pamphlets and a newspaper
representing every shade of liberal and left opinion except Communism,
which the movement opposed almost as resolutely as it opposed the

Fascists. Indeed, it was precisely this spirit of opposition to totalitarianism in all its forms that made Giustizia e Libertà an object of particular fear and hatred on the part of the Italian government, which employed every means to bring about its destruction. It was eventually successful, for in June 1937 the Rosselli brothers were assassinated in France, in peculiarly horrible circumstances, by agents of Mussolini's secret police, the ubiquitous OVRA, in collaboration with the French Fascist terrorist gang Les Cagoulards ('The Hooded Ones'). In the late 1920s and early 1930s Giustizia e Libertà had organized several daring anti-Fascist propaganda flights over Italian cities, in imitation of Gabriele D'Annunzio's flight over Vienna in August 1918, during the Great War.[10] Associated with, but independent of, Giustizia e Libertà had been Alleanza Nazionale, whose leader, the poet-airman Lauro di Bosis, was killed when, after a daring leaflet-raid on Rome on 3 October 1931, his plane ran out of fuel and crashed at sea. He had been the lover of the great American comedienne Ruth Draper. When she died in 1956, her ashes too were, at her request, scattered in the sea off the Maine coast to mingle symbolically with his.

Thus the movement had a dozen or so airmen, aircraft engineers and mechanics living in Paris as political refugees. One man at a meeting on 28 July was an undercover agent from the OVRA, and from his report it appears that Giordano Viezzoli, an ex-military pilot whose escape from the Italian police to France in 1934 had sparked world-wide interest, and Veniero Spinelli, an observer–gunner, had already left for Barcelona. About ten more, who included as well such non-airmen as Pietro Nenni, who became leader of the Italian Socialists after the Second World War, and the distinguished Anarchist philosopher Camillo Berneri, were to leave within a week.[11]

Although there was no shortage of anti-Fascist groups of various nationalities in Paris, the number of qualified aviators and mechanics among them was small and it was clear that if enough were to be found to make a squadron, mercenaries would have to be hired and the financial terms would have to be attractive. The monthly pay of a sergeant pilot in the Spanish Aviación Militar was 900 pesetas, the equivalent of 2,592 Ffr. (£36 or $180). It was therefore decided to offer nearly ten times this amount, that is to say 25,000 Ffr., per month as well as an all-risks insurance policy for 200,000 Ffr. with CAMAT, which was arranged by Lucien Bossoutrot.[12]

By the beginning of the first week of August, when the first planes were transferred from Paris to Toulouse for their hop to Spain, about a dozen pilots and an equal number of observers, as well as a few mechanics, had been recruited. Some, including Abel Guidez (an ex-military pilot), Chiaromonte (an Italian gunner) and Sanzio (Vincent) Piatti, a mechanic, went for reasons of political idealism and accepted the pay of their equivalents in the Spanish air forces. Others were pure mercenary adventurers, such as the inappropriately named Bourgeois, who had worked for Aeropostale in South America, then flown as a bootleg pilot for Dillinger, and lastly fought in the Gran Chaco War between Paraguay and Bolivia in 1934–5; he could, he claimed, fly 'anything that had wings'.[13] Two were planted by the Deuxième Bureau, the French secret service, who wanted political, technical and military intelligence on the air fighting in Spain.

One of those planted was Jean Dary, a minor Great War ace (five victories). He was serving a year's imprisonment for car theft, but was released through the combined efforts of the Bureau and Jean Moulin, who had been a prefect of police before joining the air ministry. In Spain Dary proved to be the most serious, most skilful and bravest of the fighter pilots in the Escuadra España, as the international squadron was at first called.[14] In September he shot down at least four Nationalist aircraft and, when his contract was renewed in October, was able to double his wages to 50,000 Ffr. a month. In November the newly arrived Russians asked him to join one of their two I–15 Chato fighter squadrons. He did write two secret reports for Pierre Cot,[15] but at the end of November the Russians ordered him to leave the squadron and, when asked why, explained that he had already done excellent service and that they did not want to expose him to further risks.[16] Perhaps they had found out about his reports, possibly even through Pierre Cot himself, if Cot really was the Soviet spy he was later accused of being.[17]

The other Deuxième Bureau agent was Victor Veniel, a reserve captain of the Armée de l'Air. He likewise wrote two reports, less informative in some respects than Dary's, and in 1973 wrote a deposition for the Service Historique de l'Armée de l'Air, which was then sending questionnaires to surviving witnesses of the Spanish war period, including Pierre Cot himself.[18] In this last he was highly critical of Boussotrot, whom he accused of having profiteered from the sale of worn-out and useless aeroplanes to the Republicans, and of Malraux, whom he dismissed as 'a mere adventurer incapable of exercising effective command'. He himself was to serve with distinction in the Second World War, flying with French, British and Polish squadrons; he won the Croix de Guerre and Légion d'Honneur and retired in 1967 with the rank of colonel. By the time he wrote his deposition he had moved politically very much to the right, and his remarks therefore may have had a political colouring. His claim to have been the real commander of the squadron has been vehemently denied by others; though, since Malraux's position was never supposed to have been more than nominal, the dispute seems trivial.

As for the aircraft these men were to fly, the plan to export the seventeen old Potez 25s quickly came to grief. The aircraft manufacturers Henri Potez and Marcel Bloch, who after the Second World War changed his name to Marcel Dassault and achieved renown as the builder of the legendary Mirage series of fighters, had a joint company, Potez-Bloch CAMS, for sharing government contracts. In May 1935 Bloch had received an order to build forty-four Bloch MB 131 and the nearly identical MB 132 bombers but, owing to difficulties with the prototype, none had been started by July 1936. On 28 July Potez-Bloch CAMS received a supplementary order from the Constructions Aériennes department, where Sadi-Lecointe worked, for seven additional MB 132s. In lieu of payment the company was to receive the seventeen Potez 25s, stripped of their armaments, which, now that they were private property, could be sold by the company to the Spanish Republicans. The money would then be forwarded, after the company had deducted its cut, to the air ministry and the account books would show nothing more abnormal than an intended buy-back of old Potez aircraft for salvaging as spare parts, or perhaps for use at the Potez flying school at Orly, until this unexpected offer for them came from a foreign purchaser, probably in Mexico. The air ministry would not have to make a second payment for the MB 132s because the order would, after a discreet interval, be cancelled, as indeed it was.[19] Unfortunately, an outraged official in the Constructions department gave the details to the right-wing newspaper *Le Figaro*, which published them next morning; indeed, a transcript of the very order was soon circulated to all the newspapers.[20] Meanwhile, Major Aboal, who was now the Spanish air attaché in Paris, had discovered that only seven of the Potez 25s were airworthy and that the rest would require several weeks' work to make them so. He therefore cancelled the purchase of the aircraft, which, being scarcely less ancient than the Breguet Bre 19s of the Spanish Aviación Militar, had already caused more trouble than they were worth.

To make up the numbers of the Potez 54s, Corniglion-Molinier asked the Amiot company to sell six Amiot 143 heavy bombers, of strangely angular and cumbrous appearance, which were waiting to be delivered to the Armée de l'Air, but the board of directors refused to sell any of their products that might fall into the hands of 'Spanish Communists'. On 26 July Sadi-Lecointe visited the head office of his old employers, Loire-Nieuport, at Saint Nazaire. Someone immediately informed *Le Figaro*, which next morning claimed that this must be in connection with the supply of warplanes to the 'Reds', and Sadi-Lecointe was obliged to issue an official denial that he had visited Saint Nazaire for any other reason than to enquire about the lease of a new flying field to Aviation Populaire. In fact, he had gone to ask the Loire-Nieuport directors to allow the transfer to Spain, as soon as a third country could be found to act as ostensible buyer, of the first six Loire 46 fighters from a series of sixty that was being built for the French air force. The company agreed, but explained that, as production was months behind schedule, the fighters would not be ready for at least five weeks.[21]

There remained the fourteen Dewoitine D.372s, originally ordered by Lithuania and cancelled before the outbreak of the war in Spain, and the Potez 54s (more exactly, 540s), of which six, just completed for a French bomber squadron, were now available. The Dewoitines had been built not by the Dewoitine company at Toulouse but by Lioré et Olivier at Clichy, Paris, one of the oldest and largest aircraft factories in France. Although these fighters would have been difficult, perhaps impossible, to sell elsewhere at this late date, Henri Olivier, the co-founder of the firm, bitterly opposed their sale to the Spanish Republicans. He was overruled, but his opposition was remembered six months later, when the company was nationalized in January 1937 and the new administrative committee, with a preponderance of Cot's nominees, forced his resignation from the board of directors.[22]

The agency handling the transaction was the Office Générale de l'Air, a leading aircraft sales and repair organization in Paris whose director, André Faraggi, was a friend of Pierre Cot. Malraux received some financial advice from Clara's uncle, the banker Jacques Goldschmidt, and Edy du Perron, a Dutch novelist and friend of Malraux, acted in some capacity in the buying of the Potez 540s.[23] The export permit names Andrés García de la Barga (Corpus Barga) as the buyer in France on behalf of 'Andrés Ramirez, de Formento 21, Madrid'. The valuations on the permit, which take no account of agents' commissions or the fact that the aircraft lacked all equipment for their weapons (sights, firing mechanisms, mounts, racks, etc.), show that the prices paid for the machines were steep indeed. The valuation at the equivalent of $40,211.84 per Dewoitine represents an increase of 27.6% over the $32,541.71 that the Lithuanians had contracted to pay for them, and the $107,780.91 per Potez an increase of no less than 73% over the $62,295.29 that a *complete* aircraft would have cost the Armée de l'Air. At that time a brand new Douglas DC-2, a much more advanced and expensive aeroplane to produce, could be bought on the export market, with all its equipment and seating, for between $74,000 and $92,000 depending on the quantity ordered.[24]

8

Setbacks

AT NINE O'CLOCK on Tuesday morning 4 August 1936, six of the fourteen Dewoitine D.372 fighters built for Lithuania were wheeled on to the tarmac in front of the CEMA hangars at Villacoublay.[1] They were high-wing 'parasol' monoplanes, with large radial engines and 'spatted' undercarriages,* of that dunkily attractive appearance possessed by many aeroplanes of the mid-1930s, but, to judge by two snap-shots taken that day, their metal surfaces had been sprayed to dull their shiny reflectiveness and the Lithuanian 'double-crosses' and all other markings, except for tiny production serial numbers stencilled beside the cockpits, had been removed. Although the Lithuanians had cancelled the contract in favour of the more advanced D.510s, these were still modern fighters with a performance similar to that of the Gloster Gladiator, a type which was not to enter RAF service for another five months. Their virtue was a superb rate of climb; their vices were that they were unforgiving to novices and were especially tricky to land,** and throughout the morning three company test pilots explained to three French air force reservist sergeants (Bois, Halotier and Guidez) who had joined Malraux's squadron the idiosyncrasies of these rather temperamental machines.[2]

The six fighters, flown by the three company pilots and the three reservists, left for Toulouse-Francazal aerodrome that afternoon. Halotier lost his way, however, and came down in a field about 120 km to the west,

---

* 'Parasol': a monoplane whose wing stood clear above the fuselage, supported by struts. 'Spats': the streamlined cowlings over the wheels of aircraft with fixed under-carriages.

** Like the gull-wing Loire 46s delivered in September, they had a tendency to 'float' just before touching down to land, which needed practice to correct. Lacalle relates that when two experienced Russian pilots, 'Julio' (Ivan Kopets) and 'Pedro' (probably Evgeni Erlikin), tried out two Dewoitines for the first time at Getafe in September, there was a cross-wind that obliged them to make five or six attempts before bringing the planes down safely (Andrés García Lacalle, *Mitos y verdades*, p. 135).

breaking the undercarriage and a wing. The pilots returned to Paris, where they were joined by four more volunteers, flew three fighters to Toulouse on Wednesday and the last five on Thursday 6 August. On the same day, the first two Potez 54 bombers arrived at Toulouse from the Potez airfield at Meaulte, near Albert in northern France. Toulouse-Francazal was divided into two halves, one being the civil airport and flying club, the other a military airbase which was also used as a test field by the Dewoitine company, whose hangars and workshops stood alongside. However, whereas the fighters had immediately been wheeled into the Dewoitine hangars and out of sight, the two large Potez bombers, not being company property, were left in the open for all to see. A crowd soon gathered along the dividing fence and next day a local right-wing daily, *L'Express du Midi*, observed that, while the pilot of one was a Potez employee, the pilot of the other was a Russian and that his passenger was Marcel Bloch. 'What a coincidence! A Russian and a Jew! *Toute la graine du bolshevisme!*'[3]

The export manager of the Office Générale de l'Air, Maurice Quedru, had come down to Toulouse to carry out the 'sale' of these aircraft to Corpus Barga and, together with Bloch, telephoned Edouard Serre at the Air France office in Paris. Serre gave permission for the two Potez to be transferred to the nearby airport at Toulouse-Montaudran, where, as it was the private property of Air France, entry could be forbidden both to snoopers and to the police, many of whose officers were suspected of being opposed to what was going on. Indeed, that very night (6–7 August) Frédéric Atger, the prefect of police for the department of Haute-Garonne, of which Toulouse was the capital, received a telephone call from the Sûreté in Paris instructing him to place the aircraft under guard and prohibit their departure. He was about to obey this order with enthusiasm when a call from the ministry of the interior told him that the aircraft must be allowed to leave for Barcelona. A few minutes later the customs office at Toulouse phoned to say that any flights to Spain without customs clearance must be prohibited. Later that night Jean Moulin rang from the air ministry to say that the flights were authorized and must be permitted. Next morning the Sûreté sent written instructions that the flights must not be permitted and that the planes must be put under strict guard.[4] By then, however, the two Potez 54s had flown to Montaudran, a few kilometres away beside the road to Béziers. The Dewoitines, meanwhile, were still in the company hangars, where Atger's gendarmes were unable to enter without a special warrant. A third Potez landed that evening, but, when someone ran out and shouted warnings, the pilot turned her round and took off again for Montaudran.

Throughout the week the newspapers had been reporting some untoward events at Bordeaux and the high-handed seizure by 'Spanish Reds' of French aircraft at Alicante. On 28 July four Fokker airliners, which

British Airways had sold to the Nationalist General Mola, had been grounded at Bordeaux airport on their way to Burgos and, after a diplomatic contretemps embarrassing to the Foreign Office in London, had been sent back to Gatwick on 2 August. This outcome had infuriated the Bordeaux city corporation, who, in sympathy with the Spanish rebels, had wanted the aircraft to be sent on to Mola (see below, Chapter 9). Next day, the *Atxuri Mendi*, a Basque coaster, arrived in the estuary to take on the arms that had originally been requested by Aboal and Warleta on 21 July. The list had since grown to 2,000 Lebel rifles with 2 million cartridges, 50 Hotchkiss machine-guns with 5 million cartridges, 8 Schneider 75 mm field-guns with accessories and ammunition (probably 1,000 shells apiece), 5,000 5 kg aircraft bombs and 5,000 10 kg bombs, from which it would seem that Rios had got his way in restricting the size of bombs to under 15 kg.[5] To judge by contemporary prices, the total value of the cargo would have been about 22 million Ffr., of which the Spaniards had already paid 11 million to the French defence ministry. The Spanish consul at Bordeaux, don Alfonso Otero Barceda, a Nationalist who had deliberately not informed the Madrid government of his true sympathies, alerted the port authorities and the city corporation, who, seeing a chance to get their own back on the government in Paris, refused the ship entry until her captain had obtained the necessary permits. Two Basques at the Paris embassy, Picavea and Aldasoro, hastened down to Bordeaux and, with the aid of sheafs of orders and numerous phone calls, were able to force the authorities to grant the permits. Since the consul himself had not yet been officially dismissed and replaced, the government in Madrid having more urgent things to attend to, they were not able to evict him from the consulate building, where he continued to make mischief for several weeks more. The *Atxuri Mendi* docked and began to load the arms, the stevedores, fervently pro-Republican, volunteering to work round the clock to shorten a job that otherwise might take a week.[6]

At Alicante, the rebellion had not been finally crushed until 24 July. Four days later Air France began to send passenger planes down to its private airfields at Barcelona and Alicante to evacuate French citizens, using for the purpose some old Latécoère 28s and Fokker F.VIIb3ms taken out of reserve. On 29 July a group of CNT (Anarchist) militants walked onto Alicante airfield and commandeered two Latécoères and a Fokker, declaring that flying troops to the front had a higher priority in the world struggle against Fascism than helping French capitalists to escape to safety.[7] The next day a fourth Air France machine, probably a Latécoère, came down in open country near Alarcón, in the province of Cuenca, from which village a group of the local controlling party, which happened to be the PSOE (Socialist), went to see what the trouble was. The passengers turned out to be two members of the Comintern, the

Bulgarian Boris Stefanov, Stalin's chief agent in Spain since the early 1930s, and Grigory Stern, and the aeroplane to have been commandeered at Barcelona to fly them to Madrid. Stefanov ordered them to get him to Madrid immediately, speaking in so overbearing a manner that the Socialists took them instead to Valencia in a lorry, a humiliation which Stefanov never forgot or forgave – he was later to play a sinister role in the overthrow of Largo Caballero and, in 1938, the dismissal of Prieto. The plane, meanwhile, was refuelled and, after an airstrip had been cleared by the villagers, flown to Getafe military airbase at Madrid.[8]

The French government made a formal protest to the Spanish government, which in turn demanded the release of the aircraft at Alicante. The Anarchists, supported by the city governor, refused and a crisis was averted only by Edouard Serre, who arranged for the Latécoères to be sold to the Republicans as soon as the task of flying out French citizens was finished.

The newspaper reports of these incidents were pointed out to the British ambassador, Sir George Clerk, who accordingly visited Yvon Delbos at the Quai d'Orsay on Friday 7 August. He had come, he said, to have a private and informal conversation for which he had not sought the approval of His Majesty's Government. If the French government had rightly prevented the sale of the four British airliners to the Spanish insurgents on the grounds of Non-Intervention, how could it now justify these arms sales, including that of the *military* aircraft at Toulouse, to the Spanish government? Apologizing for speaking so frankly, he put before Delbos 'the danger of any action which might definitively commit the French government to one side of the conflict and make more difficult the close co-operation between our two countries which was called for by this crisis'.[9] Delbos took the hint, thanked Clerk for speaking openly and said that, while he himself was deeply concerned at the situation, the French government had every reason to fear that Franco had offered the bait of the Balearic Islands to Italy and the Canaries to Germany, and if that materialized, 'goodbye to French independence!' Without saying how he had dealt with that last remark, the ambassador ended his report to Eden by apologizing for having spoken without instructions, 'but I had reason to believe that the extremists in the (French) government were putting pressure on M. Blum and I felt sure that what I said might strengthen the hands of the moderate and sober elements.'

After reading this, it is hard to understand how Eden or anyone else in later life could insist that the British put no pressure on the French government. Moreover, it was on that same morning that the two French admirals returned from their fruitless mission to London, and it was their account of this which finally convinced Blum that 'talking about Spain to the British was as productive as talking to a brick wall.' Blum immediately called an emergency meeting of his closest allies and went over the problems once again. The attitude of the British was only too evident, and most of the other governments in Europe were openly or tacitly in sympathy with the Spanish rebels. Opposition at home, whipped up by the right in parliament and the press, was growing more clamorous and threatening every day. Even if all these were defied, could the French arms industry – let alone the aircraft industry, long disrupted by strikes and about to suffer the upheaval of nationalization – seriously match the combined productive capacities of Germany and Italy if it came to a free-for-all contest in the supplying of arms to Spain? After a long and impassioned argument, Blum and his friends decided that the only course open to them was for France to declare Non-Intervention unilaterally and without waiting for the agreement of the other European governments, who might indeed be influenced by such an example of restraint. A cabinet meeting was due next day, Saturday 8 August, at which the decision could be ratified and brought into force at midnight. This at least would allow time for the aircraft at Toulouse to leave for Barcelona, though probably not for the ship to finish loading at Bordeaux.[10]

When he saw which way the meeting was going, Pierre Cot slipped out and telephoned Malraux to warn his pilots to fly the aircraft to Spain as quickly as possible. Malraux phoned Toulouse and then, hiring a Caudron Simoon air taxi, flew down there himself.[11] The pilots, who had just received their departure money, had planned a night on the town and refused to leave, saying it would be dark before they reached Barcelona, although in fact it was only half-past five and the flight would take less than an hour. Sergeant Bois, struck by his conscience or perhaps by the thought that an extra flight to Spain would earn him several thousand more francs, changed his mind and took off in Dewoitine no. 7 at half-past six and landed safely at Prat de Llobregat, Barcelona, at about twenty-past seven. Malraux then flew back to Paris to collect the three last Potez 54s and the remaining volunteers and mercenaries.

That same evening, the French minister of finance, the Socialist Vincent Auriol, telephoned the Spanish Socialist Luis Jiménez de Asúa, who had recently arrived in Paris, to warn him of the new situation in general and concerning the arms at Bordeaux in particular, for these, he explained, would have to be stopped 'because of the British'.[12] Asúa, it will be remembered, had supervised the writing of the Republican constitution, was vice-president of the Cortés and had been the target of an assassination attempt the previous March which had resulted in the imprisonment of the leaders of the Falange. As an internationally respected expert on penal law, he had been invited to address a conference of criminologists in Prague on 20 July. While passing through Paris on 18 July he had called on Blum and other French Socialist leaders and told them that the political situation in Spain was 'excellent' and that 'we are well pleased'. Although news of the uprising, which had begun the previous night, had not yet reached the outside world, this was an extraordinary thing to say only six days after the murders of Castillo and Calvo Sotelo, for Asúa was a man of high intelligence whose ear was usually close to the ground. When he had arrived back in Paris on his way to Spain, the Madrid government had asked him, in view of his long-standing friendships among the French Socialists, to stay in Paris and assist Rios and Albornoz with legal and financial advice in the buying of arms, and it was he who had remitted the 11 million Ffr. to the French defence ministry in payment, or part-payment, for the arms now at Bordeaux. He called on Blum and was told how Baldwin had gone over Blum's head and threatened President Lebrun with the consequences that would ensue if the arms sales went ahead.

Then Blum said to him 'word for word, "we are *salauds* if we do not keep our promises; and since we cannot, we Socialists will leave the government. The crisis is about to begin!"' Asúa returned to the Spanish embassy and consulted with Albornoz and Rios, both of whom were convinced that it was essential that the Blum government stay in office. Trying to think of ways of avoiding its fall, one of them suggested that Asúa take the cheque back and tear it up in Blum's presence as a sign of their renunciation. Asúa vehemently disagreed, arguing that they should tell Blum that if the French Socialists meekly accepted what Baldwin had imposed on them and still remained in government, they would have failed in their duty. Besides, the Socialist party, which was strong in the Chamber of Deputies, would do more for Spain in opposition than in office.

Unable to decide, they telephoned Madrid and were told that the Spanish foreign minister, Augusto Barcía, agreed with Albornoz and Rios. 'Very much against my will', wrote Asúa in 1963, 'I went to see Léon Blum at his home and tore up the cheque as a sign of our renunciation. I did not fail to tell the premier what had happened. With a sad smile and speaking in a very low voice, he replied "I think you were right!"'[13]

The first of the three remaining Potez 54s landed at Toulouse early on Saturday 8 August, and during the morning four more Dewoitines and the three Potez that had arrived on Thursday left for Spain. The pilots were then flown back to Toulouse-Montaudran, presumably in one of the Latécoères bringing out French citizens, and those needed for the rest of the Dewoitines were driven to Francazal by car. Meanwhile, Malraux spent the morning frantically collecting the volunteers and mercenaries still in Paris, while Clara waited for him in the bar at Villacoublay, where, at lunchtime, she overheard some air force officers protesting at this 'treason' and trying to think of ways of stopping it.[14] By early afternoon the whole group, now joined by the *Pravda* correspondent Mikhail Kolzov, was ready and the two Potez, one of them piloted by Corniglion-Molinier, took off for Toulouse-Francazal, where they landed shortly after five. When Malraux and Corniglion went to the duty office, they were surprised to be greeted by Captain Jean Esparre, whom they had met at Djibouti in 1934 during their flight to the Yemen. They were both in flying clothes, with parachutes trailing behind, and Malraux, who was looking tired, asked Esparre if he could spare some mechanics to check one of the Potez, which was giving trouble. Esparre told them regretfully that he had just received orders not to assist any of the party leaving for Spain. In his account Esparre writes that they had his deepest personal, but not his political, sympathy, adding that in those days 'officers did not meddle in politics!'[15] Yet it would seem they did, for Esparre had received these orders from his superior officer before Non-Intervention was due to come into force. Malraux and Corniglion returned to their machine and took off for Montaudran, leaving for Barcelona at a quarter-to-seven. Kolzov has described how, as the Potez in which he was flying circled the field before turning for Spain, he looked down and saw Malraux standing on the tarmac below, 'legs spread, hands in pockets, cigarette in mouth, just like the proprietor of a music hall during a dress rehearsal.'[16]

Meanwhile, the last eight Dewoitines were preparing to take off from Francazal, seven of them to be flown by the pilots who had just returned from Barcelona and the eighth by Roger Nouvel, a wealthy sports flyer who was to earn a lot of money in the next few months by ferrying aircraft to Republican Spain. The engine of one would not start, however, and Bois was brought back, for the second time, at first light next morning to see if the fighter could be collected. Although Non-Intervention had come into force the previous midnight, he was allowed to leave, and took off at 9.45.

A few days later the US cruiser *Quincy*, which was taking American citizens from Barcelona to Marseille, sent a radio message to US naval communications, which was passed to the State Department, reporting the arrival of this force at Barcelona and noting that three of the Dewoitines 'cracked up' on landing:

> They carried places for machine-guns, two on fuselage and two on upper wings. Planes came with French pilots some or all of these believed intending to stay in Spain. Two pilots are Italian, one or two German and three or four foreigners, no Americans. Reported to be a rough crowd and soldiers of fortune. It is stated they intend to take the planes to Madrid. Six Botet [Potez] planes also arrived, making 18 in all that started for Barcelona . . . Carried gun turrets . . . all had bomb-racks, gun mountings but no guns. Planes believed to require expert handling and Spaniards not believed capable of handling.[17]

While the damage to the three fighters was a disappointment to the Spaniards, far more bitter was the discovery that the aircraft had arrived not only without their armaments but without even the means of installing them. Each Dewoitine was supposed to have four fixed fore-ward-firing machine-guns, two Darne 7.5 mm mounted in the wing to fire outside the propeller arc and two Brownings in the fuselage synchronized to fire between the rotating propeller blades, as was standard at that time. However, in addition to the guns, the electrical firing mechanisms, synchronization mechanisms, gun-mounting plates, ammunition boxes, troughs and gun-sights had all been removed. There were no spare parts for the aircraft themselves and the data cards and cockpit instruments were in Lithuanian, which nobody could read. As for the Potez 54s, the informant on the *Quincy* seems to have been mistaken, for Colonel Veniel has related that on the first missions bombs had to be stacked on the floor and thrown out by hand, there being neither bomb-racks nor bomb-sights, a fact confirmed to the author by Vincent Piatti, who was serving with the squadron as a mechanic at the time.[18]

A day or two after the arrival of the squadron, a small team of Dewoitine company mechanics was flown over from Toulouse to repair the three damaged fighters, a service requiring payment in cash. By 16 August the armaments, which everyone believed were coming by road, had still not arrived; indeed, they never arrived, and the squadron transferred to Cuatro Vientos air depot, Madrid, where two more Dewoitines crashed on landing. Meanwhile, as a result of Asúa's tearing up of the cheque, the arms that had been loaded on to the *Atxuri Mendi* at Bordeaux had been taken off again and the ship had sailed with a normal cargo for Antwerp on 15 August.[19]

Thus far, the Nationalist appeals to Hitler and Mussolini had yielded a small air force: 29 bombers, 6 fighters and another 35 fighters on the way, complete with well over 100 trained and skilled men, anti-aircraft batteries and the logistical support needed to maintain it in the field.[20] The pilots and crews were familiar with their mounts and many of them had flown together before, an important factor in aerial warfare. All this was being supplied on credit, for which the terms had not even been discussed, for, as the Italian foreign minister, Count Ciano, said to a Nationalist emissary on 24 August, 'Not one more word about money matters! After the victory we can talk about them, but not now!'[21] By contrast, the governments of Britain, France and other democracies had responded to Republican appeals for help with a sequence of evasions, deceptions and broken promises leading to an international arms embargo in disregard of international law. Far from receiving credit, the Republicans had had to pay for everything in advance, at prices increased by nearly 50% or perhaps more, with cash raised by selling gold from the national reserve to the Bank of France.

There can be few human artefacts more useless than a fighter aircraft without its armaments. The French military aircraft in Spain failed not because they were inferior to the German and Italian, as is said in nearly all histories of the Spanish Civil War, but because there were so few of them and because they were sent without arms or the means of installing them and unsupported by maintenance back-up, trained pilots or anyone to train them. As the account and the numbers of aircraft delivered given in this book differ from those previously published in histories of the war, further details and the documentary evidence for them can be found in Appendix I, where the controversial question of Malraux's personal role is also discussed. Despite his great intelligence, he had an unfortunate tendency to encourage, or at least not to discourage, the invention of myths about himself, which, when he became de Gaulle's minister of culture in 1958, gave rise to contemptuous and much publicized denigrations of him, particularly from old Communists who had never forgiven his turning against them after the signing of the Nazi-Soviet pact in August 1939.

The Lockheed Orion in which André and Clara Malraux first flew to Madrid and in which the new Spanish ambassador was brought to France, made two more flights to Spain, leaving for the last time on 12 August. Among the passengers was the photographer Robert Capa. During the flight from Barcelona to Madrid, the Orion made a forced landing near Alcañiz in northern Teruel and suffered some damage. Telephone calls from Madrid asked the local militia to bring this valuable property of a valued ally to Barajas as soon as possible. The Orion was loaded on to two ox carts linked together by pivoted wooden planks to allow them to turn corners. However, when the convoy reached the first village, the wings prevented the Orion from passing between the houses. The militia saw that the aeroplane was constructed of wood with a plywood skin. As Madrid had stressed the urgency of getting the Orion to Barajas, they sent for the village carpenter and told him to saw off the wings. This he did, and the militia, having roped the wings to the fuselage, resumed their trek to the capital.[22]

9

The London Junta

O N THE DAY of the uprising a group of Spanish monarchists resident in London, some of whom had taken part in the conspiracy, formed a Junta Nacional for the purpose of marshalling support from the press and exploiting their connections with British politicians, civil servants, bankers and businessmen.[1] The Junta included the Duque de Alba, the Marqués de Portago, the Marqués del Moral and don Alfonso de Olano y Thinkier, a Spanish landowner with an estate in Scotland who converted his suite at the Dorchester Hotel into offices for use as headquarters. Its chief, by virtue of his influential friends in the aviation industry and his role in the hiring of the Dragon Rapide for Franco, was don Juan de la Cierva, a charismatic engineering genius remembered today as the inventor of the first practical rotor aircraft, the Autogiro, of which various models had been produced in series by A. V. Roe and Company, or Avro, at Manchester.*

While the Marqués del Moral, in charge of propaganda, canvassed the national press and received promises from the owners and editors of the *Daily Telegraph*, *Daily Mail* and *Morning Post* that their newspapers would report the events in Spain in a manner favourable to the Nationalists, Cierva and his colleagues considered ways to thwart attempts by the Giral government to buy war material. In this they had the co-operation of five of the seven consuls in the United Kingdom, most of the diplomats and staff at the Spanish embassy and, above, all, of the Spanish ambassador himself, don Julio López Oliván. Although a man of aristocratic background and monarchist convictions, he had served the Republic as a diplomat with such exemplary loyalty and the League of Nations, as a judge at the Court of International Justice, with such distinction, that in May the Popular Front had seen no risk in appointing him

---

* Including about seventy Model C.30As, of which ten were for the RAF and seven for the Spanish air forces, built in 1934–5.

ambassador to Britain. Indeed, the only person to raise a difficulty had been King Edward VIII, who, on learning that Oliván was married to a divorcee, had objected that such a person could not be received in audience. The resulting contretemps, which mystified the Spaniards since Edward's own determination to marry the American divorcee Mrs Simpson was not yet public knowledge, had delayed the new ambassador's arrival until 11 July and his presentation of letters of credence to the king until the 14th, only four days before the coup.[2]

When the fighting broke out in Spain, Oliván's conscience at first prompted him to resign. However, several members of his family were in Madrid, where the news of his resignation would almost certainly lead to their arrest and murder by one or another of the bands of 'uncontrollables' roaming the streets. Accordingly, on 23 July he sent a letter by courier to General Mola in Burgos pointing out that, while his sympathies were with the rebels, if he resigned he would be replaced by the consul-general in London, 'a person dangerous to The Cause', just as Cárdenas and the other diplomats in Paris were being replaced by Socialists who were willing to carry out orders to buy arms for the Giral government. He could serve 'The Cause' better, therefore, by staying on and adopting 'a policy of dissimulation'.[3] Having cleared himself with Mola, he told Eden next day that even if the coup failed, the present government in Madrid would soon be taken over by the Communists, a remark that Eden thought important enough to underline before relaying it to the Cabinet.[4]

By now, Oliván had taken the first measure to make things difficult for his government, should it request him to buy arms in England. Britain had been the principal supplier of weapons and equipment to the Spanish navy since the 1900s and many Spanish warships were based on British designs or had even been designed in Britain,* payment being made through the Spanish naval commission account at the Westminster Bank. The main reserve fund for Spanish state expenditure in the United Kingdom was held by the Agencia del Banco de España in London. Oliván therefore authorized the transfer of a 'considerable sum of pounds sterling' from the Agencia to the naval commission account, which placed the money under the control of the naval attaché, Captain Manuel Medina Morris, who likewise had decided to remain in post and work undercover for the Nationalists. Thus, when an order arrived on 27 July for the purchase of 5,000 shells and 4,000 shell-fuses from Vickers Armstrong,** Medina was

---

* For example, Sir Philip Watts, of Armstrong Whitworth, had designed five Spanish cruisers, including the ultra-modern *Canarias* and *Baleares*.
** These were for the *Churruca* class destroyers, similar to the British *Scott* class, of which thirteen had been built between 1928 and 1936. All remained with the Republican fleet. Displacement, 1,560 tons; speed, 36 knots; armament, five 120 mm

able to ensure that nothing was done about it.[5] When Oliván saw Eden again the next morning, 28 July, he assured the foreign secretary that no request for arms purchases in the United Kingdom had as yet been received from Madrid. What would be the British response, he asked, if such a request were received? Eden replied that it would be treated in exactly the same way as a similar request from any other friendly government. Oliván passed this reply to Madrid and on the 30th received a telegram saying that since it was now clear that the British would not refuse official requests for arms purchases from manufacturers, would Oliván please begin negotiations at once? 'A person of trust is being sent' (this was Major Carlos Pastor Krauel, to whom we shall return in due course). Eden had meanwhile gone on holiday but, before leaving, had left instructions at the Foreign Office that plausible means be found to delay or refuse export permits.[6]

Throughout August Oliván and Medina, with the collaboration of officials at the agency of the Bank of Spain, withdrew sums of Republican money from the account of the naval commission and, whenever possible, used them to buy arms for the Nationalists. For example, on 5 August, there arrived an order from Madrid to buy twenty-three sets of twin machine-guns from the Hotchkiss company in Paris, with whom Rios was already negotiating, together with a million rounds of ammunition. At contemporary prices, the whole order should have cost under £14,000.*Instead, Medina sent £30,000. Later in the month he sent £21,000 to Rafael Estrada, his counterpart in Rome, who had set up an agency for buying arms for Franco, and £16,000 to a company named Finckler in Berlin. On 19 August Medina lunched with an Admiralty intelligence officer, Commander Towers, and confessed that he was secretly working for the Nationalists, to whom he was trying to divert a consignment of French machine-guns. Towers, however, did not believe him and reported that he was convinced that Medina was 'working whole-heartedly for the Spanish government', which may explain why, when Medina finally resigned at the end of August and made a brief trip to Germany, he was, to his surprise and dismay, refused re-entry into Britain.[7]

Although British arms sales had always been controlled, the current arms export prohibition order of 1931 had made no mention of civil aircraft, and it was through this loophole that Cierva and the Junta hoped to obtain benefits more substantial than handfuls of small arms and cartridges. Their first attempt was a fiasco.

It began in the evening twilight of Tuesday 21 July, when a dark blue de

---

(4.7 in.) guns and one 76 mm (3 in.) anti-aircraft gun, all by Vickers Armstrong, and six 71 in. triple torpedo-tubes by Thorneycroft.

* About £375 per twin gun and £5 per thousand rounds, at 25.225 gold pesetas to £1.

Havilland Dragon Rapide, hired by Lord Beaverbrook from British Airways, landed at Gamonal airfield, Burgos. The pilot was Robert Henry McIntosh, the celebrated 'All Weather Mac', and his passengers were three journalists who wanted to cover the war on the rebel side, Sefton Delmer of the *Daily Express*, H. R. Knickerbocker of International News of America (i.e., the Hearst Press) and Louis Delaprée of *Paris Soir*. They were all arrested and taken to General Mola. When, in the course of questioning, Mola asked McIntosh if he knew of any large aircraft for sale, he was told of four Fokker F.XII airliners at the brand new airport of Gatwick , where British Airways, then a private company, had recently opened for business. The F.XIIs, trimotors big enough to carry fourteen passengers, had been bought from KLM, via Crilly Airways, in February for £15,000 each. It had been intended to use them on a projected service between Gatwick and Lisbon via Spain as the first step on a route from England to South America, but the scheme had come to nothing owing to the obstruction of the Spanish Popular Front, which hated the Portuguese dictator, Oliveira Salazar. They had then been put up for sale but, as they were old, their price had dropped to £2,000 each.[8]

While flying errands for Mola to Lisbon and Biarritz, McIntosh telephoned the British Airways manager in Paris, Captain Dudley Taylor, who suggested that they buy the Fokkers themselves, sell them to Mola for £60,000 and make a profit of £52,000 between them. McIntosh, unwilling to cheat a company he had only just joined, refused.[9] Taylor then rang Gatwick and told the managing director, Major Ronald McCrindle, that 'the Spanish Northern Revolutionary Army of General Mola' wanted to buy the Fokkers for £60,000 and that the famous French aircraft company of Farman was willing to act as agent.[10] However, an hour later British Airways received a cable from their Lisbon agent, James Rawes & Co., to say that a local firm, Vanzella Panhu, would pay £38,000 for the machines. This offer was accepted as likely to cause less trouble, and McCrindle asked the Air Ministry and Foreign Office for their approval. The Air Ministry said that this was a purely commercial transaction and no concern of theirs, but thought it a good idea to get four such obsolescent aeroplanes out of the country. The Foreign Office suspected a 'Spanish hand' in the affair somewhere but said it had no power to stop the sale. McIntosh sent an itinerary: as France was to be avoided at all costs, two of the Fokkers, which had fourteen hours' endurance, could fly direct to Burgos and the other two, with only seven hours' endurance, could stage at Jersey, where he would arrange for friends to refuel them. This was rejected by McCrindle, who said that payment must be in gold pesetas and placed in a Paris bank before the aeroplanes crossed the Spanish frontier. The only way to be sure that this was done properly was for McCrindle himself to fly to Paris in one of the Fokkers, as no other aircraft were at present available. McIntosh could never understand why all this could not have been done by phone and suspected that McCrindle was unable to resist the chance of a free weekend in Paris and a visit to the Moulin Rouge.[11] Whatever the truth, one aircraft took McCrindle to Paris on Sunday 26 July and the other three, one carrying a cargo of spares, flew to Teygnac-Mérignac airport, Bordeaux. It was not until 5.15 p.m. next afternoon that the Marqués de Rivas de Linares,[12] who suddenly appeared as the buyer on behalf of General Mola, was able to pay the 970,000 gold pesetas into the Paris bank and the aircraft to leave for Bordeaux.* Meanwhile, Dudley Taylor, piqued at being deprived of his profit, told André Faraggi, director of the Office Générale de l'Air, the agency that handled the sales of the Dewoitines and Potez to the Republicans a day or two later, that the Fokkers were 'going to the Fascists'. Faraggi told the air minister, Pierre Cot, who, convinced that the British were at the bottom of all his troubles over Spain, ordered the aircraft grounded, informed the press for good measure and sat back to enjoy the discomfiture of '*l'Albion perfide*'.

At Bordeaux the four machines were boarded just as they were about to take off and the crews sent back to their hotel. The airmen at Bordeaux protested to the reporters besieging their hotel, and McCrindle in Paris to the French authorities, that the aircraft had been scheduled to fly straight to Lisbon and not land in Spain. The British ambassador, Sir George Clerk, phoned the Foreign Office and Eden, disturbed at his holiday refuge, said nothing should be done until the Air Ministry had explained why it had approved the sale in the first place. Sir George Mounsey, assistant under-secretary at the Foreign Office, minuted that if British Airways got their planes back they would only fix up another deal right away. 'The company have got themselves into their own mess and must get out as best they can.'[13]

This, however, was looking increasingly difficult. The Bordeaux city corporation (who, it will be remembered, were enthusiastic for Franco and four days later were to try to prevent the Republican ship *Atxuri Mendi* from docking and taking on a cargo of arms) ordered the planes released so that they could fly on to Burgos, but when the airmen, accom-

---

* The British registrations of the Fokkers, and their crews, were: G-ADZH; pilot, Flt. Lt. J. B. W. ('Johnny') Pugh; radio operator, Philpott; passenger, McCrindle, to Paris. G-ADZI; pilot E. G. L. Robinson; radio operator, Allan Wood (whose diary of the flight was kindly lent to me by John King, historian of British Airways). G-ADZJ; pilot, A. L. T. Naish. G-ADZK; pilot, D. S. King. The price paid includes £38,000 (958, 550 ptas) for the aircraft and £450 (11,351.25 ptas) for four spare Pratt & Whitney Wasp engines and spare parts, which at 25.225 ptas gold per £1 makes 969,901 ptas gold (PRO, Foreign Office general correspondence, FO 371/20533 W 9096 and Wood's diary).

panied by some Spanish Nationalists, went to the airport and their interpreter, a *Daily Telegraph* reporter, pushed open the hangar door, they
were confronted by armed gendarmes and a crowd of mechanics, who
escorted them back to the gate shouting 'Fascistes!' That night (30 July),
during the rally at the Salle Wagram, where Blum, Malraux and others
tried to make themselves heard above the massed chanting of 'Des avions
pour l'Espagne! Des canons pour l'Espagne!' one speaker demanded that
those in the air and war ministries who were preventing the delivery of
arms to Spain should be purged. 'Let us begin by burning those four
Fokkers at Bordeaux!'[14]

Baldwin, worried by foreign newspaper reports referring to British
Airways as a government-controlled concern, called a special cabinet
meeting and decided there was nothing for it but to ask for the aircraft
back. Cot, after some expression of surprise at this crude intervention
against the legal government of Spain, and extracting a promise that the
planes would not be sold to a Spanish buyer in future, ordered their
release. No sooner had the machines landed at Gatwick on 2 August,
however, than McCrindle received a phone call from Faraggi, offering to
buy them for 1 million Ffr. (£13,158) each. The offer was declined.[15]

A week later, yet another offer came for these recently unsaleable airliners, this time from a Polish aristocrat turned arms dealer named Stefan
Czarnecki, who was staying at Jules's Hotel in Jermyn Street.[16] The purchaser was 'West Export' of Danzig (Gdansk), acting on behalf of a
mining company at Katowice in southern Poland, and the sum offered
£33,000.[17] Czarnecki was one of the Paris agents of Fritz Mandl, the
famous Austrian arms manufacturer and industrialist, and the 'Polish
mining company' may have belonged to Mandl or been briefly created by
him for this single transaction. On 14 August four Polish pilots, accompanied by G. Morawski representing 'West Export', arrived at Gatwick and
spent the afternoon spreading maps on the office floor and planning the
flight to Katowice. When they took off next morning, 15 August,
McIntosh noticed how the stately trimotors banked and yawed from side
to side as they tried to gain height and, on mentioning this to McCrindle,
was told that one of the Poles had admitted over drinks the previous night
that they were fighter pilots who had never flown large multi-engined aircraft before.

Some hours later two of the Fokkers were seen flying not over
Germany towards Poland but high over Biarritz towards the Pyrenees,
where clouds were massing and from which the rumble of distant thunder
could be heard. Shortly after the storm reached Biarritz, one of the
Fokkers, G-ADZI, came flying in below the clouds with the obvious
intention of landing on Parme-Biarritz airfield. After two passes,
however, the pilot, Count Kazimierz Lasocki, apparently decided to make

for the larger airport at Bordeaux. As the machine began to climb north-wards, there was a brilliant flash of lightning and a deafening clap of thunder directly overhead. The Fokker stalled, turned slowly onto its back and plunged vertically down, crashing with a fearsome explosion into the garden of a local English resident, Reginald Wright, joint master of the South Atherstone Hunt in Leicestershire. One of his weekend guests, the ballerina Alicia Markova, who was returning from a walk and hurrying to come in from the rain, ran down through the woods to the blazing wreckage, but, by the time she arrived, so intense was the heat of the flames that she could not get near, let alone help anyone trapped inside.* Meanwhile a second Fokker, G-ADZK, piloted by Czarkowski-Gajewski, having turned back from the mountains, crash-landed on Lagord airfield, near La Rochelle, and was damaged beyond repair. The third, G-ADZJ, piloted by Major Kazimierz Ziembinski, landed at Bordeaux and was impounded. The fourth, G-ADZH, piloted by Adam Szarek, a skilful airman who had won the Polish national light plane contest in 1935, crossed the Pyrenees and landed in the grounds of a sanatorium at Barañain, near Vitoria.[18] Next day two Nationalist pilots, Captain Angel Salas and the Duque de Prim, were sent to guide Szarek to Burgos but, when the Pole refused to go near the machine again, they decided to ferry it themselves. After some hours in the cabin trying out the controls, they took off for Burgos and, while Nationalist airmen and mechanics watched with bated breath, brought the F.XII safely down on Gamonal airfield.

At the British Airways head office in London, Mr Roberts, the chair-man, told the press, 'This is an astounding thing!' The company, he insisted, had taken every precaution to check the authenticity of West Export and had known nothing of a Spanish backer behind the deal.[19] In that case, someone suggested, the Polish ambassador might be able to throw light on the mystery since the Polish 'Colonels' Government', notwithstanding the fact that it had been the first to proclaim an arms embargo against both sides in Spain, on 23 July, made no secret of its enthusiasm for General Franco and the Nationalists. In the absence of the ambassador, who was on holiday, the Polish chargé d'affaires issued an angry statement denying any complicity on the part of his government in this criminal adventure. Moreover, he declared, it was absurd of British Airways to pretend that it had checked the credentials of the Danzig firm when they had not even approached the embassy, where they would have

---

* Most newspapers reported that the charred remains of *two* bodies had been found in the wreckage and assumed that the second body was that of Morawski. The *Manchester Guardian*, however, said that Morawksi had been seen to leave G-ADZJ with Major Ziembinski when they landed at Bordeaux.

been strongly warned that Danzig, a Free State outside Polish jurisdiction, was a notorious sanctuary for disreputable traders.[20] The statement may have been true at the time but did not long remain so, for the profit earned from handling the sale of these four airliners soon persuaded the Polish government that there was money to be made from the civil war in Spain and that most of it would have to come from arms sales not to the Nationalists, whom it morally supported, but to the Republicans.

The British air attaché in Paris, Group Captain Douglas Colyer, who detested Pierre Cot and found everything he had heard about Franco admirable, lunched with Captain Dudley Taylor a week later. Although not very informative about the Fokkers, Dudley Taylor did mention that André Faraggi, the head of the Office Générale de l'Air, had told him that Pierre Cot had 'considerable financial holdings' in the Potez company, which probably explained why he was so keen that Potez aircraft should be sold to the Spanish 'Reds'.[21] This news was greeted with satisfaction in the Foreign Office, where no one bothered to ascertain its truth, and thereafter the French air minister's name rarely appeared in a report from Colyer without some such comment as 'young crook' or 'little rascal' appearing too in the minutes, added by officials as the report passed through the departments.

On 6 September the Bordeaux city corporation took its revenge on the French government by arranging for the Fokker F.XII G-ADZJ to fly surreptitiously to Burgos, so surreptitiously indeed that its departure was unreported. The two F.XIIs served as bombers in the Nationalist air force until they were relegated to transport duties in the spring of 1937. G-ADZH survived the war and in the 1950s was probably the last airworthy Fokker trimotor in existence. In 1930, in the days when it had belonged to the Royal Dutch East Indies Airline, or KNILM, the Indian poet and sage Sir Rabindranath Tagore had been among its passengers on a 2,600-mile journey from Būshehr, on the Persian Gulf, to Calcutta. He had never been in an aeroplane before and he told reporters after landing at Calcutta aerodrome that from now on, in his opinion, flying was the only way to travel long distances.[22]

10

'Little Men in Black Suits with Bags of Gold'

I N THE 1930s the two main civil aerodromes near London were at Croydon and Heston. Croydon was the international airport, but its almost Edwardian terminus building, its lack of runways and the conservative complexion of the Imperial Airways fleet, half-a-dozen stately biplanes with cruising speeds of about 95 m.p.h., made it an object of much lament in the aeronautical press of the time. Heston aerodrome lay on a site, covered today by roads and housing estates, a little to the east of the present London airport at Heathrow. It had been built by, and belonged to, Airwork Ltd, the foremost aircraft repair and brokerage firm in Great Britain, who rented hangar space to various air transport services and used it besides for all kinds of air meetings, races and rallies. Croydon and Heston were therefore ideal places to go for anyone in need of new or second-hand aircraft.

Juan de la Cierva and his colleagues of the Junta Nacional at the Dorchester Hotel, who were badly in need of new or second-hand aircraft, soon found an able and well-situated helper in Tom Campbell Black, the world-famous co-winner, with Charles Scott in a scarlet de Havilland Comet, of the MacRobertson England–Australia air race of 1934. Campbell Black proposed to Cierva that they turn Heston, where he ran an air charter company, into a clearing-house for aircraft intended for the Nationalists.[1]

Between 25 July and 15 August the Nationalists managed to buy twelve passenger aircraft, of which six departed from Heston and all, except for the two Fokker F.XIIs that crashed in France, were delivered to General Mola at Burgos.*After 4 August however, they found themselves against

---

* Four de Havilland Dragon Rapides: G-ADCL, 1 Aug 1936; -DFY, 4 Aug 1936; -CPN and -DAO, 13 Aug 1936. One G.A. Monospar ST-12, G-ADDY, 2 Aug 1936. One Airspeed Envoy II, G-ADBB, 6 Aug 1936. Two Fokker F.VIIb3ms, PH-AFS *Specht* and -AGR *Reiger*, 13 Aug 1936. Two Fokker F.XIIs, G-ADZH and -ZJ, 15 Aug

increasing competition from the Madrid government, whose agent had arrived in London and, through contacts provided by sympathizers, engaged a firm of professional gun-runners in the City to find the aircraft for him, buy them and get them out of the country (see below, Chapter 13).

With the end of summer approaching, small air transport companies were faced by the annual nightmare of having to replace old or obsolescent machines, which nobody wanted to buy, with expensive new ones.[2] Indeed, so short was the life of an aeroplane and so numerous the hazards of commercial flying that many managers were beginning to wonder if it was possible to run a small airline profitably in England. Thus, as Alex Henshaw has recalled, when the racing pilot Bill Humble told him one morning at Heston that 'little men in black suits were on the tarmac with bags of gold buying any aircraft they could',[3] the eruption of civil war in Spain, whatever the political rights and wrongs, offered a chance of salvation not to be missed.

The British government, conscious that something like this might happen since the arms export regulations did not apply to civil aeroplanes, instructed the police sergeant at Heston to note down all suspect departures, but, as he soon reported, this was difficult because 'a great deal of secrecy is being observed at the moment by the Chiefs of Messrs Airwork Ltd regarding their transactions with aircraft.'[4] Mary de Bunsen, who was press secretary for Airwork and Heston during those years, says in her memoirs that:

> When the Spanish Civil War broke out, everybody knew perfectly well that all the unsaleable second-hand aircraft in England were being hurriedly furbished up and flown to Spain, where they were used, probably as bombers, by one side or the other. This was really a case in which the less said the better, so I lied valiantly over the telephone all morning while the aircraft took off.[5]

However, an engineer who was working at Gatwick in 1936 and 1937 has told me that 'furbishing up' was sometimes more a matter of 'furbishing down'. For example, when a Dragon Rapide or Dragon (an earlier version of the Rapide), which had been sold to a Spanish buyer at more than twice its market value, was found to have engines in good condition, 'say, with 100 hours left', it was refitted with nearly worn-out engines with perhaps only forty hours left before being flown next morning to its departure point for Spain. This, of course, was a potential death sentence on its future Spanish crew should an engine fail while flying over mountainous terrain behind enemy lines.[6]

1936. G-ADZH arrived 7 Sept 1936. Crashed in France: 2 Fokker F.XIIs, -ZI and -ZK, 15 Aug 1936. To compare with Republican aircraft sent and delivered, see below, p. 94, n.

The first machine to go to the Nationalists was a de Havilland Dragon Rapide, G-ADCL, recently rebuilt after a crash and bought through Airwork from the Anglo-American Oil Company. The pilot was Lord Malcolm Douglas Hamilton, the 24-year-old director of Air Service Training, a college for commercial air crews at Hamble, near Southampton, and the younger brother of Lord Clydesdale, who had led the Lady Houston flight expedition over Mount Everest in 1933.* The navigator was Richard L'Estrange Malone, the European sales manager of Airwork and son of the eccentric Lt.-Col. Cecil L'Estrange Malone, a sailor, soldier and airman who had planned and led the first aerial torpedo-bombing attack in history during the Dardanelles campaign in 1915 and from 1920 to 1922 had, when not in prison, sat in parliament as a Communist member for Leyton East. As the Rapide would have to reach Burgos in a single non-stop flight, its passenger seats were removed and five-gallon petrol drums stacked and fastened down in the saloon, leaving only a narrow tunnel, through which the two men had to crawl to reach their seats, and making escape by parachute impossible. The petrol was fed from the drums into the main tank through a hose, which L'Estrange Malone, in addition to his duties as navigator, had to transfer from drum to drum as each became empty, and a hand-pump, which he had to 'woggle' vigorously to keep up the flow and clear airlocks. The registration letters on the wings and fuselage sides were blanked out, false letters painted on and these in turn painted over with the genuine ones again in lamp black, the idea being that should the plane have to land in France or some other unintended place, these could be sponged off to reveal the false letters.[7] The Rapide left Heston at dawn on 1 August and reached Burgos some seven hours later. If other flights to Burgos are a guide, Douglas Hamilton was paid £150 and L'Estrange Malone £90, plus £75 each for expenses. After they had celebrated their success, they were guided by Nationalist officers, under cover of darkness, through Republican territory, across the Pyrenees and into France.

As an instance of the dangers these flights could entail, Donald Salisbury Green told me how he and T. Neville Stack, a celebrated record-breaking pilot, delivered two Fokker F.VIIb3m trimotor airliners from

---

* Possibly out of courtesy to the Fascist-admiring Lady Houston, who had sponsored the Everest flight, Lord Clydesdale joined the Anglo-German Fellowship and during these years made two visits to Germany on the invitation of Nazi leaders, with the result that in 1941 it was he, who by this time had become the Duke of Hamilton, whom Rudolf Hess hoped to meet when he flew to Scotland. Although on the right of the Conservative Party, he was not a crypto-Nazi, as some accused him of being, but used his visits to German to gather information about aircraft production and the strength of the Luftwaffe. This he passed to Churchill, of whom he was a friend and supporter.

Croydon to General Mola at Burgos on 13 August. This was a day on which no fewer than eight aircraft flew off to Spain, including, from Heston, two Rapides (one bought from British Airways) for the Nationalists and two Dragons for the Republicans.

On 10 August Stack and Salisbury Green had been invited to Claridges Hotel, where the Duque de Alba was then living, to meet a group of Spaniards, of whom one was Major Carmelo de las Morenas Alcalá, the ex-air attaché in Paris and London who had resigned and joined the rebellion. After much talk about the honour of officers and gentlemen, 'red hordes' and the importance of not creating another 'cock-up' like that over the Fokkers at Bordeaux, Salisbury Green and Stack, armed with bank drafts for 40,000 florins (£5,420, or $27,100), flew to Amsterdam to buy two old Fokker F.VIIb3ms (PH-AFS *Specht*, or 'Woodpecker', and PH-AGR *Reiger*, or 'Heron') which KLM were about to replace with Douglas DC-2s. KLM refused to sell directly to the Spanish clients, but agreed to sell indirectly through Crilly Airways, which was bankrupt and about to be bought by British Airways, provided the airliners were flown to Croydon by KLM pilots to make the deception appear more convincing. At Croydon the trimotors were fitted out with hoses and extra petrol drums, but 'some damned fool', convinced that the rarefied atmosphere high over the Cantabrian mountains would cause them to explode, punched holes in the top of each one. To work the hose and hand-pumps, Salisbury Green took on, for a fee of £100 10s., Captain Sir Anthony Mildmay M.C., late of the Grenadier Guards and a member of the brewery family. He had just completed a cure and was forbidden alcohol under all circumstances.

Everything went well enough until, approaching the Biscay coast, Salisbury Green (in -AGR *Reiger*) started his climb to reach the 14,000 ft (4,672 m, the absolute ceiling of the Fokker F.VII) that he felt he needed to clear the savage and beautiful Picos de Europa with safety. At about 10,000 ft (3,048 m) all three engines cut out suddenly and the Fokker began to drop, swaying and wobbling, towards the sea. Looking round, Salisbury Green saw 'a Niagara' of petrol pouring out of the holes in the tops of the drums and back towards the tail. Mildmay, against repeated warnings, had managed to bring two bottles of gin on board, one of which, empty, was rolling about in the petrol on the floor. The neck of the other protruded from his overcoat pocket. He was now trying to light a cigarette, fortunately in vain as Salisbury Green had had the cabin windows open and air was buffetting through the interior of the aircraft. Pretending to want a drink himself, Salisbury Green persuaded the reluctant Mildmay to hand over the half-empty bottle, which he threw out of the window, and shouted to him to start pumping *at once*. The Fokker, nevertheless, was barely 100 metres above the water before its engines burst into life again and they were able to climb to rejoin the other trimotor, in which Stack was circling anxiously to see what had happened. Once over the mountains, they dived down nearly to ground level, found the road to Burgos and roared along it at full throttle with wheels almost touching the surface, blowing up vast clouds of dust behind them and scattering donkeys and chickens as they swerved round or over villages, until they put down on Gamonal airfield.

Meanwhile, several British pilots had flown to Burgos to see what else they could offer. On 28 July Campbell Black himself left for Paris, where he collected the Marqués de Rivas de Linares, who had just paid over the gold pesetas for the British Airways Fokkers. He took him, via Burgos, to Lisbon and thence back to Burgos. On his return to England he sold his story to the *News Of The World*, which gave it front-page treatment on Sunday 9 August: 'THE SPANISH REVOLUTION FROM THE INSIDE: NIGHTMARE FLIGHTS FROM FRONTIER TO FRONTIER, by Campbell Black, the famous airman.' On their journey they often saw fighting in the villages below them – indeed, sometimes above them, for Campbell Black preferred to fly his Puss Moth along the bottoms of the valleys. They were fired on frequently, and invariably when they came down to land. He was astonished by the wildness of the landscape of Extremadura near the Portuguese frontier: 'I cannot hope to convey a picture of this forbidding country, with its colossal gorges and yawning precipices, and towns and villages perched crazily on the hillsides above', and he heard that it was in these inaccessible *pueblos* that some of the fiercest fighting and most horrifying atrocities had occurred. As an Englishman, he said, he remained strictly neutral and his sympathies impartial, 'for the political provocations of all this I do not hope to understand'; but, 'having seen murder in the eyes and weapons in the hands of women and little children', he must warn the British public that 'there is a third army in Spain today, an army born of rebellion, but fighting for no political ideals or social betterment, ... killing for the sake of killing ... which threatens to sweep the country back to pre-civilization.' He did not mention that his own reason for flying to Spain was to negotiate the sale of aero-engines to the Nationalists.[8] Campbell Black was killed five weeks later, on 19 September at Speke, Liverpool, when he accidentally taxied his Percival Mew Gull, which he intended to enter for the Schlesinger Trophy race to Johannesburg, into the fanning propellor of an RAF Hawker Hart. His death was mourned by airmen all over the world.

Campbell Black had left his de Havilland Puss Moth in Portugal, where it vanished from recorded history, and returned to Spain in a twin-engined de Havilland Dragon belonging to Crilly Airways of Croydon. The pilot, Captain Steele, told him that while passing over Gibraltar on 29 July he had nearly collided with a little Republican flying boat, whose crew had hastily put down in Gibraltar harbour and explained to the Gibraltar authorities that they had been attacked by a Fascist fighter. In London, Oliván, the Spanish ambassador, formally requested its return but was refused, the Foreign Office informed him, because that would constitute intervention.[9] Why Steele should have been flying a Crilly Airways Dragon over the Straits of Gibraltar is not known. The Rock had no airstrip at that time, no British airline ran a service in the region and, if it had, would have suspended it on 18 July. Perhaps it was in connection with Franco's order to Sr. Delgado of the Ibarrola Oil Co. at Ceuta to go to England to buy aircraft (see above, p. 17). There is no record that Delgado was in London, however, probably because the Nationalists abandoned their attempts to buy aircraft in England after 15 August.

Another airman carrying out similar missions was Owen Cathcart-Jones. He had been the first fighter pilot in the world to make a deck-landing by night on an aircraft-carrier, had broken several records, had, with Ken Waller, come fourth in the MacRobertson race, had taught several celebrities to fly, including Jack Buchanan, Sir Philip Sassoon and Lady Nelson, and recently had been personal pilot to Edward James, the millionaire patron of the Surrealists and husband of the termagant film star Tilly Losch. In July 1936 he and James Haizlip, an American racing pilot and assistant manager of the Shell Corporation at St Louis, had been in France, demonstrating a Beechcraft 17 which Haizlip had brought to Europe on board the airship *Hindenburg*. The Beechcraft 17, the design on which the Beechcraft Corporation of Wichita had founded its fortunes, was one of the fastest and most advanced light aeroplanes of its time (indeed some are still flying today[10]), but it was its remarkable range of 725 miles (1,160 km) that persuaded Victor Urrutia Usaola, a Spanish million-aire whom they met at a cocktail party in Cannes, to buy it for £3,000 and employ Cathcart-Jones to fly him first to Burgos and thence to various European capitals where he hoped to buy arms. At Burgos, General Mola ordered Urrutia to pick up the Marqués de Luca de Tena, a leading plotter of the rebellion, in Paris and fly to Mariánske-Lázne (Marienbad) in Czechoslovakia to confer with ex-King Alfonso XIII, who was staying as a guest of Prince Metternich at Königswart Castle near by.

As Mola emphatically did not want the ex-king or his son to join him, since the Carlists in his forces swore their allegiance to an opposed branch of the royal family, the reason for the meeting is not clear, but one purpose may have been to learn more about a huge cache of arms which Alfonso was rumoured to have hidden somewhere in French Morocco for a coup that was never carried out. Whether or not the cache, which was said to include several hundred thousand rifles as well as artillery, ever existed is uncertain, but there are occasional references to it in the official corre-spondence of both sides, the Republicans in particular being anxious to arm a native uprising against the Nationalists in Spanish Morocco.[11] The meeting was reported in the newspapers, the Socialists and Communists demanded Alfonso's expulsion from the country and the Beechcraft at Marienbad was grounded. Cathcart-Jones, while taking parties of reporters up for joyrides, escaped in the Beechcraft to Germany, and from there to France. There followed a few days in which he zigzagged from one airfield to another in France, Italy and Austria while British, American and French consuls demanded his immediate arrest, until he was finally cornered at Innsbruck and the machine locked away in a hangar.

He returned to England without difficulty, nevertheless, and wrote his story in the *Sunday Graphic* on 13 and 20 September. He was being watched, however, for on 4 September a Paul Bloomfield wrote to the Foreign Office to say that Cathcart-Jones and Haizlip were staying at the Beetle & Wedge Hotel at Moulsford, near Cholsey in Berkshire, where they were consulting shipping lists with an obvious view to making more money out of the Spanish war, and that Cathcart-Jones was a reader of Lady Houston's Fascist weekly the *Saturday Review*. Although Haizlip did try to sell more aircraft to Spain, Cathcart-Jones went to California, where he became a close friend of Errol Flynn and ran a racing stable at Santa Barbara until his death in 1985. As for the Beechcraft, it was sold to Alitalia and was still flying during the Second World War.[12]

In his story for the *Sunday Graphic*, Cathcart-Jones said that he had seen 'dozens' of British aircraft hidden in a wood beside Burgos airfield and, on the cross-Channel ferry back to England, no fewer than four of the 'famous English pilots' who had flown them there. The 'dozens' of British aircraft was an exaggeration, to say the least, but one of the types he names, a Dragonfly, deserves mention. It was in fact the de Havilland D.H.90 Dragonfly G-AECX, registered to Arthur Youngman of Selfridges department store in Oxford Street, London. The pilot was the Vicomte de Sibour, the representative in France of the Socony-Vacuum Oil Company (Socony, or Standard Oil of New York, was later renamed Mobil), and the passengers were his sister, her husband, Gordon Selfridge jun., and 'Peggy Shannon of Rochester', though whether this was Rochester, NY, or Rochester, Kent, is not recorded. The party arrived at Burgos on 5 August saying they were on holiday and wanted to see the war at close hand. After a day or two, replenished by eighty-five gallons of petrol allowed them by Mola, they flew down to Granada, where they told the US and British consuls that they had come to evacuate employees of Socony. This seemed odd, for the evacuation of these people was already being organized by the Nationalist authorities, and the matter was reported to Washington.[13] By then, the visitors had left for Tangier, whence Sibour returned a few days later and did indeed fly out four American ladies, after which the party returned to Britain via Portugal and

France and the incident was forgotten. Yet it would seem that Mola, who was extremely short of petrol and needed every drop he could get, would have had a more serious reason to part with eighty-five gallons from his precious supply than the evacuation of foreigners from faraway Andalucía, where he had no authority, and that the real purpose of the flight was to negotiate supplies of oil by Socony to the Nationalists, supplies we now know were expedited.

During the dictatorship of Primo de Rivera in the 1920s, the monopoly of oil sales in Spain had been granted to CAMPSA (Compañía Arrendataria del Monopolio de Petroleo S.A.), a group of banks, which in the years since had built up a fleet of nineteen tankers, the names of the ten most modern of them beginning with *Camp-* (e.g. *Campeche*, *Campoamor*). The chief supplier had been Russia until the Lerroux government had switched to the Texas Oil Company, or Texaco, in 1935, although special oils continued to be imported from other American companies, the 'Vacuum' suppplied by Socony being an engine lubricant. The uprising divided CAMPSA as it divided everything else and, during the fighting in Barcelona, Juan-Antonio Alvarez Alonso, a senior CAMPSA employee sympathetic to the rebels, escaped to Marseille, where he made contact with the chief of Texaco in France, W. M. Brewster.

It happened that the president of Texaco, Captain Thorkild Rieber, a great admirer of Hitler and authoritarian rule, was in France and a meeting with Alvarez was quickly arranged. On learning that the rebels had captured only three of the CAMPSA ships and realizing that the US Neutrality Act of 1935 did not apply to oil, Rieber immediately ordered five of his tankers on the high seas to change course for Tenerife, now in Nationalist possession, where there was a large oil refinery and the ships could unload in complete secrecy. Then, on 13 August, three tankers belonging to Standard Oil of New Jersey (later renamed Esso and Exxon), Texaco's chief rival, left Philadelphia for the Nationalist port of Algeciras.[14] Later in the month Rieber himself visited Franco and promised him all the oil the rebels would need, on credit and with no date set for payment. Three hundred and forty-four thousand tons were delivered by Christmas and, after the US Spanish Embargo Act, which included oil as a war material, was passed on 7 January 1937, Rieber showed his contempt for it by ordering his tankers, ostensibly bound for Antwerp, to go directly to Nationalist ports in Spain. A government-imposed fine of $20,000 failed to deter him and deliveries continued until the end of the civil war.

The Republicans, with sixteen tankers still in their possession, re-established the company as CAMPSA-GENTIBUS (meaning 'Campsa of the People'), and managed to bring a few shipments from Romania until they were stopped by King Carol. The CAMPSA representative in the USA,

Martínez Gallardo, told the Republican government that although Texaco had temporarily suspended deliveries, there was every hope that good relations would soon be restored. However, when the *Campoamor* docked at Philadelphia in November to take on 10,000 tons, Gallardo was told that Texaco refused to sell. The Republican consul in New York, José Gibernau Castells, began to make enquiries of his own and eventually learnt 'from friends and other sources' that Texaco had been shipping oil to the Nationalists all along. Thus it was not until Gibernau sent his dispatch to his government in Valencia on 10 April 1937, eight months after the outbreak of the civil war, that the Republicans discovered where Franco was obtaining the oil upon which his war effort depended. Gibernau reported that in recent months Texaco had made fifteen shipments to La Coruña alone, using nine tankers, of which six flew United States and three Norwegian flags. They had sailed from Port Arthur or Beaumont, Texas, and their cargoes had been consigned to 'Antwerp'.[15]

Altogether, Texaco, Shell, Standard Oil of New Jersey, Socony and the Atlantic Refining Company sold about $20 million worth of oil and petrol to the Nationalists, Texaco alone shipping 1,866,000 tons. Without these deliveries Franco's campaigns would have come to a halt in days, for at that time Germany and Italy too were dependent on the Anglo-American companies for their oil supplies.[16]

11

The Caravanserai

SOME HISTORIANS HAVE pointed, almost with relish, to the naïveté and incompetence of the Spanish Republicans in their handling of finances and their efforts to buy arms and aircraft from abroad. Yet consider their position. In the summer and autumn of 1936, when the course of the war was decided, the government was trying to bring a chaotic multitude of local revolutions under control and organize them into a unified resistance against the rebels, a task to which Giral's cabinet was unequal. By the middle of August, nearly half their already depleted stock of weapons had been captured by Franco's army during its march on Madrid and none of the handful of French aircraft had been armed, or was to be so until the end of the month. The purchase of arms and aircraft from abroad was the most urgent of priorities, but to whom could the government turn? Procuring armaments, especially aircraft, is a hazardous business even in peacetime and there is no army, navy or air force in the world that has not on many occasions suffered from misjudgements: witness, for instance, the ordering of more than 2,000 Fairey Battle bombers for the RAF between 1936 and 1939.

The Republicans, now that all the countries where arms might be bought openly were closing their doors against them, were faced with the prospect of organizing what would have to be the biggest and most complicated arms-smuggling operation in history. Nobody in or near the government knew anything about armaments or more than anyone in any other government about aviation, and although some of the officers and sergeants who were still loyal may have had some technical knowledge in their particular fields, none had any experience of arms dealing and gun-running.

Most of the embassies, legations and consulates abroad which might have served as bases for mounting such an operation, were empty or occupied by the rebels and, finally, the government was still unaware that the ambassadors and officials in London and Washington, who had given assurances of their loyalty, were working for the rebels and sending dispatches calculated to deceive it. The extent to which this lack of information misled the Spanish government is illustrated by an attempt to purchase military aircraft in, of all places, Nazi Germany.

On 1 August 1936 Hans Stürm, the representative in Spain of the Reichsverband der Deutschen Luftfahrtindustrien (Reich Federation of German Aviation Industries), told someone in the government that he had learnt from a telephone call to Berlin that the Junkers and Heinkel companies, who had been so keen to export their aircraft to Spain six months before, might still be willing to sell. Accordingly, Stürm was asked to go to Paris, collect Lt.-Col. Luis Riaño, the chief of the technical training school at Cuatro Vientos airbase, who had been sent there on 25 July to advise Fernando de los Rios,[1] and fly with him to Germany. They arrived at Berlin on 6 August and had a meeting next day with some German officers, among whom was Admiral Canaris, the head of the Abwehr or military intelligence service. Riaño requested bombers and fighters, complete with arms and bombs, and said that his government would pay in gold if desired. After the meeting von Neurath, the German foreign minister, recommended that Riaño be kept in suspense and under the impression that contracts were in the offing, for this would confuse the Madrid government and conceal the true nature of Nazi intentions in Spain. Riaño stayed, almost a prisoner, until 18 August, when he was told, 'with regret', that his requests must be refused because Germany was about to sign the Non-Intervention agreement, which indeed it did on 24 August. Riaño was allowed to return to Paris and the fact that his mission had ever taken place remained a secret until a record of it was discovered in the German archives by Dr Angel Viñas forty years later.[2]

Meanwhile, in the Paris embassy at 25 Avenue George V, off the Avenue des Champs Elysées, Professors Fernando de los Rios, Luis Jiménez de Asúa and Pablo de Azcárate, the last of whom had come from Geneva to help his two friends while continuing his duties as deputy secretary-general to the League of Nations, tried to avoid the traps and pitfalls that beset them on every side. The gold flights from Madrid had been reported in detail by the right-wing newspapers and provoked a 'gold rush' of arms dealers from all over Europe, and indeed of traders in every commodity from bicycles or scrap metal to Persian carpets, who saw in the plight of the Republic the chance to make a killing. 'The embassy', wrote Azcárate,

> was thereupon converted into an indescribable spectacle, a veritable *oriente* [caravanserai, or bazaar] where persons of the most diverse nationalities and types came and went at all hours of the day and far into the night, offering every class of weapon, ammunition and aeroplane ... How many times did Fernando de los Rios and I have to endure the anguish of not knowing whether an offer was serious and worthy of consideration or merely another base attempt to swindle us![3]

When a proposition appeared to be serious, prices and commissions had to be negotiated, payment arranged through a concealed channel and the disguising of the transportation organized. This was a world where commerce blended into criminality and none of them had conducted even an ordinary commercial transaction in his life.

Of the three, Rios, whose shock at being offered aircraft bombs heavier than 15 kg has already been noted, was nominally in charge and the most out of his depth. A legal historian and educationalist with a passion for building schools, he had been a distinguished figure of the brief cultural renaissance in Granada in the 1920s, and his daughter had married the brother of the poet Federico García Lorca. Although today he would be thought of as a rather conservative liberal, he called himself a Socialist and belonged to Prieto's moderate, or 'reformist', wing of the party. With his short beard, pince-nez, simple humour and fondness for well-cut suits, he was the image of avuncular kindness and old-fashioned moral rectitude. He abhorred violence, and after the Communist orator La Pasionaria saw him at the embassy, she wrote:

> As Fernando de los Rios stroked his seraphic beard with his right hand and hooked the thumb of his left hand into the armhole of his waistcoat, he lamented, 'Who would ever have thought that I should be here, buying weapons of destruction so that people can kill one another!' I stared at him a long while, not knowing whether to laugh or cry. Who was the idiot, I wondered, who had given this job to Brothers of Charity?[4]

Her venom, however, was spiked with a political ingredient. In the 1920s Rios had visited Moscow and, during a meeting with Lenin, had said how overjoyed he was now that justice and liberty had come to old Russia at last. 'Liberty?' Lenin had asked him sharply, 'What for?'[5] Some have denied that Lenin said any such thing, but whatever he did say was enough to make Rios regard the small Spanish Communist Party with distrust and aversion ever after. Besides, La Pasionaria knew that nobody had 'given this job' to anybody. Rios, Asúa and Azcárate had been pushed into it by providence: they had been within quick reach of Paris when Cárdenas and the others had joined the rebels, they had friends in the French government and they were men of integrity. As soon as the government could find time to re-establish the diplomatic service abroad, they would be made ambassadors, as befitted their seniority, but until then they would have to struggle on as best they could.

Alvaro de Albornoz, the new ambassador at Paris, knew even less about finance or armaments than they did and, concerned for their predicament, decided to alleviate it by delegating the most ungrateful part of the work, the negotiating with the traders congregated in the ante-rooms, to a single organization of professionals who did know what they were doing. This was the Société Européenne d'Etudes et d'Entreprises, a company which had been founded in 1930 for the purpose of building a railway in Yugoslavia. It was an associate of the Gas, Light and Coke Company in Britain, and its impressive shareholders included Schneider-Creusot, the giant arms conglomerate, the Imperial Ottoman Bank, which had long experience in arms transactions, Worms et Cie, a *banque d'affaires* which owned a chain of hotels, including the famous Crillon in Paris, and the Comité des Forges, the immensely powerful consortium of heavy industries, which was said to control seven newspapers, including the two principal national dailies, *Le Temps* and *Le Matin*.[6] The president of the Société was Jean Reveillard and its managing director was Dr Simon Marcovici-Kleja, the ex-consul of Romania at Lille and the author of articles and a book advocating Zionism as the only means by which the Jews could become a nation like any other.[7]

On 8 August, the day on which Malraux and his men flew off in their disarmed aircraft to Barcelona, Albornoz signed a contract granting the Société 'exclusive rights in the purchase in France and other countries of all the articles that must be acquired'. The Société was to 'centralize all purchases and carry them out under the best conditions and at the lowest prices' and was to receive a commission of 7.5% of the value of every contract.[8]

It has been said that when the Madrid government learnt of this contract, which placed the fate of the Republic in the hands of a single foreign commercial company, whose shareholders doubtless included some of General Franco's warmest sympathizers, it immediately rescinded it on the grounds that the Republican constitution prohibited the granting by the Republic of a monopoly to anybody. The facts, however, appear to have been not so simple. 'Cock-ups', as journalists gracelessly call them nowadays, occur only too frequently even where democracy is solidly established and when the times are orderly. In Spain in August 1936, democracy was not solidly established and the times were anything but orderly. From the fragmentary records that survive, it is evident that Premier Giral and his foreign minister, Barcía, told as few people as possible, in his own government or in that of Largo Caballero which succeeded it on 4 September, about the contract, perhaps in the hope of limiting the damage or perhaps because they were too hard pressed by other crises to give it much attention. When Luis Araquistaín went to Paris to replace Albornoz on 24 September, no one told him about the contract before he left, he did not learn of its existence until a week or two after his arrival and in November he was still trying to devise ways of annulling or getting round it without, as he said, 'antagonizing the French politicians who are protecting it'.[9] This is strange, for the French press had certainly known about it for some time and on 7 September the discovery had enabled *L'Action Française* to discharge another burst of anti-Jewish spleen:

> La Société Européenne d'Etudes et d'Entreprises, 24 rue de Penthièvre, Paris 8me, is carrying out an order for 80 million Ffr. 'It is in close contact with Blum,' declared André Blumel, director of the cabinet. The director of the Société Européenne, which is connected with Le Creusot (Schneider), is a central European Jew.

In *L'Action Française Mensuelle* for that month the editors added that a certain Spaniard attached to the embassy, Dr Otero, would meet Marcovici-Kleja daily at the Hotel du Président, 13 rue de Penthièvre, or at 2 rue Chauchat, off the Boulevard Haussmann. The editors knew that the association of Blum and Blumel, both of whom were Jews, with a Spanish 'Doctor', suggesting an intellectual, conveyed all the sinister implications required to alarm their readers.

Dr Alejandro Otero Fernández, a small hawk-faced man with the look of a worried head waiter, a great deal of nervous energy and a taste for expensive cars and the company of well-dressed women, had come to Paris at the invitation of Rios and the blessing of Prieto to assist in the ever-growing task of arms-buying. La Pasionaria wrote him off as a *madrona* ('male midwife' or 'gossip'),[10] a pun on the fact that he had previously been head of gynaecology at Granada University and a successful practising obstetrician. The 'Black Two Years' under Lerroux, from 1933 to 1935, had persuaded him to enter politics and, when the Popular Front was elected in February 1936, he took his seat in the Cortes as Socialist deputy for Granada. This gained him many enemies in a city noted for the unbending stiffness of its upper classes, who spread rumours through the *casinos* (gentlemen's clubs) that he had seduced five of the ladies he had attended as a doctor, and spread tales among the gypsies and ignorant poor who went to his free clinic on the Albaicín hill, that the chickens he kept in his laboratory for the extraction of serum were proof that he had signed a pact with the Devil.[11] He was lucky, therefore, to be in Switzerland at the time of the uprising, for at home he would have been among the first of the twenty-three councillors and several thousand lesser citizens who were arrested, beaten and shot after the Nationalists took over Granada on 20 July.[12] In Paris he was joined by José Calviño Ozores, a thin, balding, bespectacled engineer of melancholy demeanour who had written articles for the Socialist press, and Martí Estevé y Guau, a Catalan lawyer and the deputy for Solsona.

These three were the nucleus of a buying commission formed, as Calviño drily put it, 'by spontaneous generation',[13] presumably in allusion to the belief among Spanish country people that the animals, birds and insects of the wild are born spontaneously out of the ambient elements of earth, air and water. They are said to have called themselves El Servicio de Adquisiciones Especiales[14] ('Special Acquisitions Service'), though they seem more often to have been referred to as the Oficina Comercial, after the commercial attaché's office in 27 Avenue George V, an annexe to the embassy, which they used as premises. Their intention was to channel purchases made by the Société Européenne through a corresponding Spanish organization. Unfortunately, there were also arriving in Paris people who had been provided with funds, usually insufficient, by the CNT, the Communist Party, the Esquerra (Catalan separatists), the Generalitat (the Catalan regional government), the still embryonic Euzkadi (Basque) Republic or one of the regional anti-Fascist committees and sent abroad to bring back the armaments that the central government in Madrid seemed incapable of procuring. As the Oficina Comercial had no official status, such people saw no reason to pay any more heed to it or the Société Européenne than to the government in Madrid and instead went directly to the arms dealers or manufacturers.

When Dr Marcovici-Kleja heard of this, he submitted to Rios his claims for 7.5% of what he estimated the values of the contracts to be, for his contract with the Spanish government recognized him as sole buyer, and when he learnt that agents of the Spanish government had gone to Belgium before the signing of the contract, he sent two of his employees after them to ensure that everything was bought in the name of the Société. All the pieces were now in place to ensure disaster.

I2

Liège

B Y THE MIDDLE of the 1930s Belgium had become the sixth largest arms exporter in the world, with most of her arms industry concentrated round Liège.[1] There being no weapons of Belgian design to manufacture, the state Fabrique Nationale ('La FN') produced Mauser rifles, Browning machine-guns and other foreign weapons under licence for the Belgian army and for sale abroad, but the greater share of the market had been cornered by arms dealers who had their own workshops. Huge stocks of guns and ammunition left over from the Great War and previous wars lay in the armouries of all the European powers, unprofitable to scrap but hard to sell because their calibres rarely matched those required by prospective customers. British rifles and machine-guns, for example, were ·303 in. (7.707 mm), a calibre used by no other army but the Estonian, which, when replacing losses through normal wastage, preferred to buy new material.

The Belgians were among the first to see the opportunities in this and the result was a proliferation of workshops in Liège, where imported weapons were converted according to order and sold, sometimes in Europe but more often in Latin America, the Middle East and China. To encourage this free enterprise, the Belgian government had been careful to introduce no export restrictions.[2] In June 1933, however, war flared up between Paraguay and Bolivia over the disputed territory of the Gran Chaco, which was believed to contain oil, and the British government, shocked by evidence of barbarities, pleaded in the League of Nations for an international arms embargo. This, however, did not come into effect until September 1934, only ten months before the war ended in mutual exhaustion. Since several of the companies in Liège were selling arms to both sides, the British directed earnest appeals to the conscience of the king, Leopold III, who under the Belgian constitution decided foreign and military policy, but the most he would concede was a ruling that while Belgian-made arms would in future require licences for export, foreign-made arms, which generated the serious profit, must continue to pass 'in transit' freely.[3]

Before the invention of 'end-user certificates' during the Spanish Civil War, arms embargoes were not the problem they are today – not that they are so great a problem today either when a little money is available – and in the years between the world wars most, if not all, were instigated by the British Foreign Office. Apart from the Gran Chaco embargo, there was one against Lithuania during a dispute with Poland, several against China and one, usually forgotten nowadays, against Abyssinia.[4] When Mussolini, proclaiming a 'New Roman Empire', ordered the colonization of that country in October 1935, Britain reluctantly imposed oil sanctions and an arms embargo against Italy and, to show fair-mindedness, an arms embargo against Ethiopia, thus preventing Haile Selassie's warriors, armed for the most part with muskets and spears, from defending themselves against invaders armed with aircraft, explosive and incendiary bombs, machine-guns, motorized transport, artillery, tanks and flame-throwers. Of the few modern weapons that the Ethiopians did obtain, most were sold by Captain John Ball, some of them being flown to Addis Ababa in a Vultee passenger plane which, a year later, was sold to the Spanish Republicans.

Captain John Ball, a Royal Flying Corps stores officer during the Great War, had founded the Soley Armament Company, a one-man firm at 8 Park Village East, near Regent's Park, London, in the 1920s and joined in partnership with Edgard Grimard, a Belgian arms dealer, to run the Soley-Grimard et Cie workshop in Liège for converting unsaleable weapons into saleable ones. This had led to his becoming the chief sales agent for the Birmingham Small Arms Company. At the end of the Great War, BSA – which made bicycles, buses, Daimler and Lanchester cars, machine tools and steel besides arms – had acquired the rights to dispose of all War Office stocks of surplus small arms in the United Kingdom, a concession granted to save the government the cost of a subsidy during the lean years obviously ahead. BSA needed the money to train its craftsmen, for much of the production of good quality Lee-Enfield rifles still had to be done by hand.[5] Owing to the calibre problems, however, sales were disappointing and in 1930 BSA subcontracted the agency to John Ball. Business went reasonably well until the Gran Chaco War brought his name into the newspapers.

These were years of campaigns, led by the *bien pensant,* for the abolition, or at least the nationalization, of the privately owned arms industries and their related trades, which were already coalescing into what are now called 'multinationals', and when such phrases as 'merchants of death' and 'the Secret International' were becoming commonplace. In America a committee, led by Senator Nye, investigated this question from 1933 to

1935, as did a royal commission in Britain from 1935 to 1936. Letters between Ball and the American Armaments Corporation of New York, relating to an arms sale to Bolivia by devious routes, came before the Nye Committee, with the result that some American newspapers characterized Ball as being 'as devoid of morals as an Italian organ-grinder's monkey'.[6]

In London, the royal commission asked Ball for clarification. The British arms he exported, he said, were only a thousandth part of his business and they all went to Belgium. He never deceived the government, which had sources of information all over the world and would soon find out if he tried. The correspondence with American Armaments referred to a sale by a Belgian to an American company and so was of no concern to him – some of the letters quoted were not even his and had been sent to the Nye Committee by mistake – or to the British government. 'The only thing that the British government is concerned with is the letter of the law', he explained,[7] and as he had always kept within it he had never been refused a licence, except on the rare occasions when an embargo had been suddenly declared against a country to which he had just sold arms but not yet delivered them. In one instance, indeed, the embargo had not been announced properly at all, but had been reported only in a small paragraph in one newspaper, the *Daily Mail*, and he had missed it.

The hearing took place in February 1936, while Ball was trying to smuggle arms to Haile Selassie, for whom he had also managed to acquire, through a Swiss agency, three German Focke-Wulf Fw 56 Stösser fighter/trainer monoplanes and to enrol three German pilots to fly them. The Stösser ('Falcon Hawk'), a modern and expensive type of aircraft in production for the Luftwaffe, was not due to be released for export until 1937, though the Austrian air force had placed an order for twelve, to be delivered as soon as permissible. It would seem, therefore, that the Swiss agent persuaded the Austrians, with whom Mussolini was by no means in favour at that time, to ask the Germans, who were always in urgent need of foreign currency, to release three aeroplanes ahead of schedule and that the Germans agreed. It is also possible, for reasons that will become apparent later, that the agent in Switzerland was in the employ of the Russians.

The Stössers were on board ship in the Mediterranean when Ethiopia collapsed and Ball's agent sailed from port to port in search of a buyer, only to be refused permission to dock anywhere. After returning to England he tried to disembark them on Lundy Island in the Bristol Channel, which had recently been bought by Martin Coles Harmon[8] in association with Serge Rubinstein,[9] an emigré Russian financier. No sooner had Harmon bought the island, however, than he declared its independence, crowned himself King Martin I of Lundy and printed his own banknotes and postage stamps, his currency being in 'Puffins' and 'Half-

Puffins'. The Board of Trade and the Home Office, who were 'devising measures' to put a stop to this nonsense, prohibited the unloading of the aircraft and arms, and Ball sold them instead to a Spanish Nationalist conspirator, probably Cierva, in London. He then shipped them to Antwerp at the end of June to await events.

During the same week Prince Francisco Xavier de Borbón Parma, a leading Carlist, went to Germany and bought 6,000 rifles, 150 heavy machine-guns, 300 light machine-guns, 5 million cartridges and 10,000 hand-grenades in preparation for the coup.[10] His supplier, though not named, was probably Josef Veltjens,* whose role in providing arms to Mola and Franco before and during the civil war is well known,[11] but as the date of the coup was brought forward from August to 18 July, the arms, marked for 'Guatemala' and packed in nineteen goods wagons, did not reach Antwerp until 1 August, a fortnight too late.**

By then, Colonel Antonio Bolaños, a former artillery officer who had gone into politics and was now the Socialist deputy for Málaga, had arrived with two assistants in Belgium and, through the help of the Belgian Socialist Party and trade unions, placed contracts for guns, bombs and munitions for the Republic.[12] Their trainload of arms, thirty wagons carrying 300 tons of reputedly Belgian material, arrived at Antwerp a day or two later. Unfortunately, it pulled in at the same dock, no. 34, as the first train, whereupon a phone call came from Brussels ordering the first train to change to dock no. 9 at once.

King Leopold, a Germanophile who was trying to draw his country

---

* Oberführer (Colonel) Josef Veltjens had been an air ace during the Great War, with thirty-seven victories, and had later joined the Freikorps and the SA. Expelled from the Nazi Party after the SA was crushed in 1934, he appears to have enjoyed the protection of Goering. He was esteemed for his skill in camouflaging arms sales of which the German government could deny knowledge, including one, in which Goering had an interest, to China at a time when Germany was establishing closer relations with China's enemy, Japan. He was one of an iron ring of arms dealers – Josef Veltjens, Willy Daugs and Thorvald Erich (or Eric) in Berlin and Edgard Grimard and John Ball in Liège and London – which sold arms to both sides in the Gran Chaco War. Similarly, in the Spanish Civil War the same group, rearranging their partnerships with one another according to circumstances, sold German, Polish, British and Belgian arms to the Republicans and German arms to the Nationalists, laundering the money through Finland. Veltjens was also responsible for the delivery of two cargoes of arms, on the *Allegro* and *Yorkbrook*, which turned out to be rubble and rubbish. The Basques had paid for them by public subscription. In 1942–3 he served as 'special plenipotentiary' under Seyss-Inquart in the Netherlands to transfer the black market to German hands and organize the plunder of industrial plant, a task he carried out with characteristic brutality.
** That this was Prince Xavier de Borbón's consignment is almost certain: the Nationalist historian Joaquín Arraras says it was seized in Antwerp; it arrived in nineteen wagons, each carrying ten tons; 190 tons corresponds to the weight of the material bought by the prince.

closer to Germany without provoking Britain and France lest he should need their protection in future, was averse to Popular Fronts and had no objection whatever to a sale of Belgian or German arms to Spanish royalists or even General Franco. The customs at Antwerp, however, having no guidelines on the matter, impounded the contents of both trains in order to sort out which arms were Belgian-made and required licences and which were German-made and did not. This led to the discovery that the phone call ordering the first train to transfer to dock 9 had not come from the agency it was said to have done and that the papers assigning the arms to 'Guatemala' were false. Faced by the prospect of an unholy row in the cabinet – a fissile coalition of Catholics, Liberals, Social Democrats and Socialists – and in parliament, to say nothing of strikes and demonstrations by the trade unions and counter-demonstrations by the Rexistes, an extreme right party with twenty-two seats in parliament, the king was obliged to announce, on 4 and 8 August, that all arms for export would henceforth require licences and that Belgium had accepted the British and French 'invitation' to join the 'Non-Interference' scheme.[13] Meanwhile, the left-wing press in Belgium and France claimed that all forty-nine wagonloads were for Franco, as did the Republican chargé d'affaires in a telegram to Madrid,[14] and the right-wing press claimed that the whole lot had been bought by a Spanish Communist.[15] On 9 August the Belgian premier, van Zeeland, of the Catholic Party, announced that arms factories and workshops were to be put under government inspection and that energetic measures were to be taken against all extremist groups, right or left.

On 10 August, however, a Dutch steamer, the *Lodewyk* of the N.V. Europeesche Vrachtvaart Marts cargo line at Rotterdam, arrived and her master produced papers to show that the arms were a perfectly legitimate sale by a Belgian to a Brazilian company. Since the new regulations had not yet been brought into effect, there were apologies all round, the arms were released and workmen began to take the first boxes out of the wagons. Before they had time to load them on ship, however, a delegate arrived from the transport workers' federation and shouted to them to stop. He was immediately arrested and that afternoon the police said that, as there was 'silence from the Fédération office', they believed that the man had acted on his own initiative and under the delusion that the arms were for Franco. By then, all forty-nine wagons had been put under guard again.[16] On 19 August the king declared a complete ban on the export of all war material, including civil aircraft, to Spain and he ratified this by decree on the 21st.

Two other Republican agents were in Belgium in August 1936. Daniel Ovalle Gómez was the mayor of Getafe, the town adjoining the main military airfield south of Madrid, though who sent him is not known.

Accompanied by an 'expert', who turned out to be unable to tell one type of rifle from another, Ovalle went to Liège and, after an inconclusive meeting with the dealer Armande Gavage (see below, Chapter 13), called at the Soley-Grimard workshop at 19 rue Louvrex. Since he had no way of knowing whether or not Grimard's prices of 400 Bfr. ($69 or £13 8s.) per Mauser rifle and 365 Bfr. ($61.36 or £12 5s.) per thousand cartridges were fair, Ovalle returned to Paris without buying anything.[17] In fact, Grimard's prices were extortionate. A new Mauser from a German factory would have cost $30 (£6). In those days, it was professional practice to sell a thousand rounds per rifle as part of the deal, the prices of the rifle and a thousand rounds usually being equal. A new Mauser would therefore have cost $60, or £12, the rounds included. At Grimard's prices Ovalle would have paid $139, or £26, and it is not even certain that the rifles were new.

The second agent was Dorrién (Francisco Martínez Dorrién), who wrote to Juan-Simeon Vidarte, a member of the PSOE (Spanish Socialist Party) executive and the deputy for Badajoz, on 26 August to say that he had bought 'a grand lot' of arms and munitions* in Belgium in the name of the Société Européenne as instructed.[18] The director (Marcovici-Kleja) had appeared and paid the vendors but, since the ban of 19 August, had been refused the licences. The arms and the 'many millions' paid for them were therefore now irretrievably lost and all that might be saved was a small quantity of old rifles and cartridges bought in Poland. If Grimard's prices are anything to go by, and they probably are since he acted as agent in the sale of Polish arms to the Republicans despite being a Rexiste, then the money lost would have been at least 14.5 million Bfr., or $2.5 million (£500,000). Moreover, Dorrién seems not to have understood that the ammunition was quite insufficient – only 300 rounds per new rifle, 266 per old rifle and none for the Männlichers and machine-guns – and that, far from being 'a grand lot', his purchase would have been almost useless.

Although premier van Zeeland's 'energetic measures' against extremist groups, 'both right and left', continued through September, the only results reported in the newspapers concerned various lots of arms and munitions being made or collected for the Republicans. On 19 September the police raided the houses of the Socialist Revolutionary Party and the 'Socialist Reform' group in Liège, Mons, Charleroi and Brussels, seized documents relating to the export of arms to the 'workers' militias' in Spain

---

* 50,000 new Mauser M 1933 rifles with 15 million new cartridges; 30,000 old rifles with 8 million old cartridges; 16,000 Männlicher rifles, 8 mm; 63 heavy machine-guns; 2,000 light machine-guns, water-cooled; 360 light machine-guns, air-cooled and suitable for aircraft; 1,000 Bergmanns (presumably 'Schmeisser' MP 18s); 500 machine-rifles (presumably Belgian-made Browning BARs); 20,000 hand-grenades.

and found a workshop making 20,000 hand-grenades to an order from the Mexican minister in Brussels, Carlos Ogeda. This led to the boarding of the SS *Raymond* at Ostend on 22 September and the discovery of 800 rifles, bayonets, 320 carbines and 210,000 cartridges, all of which were confiscated by the police.[19]

One cargo, though not large, did get away, however. On 15 September the small Belgian coaster *Alice* left Antwerp bound for 'the Thames', carrying on board seventy-four tons of arms and ammunition. When she reached the roads of Flushing (Vlissingen), she transferred 40 crates containing 6,000 Mauser rifles, 100 machine-guns and 500,000 cartridges onto the *Iciar*, belonging to a Basque company, which sailed south to Bilbao. At Gravesend, at the neck of the Thames estuary, the *Alice* collided with the *Royal Scot* and had to sail to Ostend for repair, where the story leaked out, the ship was embargoed and the captain and owner were arrested amid much publicity.[20] The most likely explanation of how she was able to leave Antwerp in the first place is that her cargo manifest showed *British* rifles, machine-guns and ammunition being returned as 'unsaleable' by Grimard in Liège to Ball in London; all that would be needed then would be a duplicate set of papers showing the cargo to have been not seventy-four, but thirty-four, tons, not difficult to obtain with a little cash.

In contrast to the scandal over the *Alice*, the machine-guns bought in Germany by Prince Xavier de Borbón (though nothing else, according to the Nationalist historian Joaquín Arraras) were delivered to the Carlist headquarters at St. Jean-de-Luz, France, in complete secrecy, presumably at some time in September.[21]

Since neither Bolaños nor his aides knew anything about aircraft, they consulted 'Bob' Vanderveldt, the ebullient Socialist militant and amateur airman, who sent them for advice to M. Allende, the aeronautical correspondent for the Socialist daily *Le Peuple*. Allende told them of three old Fokker F.VIIb3m airliners which Sabena, the Belgian airline, wanted to get rid of and, since they were 'complètement déclassés et amortis' ('completely outdated and finished with') might be had for a song. Jules Perel, a Jewish businessman from the Netherlands fluent in French and Flemish, was employed to negotiate and a contract signed on 12 August. The price was 750,000 Bfr. (600,000 Bfr. for the aircraft and 150,000 Bfr. in commission to Perel), which worked out at $42,030 (£8,406) each, a unit price more than three times the $13,550 (£2,710) each being paid that very morning by the Nationalists to KLM for identical machines in rather better condition (see above, Chapter 10). The contract, however, stipulated that Perel must remove the aircraft within fifteen days, the time estimated that it would take to process the export licences, but when, after the ban of 19 August, this became impossible and Bolaños asked for the contract to be cancelled and the money returned, Sabena replied that they could not do that, since the sale had been to Perel, who had broken the contract by failing to remove the aircraft. Sabena then locked the three aircraft in their no. 1 hangar at Haren Airport as a precaution against thieves.[22]

The Spanish government took legal action and when the case was eventually heard in February 1938, the court judged that Sabena was morally bound to repay the money. This was not done, and on 4 May 1940 the Franco government tried to claim the Fokkers as its property, but the court argued that since it was Perel and not Sabena that had been negligent in failing to remove the aircraft, the government could do nothing.[23] The case was settled six days later, on 10 May, when Germany invaded Belgium and the Luftwaffe bombed Haren airport, destroying all the aircraft on it.

Of the few Belgian aircraft that Bolaños bought in August 1936, which included an antique Dewoitine D.9 palmed off on him by the Liège dealer Armande Gavage,[24] only an Avia BH-33 fighter, built in Czechoslovakia in 1928 and sent to Belgium in an unsuccessful attempt to secure an order, reached its destination. The flight – organized by Gaston Vedel, the Air France chief at its Barcelona airfield, and Georges Djounkowski (alias Jorge Martínez Adams, alias Jean Adamski), who may have been the Jean Adamski who was the commercial attaché at the Soviet embassy in Paris at the time – was quite adventurous. The Avia had been bought in the name of 'Bob' Vanderveldt, and the suspicious authorities had accordingly allowed only enough fuel in the tank to allow the engine to be warmed up. The pilot, Sergeant André Autrique, who had just left the Belgian air force, took off on a cold engine, however, and managed to reach Haren, from where, after refuelling, he flew towards France. It was arranged that he would land to refuel again in a field which was a mile or two away from Toussus-le-Noble aerodrome, south of Paris, but as he did so, his plane was noticed by some mechanics at Toussus who, thinking it had come down by accident, drove out to see what was wrong. He waved them off with a pistol and managed to refuel and take to the air again only seconds before the men returned with armed policemen. He lost his way and landed, out of petrol, at Ste. Foy-Le-Grand, near Libourne (Bordeaux), where this time he was arrested but, after a night in gaol, he was released through the personal intervention of Pierre Cot and Jean Moulin. When Autrique finally landed at Barcelona on 28 August, however, he found that the two Vickers guns, together with their installation equipment and ammunition, which had been hidden in the fuselage, had been stolen while he had been in prison. He returned to Toulouse to ferry one of the Loire 46 fighters, which were now ready (see p. 47), to Barcelona and then to Belgium to collect a Renard R.32, a rejected prototype which had been bought by Bolaños. Before he could do so, however, he was again arrested and, with two colleagues, Hansel and Jacobs, sentenced to six months in prison and a 25,000 Bfr. fine, which was paid by the Spanish government. After his release in April 1937, Autrique returned to Spain and flew in the Republican air force until the fall of Catalonia precipitated him once more into France. He returned to Spain yet again, when it was possible to do so, and was still living there in 1986.[25]

As for the Focke-Wulf Stössers that had been bought by the Nationalists, on reaching Antwerp they were transferred to the *Stanmore*, one of three ships of the Stanhope Steamship Company. The company belonged to Jack A. Billmeir, a London shipowner who had been trading with Spain for fifteen years and now intended to trade with both sides in the civil war. When the new licensing system was announced on 4 and 8 August, the customs had the guns, bombs and military fittings removed from the aircraft and stored on a lighter, and Billmeir, anticipating the declaration of a full embargo, ordered the ship to leave at once for Rotterdam. She had lain there for about three weeks when the Nationalists told Ball that the guns and ammunition had been stolen and that they were no longer interested in buying the aircraft, which, in fact had not yet been paid for. Ball sold them to a Republican agent in the Netherlands and the *Stanmore* slipped out by night, delivering the Stössers to Alicante on 10 October.[26] Billmeir, however, was so incensed by the behaviour of the Nationalists, whom he suspected of having stolen the weapons themselves, that he resolved to trade thereafter exclusively with the Republicans. During the course of the civil war, he became the most important blockade-runner of goods, but not of arms, although he was often accused of smuggling them. He earned enough money to acquire no fewer than thirty-seven ships, several of which were sunk by mines or bombing and others lost by capture, and to found another two companies, something he could never have accomplished by trading with both sides. As Calviño, who had served on all the successive Republican buying commissions in Paris during the civil war, wrote in 1940, 'Billmeir is the best of the rogues I had to do business with.'[27] Thus established, he continued to prosper through the Second World War and to become, by the time he died in 1963, one of the leading shipping magnates in Britain and commodore of the Royal Yacht Club at Southampton.

13

The Confidential Agent

MAJOR CARLOS PASTOR Krauel, the *persona de confianza* ('person of trust') sent by the Spanish Republican government to buy aircraft in Britain, left Madrid for Paris on 2 August and flew by Air France to Croydon airport on the 4th.[1] Thus he would have known, from the stories in all the French newspapers about the Fokker airliners that had been sold by British Airways to General Mola and sent back from Bordeaux to Gatwick on 2 August (see Chapter 9), that he would be in competition against Nationalists*, some of them former personal friends, who enjoyed the advantages of a head start and good connections with aeronautical circles in Britain. He did *not* know that two of the people at the Spanish embassy with whom he would be working closely – Captain Medina Morris, the naval attaché, and López Oliván, the ambassador, both of whom had cabled their declarations of loyalty to the Spanish government on 26 July[2] – were collaborating with the rebels, or that his room and telephone at the Waldorf Hotel in Aldwych, off the Strand, were bugged.

This had been done in 1935 during the Gran Chaco War, when Mrs Victor Bruce had tried to sell six Fairey Fox biplanes, ex-RAF, which she had bought from a scrapyard for £50 each, to the Paraguayan air force for £1,000 each. Armande Gavage, the Liège arms dealer, had come to London to procure guns and ammunition for the Foxes and had stayed at the Waldorf for three weeks, during which, as a Board of Trade official complained, the hotel had become 'the focus of all the undesirable arms trade in the country.'[3] Gavage, however, was an informer for MI5, and it had

---

* José-María Carreras, the LAPE pilot, told me that when staging at an airfield in the south of France during a gold flight to Paris, he watched a Republican 'agent' haggling over the price of an old Farman monoplane. As the price was rather steep, the agent said that he'd better phone Paris before agreeing. At that moment an old friend of Carreras's, now on the Nationalist side, came up and said with a smile, 'If you're not back in ten minutes, *I* shall have bought it!'

been his suggestion that, if some of the rooms of the hotel were wired with hidden microphones and their telephones tapped, he would spread the word through the arms-trading fraternity that the Waldorf was the safest place in London in which to do business without risk of being overheard. MI5 had approached the management, and the management, glad to do its bit for King and Country, had given permission.[4]

With the assistance of Vicente Barragán, a Colombian-born lecturer at Queen Mary's College and author of a well-known Spanish–English dictionary,[5] Pastor engaged the services of Union Founders' Trust, at 15 St Helen's Place, near St Paul's Cathedral in the City. The trust had been established in 1928 and was described in a Special Branch report as 'an ordinary commercial organization trying to make all the money it can out of gun-running'.[6] During the next three weeks the two directors, Major Malcolm Bookey Ryall, who lived in a manor house near Bath, and Arthur Collins, who had a flat on Haverstock Hill in north London, made a tour of aerodromes and bought twenty-nine machines, including twelve de Havilland Dragons (older versions of the Dragon Rapide) which could at a pinch be used as bombers, provided there were no enemy fighters in the region.

The first, a little Percival Gull monoplane, beautiful in its sky-blue finish, left Reading on 7 August. After reaching Barcelona, it was flown often by Corniglion-Molinier, who in later life remembered it as his favourite aeroplane, and was afterwards commandeered as a staff plane by senior Russian officers and 'advisers'.[7] On 13 August, by which date six other light civil aircraft had left for Republican Spain, the first two Dragons took off from Heston for Paris at about the same hour as two Rapides took off from Heston on their non-stop flight to the Nationalists at Burgos. The authorities at Le Bourget, whose behaviour since the French ban of 8 August had become quite unpredictable, ordered the two back to Britain, however,[8] and, after being fitted with tanks and hoses for a single hop, they and three other Dragons bought in the meantime took off from Croydon together in the dark at 1.30 a.m. on Saturday 15 August. All five were entered in the airport log as destined for Barcelona, there being as yet no law to prevent civil aircraft from flying to Spain. Seven hours later, a Royal Navy cruiser sailing off the Catalan coast spotted two of them, G-ACKC and -NA, as they circled in the early morning sunlight before landing at Prat de Llobregat airbase and the information was signalled to London at once.[9]

That day, the late edition of the *Evening Standard* blazoned a front-page headline, 'CIVIL AIRCRAFT FOR SPAIN: BRITAIN READY TO ACT', with a photograph of G-ACKC and -NA standing on the grass at Croydon. The accompanying story quoted a Foreign Office communiqué issued that afternoon which stated that 'His Majesty's Government is continuing to give full support to the French government' to secure an international agreement on non-intervention in Spain and that as soon as this was achieved the export of war material and civil aircraft to Spain would be prohibited. In the meantime, British subjects who assisted either side 'by land, sea or air' were making it harder to reach an agreement and could expect 'no help whatsoever should they meet with difficulties during such enterprises'. Four pilots – Haigh, Jaffe, Lloyd and Avery – were named and said to have been offered £125 ($625) each.

During the next three days editorials pointed out that although it was good for the export trade to sell British civil aeroplanes abroad, more than thirty had flown to one side or the other in Spain since 1 August (the real number in fact was twenty-six) and that at this rate there would soon be none left in the United Kingdom. Accordingly, on Wednesday 19 August, the government announced a complete ban on the export to Spain of war material, which included civil aircraft and numerous categories of technical equipment and fuel, and warned that British subjects who assisted either side in any way would be liable to fines or imprisonment and, if they were pilots, loss of their licences. In effect, it was, like the action of France on 8 August, a declaration of Non-Intervention without waiting for the agreement of the other powers.

Meanwhile, the police and other authorities were trying to find out which aircraft in Britain were still intended for Spain, who had last owned them and who owned them now. All such aircraft were to have their general licences revoked, which would render them unusable and so unsaleable until the licences were restored, and all suspect aircraft were to be grounded on any pretext. Thus, when G-ACKU belonging to Wrightways of Croydon, one of the five Dragons that had flown off on Saturday the 15th, limped back on Wednesday 19th with engine trouble, its original engines possibly having been surreptitiously replaced by old ones, it was immediately grounded. On this occasion the measure was justified, for the whole rear half of the fuselage 'reeked of petrol' which had overflowed from the tops of the drums and escaped through loose joints in the hoses. What would have resulted had the engines failed completely and the Dragon crashed in a town or village?[10]

It did not take long to discover that Union Founders' Trust owned sixteen aircraft, all recently bought and obviously intended for Spain: six were at Croydon, four at the de Havilland works at Hatfield and six at the Airspeed factory aerodrome at Portsmouth.[11] On the 20th, however, two young apprentices at the Airspeed factory decided to steal one of the machines, a little Courier cabin-monopolane (G-ACVE), sell it to 'a Spaniard' and make themselves 'lots of money'. Neither knew how to fly but, believing that a modern aeroplane could 'practically fly by itself', they took off and, after a few seconds, crashed into a fortification built during the Napoleonic War. The passenger was killed and the 'pilot', after he had recovered from his injuries, was sent to prison for a year.[12] That afternoon the authorities prevailed on the de Havilland company to cancel the sale of its four aircraft, a Rapide and three Dragons, at Hatfield.

While the authorities were busy with Union Founders' Trust and locking its eleven remaining aircraft in hangars under guard, Pastor arranged for Rollason Aircraft Services Ltd, a repair and brokerage company at Croydon Airport, to buy three more machines – two Airspeed Envoys and a de Havilland Dragon – and sell them to the Office Générale de l'Air in Paris (see above, p. 48).

The authorities blocked the sale of the Dragon, G-ACHV, bought from Railway Air Services Ltd, by withdrawing its certificate of airworthiness on some pretext,[13] but this was not possible with the first Envoy, G-ADCA, bought from a little airline called Portsmouth, Southsea & Isle of Wight Aviation, since it had just been repaired and recertified at Heston. Consequently, when the customs tried to hold it on 20 August, Captain W. A. Rollason challenged the Foreign Office to produce a single legal reason for obstructing this sale to a reputable French company with whom he had been doing business for years. They were unable to do so and he flew the Envoy to Paris next day. On its way to Barcelona on the 28th, however, it crashed near Alès in the south of France and, although the three Frenchmen on board were unhurt, was damaged beyond repair.[14] Having allowed the sale of the first Envoy, the Foreign Office could not prevent the sale of the second and Rollason flew it from Lympne aerodrome, in Sussex, to Paris on the 29th.[15] This, G-ACMT, was the original Envoy prototype and quite a famous aeroplane in its day. At Barcelona it was dismantled and its fuselage married to the wings of another Envoy (G-AEBV) delivered earlier, and in this hybrid machine Fernando Rein Loring, well known for several record-breaking long-distance flights, defected to the Nationalists on 26 September. General Mola then used it as his personal transport until he was killed in it when it crashed on 3 June 1937.[16]

On 29 August too, Pastor returned to London from a brief visit to Paris, where he had arranged for the Fédération Populaire des Sports Aéronautiques to buy the eleven aircraft from Union Founders' Trust in the hope, which was to prove vain, of forcing the British government to release them.[17]

After the loss of the two Fokkers in France, the Nationalists, unwilling to embarrass their British friends with further untoward incidents and aware by then that they would be receiving all they needed from Germany and Italy on credit, bought no more aircraft in England. On the Republican side, apart from two little Miles Hawk Major sports planes smuggled out in October, covert flights did not resume until January 1937. The tally for August 1936 was therefore as follows:

The Nationalists:
Twelve aircraft bought, of which two crashed and ten were delivered to Burgos.
The total cost was about £62,000 ($310,000) including fitting tanks, pilots, fees,
etc., an average of £6,200 ($31,000) per aircraft delivered.

The Republicans:
Thirty-two aircraft bought (twenty-nine through UFT). Of these, the sale of
four was cancelled and the money returned by de Havilland, one flew back
from Paris, two crashed in France (the second being a BA Swallow), eleven
were held in England and eventually abandoned, and fourteen were delivered
to Barcelona.* Since we know the prices of most of them – £5,000 each for the
Dragons, perhaps the same for the Envoys, £9,000 for the Airspeed Viceroy and
£2,900 each for the five Couriers (none of which left Britain) – the total cost
must have been about £120,000 ($600,000), an average of £8,750 ($42,850) for
each of the aircraft delivered.

By October the number of aircraft held by the authorities had risen to
nineteen, and a list in the Air Ministry records shows that during the
Spanish Civil War thirty-eight civil aircraft were held on suspicion at
various times. Yet, despite every precaution, a further forty-one British or
British-owned aeroplanes were delivered to the Republicans before the
end of the war, including seven Monospar ST-25 ambulances, ten de
Havilland Rapides and seventeen de Havilland Tiger Moth trainers, all
built to orders from the Spanish Republican purchasing commission in
Paris.
    Prominent among the vendors at Croydon in August 1936 was the
Hon. Mrs Victor Bruce who, having gained some repute as a motor- and
speedboat racer, had achieved fame in 1930–31 by a round-the-world
flying tour in a Blackburn Bluebird before settling down to run the Air
Dispatch group of charter companies. In her autobiography she states that

---

* One Percival Gull Six (G-ADEP, 7 Aug 1936); One Miles Hawk Major (G-ADAS, 9
Aug 1936); one Miles Falcon Six (G-ADLS, 9 Aug 1936); two Airspeed Envoy IIs (G-
AEBV, 9 Aug 1936, and G-ACVJ, 12 Aug 1936); three G.A. Monospar ST-25 Jubilees
(G-ADSN, 10 Aug 1936, -VG, 12 Aug 1936, and -PI, 13 Aug 1936); one Airspeed
Viceroy (G-ACMU, 13 Aug 1936); four de Havilland D.H.84 Dragons (G-ACDL,
-EV, -KC and -NA); and one Airspeed Envoy I (G-ACMT, the prototype, 29 Aug
1936). The Dragon G-ACKU returned on 19 August; the Envoy G-ADCA crashed in
France on the 28th. The little B.A. Swallow, which may have been G-ADBM, was
being flown to Barcelona at the end of August when its propeller flew off near
Perpignan. The pilot and passenger were two Americans, Ed Lyons (Edwin
Liebowitz) and Art Nasnit (Abraham Schapiro), on their way to join the Republican
air force. Thus, seventeen sent, fourteen arrived. With the forty-one delivered after 1
October 1936, the total for the whole war comes to fifty-five sent from Britain, plus
the three Focke-Wulf Stössers. The number sold from Britain to the Spanish
Republicans at different times was above 106, and to both sides above 118.

one evening a stranger offered to buy all her aeroplanes. She at first refused, then sold him 'two old Dragons', for which she was paid on the spot ten £1,000 banknotes. Later, she was told that the Dragons were wanted as ambulances in Spain. According to Air Ministry and Foreign Office records, however, she sold, or acted as agent in the sale of, seven aircraft which can be certainly identified and four others which were strongly suspect.[18] The total was thus not two but probably eleven, and the whole affair lasted not a few hours but many months.

The first, the Airspeed Envoy G-ADBB *Wharfedale*, went to the Nationalists at Burgos and on 15 August the newspaper *El Norte del Castilla* published a photograph of it standing behind some smiling officers, with a caption claiming that it had recently bombed 'the Marxist airport of Barajas'. Three went to the Republicans, another Envoy (G-ACVJ) and the two Dragons she refers to, which are identifiable as G-ACKC and -DL; indeed, it was the spotting of -KC landing at Barcelona on 15 August that alerted the government, who remembered the affair of the Gran Chaco War, to what Mrs Bruce was doing. The other aircraft were held in Britain, the subject of a long and often angry tussle between herself and the authorities. On one occasion, the chairman of Air Dispatch, Sir Maurice Bonham Carter, wrote to an under-secretary at the Foreign Office to protest at the treatment that Mrs Bruce, who was only trying to abide by the spirit of the regulations, was being subjected to; on another, she gave the authorities the name of a former employee who, she believed, was still ferrying aircraft to Spain.[19] It was all to no avail and her aircraft were not released until March 1937, and then only under the most stringent conditions and against the wishes of the Air Ministry.

From an interview that I had with Mrs Bruce in 1978, it would appear that politics did not enter into the matter and that her knowledge of the issues in Spain was almost non-existent. Of her two Dragon 'ambulances', for instance, she said, 'At least they went to the right side, that general, whatever his name was', to which I explained that, on the contrary, they were used for a while as improvised bombers by the Alas Rojas ('Red Wings') squadron supporting the Anarchist militia in Aragón.[20] In common with most of the other managers of small air transport companies at that time, she was desperately trying to stave off bankruptcy, especially after one of her Envoys, which had earned the main income for Air Dispatch by running a daily service of newspapers and bullion between London and Paris, had crashed at Westerham in Kent, killing its crew. Regarding the second Envoy, G-ACVJ, which left on 12 August, she told me that as the aircraft was having its engines warmed up for the Paris run, 'those horrible Airspeed people' climbed aboard while the pilot was momentarily absent, 'took the newspapers out, dumped them on the ground in the rain and then flew off without so much as a by-your-leave!'

Thus she lost yet another aeroplane. CAA records show that G-ACVJ had been bought on hire purchase from Airspeed on 10 July and that the first instalment was therefore due on 10 August.[21] She told me that she had intended to send it on the 12th and that the 'Airspeed people' must have used this as a pretext for repossessing the aircraft in order to sell it to the Spaniards.

One of the directors and senior designers at Airspeed Ltd at the time was N. S. Norway, better known today as the novelist Nevil Shute, who explains in his autobiography, *Slide Rule*, how the company was rescued from financial difficulties by the advent of the Spanish Civil War. In one passage he writes that six Couriers, which had been returned by a small airline that had gone bankrupt before being able to finish paying for them, were 'sold at better than their original prices and went by devious routes to Spain' and in another he writes that 'we made a bulk sale of practically our whole stock of unsold Couriers and Envoys to one British aeroplane sales organization and heard no more of them.'[22] That both statements are quite untrue may be attributed to a faulty memory, but he could hardly have forgotten that the five aircraft sold to Union Founders' Trust were immobilized and under police guard in the company hangar for seven months or the correspondence occasioned by the fact that the police insisted on removing the airscrews after every daily warming up of the engines, necessary to keep them in proper running condition. Continual removal and replacing of the airscrews was damaging the threads and bearings and would incur heavy expense to repair if continued.[23]

In November 1936 Airspeed received an order for three new Envoy IIIs from Fritz Mandl, who was acting on behalf of the Spanish Republicans. The deal was betrayed and the first two Envoys were impounded after reaching the Netherlands (see p. 200). The remaining Envoy and five more were then ordered by Air Pyrénées, a small airline created by Auguste Amestoy and other French supporters of the Republic to establish air communication between France and the Basque-Asturian zone. All were delivered, two were shot down and in one of them Abel Guidez, formerly of the Malraux squadron, was killed while trying to evacuate some Russians from Gijón on 7 September 1937. After the fall of the northern zone, the remaining four Envoys were transferred to LAPE in the main zone.[24]

Shute's reticence is therefore perhaps understandable. *Slide Rule* was published in 1953, when the Franco regime was still defensive and touchy over the international ostracism it had suffered, very unjustly it believed, since the Second World War. If Shute had openly admitted that in 1937 his company had built six Envoys not only for the Spanish 'Reds' but for Air Pyrénées, several of whose pilots were determined Basque separatists, his novels, which were, and still are, popular in Spain, would probably have been banned there.

Of particular interest, however, is Shute's account of the sale of the one and only Airspeed Viceroy, an Envoy which had been redesigned for the MacRobertson race of 1934. Owing to a minor electrical fault it had done poorly, however, and in 1935 Shute himself had supervised its conversion into a bomber for Haile Selassie, but, as with the Focke-Wulf Stössers, the war had ended before it could be delivered. Converted back again, it was sold to Max Findlay, a distinguished flying instructor, and Ken Waller, Cathcart-Jones's partner in the MacRobertson race, for the Schlesinger Trophy race to South Africa, scheduled for September 1936. In August, however, 'an agent of some continental nationality came and wanted to buy the Viceroy. They told him the machine was not for sale. Between friends, he said, everything could be arranged. They said they were not interested in his friendship, they were not selling.' He said that was no way to talk between friends, told them he knew the price of the Viceroy (£5,500) and of the first prize in the race (£4,000) and offered them £9,500 on the spot. They sold and flew the Viceroy to Paris for him.[25]

The agent was obviously Pastor, a man of refinement, and there seems to have been a difficulty over language. On such occasions 'entre amigos' does not have the ingratiating sound that its literal translation has in English, but is ironic and simply means 'with courtesy, everything is negotiable'. Carlos Pastor Krauel belonged to an upper-class and part-German family in Málaga, all of whose members would have been in mortal peril had he betrayed any Nationalist sympathies. As a German-speaking air force engineer, he had been sent to Germany in April 1936, ostensibly to discuss the possible ordering of material but in reality to assess how far production figures indicated preparations for war.[26] Indeed, in England his situation must have resembled that of the hero of Graham Greene's novel based on the Spanish Civil War, *The Confidential Agent*, in that he could trust no one, was trusted by no one and was constantly followed by Nationalist agents, some of whom tried to persuade him to come over to their side, where he naturally belonged. On Monday 17 August, two days after the five Dragons had flown off from Croydon, the Spanish ambassador, López Oliván, visited Sir George Mounsey, a senior Assistant Under-Secretary at the Foreign Office, told him of Pastor's activities and recommended the man be watched. Mounsey then sent a note to Eden with the warning that 'Oliván of course does not want his name revealed as the source of this information.'[27] After his return from Paris on 29 August, Pastor found it impossible not only to retrieve the aircraft he had bought or to buy new ones, but even to buy spare parts for British civil aircraft that had been in Spain since long before the war. On 4 September Walter Roberts, one of the Foreign Office officials most hostile to the Spanish Republic, recommended to the Home Office that Pastor be deported, an urgent matter since he had been informed that the new government of Largo Caballero intended to appoint him as air attaché. As communication between the embassy and Madrid had become secure after the resignation of López Oliván at the end of August, this item of information could have come only from transcripts of Pastor's telephone conversations from the Waldorf. Special Branch visited the hotel twice, the first time to question Pastor and the second intending to escort him to Croydon and put him on a plane to Paris. By then, however, he had slipped out of Britain undetected.[28]

Pastor probably never suspected the treachery of the ambassador, however. After leaving London, López Oliván went to Nationalist Spain, where he received a cold welcome and no offer of employment from Franco, who had been told, perhaps wrongly, that he was a Freemason. He returned to his post at the Court of International Justice of the League of Nations at The Hague and after the Second World War worked in a similar capacity for the United Nations until 1960. He died in 1964. In the 1970s two distinguished friends, Salvador de Madariaga and Pablo de Azcárate, who replaced López Oliván in London, praised the loyalty and discretion with which he had served his government, Azcárate attributing his resignation to the massacre by militia of seventy prisoners – López Oliván's brother-in-law Colonel Capaz being among them – in the Model Prison, Madrid, on 22 and 23 August. It was a barbarity which some later justified as a reprisal for an air raid which had caused many casualties the day before, though in fact Madrid was not bombed until four days later (27 August) and when news of the massacre reached President Azaña and Premier Giral, both wept in despair for the Spanish Republic. The truth about López Oliván's conduct in London was not published until 1990.[29]

14

The Arms-Purchasing Commission

O N 3 SEPTEMBER 1936 the Nationalists captured Irún, thereby cutting off the Basque–Asturian zone from France, and on the 4th they took Talavera de la Reina in New Castile, only 70 miles (112 km) from Madrid. Giral's government, conscious that it could neither stop the rebel advances nor bring the 'uncontrollables' in its own ranks to heel, resigned and was replaced by that of Francisco Largo Caballero, the left-wing Socialist leader. Largo, who reserved for himself the offices of prime minister and war minister, included in his cabinet not only six Socialists, there having been none in any previous Spanish government, but also two Communists and he even offered places to the Anarchists. At first they refused, since to join government was against their principles, but in November, when the Nationalists were fighting their way into Madrid itself, they agreed, with misgivings, to send four delegates.

Indalecio Prieto became minister for the navy and air force (Marina y Aire), Dr Juan Negrín, another moderate Socialist, minister of finance, and Julio Alvarez del Vayo minister of state for foreign affairs. Prieto and Negrín objected to this last appointment on the grounds that Vayo was both stupid and, though nominally a Socialist, little more than a Soviet agent. Largo agreed, but kept him there because, he said, in such a position of prominence 'we can watch him.' In a public broadcast Largo proclaimed that his would be 'the Government of Victory'.

The three professors in Paris received their ambassadorships, Pablo de Azcárate arriving in London on 13 September, Fernando de los Rios in Washington on 7 October and Luis Jiménez de Asúa in Prague on 15 October. Alvaro de Albornoz was recalled from Paris and replaced by Luis Araquistaín, Largo's adviser on socialist theory and a prominent author and editor, who arrived on 24 September.

At the embassy he found the arms-buying enterprise in confusion and the atmosphere of distrust between the persons and groups engaged in it 'truly unbreathable'.[1] The Oficina Comercial, of which Dr Otero had made himself the effective head by dint of sheer energy, consisted, so Araquistaín concluded, of men who, though inexperienced in the practices of 'the most heartless trade in the world', acted in good faith but were hamstrung by the contract with the Société Européenne. Moreover, their problems were aggravated by the almost daily arrival of people, singly or in groups, from Spain with authorizations to buy military hardware on behalf of this or that body or consequential politician, some indeed being sent without the knowledge of the government in Madrid. Belonging to antagonistic political parties or movements – such as the Communists, the CNT (Anarchist trade syndicate), the Basque Euzkadi Republic, the Esquerra (Catalan separatists) or even the opposing wings of the Socialists – they steered clear of one another and of the Oficina Comercial and tried to deal privately with the vendors. Knowing little of business, let alone the arms business, and ignorant of foreign languages they were easily ensnared by the arms traders and beguiling entrepreneurs waiting in the embassy foyers for interviews with the ambassador. After being swindled once and then, in an attempt to restore their *amour propre*, a second time and so reduced to indigency, they returned home at the expense of the embassy or, fearful of being accused of embezzlement or treason by their sponsors in Spain, became fugitives in France.

In so doing they created further unintended mischief. Believing that they could manage on their own, they had unwittingly competed against one another for the same lots of weapons, in some instances weapons for which the Oficina Comercial had itself been about to sign contracts. The dealers were thus able to raise the prices as at an auction, telling each of the parties that the other rival bidders were agents of General Franco, and so force Otero to pay an outrageous sum or cancel the contract. To pay exposed him to the charge of rigging the price to secure a higher commission for himself, though in fact he took no commissions,[2] while to cancel exposed him to the charge of treason, for the cries for arms at any price grew more desperate by the hour as Franco's forces came nearer to the capital. Meanwhile, the arms dealers and *espontaneos*, traders in other fields who had decided to try their hands at arms-dealing while the opportunity was open, importuned the ambassador with denunciations of one another and of all the Spaniards. If he could not pacify them, they travelled to Madrid and told the ministers and anyone they could buttonhole that the Paris embassy was a nest of incompetents and thieves.

As though these causes of friction were not enough, it seemed that whenever the Oficina Comercial withdrew or transferred money from a bank, the details appeared in the right-wing newspapers a day or two later. One example from many will suffice:

On 7 September an American bank in Paris' [in fact, the Chase National] made a transfer of £150,000 sterling to the Oesterreichische Creditanstalt of Vienna in the name of the Spanish journalist Corpus Barga, charged by the Madrid government with buying war material in Czechoslovakia.[3]*

The effect, at a time when co-ordination offered the only hope of success, was to make everyone suspect everyone else, as is shown in Dorrién's letter to his chief Vidarte on 26 August (see above, p. 86). Referring to the loss of the arms he had bought in Belgium, he wrote 'I'll be sure to say nothing to Otero, who has asked me about this, for I'm afraid of his indiscretions.'[4]

The Republicans were not to discover until the end of October that most of these items of information were leaking out not as the result of 'indiscretions', still less of treason, but were being passed to the news-papers by the banks themselves.

Araquistaín decided that the only solution was to establish an officially constituted arms-purchasing commission, the Comisión de Compras, under the presidency of a senior 'neutral' politician, the man chosen being Antonio Lara of the Unión Republicana, who had been minister of public works in Giral's cabinet. Otero became director of operations, assisted as before by Calviño and Martí Estevé, Lt.-Col. Luis Riaño and Major Jácome (José Jácome Marquez de Prado) were put in charge of aviation, Col. Luis Monreal, a naval gunnery officer, of artillery and explosives, and democratic procedure was to be safeguarded by a control committee of representatives from all the main political parties and regional move-ments. To house this sizeable staff, offices were rented nearby at 55 Avenue George V, a six-storey building built in 1931, in the white cement Art Deco style, near the corner with the Avenue des Champs Elysées. Its other tenants included a Quik Cafétéraire Electrique, a furniture shop, a travel agency and an advertising agency, while Socimex, the Republican purchasing commission, occupied the upper floors.[5]

The subsequent history of the building is of interest. At the end of the Spanish Civil War Socimex closed down, after removing all its records. The other tenants were evicted when the Germans occupied Paris and the building was taken over by a ferociously anti-Semitic newspaper based on Die Stürmer, Au Pilori, whose editors, Jean Lestand and the octogenarian Jean Drault, preferred to call their street 'Avenue Edouard Drumont' after

---

* This particular leak may have been attributable to the fact that the ex-director of the Oesterreichische Creditanstalt, Fritz Ehrenfest, was at this time living at Estoril, Portugal, and, in association with the Marqués de Quintanar, Franco's representative there, trying to procure war material for the Nationalists (Fundación de Pablo Iglesias, Madrid, Archivo de Luis Jiménez de Asúa, ALJA 442–6, Informe 11°, p. 90, 16 Jan 1937).

the 19th-century 'pioneer' of anti-Semitism. They were cleared out during the Liberation and today 55 Avenue George V is the Paris headquarters of the American airline TWA.

The opening of the commission was not auspicious, for after it moved in on 15 October, it had to wait another nineteen days for its first telephones, owing to the fact that no one had remembered to order them.[6] More serious was the matter of the Société Européenne. How it was resolved is not clear, although a few surviving references to the affair indicate that by the time relations were finally severed early in 1937, the company had been paid 100 million Ffr. (£1.3 million or $6.5 million) against invoices it could not justify and 64 million Ffr. in commissions on purchases with which it had nothing to do and that it was trying to extract a further 28 million Ffr. which it claimed were still owing to it.[7]

It may be convenient here to pause and take stock of how much usable war material the Republicans managed to acquire from abroad between the outbreak of the civil war and the beginning of October 1936, when the purchasing commission was formed in Paris and the first ships arrived at Cartagena with arms from the Soviet Union. Historians of the Spanish Civil War tend to be vague on this question, although those who began writing in Spain during the Franco years, and are still reiterating the arguments they proposed then, give the impression that arms flowed in to the Republic almost from the first day, if not before.

With regard to the aircraft, it is now possible to calculate the number to within a margin of two or three: twenty-six modern French military aircraft without armaments or the means of installing them; sixteen French civil aeroplanes, mostly old and either small passenger planes or trainers; and fourteen civil aeroplanes from Britain, of which only the four de Havilland Dragons, slow and practically defenceless, could be briefly used as light bombers where there was no opposition. Finally, there were four long obsolete, indeed ancient, military aircraft which – even if they had been delivered armed, which they were not – were of no military use whatever.* This brings the total to sixty, or at most sixty-two, machines of all types, of which only twenty-five were able to play any part in the fighting on the Madrid front, and then only after long delays while they were being fitted with improvised and very defective armament.

Although Blum told his friends privately that he intended to adopt a policy of *non-intervention relâchée'* ('relaxed non-intervention') and

---

* The Avia BH-33 fighter from Belgium on 27 August (see above, p. 88); a Lioré et Olivier LeO 20 bomber, possibly sometime in August, shot down on its first mission; a Blériot SPAD 91/6 fighter on 30 September; a LeO 213 military transport converted into a bomber, date of arrival uncertain. There is no evidence to support claims that two or four Bloch MB 200 bombers were delivered early in August or at any time (Howson, op. cit., under type headings).

allow material to cross into Spain provided it were done discreetly,[8] this did not prove easy in practice. There is, for example, a file of correspondence relating to bomb-racks for the Potez 540s that arrived on 8 August. When the Republicans, who thought they had paid for them, discovered that the racks had not been delivered with the aircraft, they asked the manufacturer, the Société Serquigny, to make and send sets for the six bombers. Serquigny replied that as a government-controlled company it was prohibited from doing so and suggested that the Spaniards make them themselves. The exchange of proposals and counter-proposals, including the granting of a manufacturing licence etc., dragged on until the Spaniards gave up at the end of September. There are other letters through August to October from Hispano Aviación, the aviation branch of Hispano-Suiza, at Guadalajara and CASA (Construcciones Aeronáuticas SA) at Madrid to no fewer than thirteen French aviation companies, including Dewoitine and Loire-Nieuport, requesting, in vain, the urgent deliveries of spare parts, from magnetos to undercarriage-wheel tyres.[9] Thus, no weapons came with the aircraft.

So far as weapons for the army are concerned, if any were slipped into Spain in July or the first weeks of August, the volume must have been very modest – pistols or hand-grenades in boxes small enough to hide in cars or vans, for instance – for the French police and customs kept a close watch on traffic across the frontier of France and Catalonia during the summer and autumn of 1936. The earliest delivery of which I have found any record is on or about 23 August, when 150 Brandt trench-mortars (fifty 81 mm and a hundred 60 mm) and 45,000 mortar-grenades were brought to Alicante by the *Jalisco*. This ship, formerly the *Berbère* (1,700 tons, built in 1891), had been lying, considered little better than a hulk, at Marseille for several years and had been bought, on 5 August with Spanish Republican money, by Captain Manuel Zermeno Araico, of the Mexican gun boat *Durango*, which happened to be in the Mediterranean. Renamed *Jalisco*, she sailed on 21 August from Marseille to Alicante, left Alicante for Marseille on the 29th and sailed for Spain with a second cargo of arms on 10 September, this time taking, apparently, fifty Oerlikon 20 mm anti-aircraft cannons (see above, p. 17, n.) and 75,000 shells.[10] The next delivery of arms, likewise by courtesy of the Mexican government, came on 2 September, when the Spanish liner *Magellanes*, after an adventurous journey in which she had been twice attacked by Italian bombers, docked at Cartagena and disembarked 20,000 Mauser rifles and 20 million cartridges, sent as a gift by the president of Mexico, Lázaro Cárdenas. Although old, the rifles and cartridges at least had the virtue of being of the same calibre as Spanish army Mausers (7 mm) and the Republicans insisted on paying for them. The Mexicans, however, refused to accept more than 3,500,000 pesos (£192,400 or $962,000), that is, £4. 6s. 2d. ($24.05) per rifle and the same per thousand rounds.[11]

For the rest, most of the weaponry, apart from Soviet material, obtained by the Republicans during the next year came from eastern Europe and all but a small part of it from Poland; some indeed came through agencies in Nazi Germany. These are extraordinary facts of which, so far as I can discover, there is no mention in any history of the Spanish Civil War.

15

Warsaw

THE GENERALS AND colonels of the military junta that ruled Poland at this time had been put in power in 1926 by Marshal Pilsudski, the hero of the fight for independence from 1916 to 1920, and had remained in power after his death in 1935. His successor, the blimpish Marshal Smigly-Rydz, was a mere figurehead, and the president, Dr Mościcki, a shadow; the dominant personality of the regime was the foreign minister, Colonel Jozef Beck. They called their government *Sanacja*, meaning 'sanitation' or 'moral renewal'. The problems they faced threatened to, and within three years did, overwhelm them.

After more than a century of partition under Russia, Austria, Prussia and Germany, Poland had been independent for less than eighteen years. Much of the population consisted of large and restive minorities; the landed aristocracy was entrenched, the peasantry 'backward', the Catholic Church strong, industry underdeveloped and the treasury impoverished. The country had no natural defences, yet lay between two great powers, Nazi Germany and the Soviet Union, both of which agreed, while they agreed on nothing else, that Poland ought not to exist and were intent on seizing back, as soon as the moment presented itself, territories which had formerly belonged to the German and Russian empires. Most menacing of all was the question of the 'Polish Corridor', created by the Treaty of Versailles to allow Poland access to the sea through the specially established Free Port and Free State of Danzig (Gdansk), a city and region whose people were almost entirely German and many of whom had recently become fervent Nazis. To reinforce their presence in the 'Corridor', which separated Germany from East Prussia, the Poles had built a new port at Gdynia.

With an increasingly unreliable France as their only ally, the Poles had decided that their best hope of defence was to build up their armed strength. The difficulty was paying for it. After the fighting for independence had come to an end with the driving back of the Russian

Bolsheviks in 1920, the Polish army had found itself in possession of a dis-
maying variety of French, Russian, German, Austrian, Italian, British and
American armaments which it had captured, bought or been given. Since
1930 it had made efforts to standardize by replacing old weapons with
new from the state arsenals at Radom and Warsaw and by importing new,
or old but refurbished, material from Belgium, Germany and
Czechoslovakia. Its Mauser 7.92 mm rifles, for instance, were made not
only in Poland but in Czechoslovakia by the Zborojovka (Zb) factory at
Brno and by the Fabrique Nationale at Herstal in Belgium, while refurbished German Mausers were supplied by Soley-Grimard at Liège. This
did not matter since the rifles were for all practical purposes identical to
the Mauser 98, the standard German army rifle of both world wars.

The Poles had expected to meet at least some of the cost of rearmament
by selling off the 'old stocks' of arms and munitions, but, apart from Saudi
Arabia and a few Chinese warlords, there had been no customers. Indeed,
the only success had been in aviation, thanks largely to the genius of
Zygmunt Pulawski, the young aircraft designer whose series of gull-
winged fighter monoplanes, a configuration invented by him and much
copied abroad, had briefly put Poland into the forefront of world fighter
aircraft development during the early 1930s and brought substantial
export orders from Bulgaria, Greece, Romania and Turkey.*

The agency responsible for these sales was SEPEWE (Syndicat Exporti
Przemyski Wejennego, or 'Export Syndicate of War Industries') at 65
Wilcza Street, Warsaw. In theory a private company but in fact owned and
controlled by the government, it had been founded in 1926 to dispose of
surplus war material, but in 1928 had expanded into general arms-dealing
and by 1936 had branches in thirty-five countries.[1] Its director was Lt.-
Col. Wladyslaw Sokołowski, a former chief of the arms production division of the ministry of military affairs, though the driving force in the
company was said to be his deputy, Major Zarębski.[2] The overriding
problem facing both, however, was that the bank balance of SEPEWE was
permanently in debit.

As related in Chapter 9, the sale of four Fokker F.XIIs by British

---

* In 1935 the Poles negotiated with the Spanish government over the sale of P.Z.L. P.24
fighters to the Aviación Militar, which would have been built under licence in Spain.
Negotiations broke down over the failure of the Poles to send a demonstration aircraft, since all those available were in the Balkans, and over the difficulty of obtaining
engines from the Bristol company in England, and the Spaniards bought the Hawker
Spanish Fury instead. (My colleague Pawel Swieboda found two brief references to
this in the Archives of Modern Records in Warsaw: Ministry of Foreign Affairs,
Political Department, Western Division, Spain; File 4046, P 11 H57/8/36 and P 11
H57/21/36, letters from the Polish Mission in Madrid, 21 and 28 Jan 1936. There are
others in the SEPEWE file [B. I. 113] in the Polish Institute Archive, London, e.g. the
depositions of Sokołowski, Kowalewski and Abczynski; see n. 1 below.)

Airways to General Mola in August 1936 was handled by the aristocratic Polish arms dealer Stefan Czarnecki, supposedly on behalf of a Polish mining company, but the man who alerted the Polish government to the possibilities offered by the fighting in Spain seems to have been Major Kazimierz Ziembinski, the pilot of the Fokker G-ADZJ who, defeated by the thunderstorm over the Pyrenees, turned back and landed his machine at Bordeaux, with or without the mysterious 'G. Morawski' as his passenger. Ziembinski, a retired fighter pilot, was the sales representative for SEPEWE in the Middle East and an agent for the Polish military intelligence department of the general staff, to whom, according to one of their officers, he gave information about the rebellion in Spain 'which was of great value to us'.[3]

In the discussions that followed Ziembinski's report to SEPEWE, Sokołowski tells us:

> Economic imperatives dominated the decision-making. The Spanish White government had no money and was in any case being supported by the governments politically allied to it. The Red government, on the other hand, had plenty of money but lacked sufficient reserves of war material and, in view of the difficulties of procuring arms, would have to pay high prices for them in hard currency. So far as I remember, political considerations were not important.[4]

That was not quite true. Colonel Beck, the foreign minister, was trying to construct an intricate arrangement of pacts and treaties in the hope of placating the Germans and Russians without alarming Britain and France and, when the civil war broke out in Spain, the Polish government had been the first in the world to declare, on 23 July, an arms embargo against both sides. Nevertheless, the colonels sympathized wholly with General Franco and saw to it that nothing critical of the Nationalists or favourable to the Republicans was published in the press or broadcast on the radio. Their arms sales to the Republicans would therefore have to be kept a dark secret indeed and to this end Beck insisted that negotiations with Spaniards must never be conducted directly but only indirectly through a chain of foreign intermediaries, preferably those with whom SEPEWE already had good relations. He also reserved the right to stop any transaction that might spoil his foreign policy.[5] However, once it was decided that the bulk of the sales must be to the Spanish Republicans, things moved quickly and preparations for delivery were already under way when the Polish government signed the Non-Intervention agreement on 26 August. The shipping side of the traffic was handled through the naval counterpart of SEPEWE, the Polska Agencja Morska (PAM).

The KZU (Armed Services Supplies Division), which was responsible for the 'old stocks', already had a standing list of export prices for surplus materials, approved by the chiefs-of-staff and graded as follows:

a) unusable;
b) withdrawn for being untypical or incompatible;
c) worn out;
d) dangerous owing to design or manufacturing faults;
e) withdrawn for having been stored too long.[6]

Obviously, the prices for such materials were extremely low. However, the Spanish Republicans needed the arms very urgently, wrote Sub-Colonel Ostrowski, the chief of the KZU, 'and I thought this advantageous situation made it feasible to charge prices for these weapons that were significantly higher than those on the price list.'[7] Sokołowski objected that this would reflect poorly on SEPEWE, for the standing price list was already known to foreign clients but, after his deputy, Major Zarębski, went over his head to the chiefs-of-staff, was overruled.[8] It was at this time too that Sokołowski learnt that Ziembinski had given information about Spain to the military intelligence department and, ignoring the protests of the intelligence chiefs that it was the patriotic duty of every officer serving abroad to bring back information useful to his country, dismissed him on the grounds that no officer could serve two masters simultaneously. Inter-departmental squabbling of this kind was endemic to the *Sanacja* regime, where every general and colonel treated his ministry or department as a private fief, and it soon became common gossip in the cafés of Warsaw that the directors of SEPEWE and other senior members of the government had formed a 'family' to keep a firm grip on the 'Spanish trade' and to limit the number of people who might profit from it to as few as possible.[9]

It is extraordinary to relate that on 6 September 1936 Léon Blum advanced a loan of 2,000 million Ffr. (*c.* £19 million, or $95 million), to be paid over four years, precisely to help the Poles finance their rearmament. He hoped thereby to stem the Polish drift towards Germany, which had increasingly worried the French since the non-aggression pact signed by Hitler and Beck in 1934.[10] One would have thought that this huge infusion of money might have caused the Poles to reconsider the dangers of their policy on Spain, but obviously it did not. Indeed, none of the deponents to the Sikorski inquiry so much as mentions it.

Appendix II contains a list of the thirty-one arms shipments from Poland to Spain from 9 September 1936 to 25 September 1937. Twenty-six voyages were made to the Republicans: three ships (the *Sylvia*, *Rona* and *Hordena*) fell into Nationalist hands and one, the *Lola*, was impounded by the Romanians at Constanta. Four deliveries were to the Nationalists. The figures for the arms require careful interpretation, however. Of the 100,000 rifles delivered to the Republicans, only the 25,000 Polish-made Mausers (PWU 29s) were even reasonably new. Of the 11,123 light machine-guns and machine-rifles bought by the Republicans, only 992 were delivered. Of the 180 million cartridges bought by the Republicans, only 68 million were delivered. Thus if the medium machine-guns had their due quotas of 10,000 rounds each, the light machine-guns had only 5,000 rounds each, enough for eleven minutes total firing time, to be spread across the entire war, and the rifles only 624 rounds each instead of their 1,000.

Of the 294 artillery pieces on the list, all were old; only eight had their panoramic sights, without which guns could not be aimed properly; none had their wagons or limbers, without which guns could not be moved properly, and all had insufficient ammunition. As rifles were sold with 1,000 rounds and machine-guns with 10,000, so artillery pieces were customarily sold with 2,400 shells each, on the calculation that for normal use each gun would require 120 rounds per day up in the battery, with ample reserves within quick reach. Particularly noticeable is the shortage of shells for the 75 mm field-guns and howitzers, a calibre in common use all over the world. The first four guns arrived in November 1936 with only 242 shells each, enough for two days' action, and when these were used up the guns would have to be withdrawn from the front. No more 75 mm ammunition arrived until March 1937, five months later, when three ships delivered sixty-eight Italian guns with only 595 shells and 176 shell charges each. In October 1937 the *Ploubazlanec* delivered 40,000 shells at Bordeaux, but these may not have crossed into Spain until considerably later, or even until February or March 1938, when the French frontier was opened. Finally, fifty-four Italian 75 mm field-guns on the *Jaron*, with 1,000 rounds each, did not reach Spain, assuming they all did, until taken to Le Havre by the *Diana* in April and May 1938 (see Appendix II).

As the guns were old and already much used, there must have been considerable wastage through premature explosions or the expanding of barrels caused by defective ammunition, and through capture by the enemy resulting from the sheer difficulty of moving the guns without their proper transportation equipment. Some historians have remarked on the erratic character of Republican artillery fire and on the disproportionate number of artillery pieces captured by the Nationalists during the course of the war, attributing them to Republican incompetence, lack of discipline and poor leadership. These facts provide a more likely explanation.

In some of the instances where it is possible to compare the Polish lists with Spanish records, the quantities sent in reality were less than both those paid for by the Republicans and those listed by the Poles as having been sent. If these were isolated cases, they are of little importance, but if they represent a continuing trend, then the cumulative effect of such short-changing would have been considerable.[11]

More significant is the fact that most of the prices on the SEPEWE
delivery list are low, new Polish Mausers being charged at $21.40 each and
old rifles at from $14.40 down to only $4 each. Ostrowski stated that he
raised all prices significantly above those on the official price list and those
Polish officers and agents who mention the subject in their depositions
corroborate this. A Major Buchowski, for example, refers to some Italian
M 1905 guns (probably Skoda 76.5 mm M 1905 light field-guns) with only
1,000 shells each and with no communication equipment, which were to
be sold at a unit price equivalent to that of a modern Italian gun, bought
new from the factory in 1937, plus 25%! When he protested that this was
outrageous and dishonest, Major Zarębski, Sokołowski's deputy, replied,
'Why should you worry? It's only to the Spanish Republicans!'[12] In the
Spanish archives in Madrid is a copy of an offer from SEPEWE to the
Republicans (July 1937) of new Polish Mausers at 225 zlotys ($45, or £9)
each, which was one third higher than the market price of a new German
Mauser ($30, or £6).[13]

Then there are the eight Russian mountain-guns (M 1904/09, 76.2 mm)
brought by the *Hillfern*, which, according to the Polish voyage list, cost
20,000 zlotys ($4,000, or £800) each. As we shall see (pp. 216, 282 and 334),
they were bought from SEPEWE by a Soviet agent code-named 'Tomson'
for $6,500 (£1,300) each[14] and, after being included by the Russians on
their own list as Soviet material, were finally sold to the Republicans at
$6,580 each,[15] which is nearly 40% above their price on the Polish list.

It seems that the prices recorded in the SEPEWE account-books and
preserved in the archives are those of the original standing price list, before
Ostrowski had increased them, and that the prices paid by the
Republicans were between 30% and 40% higher. The undeclared surplus
would then be 'laundered' abroad; indeed, one of the deponents refers to
the payment of such a sum into a bank account in Finland.[16]

The list in Appendix II shows that armaments to the value of about $24
million (£4,800,000) were sold to Spain by the end of September 1937, of
which only about 2%, or about $518,000, represented sales to the
Nationalists. According to Sokołowski, sales stopped in March 1938,
though it seems that a few deliveries were made during the summer, presumably of material that had been held up in Poland. It became a practice
of the Polish authorities at Gdynia, Danzig not being used after January
1937, to hold goods in the warehouses on one pretext or another in order
to charge the Republicans higher storage fees, some amounting to tens of
thousands of pounds.[17]

A great deal of money was consumed as well by the intermediaries in
the form of commissions and various other charges. The agencies used at
first by SEPEWE belonged, with the possible exception of Klaguine, to a
ring of arms dealers including Josef Veltjens, Willy Daugs and Thorvald

Erich* in Berlin and Edgard Grimard in Liège. Of these, Veltjens was a Nazi, Daugs and Erich probably Nazis, and Grimard a member of the Rexiste monarchist-Fascist party in Belgium, which explains, no doubt, why two shiploads of arms turned out on arrival to have been sabotaged and four shiploads were delivered to the Nationalists instead of the Republicans (see below, pp. 195–7). Alexandre Klaguine seems unlikely to have had much sympathy for the Republicans either, being a Lithuanian Tsarist emigré who had built up his arms business in Liège and Paris by using contacts, inherited from before the Russian Revolution, in the Baltic states.[18] Another whose name appears in the depositions is Fritz Mandl, for whom Stefan Czarnecki acted as an agent in Paris (see pp. 63 and 200).

If the Republicans in Paris were worried by the fact that they were procuring arms through such people, of whom three were based in Berlin, there was little they could do about it in the autumn of 1936. Poland was the only country to have offered arms in any quantity and demands from the front, as the Nationalists came closer to Madrid, grew every day more frantic. They were not told that the Soviet Union had decided to intervene, for that was a closely kept secret confined to a few members of the government. Beck had insisted that SEPEWE effect its sales through intermediaries. Arms dealers, individually or in rings, tried to carve out their territories and when one sold arms to a country where another dealer had already put down his stakes, he had to sell the arms through him. Grimard, Ball and Veltjens (I do not know about Daugs) had been selling arms to China and the Middle East since the early 1930s and when SEPEWE sold their old weapons to these buyers in the 1930s, they would have to have done so through one or another or all of these men, or by coming to some arrangement with them, and it was naturally the same people to whom the company turned when setting up the 'Spanish trade'. Dr Otero and his colleagues at the buying commission may have been children in this predatory world, but it is improbable that the most hard-

---

* Daugs and Erich are referred to in the Polish depositions as a single company. Ian Hogg kindly supplied me with the little information to be found about Daugs during the Second World War and after. In 1942 he was director of the Tikkakosi arsenal in Finland; in 1945 he moved hastily – via Sweden and the Netherlands – to Spain, where he worked for the Oviedo arsenal. With Ludwig Vorgrimmer, an ex-employee of Mauser who had similarly fled from Germany to Spain, he tried to market the DUX 53, their improvement (i.e. licence-dodging) version of the Finnish M 44 sub-machine-gun. Having sold some to the West German police, he was employed by the Anschatz armaments company at Ulm in the 1950s, when he helped to redesign the DUX 53 as the DUX 59. Without telling his employers beforehand, however, he sold the licence for this gun to an unidentified party, vanished and, so far as is known, has never been seen since. Thorvald Erich, as Daugs's partner, sold guns to the Paraguayans during the Gran Chaco War and in 1937 bought some of them back for the Spanish Republicans (see below, pp. 234 and 276).

ened professionals would have been able to do very much better. In any case, things improved when, after ridding themselves of the services of export-import companies such as Fuller Frères and Langstaff-Ehrembert[19] in Paris and the Société Européenne at the end of 1936, the Republicans handed over the Polish traffic to Daniel Wolf.

According to both Sokołowski and Colonel Stanislaw Witkowski, the chief of the armaments bureau in the Polish ministry of military affairs,[20] the turnover from arms sales during the Spanish Civil War came to about 200 million zlotys, that is to say about $40 million or £8 million. If to that we add all the extra charges mentioned above, as well as transport costs, it is hard to see how the armaments from Poland cost the Republicans less than $60 million (£12 million), especially when it is remembered that many of the arms and munitions, of which a large proportion was not delivered or proved almost useless, appear to have cost 30–40% more than their list prices. In his deposition Colonel Witkowski comments rather sourly that 'the turnover of 200 million zlotys ($40 million) ought to have been much higher, and would have been but for the fears of the foreign ministry and the chiefs-of-staff.'[21] The evidence relating to Colonel Beck's role in the affair is conflicting, however. For example, on 28 December 1936 Luis Jiménez de Asúa, the Republican ambassador in Prague, received a verbal message from the Polish chief of general staff, General Waclaw Stachiewicz, concerning a proposal to sell 150,000 Polish Mauser rifles, all in their factory wrappings and complete with ammunition (indeed, up to 100,000 rounds each!), recently produced as part of the Polish rearmament programme. Asúa had heard reports that some agents acting for the Republicans had been trying to buy arms in Poland, but had attached little importance to them in view of the known hostility of the Polish colonels to all left-wing governments. The message was therefore the more surprising, and in his dispatch to Vayo, the Republican foreign minister, he wrote:

> It is important to advise you that, according to 'Palacios' [Lt.-Col. Pastor Velasco; see below, pp. 153ff], things have changed dramatically in Warsaw. Previously, Beck has wanted nothing to do with the Spanish Reds, but now the attitude of Germany has made him decide to help us, in order to avoid the Germanization of Europe that is causing such enormous anxiety in Poland.[22]

Had these words been said in 1938, after Hitler's march into Austria and when the crisis over Czechoslovakia was already brewing, they might possibly be seen as consistent with Beck's attempts to steer between the German Scylla and the Russian Charybdis. But in December 1936 they are at variance with everything that is known about Beck's foreign policy, which was regarded by many Poles, and by many outside Poland, as too conciliatory to Hitler for the good of his own country. Moreover, by then the Poles had been shipping arms to the Republicans, as well as to the Nationalists, for three full months. Was General Stachiewicz speaking out of turn, or was the message concocted by Beck merely to put a respectable face on a shady business?

Another deponent, Wladyslaw Cmela, writes that 'when Colonel Beck and Ignaci Mościcki [the Polish president] approved the export of arms, they did not do so without an interest' and goes on to say that during the course of the Spanish war both 'received large provisions from SEPEWE.'[23] Cmela names as his authority for this allegation Andrjez Dowkant, the vice-director of the state arms factories, whom he describes as 'an honourable man' who had become indignant at the turn events were taking. It was one thing to sell off old and useless material, even to the Spanish Republicans, but quite another to sell brand new weapons during a programme of urgent rearmament, when the state factories were as yet unable to meet the requirements of the Polish army itself. No less baffling, therefore, is the offer by the Polish government to build a series of fifty P.Z.L. P.37 bombers for the Republicans. The P.37 Łos was one of the most advanced aircraft of its time and its very existence was still top secret when the offer was made in July 1937 (see below, Appendix IV C).

Although many details remain obscure, it is clear that the regime of the colonels' group in Poland, which called itself 'Moral Renewal' (and was ideologically close to Franco), became the second largest supplier of arms to the Spanish Republic after the Soviet Union. The colonels wanted the money to pay for rearmament, in addition to the huge French loan, and the message to Asúa may have been partly sincere. The shifts to which they had to resort to ensure secrecy, however, presented innumerable opportunities for corruption and, as the dangers gathered round Poland on all sides and the more perceptive foresaw the inevitable catastrophe, the temptations to some to cream off money to provide means of refuge abroad must have been irresistible. During the Second World War, those involved sent their testimonies to the committee set up by the Sikorski government in exile to inquire into the causes of the Polish defeat in September 1939 and either blamed one another or justified the selling of worthless material at high cost to the Spanish Republicans as an act of patriotism. As Stefan Katelbach, the Polish arms trader who became Daniel Wolf's principal agent, boasted in his deposition, 'by selling junk to the Spaniards at fantastic prices, we were able to restore the Polish bank to solvency.'[24]

16

The Non-Intervention
Committee

O N SUNDAY 6 September 1936, while Blum was explaining Non-
Intervention to 60,000 Socialists at a rally in Luna Park, Paris,
and being heckled once more with shouts of 'Des armes pour
l'Espagne', the British Labour Party was holding a rally in Trafalgar
Square, London, where 15,000 Socialists stood bare-headed in the pouring
rain to honour the Spanish dead.

In Britain the leadership of the Labour movement, that is to say the
party executive and the Trades Union Congress (TUC), was in a
quandary. Since the advent of Hitler it had called, as had Maxim Litvinov,
the Soviet delegate at the League of Nations, for 'collective security' to
meet the threat of international Fascism, but had voted against any proposal for expenditure on armaments because, it said, an increase of arms
would increase the probability of war. Those in the leadership, such as
Hugh Dalton, the chairman of the party executive, who were not inclined
to pacificism pointed out that while all democrats agreed that the Spanish
government should be allowed to buy arms, as was its legal right, Britain
had none to spare, for the productive capacity of the British arms industry
was fully booked for years to come with orders for the country's own
rearmament programme. Thus, for one reason or another the Labour
leaders, despite the misgivings of many of the rank and file, went along
with Non-Intervention, especially after Eden had assured them that the
policy would be enforced with equal strictness upon both sides in the
Spanish Civil War.[1]

The British Communist Party, having as yet received no clear line from
Moscow on what to say, said nothing that was clear, but had already begun
to organize the surreptitious recruitment and transport of volunteers for
what would soon become the International Brigades.

On 9 September the Non-Intervention Committee met for the first
time at the Foreign Office in Whitehall, London. It had twenty-seven
members, one from each of the European countries that had signed the

agreement,* but after the second meeting the weekly work was delegated to a sub-committee (hereafter the 'Committee') of nine members representing the three countries with frontiers adjoining Spain – France, Portugal and Britain (at Gibraltar) – and six major European arms-producing countries: Belgium, Czechoslovakia, Germany, Italy, Sweden and the USSR. The chairman (Lord Plymouth, who also represented Great Britain), secretary (Francis Hemming) and supporting staff were all British.

The duties of the Committee were to investigate reports of arms-smuggling and other violations and devise measures to prevent further foreign intervention. The purpose of Non-Intervention was to contain the fighting within Spanish territory and, by coming to an understanding with Hitler and Mussolini, relax the tension in Europe. However, since Spain was swarming with journalists, spies and observers of all nationalities, evidence of German and Italian intervention was only too abundant. To present this to the Committee would lead to a head-on collision with the dictators and ruin any chance of reaching the understanding hoped for. If the Committee did its work honestly, therefore, it would not lower the tension but heighten it. On the other hand, unless it investigated violations it could not propose measures to prevent their recurrence. The Committee tried to resolve this dilemma by instituting rules that evidence could not be accepted from any government that was not a party to the agreement, or from any private individual such as a journalist or observer, or from any international body such as the Red Cross or World Council of Churches, or from anyone who was serving in, or even present among, the armed forces of either side, which effectively barred everyone in Spain from giving evidence, apart from a handful of diplomats.

It happened that the Republican foreign minister, Julio Alvarez del Vayo, had recently handed to the British chargé at Madrid a report on German and Italian intervention on behalf of Franco, complete with photographs of an armed Junkers Ju 52 that had come down in Republican territory, a photograph of the number-plate of a captured Fiat C.R.32 fighter shot down, copies of captured documents and a signed statement by a captured Italian pilot.[2] Vayo warned that he intended to present this evidence to the League of Nations. At the Foreign Office, it was at first decided not to pass these documents to the Committee, for, as Sir George Mounsey, Assistant Under-Secretary of State at the Foreign Office, put it,

---

*Albania, Austria, Belgium, Bulgaria, Czechoslovakia, Denmark, Estonia, Finland, France, Germany, Greece, Hungary, the Irish Free State, Italy, Latvia, Lithuania, Luxembourg, the Netherlands, Norway, Poland, Portugal, Romania, Sweden, Turkey, USSR, United Kingdom (including the Commonwealth and colonies) and Yugoslavia. Switzerland was not a signatory, having embargoes already in place. The USA imposed a 'moral embargo', later a full one. The Latin American countries, except Mexico, imposed embargoes of their own.

'the discussion of such delicate questions may at any moment break up the Committee and with it the agreement.'[3] Besides, as William Pollock, a Second Secretary, pointed out, when looked at with an unclouded legal eye, 'The Spanish Govt's note . . . & its enclosures do not contain *a single piece of clear evidence* of the breach of the terms of the agreement by Germany, Italy or Portugal'[4] (my italics), while Walter Roberts gave his opinion that 'to allow the Spanish government, which is not a party to the agreement, to prefer a complaint would not only be against the rules but would amount to *discrimination against the insurgents*, who have no international status at present . . .'[5] (my italics). Meanwhile, Vayo delivered his speech, with the evidence, to the League of Nations, where it was rejected and quickly forgotten, and Sir Robert Vansittart, the permanent head of the Foreign Office and one of its few senior officials who believed that war with Germany was inevitable sooner or later, minuted 'We have certainly got to take action on these charges. There wd be a scandal if we didn't.'[6]

On 1 October the War Office gave its view that 'Germany, Italy and Portugal are clearly on the side of the insurgents and there is no doubt that the first two are supplying the arms, the material and especially the aircraft that are enabling the rebels to gain their successes.'[7] Eden therefore authorized Lord Plymouth to lay the evidence before the Committee, but 'in the most inoffensive and discreet manner possible in the hope that the Committee remain intact',[8] and it was finally presented on 9 October, nearly a month after its arrival in London. The German delegate, Prince Bismarck, explained that the Junkers was merely one of those passenger planes evacuating German citizens from Spain and that it had been armed because it had been sent to a war zone, where it might have had to defend itself against French fighters. Reports of Heinkel fighters etc. in the dossier, he said, were all untrue. Lord Plymouth thereupon declared that all the allegations were unsubstantiated.

This set an encouraging precedent for subsequent meetings, at which complaints were put aside as irrelevant, inaccurate or unproven. Indeed, many were indeed inaccurate, for they came from informants ignorant of the most elementary facts, especially where aircraft were concerned. Moreover, the Committee allowed itself to consult no other body than its own technical advisory committee, which met but once a month, with the result that whenever matters became 'technical' the delegates, who knew less about aircraft, guns, tanks or ships than most schoolboys, repeatedly found themselves at a nonplus.

Arguments grew more heated and confused when reports began to come in, at first prematurely, that Russian aircraft and arms were being unloaded from Russian ships at Republican ports. On 10 October, for instance, Norman King, the British consul-general at Barcelona, who had recently been subjected to a scathing attack by Stephen Spender in the *News Chronicle*,[9] wrote in his dispatch that he had just heard 'from a source that *might* be reliable' that seventeen Russian bombers of the latest type, 'each with five engines and fighting-turrets', had been disembarked at Barcelona. It took ten days for the Foreign Office to learn from the air attaché in Moscow that 'no five-engined bombers with fighting-turrets exist in the Soviet Air Force.'[10] A few days later Walter Roberts was informed by the Admiralty that two Russian steamers, the *Neva* and *Volga*, had unloaded no fewer than 150 large Russian aircraft at Cartagena on 24 October. Without pausing to consider if such a thing were physically possible, Roberts minuted, 'I fear that the inequality of the government forces is being rapidly redressed.'[11]

At the Committee meeting on 4 November, Prince Bismarck accused the Soviet Union of sending 'Gorky' bombers to Spain. Ivan Maisky, the Soviet delegate and ambassador to the United Kingdom, replied that this could not be, for no such bombers existed. Prince Bismarck suggested that the bombers might have been built 'at the Gorky factory'. Maisky denied that there was such a factory. Count Grandi, the Italian delegate, who had been leafing through a copy of *Jane's All the World's Aircraft*, which in those days was neither a complete nor an accurate publication, found a reference to a factory at Gorky in the section dealing with the Russian aviation industry and showed it to the delegates. Maisky insisted that *Jane's* was in error. Grandi countered this by saying that, however that may be, the Russian ship *Komsomol* had been seen to unload tanks. Maisky, who may not have been informed of this fact by the Soviet government, declared, with quick presence of mind, that they were lorries. 'But there were eye witnesses!' Grandi protested. 'Who? Paid spies, no doubt!'[12]

During such altercations, Baron Eric Palmstierna, the Swedish delegate, would sometimes fall into a species of trance, for he was busy composing a book, *The Horizons of Immortality*, in which he recorded his conversation with 'the messengers from the other world', and whenever these spirits spoke to him he had to concentrate on what they said in order to write it down later. When his book appeared in 1938, he had reached retirement age and the Swedish government, apprehensive that its instructions might not always accord with those of the messengers, recalled him.

From the tanks on the *Komsomol* the argument moved on to the tonnages of the two Russian vessels, the *Neva* and *Volga*, which had reportedly carried arms concealed in their cargoes or, according to the Admiralty report that had upset Walter Roberts, seventy-five large aircraft each. At 10.15 p.m. the Committee, exhausted, decided to consult *Lloyd's Register of Shipping* for the relevant information before the next meeting. However, as Lord Plymouth remarked, even with the facts and figures they would not be able to come to a useful conclusion, for in truth the

Committee could neither impose sanctions against governments that violated the agreement nor publish reports other than a bland communiqué
after each session, from which everything of a factual, and so possibly
contentious, nature had been excluded. What was needed was an international system of supervision and control.

Throughout these first weeks of the Committee the Soviet delegates,
first Samuel Kagan, the Soviet embassy counsellor and, after 23 October,
Ivan Maisky, the new ambassador, had repeatedly warned that unless
something was done to expose and stop German and Italian intervention
in Spain, the Soviet government would consider itself free to assist in
defending the Spanish Republic, although neither he nor the Soviet
government nor yet Stalin would openly declare that this assistance would
amount to military intervention. By 4 November not only had Soviet
material been arriving in Spain for exactly a month but the Germans had
decided to respond by creating a complete expeditionary force, code-
named Legion Kondor and consisting of a permanent strength of one
hundred aircraft, supported by anti-aircraft batteries, field artillery, tanks
and training, technical, medical and supply units. In addition, there were
to be two small experimental air units in which the latest aircraft types
could be assessed under conditions of real warfare. In December
Mussolini decided to upstage Hitler by sending the Aviazione Legionaria,
an air force with a permanent strength of 250 aircraft, and the Corpo
Truppe Voluntarie (CTV), an army of about 48,000 troops with artillery
and tanks, and to order the Italian navy to assist the Nationalist navy in
attacking and sinking Russian and Republican ships in the Mediterranean.
By the end of the war Italy had sent between 632 and 642 military aircraft,
all armed and supported, 57 training aircraft, a little under 2,000 artillery-
pieces, about 150 light tanks and 72,827 troops.[13]

Geography too helped the Nationalists in what is commonly called 'the
farce of Non-Intervention'. Men and material for Franco were delivered
straight to Nationalist ports where, under the rules of evidence, their
arrival could not be reported to the Committee or, in consequence, admitted by the British government during prime minister's question time in the
House of Commons. On the other hand, material for the Republicans
leaving the Baltic or crossing the Spanish frontier from France could be
easily watched and reported to the Committee under the same rules.
Similarly, ships carrying supplies to the Republicans from the Black Sea
had to pass through the Bosphorous and the Dardanelles, which enabled
the German, Italian, British and French consuls to send lists and descriptions to their governments, although the British later discovered that they
were all buying the information from the same man, who was doctoring
his reports to suit the expectations of each of his clients. The British thereupon dispensed with his services.[14] Even by 19 November 1936, therefore,

Eden had received enough misinformation to tell the House of Commons that, so far as breaches of the agreement were concerned, 'I wish to state quite categorically that there are other governments more to blame than Germany and Italy.'[15]

At the War Office, Major C. S. Napier, who was responsible for collecting data on foreign intervention in Spain, was surprised that Eden, to whom he had sent a report on 5 November showing the contrary, should have said this and on 23 November submitted to the Foreign Secretary a summary of all breaches of the agreement so far known, in which he concluded 'The War Office has no evidence to show that there are other governments more to blame than those of Germany and Italy.'[16] By 'other governments', Eden, of course, meant the Soviet Union, whose aid to the Republic has provoked more questions, mystification and bitter controversy than any other subject in the history of the Spanish Civil War.

17

Stalin

S INCE THE SOVIET Union was the only power to assist the Spanish
Republic with substantial military force, a great deal has been written
about why and when the Soviet government, which is to say Stalin,
took the decision to do so. Almost all of it is conjecture. Neither Stalin's
private thoughts on the matter nor the minutes of Politburo meetings,
assuming any were taken, have ever been published and all we have to go
on are the memoirs of two NKVD* officers who later defected, Walter
Krivitsky and Alexander Orlov, various items of gossip and a few references in the diary of Maxim Litvinov, the Soviet foreign minister, which
some experts in any case dismiss as a forgery.

Equally problematical has been the extent of Soviet aid. Throughout the
entire life of the Franco regime, historians and journalists writing under its
watchful eye in Spain produced figures, supposedly based on captured
Republican documents, to show that Soviet aid had been at least as great
as, or even greater than, that supplied to the Nationalists by German and
Italy combined (see below, p. 249). Many of these figures can still be found
in general history and reference books all over the world, with no indication of whether they derive from fact or wishful thinking. Spanish
Republican writers, some in exile and others after they had returned to
Spain in the 1960s, and historians in other countries who wanted to
research the subject seriously, doubted these findings, but could not
support their case with evidence, for the Spanish archives were open only

---

* The Soviet security services underwent numerous changes of names and abbrevia-
tions: Cheka, 1917–22; GPU, 1922–3; OGPU, 1923–34; NKVD, 1934–43; NKGB,
1943–6; MGD, 1946–53; MVD, 1953–4; KGB, 1954–94. Miliary intelligence was the
responsibility of the RU-RKKA, created in 1924. A third service, the GUGB, was
created in 1934, but when Yezhov took command of the NKVD in 1937 both the
GUGB and RU-RKKA were subordinated to him as well and were eventually combined, hence GRU. Its name, 'Fourth Department', thus derived from the fact that it
was the fourth of the many departments of the NKVD state within the state.

to approved official historians until the 1980s, and the Soviet archives until the 1990s. When the Soviet government itself published two sets of figures in the 1970s, in two separate books, the quantities in both were far lower than any published in the West, but otherwise differed in almost every particular and, since they were unaccompanied by breakdowns or indications of source, there was no telling if either could be trusted (see below, pp. 141–2). As a result, they were no help at all and 'What did the Russians really do?' is the most important question about the history of the Spanish Civil War that has remained without a satisfactory answer.

Finally, despite the numerous books and articles that have been written about the subject, we do not yet know the full truth about the 510 tons of Spanish gold, valued at $518 million, that were sent to Russia at the end of October 1936. According to the Franco regime, Stalin effectually blackmailed the Republican leadership into surrendering the gold before agreeing to send military aid. As this 'Moscow gold' represented three-quarters of the entire Spanish reserve, which until then had been the fifth largest in the world after those of the United States, Britain, France and the Soviet Union, the transfer was denounced as an act of unforgivable folly, or treachery, on the part of the Republicans and of unparalleled criminality on the part of Stalin. A newsreel of 1954 shows General Franco laying the blame for the continued poverty of his country upon 'this robbery'. With arms upraised, he cries, 'We found a ruined Spain! The Marxists stole the gold and wealth of Spain and took them to Russia! They left Spain empty!'[1]

During the following decades a more complex picture gradually emerged, according to which it was not Stalin but the Spanish Republicans themselves who had first proposed the transfer. On 16 September 1936 Dr Juan Negrín, Largo Caballero's finance minister and later the Republican premier, had had the gold reserve moved for its better safety from Madrid to the port of Cartagena, in the extreme south-east corner of Spain. Meanwhile, the Republicans were finding it increasingly hazardous to employ the gold that had been sent to France for the purpose of buying arms. The banks in Paris, London and New York were refusing to accept Republican money, were leaking information about Republican transactions to the press and governments and were obstructing the movement of funds from country to country (see below, pp. 169–71). Moreover, the gold was still not safe at Cartagena, where it might be seized by a Nationalist raid or even by the Anarchists, who were known to be considering such a coup. Nor could it be sent to one of the Non-Interventionist countries, whose government might 'freeze' it in order to bring the war to a quick end with a Nationalist victory. Accordingly, on 14 October, when the first Soviet ships bringing arms and aircraft were already arriving, Largo Caballero asked the Soviet government if it would agree to the transfer of a part of the gold reserve to the USSR. An affirmative reply was received on the 17th and the gold departed, in circumstances of high drama, by night on the 26th.[2] Very few members of the Republican government were informed and the whole affair was kept as secret as possible. In Moscow part of the gold was used to cover the cost of Soviet aid and the rest sent back, in the form of foreign currency, to the Soviet bank in Paris, the Banque Commerciale de l'Europe du Nord (BCEN), to enable the Republicans to buy additional supplies outside the USSR in secrecy and without interference from Western banks or governments.

During the 1950s certain Republican leaders in exile who had been responsible for arms procurement during the civil war, notably Indalecio Prieto (the minister for the navy and air force and later the minister for defence) and Luis Araquistaín (the Republican ambassador in Paris under Largo Caballero), began to claim that the Soviets had cheated the Republicans, for the value of the material sent must have been well below the money that the Soviets had deducted from the $518 million to cover its cost. Wrote Prieto, 'We are in the presence of colossal fraud and embezzlement.'[3] Neither he nor Araquistaín, however, had any figures at their disposal – Araquistaín, indeed, had never had any knowledge at all of what the Soviets might have supplied[4] – and the allegations were not taken seriously. By 1980, the painstaking researches of Dr Angel Viñas appeared to have settled the matter at last. From the available evidence, it seemed that the quantities of material supplied corresponded very closely in value to the money charged for them and that the Soviets had behaved correctly after all. Viñas was nevertheless aware that the evidence – which consisted of documents in the Spanish ministry of finance, the Bank of Spain and in the possession of Dr Marcelino Pascua, who had been the Republican ambassador in Moscow for much of the war – was incomplete and warned that until the full records of the Soviet government and of the BCEN in Paris were opened to researchers, no one could be sure that the whole truth was out. The figures for most of the Soviet aid and for nearly all of the arms, aircraft and munitions bought in other countries were derived from data compiled by historians whose sympathies had always been with the Nationalists; suspicion of Soviet malpractice could not be utterly dispelled; nor was it absolutely certain that the chance of obtaining the Spanish gold had not influenced Stalin's decision or that Largo Caballero had made his request of his own free will and not under Soviet pressure,[5] for there was still much ignorance of Soviet motives.

Although we do not have Stalin's word for it, there is little doubt that the outbreak of civil war in Spain presented the Soviet government with dilemmas as excruciating as those which faced the British and French governments. Ruling circles in Britain and France might be apprehensive that the Soviet Union would one day succeed in precipitating a general war, from which it would stand aloof until it could move in and erect

Dictatorships of the Proletariat amid the ruins of a devastated Europe, but Stalin feared the 'bourgeois encirclement' against which Lenin had warned. One day within the next ten or twenty years the European powers might sink their differences and, with Nazi Germany to the fore, launch a concerted attack on the Soviet Union. Stalin's options therefore were to try for better relations with the democracies – hence the Popular Front scheme and the French–Soviet pact of 1935 – or by some means come to terms with Hitler, and entanglement in Spain could well jeopardize both.[6]

On the other hand, the first of the great show trials – that of Kamenev, Zinoviev and fourteen other 'Old Bolsheviks' – was due to start on 19 August and, in view of the crises of faith that this might provoke in the foreign Communist parties, it was essential for Stalin to preserve the loyalty of their leaders during the months ahead. Failure to defend a Popular Front government attacked by the armed forces of Fascism could fatally weaken his standing as the leader of the world movement and it was probably this consideration which outweighed the rest. Stalin manoeuvred, as Hugh Thomas puts it, 'with crablike caution',[7] making gestures of reassurance to the democracies and authorizing secret measures to quieten the militants in the Comintern, an organization he held in contempt. On 25 August – the same day on which Kamenev, who had confessed to the preposterous accusations against him on the understanding that his life and his family would be spared if he did so, was condemned to death – the Soviet Union signed its adherence to Non-Intervention 'in the interests of world peace'. Diplomatic relations with Spain, which had been broken off during the Russian Revolution, were restored and Marcel Rosenberg arrived in Madrid as Soviet ambassador on the 27th. The two most important men on his staff were Arthur Stachewsky, who was both 'trade attaché' and Stalin's most trusted personal representative in Spain, and General Jan Berzin, who was to advise the Republicans on military tactics and strategy.* On the 28th, as Kamenev, Zinoviev and the others were

---

* A Latvian, Berzin's real name was Peteris Kjusis. He was imprisoned for taking part in the 1905 revolt, but escaped, using the documents of a dead man named 'Yan Karlovitch Berzin' and kept that identity thereafter. He commanded the GRU from its foundation in 1924 until, according to some accounts, he was succeeded by Uritsky in 1935. According to others, however, he was sent to eastern Siberia in January 1932 to carry out a central committee resolution of 11 Nov 31 to create Dal'stroy, a complex of mines and 160 forced labour camps at Kolyma, a name now coupled with Auschwitz and Treblinka as scenes of the most horrific nightmares of this century. He built the arrival port of Magadan and named its first street after himself (Ryszard Kapuściński, *Imperium*, pp. 200–9, quoting from Varam Shalamov's *Kolyma Nights* and Evgeniya Ginzburg's *The Steep Wall*). His service in Spain was distinguished and most historians of the war have written of him sympathetically; Col. I. G. Starinov, who conducted guerrilla operations behind Nationalist lines, writes of him with admiration and affection in his book *Over The Abyss* (Ivy Books, New York, 1995, pp. 74–5). Berzin is said

being shot in the execution cellars of the Lubyanka prison, Stalin signed a decree prohibiting the export of war material to Spain and volunteers from offering their services to the Republicans. In the meantime, however, workers' commissariats all over the Soviet Union organized the collection of funds to pay for food, clothing and medicines for the Spanish Republic. Mass meetings, complete with banners and huge portraits, were held in every major town, the occasions were filmed, the newspapers printed hundreds of letters, especially from schoolchildren, expressing admiration and love for the Spanish working people and *Pravda* (16 October) published an open letter from Stalin to the Spanish Communist Party, saying:

> The workers of the Soviet Union are doing no more than their duty in rendering all possible aid to the Revolutionary Masses of Spain. They are well aware that the liberation of Spain from the yoke of Fascist reactionaries is not the private concern of Spaniards alone but the general concern of all progressive humanity.[8]

Yet it is noticeable, in the films and newspaper reports of the meetings, that on the banners the word 'Spain' is nowhere visible, that the portraits are not of Spanish leaders but of Marx, Lenin and Stalin, mostly Stalin, and that Spain is nowhere mentioned in the prepared speeches, which are devoted entirely to praising the far-sighted sagacity and benevolence of the Great Leader.[9]

According to Krivitsky, on 2 September Soviet agents in Europe were ordered to create a clandestine organization, which must have no visible connection with the Soviet government, for the purchase and transport of war material to Spain (see below, p. 208).[10] A week or two later an advance party of airmen, having travelled across Europe by rail, arrived in Spain to assess the logistics of sending an expeditionary air force, choose possible airfields and carry out orientation flights.[11] On the 16th Alexander Orlov, a senior major (equivalent to brigadier general) of the NKVD, arrived, officially to take up the post of 'political attaché', but in reality to organize security, counter-intelligence and the formation and training of guerrilla groups to operate in Nationalist territory and to take charge of any other behind-the-scenes business.[12] Yet Litvinov's diary, if it be genuine, records

---

to have incurred Stalin's displeasure when he endorsed a letter by Stachewsky warning that the high-handed behaviour of Orlov and the NKVD in Spain was alienating the Spanish government and people. He and Stachewsky were recalled to Moscow in June 1937 and disappeared. However, a letter dated 19 July 1937 shows that he was by then directing the sending of war material to Spain (RGVA, F33897 O 3 D 1656 L. 40). Kapuściński may be mistaken in saying that Berzin was recalled to Moscow from Magadan on 1 Dec 1937 (1935?), unless Berzin, after a period with 'Operation "X"', was sent back to Magadan and then recalled from there. It is now known that he was executed in July 1938.

a Politburo meeting on 10 September at which Stalin still inclined to neutrality. He was opposed by Molotov and Marshal Voroshilov, who argued that the Non-Intervention Committee in London had held its first meeting the day before and that 'as we have a seat on that committee, we should seize the first opportunity that arises to help Largo Caballero, even though we have little confidence in him personally.'[13]

According to Krivitsky again, Stalin, determined that all operations on behalf of the Spanish Republic should be absolutely secret, placed them under the control of the NKVD and instructed its chief, Gendrik Yagoda, to call a special meeting in the Lubyanka on 14 September to set things in motion.[14] Present were Abram Slutsky, the director of the INO (the foreign department of the NKVD), General Mikhail Frinovsky, commander of the military forces of the NKVD and the frontier guards, and Corps Commander (equivalent to three-star general) Semon P. Uritsky,* the chief of the GRU (the Red Army intelligence service, also called RU-RKKA or 'Fourth Department'). All four were experienced interrogators who had helped to extract 'confessions' from the accused in the recent show trial and all four, together with Stachewsky, Rosenberg and General Berzin, were to be swept away in the Great Terror, Yagoda himself, the first, being dismissed and replaced by the half-insane Yezhov barely a fortnight after this meeting. Slutsky, after distinguished service in Spain, died in Frinovsky's office, supposedly of a heart attack but probably poisoned by Frinovsky himself. Uritsky was dismissed in the summer of 1937, replaced by Berzin, his former commander, and then both were arrested in the winter and executed after torture. Frinovsky, having executed nineteen of his own staff in a vain attempt to keep in Stalin's favour, was shot during one of the last wholesale massacres of senior Red Army and NKVD officers in 1940.[15] Nobody seems to know why or when Stachewsky and Rosenberg were shot, except that it was in 1937.

The relevant documents in the Russian State Military Archives show that two days after this meeting, on 16 September, 'Operation "X"' (that is to say, 'The Transportation of Special Goods to Our Friends in "X"', 'X' denoting Republican Spain) was born and a Section X – consisting of offi-

---

* Semon P. Uritsky was the son of Moise Uritsky, the founder and head of the Leningrad Cheka until he was assassinated on 30 August 1918, the day of the first attempt on Lenin's life. Semon Uritsky replaced Berzin at the GRU in April 1935 and took command of 'Operation "X"' (see below) on 16 September 1936. When the American journalist Louis Fischer interviewed him in January 1937 (*Men and Politics*, p. 384), Luli Cisneros, the young daughter of General Hidalgo de Cisneros, the Republican air chief, and another little Spanish girl were staying at his home. Although denounced as a Trotskyite in May 1937, he was not arrested until 11 November. After prolonged beating, he was executed without trial. It is unlikely that Hidalgo de Cisneros, one of the most senior aristocrats in Spain who, with his wife, turned communist and remained so until his death in 1966, was ever aware of this.

cers of the NKVD, the GRU, and the army, navy, air force, transport and finance departments responsible for choosing, transporting and auditing the costs of the materials and personnel to be sent to Spain – was set up under Uritsky. The officers submitted their lists of materials, personnel, costings, progress reports, recommendations and requests to do this or that to Uritsky, who passed them to Voroshilov, the overall commander of the operation, who in turn passed them, with his own comments, suggestions and requests, to Stalin for approval or rejection. Indeed, one of the surprising revelations of these documents is the extent to which Stalin retained personal control over the whole operation, at least during its first year, for it seems that all decisions, even such minor ones as the withdrawal of quite small sums of money, were referred to him before being implemented.[16]

Another revelation is that, apart from the aircraft, tanks and 150 Degtyarev light machine-guns, all the weapons sent in 1936 were old and nearly worn out, more than half of them being ancient museum pieces supplied with so little ammunition as to be practically useless (see below, Chapter 19). One possible clue as to how this came about is in Krivitsky's memoirs, where he says that Stalin insisted that none of the weaponry should be traceable back to the USSR. Yagoda thereupon summoned Captain Misha Umanksy, a Polish NKVD agent who had been the interpreter during H. G. Wells's famous interview with Stalin in 1934 and escort to both Anthony Eden and Pierre Laval, then the premier of France, during their visits to the Soviet Union in 1935. In Odessa, Yagoda said, were three high Republican officials who had come to buy arms and had been cooling their heels there for some time. Umansky was to go to Odessa and 'create a neutral private firm for them to deal with'.[17] Since there is no record of any Spanish Republican high officials in the USSR during August or September 1936, this story has been doubted. However, if Krivitsky, or his ghost-writer, was mistaken merely in describing the Spaniards as 'high officials' rather than as the humble arms buyers they would have been, then the story may be true, for on 26 September Stalin telephoned Voroshilov from his dacha at Sochi in the Caucasus, where he was on holiday, to order that the Spanish tanker *Campeche*, which had taken on a cargo of arms at Feodosia in the Crimea, should now sail.[18] She left the same day, arrived at Cartagena on 4 October and thus became the first ship to carry Soviet arms to Spain.

The arms, however, were an assortment of old and ancient rifles and machine-guns of various nationalities and 240 German grenade-throwers.* The most useful weapons were six, but only six, Vickers light

---

* A *granatenwerfer* ('grenade-thrower') was a small German device fired by a cartridge and spring, for throwing stick-grenades across short distances. Introduced in 1915, it was soon rendered obsolete by the more efficient trench-mortar of 1917.

howitzers. This material may have been bought by three Spaniards through a fake company in Odessa, presumably with the intention that should the *Campeche* be intercepted in the Mediterranean by a Nationalist warship, her captain could at least produce forged documents to show that the arms had been bought in Turkey or one of the Balkan states, but this raises the question of why such a deception should have been kept up, as it was, after the arrival of modern Russian aircraft and tanks, with Russian crews, on the Madrid front at the beginning of November. An answer may perhaps be in a note which Voroshilov wrote to Stalin on 2 November, when the second series of deliveries, due to start in December, was being planned:

Dear Koba,
   I am sending you [he uses the familiar 'thee'] a list of the goods that we can sell, though it hurts us, to the Spaniards ... If France doesn't behave despicably, we shall manage to get everything to its destination in the shortest possible time. You will see that the list contains a lot of artillery pieces, owing not only to the fact that the Republican army needs them but to Kulik's* (I think correct) decision to rid ourselves, once and for all, of the artillery of foreign – British, French and Japanese – manufacture – that is, 280 guns, or 28% of the weapons of this category in our artillery parks. Most painful of all is the aviation material we are sending but, as they can't do without it over there, it must be sent. I request your permission, should you see fit, to commence the transportation of material to Murmansk.
                                                                                                  Yours,
                                                                                    K. Voroshilov.
   P.S. I will inform you under separate cover of the value of the supplies, which comes to about 50 million US dollars.[19]

Stalin's response was to cut everything on the list, except the aviation material, by a half. Nor was any material embarked from Murmansk until a year later.

According to an article by the Russian military historian Lt.-Col. Yuri Ribalkin, published as recently as April 1996, it was not until 29 September that 'the Politburo voted a surprise resolution to render aid on

---

* General (later Marshal) G. I. Kulik. Every memoir speaks of him as incompetent and a bully. A crony of Stalin's since the Revolution, he was at one time chief of artillery. During the Spanish Civil War he was sent for a while to Spain, where he was known as 'General No-No', 'no' being the only Spanish word he was able to master. In 1941 he commanded an army under orders to keep the Germans back from Leningrad, but, since he had never commanded a serious military operation before, let alone one against the Wehrmacht, his army was quickly surrounded and destroyed. He managed to escape into Leningrad, however, where he became notorious for blaming others for his mistakes and having them executed. After the war Stalin promoted him to marshal, then tired of him and had him shot in 1950.

a grand scale to the Spanish Republic'.[20] The explanation that Ribalkin offers for this date, which is far later than historians have hitherto assumed to have been the date of Stalin's decision, is that Stalin finally made up his mind only after learning that the Spaniards were willing to transfer their gold reserve to Russia and that he consequently had a guarantee that the full cost of Soviet aid would be met by the Republicans themselves. In support of this, Ribalkin points to the fact that Largo Caballero received an affirmative reply to his request of 14 October within three days. Such speed, says Ribalkin, unheard of in Soviet diplomacy before or since, strongly suggests that discussions about the gold had been going on for some time, probably since the middle of September, and that Largo's request and the Soviet reply were mere formalities. This, in turn, though Ribalkin does not say so, would revive the notion that the original pro- posal to ship the gold to Russia was made not by the Spaniards, as is now generally believed on the known evidence, but indeed by the Russians. It also suggests that the transfer of the gold from Madrid to Cartagena, which was carried out entirely by Spaniards, was in reality a preparatory measure of which, among the Spaniards, only Negrín and perhaps Caballero were aware, for its eventual transfer to the Soviet Union.

Ribalkin gives no source for his assertion, but since he is a member of the Russian Institute of Military History and has access to the relevant archives, one assumes that it is based on documentary evidence. If he is right, therefore, one can make a tentative reconstruction of what hap- pened.

Stalin put off the decision from week to week while preparations were begun in such a way as to enable him to cancel at any moment and leave the world none the wiser that the Soviet Union had ever planned to inter- evene at all. These included a shipment of old arms, disguised to conceal their Soviet origin, on the *Campeche*, a CAMPSA tanker that may have been already in the Black Sea to take on a cargo of oil at Batum. That there were indeed discussions about the gold is very likely, for the Spaniards must have told the Russians that payment for the arms would be made in gold, as it was being made elsewhere. However, on 28 September, two days after the *Campeche* sailed, Toledo fell to the Nationalists amid world-wide publicity over the relief of the besieged in the Alcázar fortress, and it became obvious that if the Soviets were going to do any- thing to save Madrid and prevent a Republican defeat, they must act quickly, for otherwise the damage to Stalin's authority over the foreign Communist parties would be irreparable. The operation to send arms, planes, tanks and men then went ahead. By the middle of October the effects of 'sabotage and boycott' by European and American banks, which Negrín later told the Republican ambassador in Mexico had become 'barely imaginable',[21] were now apparent and the placing of a part of the gold reserve on deposit and for safe-keeping in the USSR seemed an effective means of countering them. Orlov says that:

> When the loading was smoothly under way, I finally asked the question I had carefully avoided until then: 'How much of the gold are we supposed to ship?' So haphazardly had the operation been prepared at the Spanish end that a Treasury official replied 'Oh, more than half, I suppose.' It would be, I said mentally, a lot more.

Before dawn on 25 October there was an enemy air raid in which a Spanish freighter, moored close to the four Soviet ships* on which the gold was being loaded was hit and Orlov 'decided to terminate the operation and send my ships out of the bay as fast as possible'. They left the next night.[22] Orlov's story has been vigorously denied on the grounds that the Spanish end of so important an operation could not possibly have been haphazardly planned. Even so, it is not impossible that the Russians loaded more of the gold than the Spaniards had intended. Meanwhile, in Moscow, Voroshilov and his staff were taking the same view as the Polish colonels, that here was an opportunity to unload the old stocks in the arsenals onto the Spaniards and, having started with the *Campeche*, saw no reason not to continue. Moreover, once the gold was safely in Moscow, they saw that while they were about it they could present bills for the arms in such a way as to cheat the Republicans out of millions of dollars, which, as the documents in the Russian State Military Archives (RGVA) now show, they did (see below, Chapter 20).

Histories of the Spanish Civil War give the impression that, once Stalin had given the orders, the men and material were simply sent, as they would have been in any military operation, and that the most serious problems were the length of the sea journeys between Russia and Spain and the danger of interception by hostile warships. This impression is strengthened by accounts of the sudden and dramatic appearance, as it seemed from nowhere, of Russian aircraft and tanks when the Nationalists opened their full-scale attack on Madrid at the beginning of November, an appearance which gave such a tremendous boost to Republican morale that it probably did as much as anything else to save the city from falling. The records in the RGVA show, however, that as a result of the lateness of the decision everything had to be done in the utmost haste and at the cost of considerable disorganization.

---

* The *KIM, Neva, Volgoles* and *Jruso*. In his article in *Argumenty i Fakti* (4 April 1996), Lt.-Col. Ribalkin names the fourth ship as *Kuban*, instead of *Jruso*.

18

'Operation "X"'

THE FILES IN the Russian State Military Archives (RGVA) show that the quantity of armaments supplied by the Soviets to the Spanish Republicans was far less than hitherto believed, that many of the ancient weapons that the Republican army was obliged to use were not obtained through unscrupulous arms dealers in various parts of the world but came directly from the USSR itself, and that Soviet ships participated in the delivery of arms only briefly and in small numbers.

Historians have estimated the number of arms deliveries by Soviet ships alone during October, November and December 1936 to have been twenty-three or twenty-five, though some have put it as low as nineteen and others as high as thirty-three.[1] The real number was *eight*, of which the last, the *Blagoev*, arrived on 4 November and these eight were the only arms deliveries by Soviet ships during the entire war. In addition, between 4 October and 30 November, when the first series of deliveries ended, five Spanish and two foreign ships delivered arms (though the arms on the foreign ships did not come from the Soviet Union), one Soviet ship brought petrol and another personnel. After that, nothing was received until the second series began to arrive on 30 December, a full month later.

A complete list of all the 'Operation "X"' voyages will be found in Appendix III, of which a summary is given below. Every voyage was allotted a number in chronological order, regardless of whether the ship was Soviet, Spanish or foreign and of what it was carrying. Dossier numbers, prefixed by 'Y-', were allotted only to Soviet or Spanish ships carrying arms. The voyages were in six series, of which the first five only need concern us:

I 26 Sept–30 Nov 1936   Seventeen voyages, of which one (*Serge Ordzonichidze*) carried petrol and one (*Chicherin*) personnel; eight were by Soviet, five by Spanish and two by foreign ships. Of the fifteen arms deliveries, thirteen were to Cartagena in the main zone and two to Bilbao in the isolated northern zone.

II   23 Dec 1936–14 Feb 1937   Four voyages.

III 16 Feb–13 March 1937   Four voyages, of which one (*Turksib*) brought personnel only.

IV   21 April 1937–10 Aug 1937   Twelve voyages.

V   14 Dec 1937–11 Aug 1938   Fourteen voyages, all but two by ships of France Navigation, a company created by the Republican government with the help of the French Communist Party.

VI   Jan–Feb 1939   Three or perhaps seven voyages from Murmansk to Le Havre, France. By the middle of February, however, Catalonia was completely overrun by the Nationalists, who immediately captured the few arms that had crossed the frontier. These deliveries, therefore, did not affect the course of the war.

Thus there were forty-eight deliveries of Soviet arms in all, with some long gaps between the series: a month after 30 November 1936, five weeks after 13 March 1937 and four months after 10 August 1937; nor were there any deliveries after 11 August 1938, since those of February 1939 arrived too late to be used.

Some of the difficulties of mounting the operation are apparent in a report which General Efimov, the chief of artillery and deputy chief of the armaments department of the Red Army, wrote to Voroshilov on 29 December 1936.[2] Orders, he said, would arrive with demands that they be expedited within a few days, or even within a few hours, but without warning and leaving no time for preparations. It was impossible for his department to communicate directly with the army depots where the arms were stored, for they had no deciphering facilities and secrecy was paramount. Finding and sorting the required weapons, all foreign, dating from the First World War or earlier and lying in depots which were hundreds, or thousands, of miles distant from one another and the ports of embarkation, were added complications, to put it mildly. Millions of cartridges and shells of various nationalities, calibres, types and ages had to be sorted through and all likely duds removed. The weapons had to be tested and when necessary repaired. All identification marks that might make them traceable back to the USSR had to be filed off or destroyed. The artillery presented less of a problem because, luckily, his department had already repaired most of the pieces during the first six months of 1936. For his department's materials alone, the NKVD railway transport department had commandeered one thousand goods wagons, but a further 270 were urgently needed for the despatch of thirty-two anti-aircraft guns (eight batteries of four each) and 50,000 modernized Russian rifles and the requisite ammunition.* All Russian weapons, he added, were brand new from 'last year's production-batch'. Nevertheless, he was pleased to report, despite all these obstacles everything had been sent off in good condition and there had been no delays. Efimov ended by requesting that all the officers and staff engaged in the operation, both in his department and at the depots, be awarded for their round-the-clock tireless labours, that cipher facilities be installed at the depots as soon as possible in 1937 and that his department be sent reports on the performance of the weapons in Spain, which was vital to future research, development and training.

Efimov's assertion that all the Russian material was brand new was an exaggeration, for the only new weapons sent in 1936 were the 150 Degtyarev light machine-guns (see below, Chapter 19). Nor was his claim that there had been no delays quite true. For example, a list, signed by him, of 'material sent before 29 October 1936' includes 1,500 American Colt M 1895 heavy machine-guns, which in reality left on the Spanish ship *Cabo Palos* on 15 November.[3] Indeed, one has the impression from these reports that Stalin would sign an order that so many thousands of this, that and the other must be shipped 'by tomorrow' and that when he remembered a day or two later to ask if they had gone yet, the answer was naturally 'Yes, Comrade Josef Vissarionovich', when in fact much of the material was stranded in a train at some remote spot on the steppes or had been lost track of altogether. That happens in every army, but in the Soviet army in 1936 no one was likely to admit a mishap for which the penalty was a firing-squad or fifteen years in a labour camp for 'wrecking' and 'sabotage'.

General Efimov does not mention what appears to have been the most intractable problem of all, that of shipping space. Indeed, the only Russian who refers to it even in passing is Admiral Nikolai Kuznetsov, who had

---

* Yet, according to the voyage lists, no modernized Russian rifles reached Spain until 10 August 1937, when the *Cabo San Agustín* delivered 10,450 Mosin-Nagant M 91/30s. They were followed by another 75,000 delivered in three lots in 1938 (see Appendix III).

served as the Soviet naval attaché to the Spanish Republic during the civil war and in a memoir written thirty years later recalls, 'During the events in Spain we were unable to do all we should have done ... because there were not enough adequate ships.'[4] He does not elaborate on this, but a moment's reflection confirms its truth. In the autumn of 1936 the total tonnage of the Soviet merchant fleet of vessels of over 100 tons was 939,308, or a mere 489 ships, as compared, for instance, to the 20.6 million tons (9,280 ships) of the British, the 9.8 million tons (2,560 ships) of the American or the 4 million tons (c. 1,900 ships) each of the Norwegian and Japanese merchant fleets.[5] The Soviet total, of course, included river steamers, which constituted a large proportion of the fleet, as well as the ships used on the Caspian and Aral seas. The remaining merchant fleet was divided between the Arctic and White seas, the Baltic, the Black Sea and the Pacific, with all their ships engaged already on their normal trading duties in various parts of the world, in loading or unloading their cargoes in Russian ports or undergoing repairs.

The number of ships at the Black Sea ports available for the immediate transportation of arms and aircraft to Spain, Stalin's orders notwithstanding, must therefore have been extremely limited. There was also the problem of capacity. It may be remembered that at the Foreign Office in London, Walter Roberts had been distressed by the Admiralty message saying that two Soviet ships had recently unloaded a hundred and fifty large aircraft at Cartagena (see above, p. 117). In reality the Russians had thought it essential to send an air regiment (thirty-one aircraft) of SB medium bombers with the very first deliveries. The most convenient way to pack an SB was in two crates, one measuring 40 × 25 × 12 ft (12.2 × 7.6 × 3.7 m) for the fuselage, centre section and tail-fin and the other 26 × 15 × 7 ft (8 × 4.6 × 2.1 m) for the outer wings. In those days cargo hatches on most cargo ships measured only 31 × 21 ft (9.4 × 6.4 m), which would have created the additional problem of finding ships with hatches large enough to allow the crates to be lowered through them. Holds needed to be capacious enough to accommodate a worthwhile number of bombers as well as the material to go with an air regiment, which included bombs, guns, ammunition, spare engines, spare parts, 500 tons of petrol, fifty tons of oil, four tons of coolant, six petrol-tanker lorries, nine Hucks Starters (a vehicle with a powered crankshaft mounted high for spinning the propeller shafts and starting the engines), tools and space-filling jacks and jigs.[6] In the event, the *Stari Bolshevik*, *KIM** and *Volgoles* brought ten SBs

---

* On her return journey, the *KIM* was one of the four ships that took the Spanish gold to Odessa. In the winter of 1937 she transported 3,000 political prisoners to Magadan in the Far East. They mutinied and the guards flooded the holds. It was −40°C and the prisoners arrived as frozen blocks.

each in October, the thirty-first (commander's) machine being left behind for want of room. By the time that the next air regiment of SBs was sent, in June 1937, Spanish ships only were being used and a letter from Uritsky to Voroshilov explains that as those which were at present in Russian ports were too small, it would be necessary to pack each SB in three crates, which would mean that each ship would be able to take only two aircraft. He therefore requested Voroshilov to arrange for the Spaniards to send at least four or five ships more as a matter of urgency.[7] The Spaniards responded by sending two of their largest bulk-carriers, the *Artea Mendi*, which took ten (voyage 33), and the *Aldecoa*, which was able to take twenty-one (voyage 34).

All of this explains, I suspect, why the Soviets allowed so few of their own ships to take part in the operation, a decision probably forced on them by the sinking of the *Komsomol*, during her second voyage, by the Nationalist cruiser *Canarias* on 14 December 1936. According to some reports she was sunk by gunfire; according to others, she was scuttled to avoid capture; in either case, it seems likely that she was carrying arms, although her second voyage is not on the voyage list.[8] Nevertheless, this act of war by the Nationalists was sufficient to persuade the Russians that they could neither risk an international incident, for the next sinking might be by a German or Italian warship, nor afford to lose any more of their merchant fleet. Nevertheless, Soviet ships did continue to bring food, clothing and other goods not proscribed by the Non-Intervention agreement throughout the rest of the war, about $30 million worth of the goods being paid for by contributions raised by the workers' commissariats.[9]

Quite elaborate measures were devised to avoid interception, though whether these were adopted at the beginning or over a period of time is not clear. A system was established by which every ship – Russian, Spanish or foreign – had on board a team of Russian telegraphists and cipher clerks under the command of a Russian officer responsible for the safety of the voyage. After the ship passed through the Dardanelles, her name, colour, silhouette, flag and documents would be changed. I have a copy of instructions to the *Aldecoa*, for instance, when she was taking the twenty-one SB bombers in June 1937 (voyage 34). After passing the Dardanelles, she was to change her colour, paint a white band 0.5 m wide on the level of the hawser-holes, change her name to *Bhytan* and raise a British flag. If necessary later, she was to change her name again to *Byzadzen* (British flag) and *Blanca* (Norwegian flag).[10] A chain of radio stations, equipped with the latest high-powered short-wave transmitters, was established along the Black Sea coast at Poti, Novorossisk, Yalta, Sevastopol and Nikolaev, with the four principal stations at Odessa. These would send brief signal bursts, or 'flash messages', twice a day as she crossed the Mediterranean well to the south of the 35th parallel to keep clear of Malta, until she reached an appointed longitude off the Algerian coast. Her captain would then be ordered to disguise the ship and replace his documents once more. It was now for him to change course north by north-west and run the blockade outside Cartagena, Alicante or Valencia and the ship thereafter would move only between sunset and sunrise, with all lights extinguished. During these tense hours, the radio stations on the Black Sea coast, others on the Spanish coast and any Russian ships that happened to be in the western Mediterranean or eastern Atlantic would send out a barrage of messages to confuse the blockaders. If such a Russian ship was sighted by Nationalist, German or Italian warships, she was ordered to behave as though trying to escape interception and so lure them away from the arms-carrying ship.[11]

During an interview granted to the American journalist Louis Fischer, Uritsky told him that 'Moscow had a big bureau which did nothing else but devise means of disguising war munitions and the vessels that carried them. They sometimes rebuilt freighters, giving them a false deck, and placed the arms between the decks. Tanks were immersed in the oil of tankers, and so on.'[12] This last must have been an experiment which was abandoned, for none of the eleven ships that took tanks to Spain was an oil tanker.

Despite these tactics, eighty-six Soviet ships were intercepted during the first year of the war, of which ten were captured and escorted to Nationalist ports and two more, the *Timiryazov* and the *Blagoev*, were sunk.[13] None, however, was carrying arms.

19

Soviet Arms

O N 29 OCTOBER, while the Italians in Franco's service and dignitaries of the Falange were celebrating the fourteenth anniversary of Mussolini's march on Rome, three sleek twin-engined monoplanes appeared without warning over the Nationalist airbase at Tablada, Seville, dropped their bombs across the field and then escaped northwards at a speed which no Nationalist fighter could hope to match. Larger formations of the same 'mystery machines', which in fact were SB Katiuskas, repeated this performance rather more effectively during the next few days with attacks on other Nationalist airfields nearer Madrid, damaging several aircraft and hangars. Since the Nationalists knew that Russian ships had been arriving at Cartagena since the beginning of the month, they presumed the bombers were Soviet. However, everybody in the Western world knew for a fact that the Russians, being a technically backward race, were incapable of producing, let alone designing, modern aircraft and that their air force, like the Japanese, was equipped with inferior copies, based on 'stolen plans', of European or American originals.*
Therefore, they could not really be Russian but must be American. Indeed, from the brief sightings of them, they looked rather like the Martin 139W bomber that the Spanish government had ordered before the

---

* In the leading British aeronautical magazine of the period, *The Aeroplane* (18 Nov 1936), its editor, C. G. Grey, wrote of the Soviet aircraft at the Paris air show, 'the whole Russian exhibit is comic and rather consoling to those who regard Russia as the authentic Yellow Peril rather than as a large-sized nuisance which we must be prepared to squash when it becomes too offensive.' The workmanship and finish on them were crude and 'awful'. Of the fighter – a Polikarpov I-17 monoplane, which had a liquid-cooled engine in place of the usual radial – he wrote that it seemed to be 'a mixture of the Hurricane, Spitfire and Battle and to have missed all three pretty badly'. In short, 'the three aircraft are so obviously the product of an Oriental people trying to appear European that they would be pathetic if we could feel any sympathy with Russians.' This was written in the very week when, unknown to him, Russian fighters were gaining air superiority over Madrid.

war. That was it! They were Martins, or crude Russian imitations of them, and 'Martins' or 'Martin Bombers' they were thereafter called, although some preferred 'Martin Bombergs', which had the right-sounding connotation with the 'Bolshevik-Jewish-Free-Masonic-International-Financiers' Conspiracy' against which the Nationalists were crusading.

The same thing happened after the appearance of the Russian fighters in November: the little I-15 biplane, which had a flat-fronted radial engine and was named Chato ('snub-nose') by the Republicans, was called 'Curtiss', after the American Curtiss F9C Sparrowhawk, to which it bore a slight outward resemblance, and the stubby little I-16 monoplane fighter, which the Republicans called Mosca ('fly'), was called 'Boeing', after the famous Boeing P-26A, to which it bore no resemblance whatever, inward or outward.* Even American mercenary pilots, such as Frank Tinker and Harold Dahl, who flew these machines in the Republican air force, believed, or pretended to believe, this, and in the American newspapers journalists declared that the success in Spain of these American types 'built under licence', in the USSR proved the superiority of American aviation.[1] On the Republican side, meanwhile, Communists were spreading the story about, during a campaign to discredit everybody else, that the success of Soviet and the failure of French aircraft in Spain proved the superiority of 'proletarian' over 'bourgeois' technology.

Myths about the originality or otherwise of aircraft designers in different countries and stories of stolen plans and the like, such as those told about the Japanese 'Zero' fighter or the Russian 'Konkordsky' supersonic airliner, are mostly nonsense. The Tupolev SB, which the Republicans called Katiuska, and the Polikarpov I-16 monoplanes were both in advance of anything in service in other air forces at the time and their principles of construction were fundamentally different from those of their presumed originals – indeed, the only non-Russian features were their engines, which *were* American (Wright Cyclone) and French (Hispano-Suiza 12), at first built under licence and then developed. Even so, in the 1930s the pace of aeronautical development was so hectic that a military aircraft might become obsolete within a year or two of entering service, or even before entering service, and the SB Katiuska, recognized now as the world's first modern bomber, and the I-16 Mosca, the first modern fighter, were soon to be surpassed by new 'state of the art' machines already being tested in Europe, America and Japan. The Soviet aircraft in Spain, then,

---

* Another Nationalist name for the I-16 was Rata ('rat'). In the early days of the air fighting over Madrid, the I-16 pilots, instead of escorting the I-15s from above, flew in almost at rooftop level and, exploiting their rapid rate of climb, attacked the Nationalist aircraft from the direction least expected – below – and appeared to have come out of holes in the ground, 'like rats'.

were good, although there were not enough of them. So too were the first
contingents of Soviet airmen, although, according to Lacalle, their quality
declined after the summer of 1937.[2] Spanish and even a few foreign pilots
were taken into the Russian squadrons almost immediately, in November
1936, and about 600 Spanish airmen, as well as tank crews and other
specialists, were trained in the USSR during the course of the war; indeed,
the process by which the Spaniards established their own air arm was as
rapid on the Republican as on the Nationalist side.

The Russian T-26 tank, weighing 9.5 tons and armed with a 45 mm gun
and three machine-guns, was the equal of any in its category at the time. It
was developed from a Vickers design and 280 were sent during the war,
106 of them in 1936. The other type of Russian tank used in Spain was the
BT-5, the predecessor of the T-34s that won the Battle of Kursk in 1943.
Adapted from the American Christie tank, on which the tracks were
driven by large-diameter wheels, the BT-5 was remarkably fast, having a
top speed of nearly 40 m.p.h. (64 km/h) across country and, with the
tracks removed, nearly 70 m.p.h. (112 km/h) along metalled roads. Fifty
were delivered in August 1937. On neither side, however, did tanks play a
major role in any of the campaigns. There were not enough of them, nor
did the logistical conditions in Spain make it possible to develop the strategy and tactics employed in the Second World War. Many of the Russian
tanks, for example, had no radios.

The picture is very different, however, when we turn to rifles,
machine-guns and artillery. The 48,825 rifles of Soviet origin delivered in
1936 were of at least eight different nationalities, ten different types and
six different calibres.* Thirteen thousand, three hundred and fifty seven
of them, for instance, were 11 mm Vetterlis. The Vetterli, a Swiss design,
was the world's first bolt-action rifle, designed in 1868–9 and predating
the famous Mauser by a year or two. This particular batch had been

---

* They included:

Austria	Gras-Kropotchek 11 mm (1878)	1,821
	Männlicher 8 mm (1888–95)	3,658
France	Gras 11 mm (1874–84)	10,000
	Lebel 8 mm (1886–1907)	1,242
Italy	Vetterli 11 mm (1871)	13,357
Japan	Arisaka 6.5 mm (1897)	?
Poland or Germany	Mauser 7.92 mm (1886–1916)	6,000
United Kingdom	Lee-Enfield 7.707 mm (1895–1913)	3,202
Canada	Ross 7.707 mm (1897–1902)	?
USA	Winchester 7.62 mm (1860–95)	9,000

The figures in parenthesis indicate dates of manufacture, not design. Some 20,350 of
these rifles were shipped on the *Campeche* (RGVA F 33987 o 3 D 83 L 240–1).

made at Brescia, Italy, in 1871 and sold to Turkey. The most likely explanation of how so many came to be in a Soviet store in 1936 is that the Russians had captured them during the Russo-Turkish War of 1877, probably when they took the garrison at Kars. Moreover, the production records show that they were single-shot.[3] Another 11,821 of the rifles were 11 mm French Gras and Austrian Gras-Kropotcheks made in the 1880s. This calibre had been obsolete the world over for forty years. The Vetterlis came with only 185 rounds each, the Gras with only 395 each. Their cartridges were not interchangeable and when this supply of ammunition ran out, which it would do after a day or two, all these rifles would have to be thrown away.[4] The 6,000 Mausers (7.92 mm) too came with only 500 rounds each and, since the Mausers arriving from Poland (see above, p. 109) were also under-supplied, their ammunition could not be replenished. In short, of the 48,825 rifles sent from the USSR in 1936, nearly 26,000 were ancient museum pieces with hardly any ammunition and another 6,000, also much used, had only half their required supply.

The only modern machine-guns sent at this critical moment of the war were the 150 Degtyarev DPs, the thin light machine-guns, familiar from innumerable Red Army photographs, with large, flat, disc-shaped magazines. There were also 200 Maxim heavy machine-guns on their two-wheeled carriages but, although General Efimov assured Voroshilov that all Russian material was new, the British International Brigade volunteer Jason Gurney records that in his battalion none of the Maxims had been made later than 1916 and that they were consequently very inaccurate.[5] Gurney also says that the elderly Lewis guns in his battalion were quickly replaced by Colt machine-guns, which would have worked had not their ammunition belts all perished. Rumour had it that the Americans had sold the Colts to the White Russians, but the guns had gone to Archangel and the ammunition and belts to Odessa, and the twain had never met until October 1936.[6]

Among the other old machine-guns cleared out of the stores were at least 300 Saint-Etiennes and 400 Chauchats.[7] The Saint-Etienne 8 mm M 1907 had been an unsuccessful attempt by the French state factory in the town of that name to improve on the Hotchkiss and avoid the payment of patent-licence fees by reversing the mechanism. After a few months of disastrous service on the Western front in 1914, all had been withdrawn. These guns may have been captured from the Poles in 1920 or sold to the White Russians during the Allied intervention against the Bolsheviks. John Sommerfield, another volunteer in the International Brigade, says of them, 'They were the most extraordinary machines – beautifully made, insanely complicated, the lock (whose principles we never really understood) working on a system of cogs and slides that had the complexity of one of those old-fashioned clocks whose mechanism also indicates the days of the month and eclipses of the moon.' They jammed frequently and were so heavy that it required two or three very large and very strong men to lift one, with great difficulty, from place to place on the battlefield under fire.[8] As for the Chauchat 8 mm M 1915, this is remembered now as one of the worst automatic weapons invented by the mind of man. When it was rushed into service in 1915, the French soldiers found not only that it was slow and inaccurate, but also that it jammed after every four or five rounds and, to clear it, it had to be completely dismantled, in the mud of the trenches and with a German bayonet charge coming at them through the rain. Like the Saint-Etiennes, they were quickly withdrawn and, along with nearly a quarter-of-a-million that had been manufactured as a result of financial chicanery, were sold off to unsuspecting buyers all over the world. The British and American International Brigadiers called them 'Shoshers' or 'Shossers' and Gurney tells us that the men in his unit threw all theirs away on the first morning of the Battle of Jarama in January 1937.[9]

The adjoining tables show the various sets of figures for the quantities of Soviet arms sent to Spain that have been published at different times, so that the reader may compare them. Table 1 is representative of those published in the West during the past thirty-five years. Tables 2 and 3 are from two books published in the Soviet Union in 1974 and Table 4 shows figures calculated from the voyage lists in the RGVA, of which fuller details can be found in Appendix III. Yet even the figures in Table 4 are deceptive, especially those for artillery. Table 2 puts the number of guns at 1,555 and Table 3 at 1,186, which is also the number that the Russian military historian Lt.-Col. Yuri Ribalkin stated in an article published by the Spanish official journal *Ejército* in January 1992. In November 1992 the same journal published a reply by the Spanish military historian José Luis Infiesta Pérez, who insisted that Ribalkin was mistaken and that the true number was as high as 1,968. Table 4 shows that the true number seems to have been only 988, i.e., 980 fewer guns.

To the lay reader, 'artillery pieces' means field-guns and howitzers for putting down barrages, softening-up enemy strong-points and the like. Of such pieces, however, there were only 493, that is, 302 field-guns and 191 howitzers, of which 30 field-guns and 8 howitzers did not come from the Soviet Union (see below, p. 302). The rest consisted of small anti-tank guns*

---

* The Russians sent two types of anti-tank gun to Spain:
   Model 30 L. 45, 37 mm. This was a licence-built Rheinmetall 37 mm Pak 35/6, identical to the German gun but for its wire-spoked wheels. Two hundred and fifty were sent in April 1938. The Germans also used small numbers of Pak 36s in Spain.
   Model 32 L. 46, 45 mm. A scaled-up Model 30. One hundred and forty-six were

and sixty-four anti-aircraft guns which, unlike the famous German 88 mm, could not be used as field artillery.

TABLE I

Estimates of Soviet war material supplied to the Spanish Republicans as found in numerous publications between 1950 and 1996

Aircraft	1,000–1,400
Tanks	*c.* 900
Armoured cars	*c.* 300
Artillery pieces	1,500–*c.* 2,000
Machine-guns	*c.* 30,000
Rifles	*c.* 500,000

Plus huge quantities of munitions and military equipment of all kinds.

TABLE 2

Soviet war material supplied to the Spanish Republicans, as stated in *International Solidarity with the Spanish Republic*, p. 329 (Academy of Sciences of the USSR, 1974)

Aircraft	806
Tanks	362
Armoured vehicles	120
Artillery pieces	1,555
Rifles	500,000
Grenade-launchers	340
Machine-guns	15,113
Aerial bombs	110,000
Rounds of ammunition	3,400,000
Grenades	500,000
Cartridges	862,000,000
Tons of gunpowder	1,500

Torpedo-boats, torpedoes, 772 airmen, 351 tank-men, 222 army advisers and instructors, 77 naval specialists, 100 artillery specialists, 52 other specialists, 130 aircraft factory workers and engineers, 156 radio operators and signallers and 204 interpreters (2,064 total).

---

sent: 119 in 1937, 24 in 1938 and 3 in 1939. Both the Model 30 and Model 32 were excellent and were used by the Red Army throughout the Second World War and after. While the Model 30 was small enough to be pulled around by hand, the Model 32s in Spain arrived without the vehicles to tow them. Moreover, the first shipment (fifteen on the *Escolano*) did not arrive until 29 April 1937.

TABLE 3

Soviet war material supplied to the Spanish Republicans, as stated in
Istoriia vtoroi mirovoi voiny, 1939–1945, vol. 2, p. 54, 'Nakanune voiny'
(Institute of Military History of the USSR, 1974)

Weapons	*1 Oct 1936–* *1 Aug 1937*	*14 Dec 1937–* *11 Aug 1938*	*25 Dec 38–* *28 Jan 1939*	*Total*
Aircraft	496	152	–	648
Tanks	322	25	–	347
Armoured vehicles	60	–	–	60
Artillery	714	469	3	1,186
Machine-guns	12,804	4,910	2,772	20,486
Rifles	337,793	125,020	35,000	497,813

The Russian authors state that the USSR 'managed to send' ('udalos
napravit') to the Republic 52 ships between 1 Oct 1936 and 1 Aug 1937,
in contrast to 13 ships between 14 Dec 1937 and 11 Aug 1938, and only
three ships between 25 Dec 1938 and 28 Jan 1939. They do not mention
the number of personnel.

TABLE 4

Soviet war material supplied to the Spanish Republicans, as shown by
the documents in the Russian State Military Archives (RGVA). Material
sent in 1939 excluded

Aircraft	623 plus 4 UTI trainers
Tanks	331
Armoured cars	60
Artillery:	
Field-guns	302 (–30)
Howitzers	191 (–8)
Mine-throwers	4
Anti-aircraft guns	64

Infantry-support and
  anti-tank guns, 37 mm
  and 45 mm
	427

Grenade-throwers	240 or 340
Small arms:	
Machine-guns	15,008 (–2,430)
Rifles	379,645 (–85,000)

N.B. Figures in parentheses show material that did not come from the
USSR. Total medium and light artillery=493 pieces. For breakdowns of
above, see Appendix III, p. 302.

In 1936 the Russians sent ninety-four 'English 115 mm howitzers', twelve Armstrong 127 mm field-guns and thirty Russian Maklen 37 mm M 1917s. The 'English 115 mm' is almost certainly the Vickers 4.5 in. M 1910 Mk I howitzer (the Mk I was made by Vickers at Coventry, the Mk II at Woolwich Arsenal). About a thousand were exported before and after the First World War. These might have been bought before 1914 or captured in 1919. The Armstrong 127 mm was known in the British Army as the '60-pounder'; fifty-two were bought by the Russians in 1912. The Maklen 37 mm, which resembled a toy field-gun, was intended as an 'infantry-support gun', a type born of trench warfare and found to be of not much use for anything. Perhaps the Russians sent them to fill in as anti-tank guns until real ones could be sent, though their shells are not listed as armour-piercing.

The British guns came with their wagons and limbers but not much ammunition. The Armstrong 127 mm, for instance, had about a month's supply to last the entire war. The first ninety-four 115 mm guns had about nine days' supply to last until another twenty guns arrived, with some ammunition, in February 1937, with more ammunition arriving in March, April and May. Nothing more arrived after that until the end of February 1938.[10] In other words, these hundred and fourteen guns had to stretch out ammunition sufficient for twenty-seven days over a period of fifteen months, which included the battles of Madrid, Jarama, Guadalajara, Brunete, Belchite and Teruel.

It is not clear from the records that the other artillery pieces sent in 1937 and 1938 all had their wagons and other vital accessories. It seems unlikely. Some had been captured during the Russo-Japanese War of 1905, others from the Germans and Austrians during the First World War, others from the British, French, Americans, Poles and Japanese during the Allied intervention against the Bolsheviks and the Polish war in 1919 and 1920. Seven different calibres appear on the lists (75, 76.2, 77, 105, 107, 152 and 155 mm) and, although the types are not specified, at least a dozen are known and include twenty prehistoric French de Bange 155 mm M 1877 field-guns. They are easily recognizable in photographs by their long barrels with a handle on the top and the heavy flat metal plates, or 'pedrails', fastened round the wheel-rims. A well-known photograph shows one standing in the Plaza de España, Madrid, at the end of the war with a Nationalist flag stuck derisively in its muzzle.

The authors of *International Solidarity*, in which the figures of Table 2 appear, say that they represent 'the total extent of Soviet military supplies', and the authors of the book in which the figures of Table 3 appear say '... we managed to send ...'[11] In fact, however, three shipments and four part-cargoes were not of Soviet material but of weapons and munitions bought in Europe and shipped from European ports. They had been paid for, however, by Soviet agents with cash lent by the Soviet government* and then charged to the Spaniards when the gold in Moscow had been converted into currency. However, since 'they have been bought with our money', as Voroshilov told Stalin,[12] they were treated as a part of 'Operation "X"', which had the double advantage of making it seem that the Soviets had sent more of their own material than they really had and of enabling them to charge higher prices (see pp. 110, 282 and 334–5). To arrive at a more accurate figure for the Soviet material, it would be necessary to subtract the 10,000 Männlicher rifles, the 420 old machine-guns and 8 howitzers on the *Hillfern*, the 30 artillery pieces on the *Linhaug*, the 25,000 rifles on the *Vaga* and the 50,000 rifles and 2,000 machine-guns from Czechoslovakia at the beginning of 1938, all of which would reduce the Soviet total further.

I cannot reconcile the discrepencies between Tables 2, 3 and 4 or explain, for instance, how the authors of Table 2 arrived at a figure of 806 aircraft or the authors of the figures in Table 3 at 648, when the voyage lists show the number to have been 623 military aircraft and four UTI trainers.** Equally puzzling is the difference between the 500,000 or so rifles stated on the published lists and the 364,625 sent in reality, of which 85,000 came not from the USSR but from Europe. Of the 279,625 that did come from the USSR more than 25,000 were ancient museum pieces with barely a day's supply of ammunition. No Russian rifles arrived until 16 January 1937 (on the *Sac 2*), no modern Russian rifles (Mosin M 91/30) until 10 August 1937 and no more after that until 23 January 1938. Finally, if we subtract the thirty-eight guns procured in Europe, we are left with 272 field-guns and 183 howitzers – most of them with very insufficient

---

* The three ships were: *Hillfern* (voyage 10), *Linhaug* (voyage 11) and *Vaga* (26). The cargo on the *Hillfern* was bought from SEPEWE by 'Tomson', that on the *Linhaug* by 'Argus'. In March and April 1938, four ships – *Gravelines* (43), *Bougoroni* (44), *Winnipeg* (45) and *Bonifacio* (46) – brought the rifles, machine-guns and ammunition that the Republican ambassador in Prague, Luis Jiménez de Asúa, had bought in Czechoslovakia. The material had originally been ordered in November 1936, and the Soviets had been largely to blame for the delays that had ensued from their refusal to act as ostensible buyers. When they finally agreed to do so, they included the material on their own lists as though they had supplied it themselves (see below, p. 160).
** 'Argus', who bought the artillery on the *Linhaug*, also bought the four Swissair American airliners (see below, p. 214). In addition, the Russians included as their own material the eight American aircraft shipped by Robert Cuse on the *Mar Cantábrico* from New York and captured by the Nationalists in the Bay of Biscay (see below, p. 182). If the thirty I-152 fighters delivered in January 1939 are included, although they took no part in the war, then we should have a total of 669 aircraft for which the Republicans were chargeable. It is impossible to bring the total to 648 no matter how one calculates it, a matter more of curiosity than importance since the differences are small.

ammunition, all old and twenty or thirty of them between fifty and sixty years old – sent from the USSR itself.

The inferiority of the Republican artillery, certainly not redressed by the material bought at great expense in Poland or by the few guns bought elsewhere, is demonstrated by the fact that when the Nationalists opened their counter-offensive on a *one-mile* front on 30 October 1938, towards the end of the Battle of the Ebro, they commenced with a concentrated three-hour bombardment by 700 guns (175 batteries of four guns each). In theory, as the rate of fire of a field-gun or howitzer at that time was about four shells a minute, they would have expanded 504,000 shells before their infantry advanced. Even if the real number was only 100,000, the offensive lasted another sixteen days.

20

Soviet Prices

O N 27 JANUARY 1937 a Spanish officer, whose name does not appear on the document, prepared a report for the Republican war ministry concerning three different evaluations of the cost of the war material delivered by the USSR in 1936. They had been submitted by the Soviet government and he had had difficulty in making sense of them. The lists, he wrote, did not agree on the quantities of material delivered. There was nothing to say which materials were new, or old, or used, or how much used. Whole groups of weapons had been lumped together with no unit prices given. There was no indication as to whether or not the weapons and aircraft had come complete with their accessories or, in particular, the artillery pieces with their transportation and aiming equipment. Above all, the evaluations were in pesetas, with nothing to show what exchange rate had been used. He was assuming, nonetheless, that it would be 12.3 pesetas to the US dollar and 60 to the pound sterling.[1]

Since the matter had been kept so secret, he was probably unaware that the gold reserve had been in Moscow since 5 November 1936 and was still in the process of being counted and melted down into ingots, including, apparently, even rare antique coins of great numismatic value. The Soviet lists, therefore, were simply statements of the credits that the Soviet government was granting until such time as the process was completed and the debt paid off against the gold.

The Soviets, however, had assured the Republican government that, since the war was being fought on behalf of all progressive humanity, they were allowing generous discounts on all items; indeed, for the greater part of the war the mass of the Republican people was led to believe that the arms and aircraft were being supplied free, in a spirit of solidarity. The percentages of these discounts are mentioned in a letter from Voroshilov to Stalin on 13 December 1936, in which he says that 'to forestall any complaint that our prices are too high, the prices have been based on average European prices for arms, less 10–15–20%, calculated article by article.

On material that is *not* ours, we have given discounts of 40–50%, despite the fact that all the articles have been repaired and dispatched in perfect condition.'[2] Written in ink across the bottom is Stalin's reply: 'Prices approved. Make translation and send to Rosenberg [Soviet ambassador in Madrid] soonest.'*

Of the condition of the material, something has already been said in the previous chapter. As for the discounts, the RGVA documents show that on Soviet-made material there were none at all. Having set rouble prices for all the items, whether discounted or not, the Russians then devised a system of converting the roubles into dollars and dollars into pesetas which ensured that the Spaniards, who never saw the rouble prices or the calculations for conversion, ended by paying a great deal more than they should have done and that the Russians were left with a hidden, but very substantial, profit.

Unlike arms and aircraft manufacturers in the West, the Soviets had no accurate means of costing their products. Their aviation industry, though not lacking gifted and original designers, was behind the West, particularly the United States, in sophisticated methods of mass production. For example, many of the refinements on the SB Katiuska prototypes, such as the flush-rivetting, had to be abandoned on the production aircraft, owing to a shortage of skilled workers, with detrimental effects on performance.[3] The Soviet Union was also behind in the design of aero-engines, but this could be said too of most countries. Tank and artillery production was still primitive and slow, which makes the tremendous achievements of the Russians during the Second World War the more extraordinary. Thus, despite Voroshilov's assurance to Stalin that prices to the Spaniards were based on average European prices, the prices shown on the lists in the 'Operation "X"' files often bear no relation to them and, indeed, seem quite arbitrary. A Russian T-26 tank ($21,500), for example, was about half the price of its German equivalent, the Panzer III ($41,000), a Russian 76.2 mm M31 anti-aircraft gun ($20,000–$30,000, depending on fittings) was nearly, or more than, twice the price of the far more complicated German 88 mm Flak 18 ($13,000), a weapon which, unlike the Russian, could serve as efficient field-artillery. Nor does there seem to be any reason why a Degtyarev DP light machine-gun should have cost $225 when its German counterpart, the MG 34, cost only $135.[4]

These three examples are the dollar prices charged to the Spaniards after being converted from roubles. The rouble had been stabilized internationally since late October 1936 to 5.3 roubles to $1, at which level it was maintained until 1940.[5] This was the official rate, according to a report to

---

* Not in Stalin's handwriting, but believed to be in that of Colonel Langevoi, 'Chief of Missions of Special Importance, People's Commissariat of Defence'.

Voroshilov on 25 January 1938, and for this reason it was used for calculating the costs, upkeep and pay of all Soviet personnel sent to Spain.[6] The Spaniards had no reason to doubt that this was the exchange rate used for all calculations or, when they were told that they were getting a 20% discount on one article and a 50% discount on another, that that was what they were getting. Not so.

Spread on my desk are four separate Russian lists of the same consignments of rifles, machine-guns, artillery and ammunition sent to Spain in October and up to 15 November 1936, the very same material, in fact, discussed in the report by the Republican officer quoted at the beginning of this chapter. Each page is signed by General Efimov.[7] The unit and total prices of each lot are shown in roubles on the left half of the page and in dollars on the right. Down the right side of the page is a column which is blank on the first two lists, but on the third and fourth is headed, in Cyrillic, 'Coefficient of deduction'. All the way down this right-hand column are small numbers, such as '3.6' or '2', one against each lot or item. These 'coefficients' vary from item to item. Omitting the total prices to save space, here are three examples:

Type	Roubles	Dollars	Coefficient of deduction
Foreign rifles	90 / 45	25 / 12.50	3.6
Russian Maxim machine-guns	1,500	600	2.5
English Armstrong 127 mm field-guns	70,000 / 50,000	35,000 / 25,000	2

The upper figures for the rifles and 127 mm guns are the set prices, the lower the prices after discount. It is obvious, however, that the 'coefficients of deduction' are the exchange rates used for calculating the dollar price of each item or lot in turn, different for every item but kept below 5.3. At 5.3 roubles to the dollar, an old foreign rifle would have cost the Republicans not $12.50 but only $8.49; a Maxim, for which there was no discount since it was Russian-made, would have cost not $600 but $283, and a 127 mm gun not $25,000 but only $9,433.96. Put another way about, the Republicans were paying not 45 roubles for a rifle but 66.25, and not 50,000 roubles for a 127 mm gun but 132,500.

Looking back at the first two lists and dividing the dollars into the roubles item by item, one can now see what was being done. On all four lists the rouble prices are unchanged while the dollar prices vary. On the first list, for instance, the Maxim, at 1,500 roubles, is priced at $800, that is, at only 1.9 roubles to the dollar. On the second list, it is still 1,500 roubles but reduced to $400 at 3.75 roubles to the dollar. On the third and fourth lists it is still 1,500 roubles, but the dollar price has gone up again to $600, at 2.5 roubles to the dollar, and we know from other documents that $600 was the price at which the Maxim was sold to the Republicans throughout the war. On the fourth list, however, among other changes, the price of $25,000 for the 127 mm gun is crossed out in ink and reduced to $20,000 and the 'coefficient' therefore becomes 2.5.

In a second set of lists giving rouble and dollar prices for the material sent at the end of the war, in January 1939, the same system is still applied.[8] This time, however, one or two rouble prices are reduced while the dollar prices remain the same, thus rendering the deception even greater. For example, the Vickers 115 mm Mk I howitzer (M 1910), which in December 1936 was priced at 58,440 roubles or $12,000, is now only 40,000 roubles but still $12,000, which means that by raising the exchange-rate from 4,87 to 3.3 roubles to the dollar, they increased the overcharge from a mere $974 per gun to $4,453 per gun.[9] For some reason, the Vickers 115 mm was not subject to discount, although it was not a Russian-made weapon, and the overcharge therefore represented a clear profit. It is unclear when the rouble price was lowered. If, for example, it was changed after the delivery of the first ninety-four, then the remaining sixty-five delivered in 1937 and 1938 would have raised the hidden profit on the 159 delivered altogether to nearly $400,000.

Most remarkable of all is the hidden profit that the Soviets made on the aircraft, which, being Russian, were not subject to discount. Their dollar prices to the Republicans have been known for a long time: an SB Katiuska bomber cost $110,000, an I-16 Mosca fighter and a UTI trainer cost $40,000 each, an I-15 Chato, an R-5 Rasante and an R-Z Natacha cost $35,000 each.[10] The 1939 list, however, fortunately includes the rouble–dollar prices for three of them: SB Katiuska, 435,000 r. converted into $110,000 @ 3.95 to $1;* I-16 Mosca, 128,000 r. converted into $40,000 @ 3.2 to $1; UTI: 124,000 r. converted into $40,000 @ 3.1 to $1.

Thus there was a hidden profit of no less than $27,925 on every one of the ninety-three SB Katiuskas delivered during the war, of $15,850 on every I-16 Mosca (276 delivered), and of $16,603.80 on every UTI (4 delivered). The spares and equipment – from the largest, such as engines, undercarriages and propellers, down to the smallest, such as carburettors, sparking-plugs and ball-bearings – were likewise calculated separately,

---

* The Russians may have settled on $110,000, 34% above the set price of $82,075.47, after learning that this was the unit price that the Republicans were willing to pay for Martin 139W bombers secretly offered in the USA (see below, p. 188).

article by article, the conversion rates varying between 2.3 and 3.1 roubles to the dollar. Indeed, among the hundreds of items in the two sets of lists, only seven are worked out at the official rate or slightly above it, these being some bales of old cartridges and boxes of gunpowder.[11]

There can be no innocent explanation for such figures. They show, on the contrary, that once it had the gold safely in its possession, the Soviet government, having promised generous discounts on the prices of arms as a proof of its solidarity with the Spanish Republic, reduced the number of discountable articles to as few as possible, then resorted to Byzantine jiggery-pokery in order to claw back most of the discounts on the materials that were discountable and to make handsome profits on those, the majority, which were not. It was able to pull this off by ensuring that the Spaniards never saw the rouble prices, most of which were more or less arbitrary in any case, and by using a different rouble–dollar conversion rate for every article. The process can be seen from the four 1936 lists: the clerks of the NKVD – who, to judge by the various elementary mistakes in addition and long-division and the scribbled corrections over them, were not very good at arithmetic – made a list of materials with suggested dollar prices for fleecing the Spaniards. On checking these, a higher authority decided some were high enough to provoke a protest and sent them back to be worked out again. This went on until prices were reached which the higher authority thought they could get away with. There is probably a fifth list somewhere in the archive, all typed out in fair copy. There are no rouble prices for the I-15, R5 and RZ aircraft, which cost $35,000 each and of which 255 were delivered in all, or for much of the material delivered in 1937 and 1938. However, when comparing the sets of totals in the 1936 and 1939 lists, I found that out of every $20 million charged to the Republicans, about $6 million represented an overcharge.

The sum that the Soviet government charged to the Spanish Republican government for war material supplied up to 8 August 1938 came to $171.2 or $171.4 million,* and this was deducted from the value of the Spanish gold reserve, worth $518 million, in Moscow. The balance of $346.6 or $346.8 million was in the meantime sold to the Soviet government during 1937 and the first half of 1938, and the foreign currency earned thereby transferred to the Soviet bank in Paris, the Banque Commerciale de

---

* According to the voyage lists, the total up to 5 August 1937 came to $131,567,580.70 (RGVA, F. 33987, O. 3, D. 1056, L. 117). The fourteen deliveries in 1938 came to $39,871,209 (the 1938 voyage lists are on three typed sheets, no date or file reference, possibly compiled and typed in the 1970s by a researcher from the Institute of Military History of the USSR), making $171,438,789.70 in all. According to Ribalkin (*Ejército*, Jan 1992, p. 45), the total cost of materials came to $166,835,023, which the Republican government amortized by paying $171,236,088. There is thus a difference of only $208,479 between the two totals.

l'Europe du Nord (BCEN), to enable the Republicans to buy arms, air-craft and general supplies in other parts of the world. Thus the Soviet government was able to claim that by 8 August 1938 the Republicans had spent nearly all the gold and that only 1.5 tons remained against which they could draw currency. However, if the $6 million overcharged out of every $20 million charged represents an average carried across the period between October 1936 and August 1938, then the total overcharge on the war material would amount to at least $51 million (171 ÷ 20 × 6). Had the Soviet government behaved honestly, it would have deduced not $171 million from the gold but $121 million, or even less. Of all the swindles, cheatings, robberies and betrayals that the Republicans had to put up with from governments, officials and arms traffickers all over the world, this barrow-boy behaviour by Stalin and the high officials of the Soviet *nomenklatura* is surely the most squalid, the most treacherous and the most indefensible.

Since any attempt to fiddle the books when costing the sending of Soviet personnel to Spain and the training of Spaniards in Russia, would have led to immediate exposure, the Soviet government, as already men-tioned, stuck to the official exchange rate and compensated for this by charging for everything they could think of, to the last kopek. In addition to the war material, the Spanish Republicans were charged: the travel, pay and costs of all Soviet personnel in Spain; the upkeep of their families at home while they were there; a month's holiday for them and their families on return; the pay of all Soviet personnel engaged on 'Operation "X"', including, apparently, not only the crews of the Russian ships but also Russian railwaymen and dockers; the costs of training the Spanish airmen, tank crews and others in the USSR; the pay of all Russians employed at the training airfields and camps, from commanders and instructors to cooks and cleaning women; the maintenance and repair of aircraft, vehicles, equipment, buildings, furniture and fittings; the petrol, oil and heating-fuel consumed; and, finally, the renovation of the airfields after the Spaniards left, which included not only the refurbishment of hangars and buildings etc. but also the laying down of tarmac aprons in front of the hangars where there had been only grass before.[12] Not enough data is available to make an estimate of what these additional expenses came to; I have been told that they came to about $30 million and brought the total cost of Soviet aid to a little over $200 million. On the few figures that are known, it seems more likely that they came to about half that amount, but until more records are seen, the question is better left open.

Since it is now certain that the Soviets cheated over the arms sales in order to acquire the gold as cheaply as possible, the question must be raised of whether they also cheated the Republicans over the rest of the value of the gold sent to Paris from Moscow. Before this can be answered,

a great deal of information hitherto concealed will have to become access-
ible. The BCEN in Paris will have to open its accounts to researchers; we
shall have to know more exactly how much the Republicans spent on oil
supplies, both from the USSR and elsewhere, and how much on shipping
charters and the like. (The average price for chartering a ship in the 1930s
was about £5 or $25 per ton of the ship's tonnage, though the fees were
probably much higher for carrying cargo to Spain during the civil war.)
One can only say that the cost of war materials bought from countries
other than the Soviet Union was probably about $82 million ($30 million
on aircraft and $52 million on armaments) or, if as much as $60 million
were spent in Poland, $102 million. A lot of this money was consumed in
commissions, bribes and payments for materials never delivered, including 126 aircraft. Finally, we should have to ascertain how much money –
$350 million? $450 million? – remained for buying such commodities as
food, clothing and the like and to see whether or not those expert in the
economic aspects of the history of the Spanish Civil War believe such a
figure likely. It is now for the Russian authorities to make a start, therefore, by opening all their Spanish Civil War records to the public, for the
sake of establishing the facts at last and, from them, the historical truth.

21

Prague

THE MADRID GOVERNMENT believed Professor Luis Jiménez de Asúa's appointment as its minister* at Prague to be exceptionally important. Czechoslovakia was a prosperous democracy surrounded by countries – Nazi Germany, Poland, Romania, Hungary and Austria – whose rulers were far from democratic and no friends of the Spanish Republic, and a minister at Prague would be strategically placed to gather intelligence about the politics of eastern and central Europe which would otherwise be unobtainable. Czechoslovakia, however, was also the largest exporter of arms in the world, and it was proverbial among her politicians that without arms exports the economy would collapse in a month.[1] Since her government was a coalition of parties from right (Agrarian) to left (Social Democrat, as the Czechoslovakian Socialists called themselves) under a president, Eduard Beneš, who, despite having signed the Non-Intervention agreement, was known to be sympathetic to the Spanish government, the Republicans hoped that it might be possible to buy, if the business were managed discreetly, arms and aircraft in Czechoslovakia. To this end Lt.-Col. Angel Pastor Velasco, one of the two Republican sub-secretaries for air, had gone to Prague in September. Like his namesake, Major Carlos Pastor, he was a well-born officer who had remained loyal to the Republic and, in view of the distrust with which such men were regarded, had been sent abroad for his own safety.[2] He was provided with a 'starting fund' of £150,000, channelled through a bank in Vienna to avoid Germany and taken to Prague by Corpus Barga. (It may

---

* As a lesser and younger state, Czechoslovakia was represented abroad not by ambassadors at embassies but by ministers at legations, their full title being 'Minister Plenipotentiary and Envoy Extraordinary'. Conversely, the foreign representatives at Prague held the same rank. These distinctions, laid down at the Congress of Vienna after the Napoleonic Wars to avoid disputes over precedence, were gradually abolished after the Second World War. In the United Nations Assembly, for instance, they would have been ridiculous.

be remembered that the details of the transfer were leaked by one of the banks involved to the French right-wing newspapers; see above, p. 101.) Since Mexico had agreed to provide 'cover', that is to say, act as the ostensible buyer of the material, Pastor Velasco carried a Mexican passport in the name of Alfredo Palacios, which would also lessen the risk of his being seized by the Gestapo or OVRA, should an airliner in which he was travelling on one of his journeys across Europe land in Germany or Italy.

The previous Spanish minister, Luis García Guijaro, had departed without a word in August, and since then the Spanish secretary, Gaspar Sanz y Tovar, had been using the legation as a centre for Nationalist propaganda. When Asúa arrived in Prague on 14 October 1936, he was told that Sanz y Tovar was refusing to leave the building until he had received a declaration signed by Kamil Krofta, the Czechoslovakian foreign minister, that Czechoslovakia recognized the Republic as the only legitimate government of Spain. This was intended to embarrass the Czechoslovakian government, which had no desire to provoke its Nationalist-sympathizing neighbours, let alone Hitler and Mussolini, by issuing statements of this kind. As a result of the ensuing delay, Asúa and the new secretary, Julio López Rey, were unable to go to the legation until late the following afternoon, and then only surrounded by a police guard to protect them from a jeering crowd mustered by Sudeten Germans and other parties of the extreme political right. Inside, they found unpaid bills but everything of value, including the records, inventories and the money from the safe, gone. Nor had Sanz y Tovar left any money in the Prague bank account of the Spanish government, and Asúa and his staff thus had to manage on the cash they had brought with them, some francs and pesetas worth about £40 ($200), until funds arrived from Madrid on the 21st.[3]

The Social Democrat ministers and politicians whom Asúa saw during the next few days all promised help in the matter of procuring war material. Beneš and Krofta warned, however, that after reports in the press that some Czechoslovakian arms, supposedly ordered by Mexico, had been taken by the ship *Azteca* to Bilbao instead (Appendix II), a ban had been imposed on further arms sales to Mexico. Any arms purchases by the Spanish government must be made legally and with the authorization of the national defence committee, most of whose members, they thought they should mention, belonged to the right wing of the Agrarian Party.[4]

On 27 October Pastor, whom Asúa was obliged to meet in obscure cafés since he was not supposed to know of his existence, reported that he now had a firm offer of fighter aircraft, tanks, artillery, small arms and ammunition, all ready to go at short notice.[5] The problem of 'legality' could be solved at a stroke if the Soviet Union would agree to provide 'cover' and send this material with the material it was sending to Spain already. The matter was therefore put to Sergei Alexandrovsky the Soviet minister in Prague, but he described the proposal as 'very strange' and the offer itself was probably suspect, and regretted that in any case this particular form of assistance would not be possible.[6]

An offer of 'cover' was received from Madame Lupescu, the famous mistress of King Carol II of Romania, whom she had accompanied on a state visit to Czechoslovakia, but the size of the commission she demanded was enormous (see below, p. 214). The Prague chamber of commerce then introduced Asúa to Hugo, Baron von Lustig, a prominent industrialist, and his colleague Fesdji, a retired Turkish army officer who had once saved the life of Kemal Ataturk, the Turkish ruler, and was therefore said to be a man of great influence, who undertook to arrange 'cover' with the co-operation of certain officials in the Turkish government. General Čižek, the secretary of the national defence committee, on whose signature of the permits everything depended, raised no objection and it was expected that all the material would be on its way to 'Turkey' by the end of November at the latest.

As the weeks went by, however, General Čižek gave one reason after another for being unable to sign the export permits: he had noticed technical discrepancies in the orders; he needed written confirmation from Ankara that the weapons were for Turkish use only; he needed more copies of the confirmations for Technoarma, the company handling the export, and for the factories – Skoda, Avia (the aircraft division of Skoda), CKD (which made tanks) and ZB (Zborojovka at Brno, whose ZB 30 was developed into the Bren-gun); the confirmations had to be endorsed by five ministers, all of whom were away for Christmas, and then the sales had to be legalized by Krofta, the Czech foreign minister, which would cost £1,000.[7] This last was especially surprising, for Pastor had already had to pay out £77,500 in commissions and bribes – £40,000 to von Lustig and Fesdji 'to meet the expenses' of the officials in Turkey and £37,500 to various officials in the Czechoslovakian administration – besides the commissions (the sums are not specified) to von Lustig and Fesdji themselves.[8]

At the beginning of January Asúa managed to put a tactful complaint, via a bank director, to Dr Milan Hodzá, the prime minister, who expressed shock and promised to remonstrate with 'that corporal' (General Čižek), but when, after a week, it appeared that Hodzá had done nothing, Asúa appealed to General Bekarek, the vice-president of the defence committee and Čižek's superior. He too promised to put a stop to these unconscionable delays by calling a special meeting, but a few days later von Lustig told Asúa that instead of calling a meeting Bekarek had privately tried to pressure those who had received commissions to do their patriotic duty and invest the money in the Czechoslovak copper mines, a proposal that went down badly since they all knew that he was a major shareholder in the mining company.[9]

During these months arms dealers and would-be entrepreneurs of various nationalities, as well as Spanish Republican arms-buying agents, arrived in Prague amost weekly, some alone or in pairs, some in groups of four or five. Some had been, or claimed to have been, sent by this or that politician or political party, others by the Republican buying commission in Paris. One group, consisting of Louis Mortier, a leading Paris arms dealer, Major Bordelet, a Belgian arms technician, and Adler and Lederer, two German Jews, came with orders for material of which a large part turned out to be the same as that which Pastor was trying to send out under Turkish 'cover'.

This, wrote Asúa to his chief, Julio Alvarez del Vayo, the Republican foreign minister, was absurd and it looked as though the lack of co-ordination that had bedevilled things in Paris was going to bedevil things here too. There was no need in Czechoslovakia for intermediaries and their costly commissions, for arms could be bought directly from the factories through Technoarma (the Czech equivalent of SEPEWE). The real problem was to get the arms out of the country. This was a complicated, not to say illegal, business and the fewer the people who were engaged in it the better. Vayo must therefore tell him whether arms procurement was to be controlled from Paris, in which case well and good since Pastor and the legation could cease operations immediately and would be relieved of responsibility for the inevitable disaster, or Prague was to act independently, in which case the Spanish government must prevent any more of these intermediaries from coming to Czechoslovakia. No such clear instruction was ever sent, for neither Vayo nor the government as yet had the power to enforce the necessary measures.[10]

While all this was going on – or rather, not going on – there appeared in Prague a 'Marchese di Castelli' with an order for arms and aircraft signed by the Turkish consul at Milan, which suggested that the Spanish Nationalists were likewise trying to obtain arms under Turkish 'cover'. At the Turkish legation in Prague, he explained that the papers had been approved by General Čižek, requested that they be signed by the Turkish minister and said that he was staying at the Hotel Esplanade. The Turks told him to return in twenty-four hours, when everything would be ready. That night, however, they discovered that the order was a fake and informed both Asúa and the press. Pastor, worried lest this affect his own transaction, rushed round the newspaper offices, paying some 20,000 koruna (£150, or $750) in all to have the story spiked, only to see it on the front pages of several right-wing dailies next morning.[11]

Rudolf Slánský,* the leader of the Communist Party of Czechoslovakia,

---

* In the absence of Klement Gottwald in Moscow, joint leadership of the Czech CP was delegated to Slánský and Jan Sverma, although both were under Stalin's constant

had supplied Asúa with a private investigator named Skorpil, the Communist son of a local theatre manager, who was useful owing to his numerous friendships among the waitresses, chambermaids and receptionists at the hotels, restaurants and bars frequented by foreigners 'on business'. He was put to work and soon discovered that the 'Marchese' was not an Italian minor aristocrat but Spanish, a Señor Machuca who was a confidant of ex-King Alfonso XIII and, with Louis Mortier and von Lustig in 1935, had got together Alfonso's hoard of arms now said to be somewhere in Morocco (see above, p. 71). Machuca was not at the Esplanade but at the Hotel Ambassador, and was observed having meetings by night with Louis Mortier, an 'Engineer Pfeiffer' and a young Polish woman, Erna Davidovic. Skorpil's *informes* to Asúa illustrate the truth of Graham Greene's remark that 'real life' is sometimes more like the stuff of a spy novel than most of us, especially historians, are disposed to believe: Mortier is described as 'robust, full-faced, moustache clipped short in the English style, wearing a blue suit, grey overcoat and hat and *dark red* shoes'; 'Engineer Pfeiffer' he describes as 'stout, round-faced, clean-shaven and bald, light grey suit, blue shirt, red tie and *yellow* shoes'; and Erna Davidovic as 'thin-faced, long nose, blonde hair combed back over her head, pink blouse, black skirt, black hat, short coat with a leather belt'. They would go back and forth between the hotels Esplanade, Ambassador and Alcron, constantly changing taxis, Machuca hiding behind a car or round a corner while they were waiting, and one night (8 January) Mortier and 'Engineer Pfeiffer' were watched through the window, while they talked in a bar at 22 Stepanska Street, by a mysterious man in a grey overcoat and hat. Pfeiffer was seen to go to the Hotel Sax and Café Imperial, where Sanz y Tovar had set up a headquarters for Nationalist agents in town. From eavesdropping waitresses and a search of Machuca's room while a chambermaid changed the sheets on the bed, and even by striking up a relationship which Miss Davidovic herself, Skorpil or one of his agents learnt that the clumsy faking of the documents had been deliberate in order to create a scandal and to sabotage any dealings the Republicans might be having with the Turks. Machuca, Mortier and Pfeiffer, who may have been the 'Baron Pfeiffer' who had tried to buy aircraft from Mrs Victor Bruce in November (see below, p. 200), were all in touch with Fritz Ehrenfest, the ex-director of the Oesterreichische Creditanstalt bank in Vienna, which brings us back in a circle to the matter of the leaking of information about the £150,000 that Corpus Barga took to Prague for Pastor (see above, pp. 101).[12]

---

suspicion. Slánský was the protagonist of the show trials of 1952, when Stalin put to death most of the Czech party leadership. Asúa says little about Slánský's activities on behalf of the Spanish Republic, the details presumably being in the now vanished reports sent to Prieto, for which see the end of this chapter.

This was the group, then, that brought the Turkish deal to grief. For a week or so, it seemed that the press reports about the faked order might be shrugged off as another 'Fascist provocation', but von Lustig and Fesdji, anticipating trouble after Bekarek's attempt to make them invest their 'commission' money in the copper mines, sent more details to the Turkish war ministry, which was thus obliged to announce an inquiry. While the Czechoslovakian government, now deeply embarrassed and annoyed, awaited its findings, General Čižek passed word through yet another intermediary* that if the report that he and the defence committee would have to prepare were to put a gloss on the affair which was favourable to the Spanish government and by this means perhaps still save the situation, he and General Netik (an important member of the committee) would need another million francs in cash. This was paid on 18 February, but to no avail, for by then the Turkish report had already arrived, as Čižek well knew, and pronounced all the papers to be forgeries. Pastor, who had already been arrested on a trumped-up charge and released on bail in December, left for Paris to avoid a second arrest, telling Asúa that he knew the papers to be genuine; it was merely that the Turkish war minister himself had not signed them.[13] This was probably true, for Turkish officials continued to provide 'cover' until the 'Grumman scandal', which led to the resignation of the war minister, put an end to their assistance in the spring of 1938 (see below, pp. 222). Von Lustig and Fesdji took the first train to Vienna and Asúa discovered, too late, that Fesdji had agreed to come in on the deal only in order to earn enough money to buy the monopoly over the export of Turkish tobacco to central Europe and that von Lustig was known to the British in Shanghai and Hong Kong for shady arms deals in China which had bankrupted him. In Vienna, Asúa now heard, von Lustig was boasting to his cronies that it was only the naïveté of the Spanish Republicans that had restored his fortunes.[14]

After the Turkish deal collapsed, the aircraft, now numbering about eighty machines of various types, were taken over by Estonia, though with only partial success (see below, p. 212). Iran, which had agreed to release thirty-three tanks as part of the deal, now decided that it wanted them after all.[15] The artillery pieces too seem to have been abandoned, at least there is no further mention of them. There remained 50,000 Mauser 7.92 rifles, 2,000 machine-guns, 70 million cartridges made by ZB and its subsidiary, Sellier and Bellott, an ammunition factory founded in 1826 and

---

* This was Lt.-Col. Smit (or Smid), a Czechoslovakian army officer who in Spain had told Prieto that he could obtain several batteries of artillery. Prieto guardedly authorized him to go ahead and, being neither stupid nor without humour, assigned him the code-name *Zapatero* ('Cobbler') by which Asúa refers to him throughout his dispatches. The batteries never materialized, though *Zapatero* was continually visiting the legation until the summer of 1938.

still in business today. After months of seeking 'cover' through Iraq, China, Uruguay, Columbia, Chile and even Mexico again, Asúa and Pastor's replacement, Domingo Martínez de Aragón, concluded a deal in July 1937 with the Bolivian government, which had already agreed with the Republican ambassador in Mexico to provide 'cover' for twenty-eight American aircraft waiting for a ship at Veracruz.[16] The scheme was that the Bolivians would sell off some old army material and send it out through Peru. The Bolivians in turn would order, as though for themselves, the rifles, machine-guns and ammunition bought by the Republicans from ZB. Luis Añez, the Bolivian minister of agriculture, thereupon arrived in Germany 'to negotiate the hiring of technicians to assist in opening up a province of the interior for development' and, during a visit to Prague, settled the terms with Zdanek Fierlinger,* the chief of the political division of the Czechoslovakian foreign ministry, and a 'Señor Rioja', that is to say Martínez de Aragón.[17] The American side of the affair is discussed later (see below, Chapter 30). All that need be said here is that the 'Bolivian deal' cost the Republican legation in Prague a further £134,680 (20 million Ffr.) in bribes and commissions to Añez and his colleagues, two of whom – Erainn Lillienfield and Dr Guillaume Pohoreille (or Pohorylle) – were said by one of Sanz y Tovar's agents to have received £8,600 each.[18] Once again, the money was spent for nothing.

Robert Flieder, the Czechoslovakian minister to Spain before the civil war, was, like his British counterpart Sir Henry Chilton, a firm supporter of the Nationalists and, like Chilton, refused to return to Madrid and instead set up a make-shift embassy in France near the frontier. His father-in-law, Senator Wessaly, was the administrator of Beneš's personal fortune, with the result that when he returned to Prague in the summer of 1937, Flieder, as a member of the president's inner circle, found a senior post in the foreign ministry and became chief of the political department when Fierlinger was sent as minister to Moscow.[19] To comply with Beneš's instruction that all arms sales must be checked for legality in case Czechoslovakia was accused of violating Non-Intervention, all docu-

---

* Colonel Zdanek Fierlinger was a veteran of the Czech Legion that, with its famous armoured train, had fought in Russia against the Bolsheviks in 1918–20. By 1936, however, he had changed his views completely and become a philo-Communist, if not already a Soviet agent. In the autumn of 1937 he was appointed Czechoslovakian minister in Moscow. After nine years in Moscow, he returned to Czechoslovakia and played a sinister role in the Communist take-over in 1948. Asúa, who mentions him frequently in his dispatches, on one occasion refers to him as 'my friend'. Pastor, on the other hand, thought Fierlinger 'a Jesuit'. It is uncertain how much Fierlinger, Slánský or, for that matter, Alexandrovsky actually did to help the Spanish Republicans, however, apart from denounce almost everyone in sight who was not a Communist as a traitor or Fascist spy, as often as not wrongly accusing those who were innocent and failing to notice those who were indeed crooks.

ments relating to them had to go through numerous departments of the foreign ministry. When they reached Flieder's desk, he passed the details to Sanz y Tovar, who included them in his dispatches to Franco's foreign minister at Salamanca, who passed them on to the German and Italian governments. In the autumn Flieder and Dr P. Cermak, the head of a department in the ministry of public works and temporary acting chief of police, who had always been a friend to the Nationalists, confronted Krofta with evidence to show, they said, that Bolivia was acting as a go-between for the Spanish Reds whereupon Krofta, apprehensive of another scandal, cancelled the export permits.[20] The Bolivians, sensing an opportunity to obtain the arms for themselves and at no cost since the documents purported to show that it was they who had paid for them, claimed the material on the grounds that their order had been genuine, but, since the Czechs were unwilling to become further entangled in this unsavoury business, were rejected.[21]

In despair the Republicans turned again to Alexandrovsky, whose refusal, presumably on Stalin's orders, to provide 'cover' in October 1936 had been the cause of all their tribulations since. In December 1937 the Soviets finally relented, probably because they were, in any case, about to send their second and last wave of supplies to Spain. The rifles, machine-guns and cartridges left via Poland in February and were carried to Bordeaux by four ships of the Republican-owned France Navigation company (see below, p. 298): the *Gravelines* (sailed 13 March 1938), *Bougaroni* (2 April), *Winnipeg* (6 April) and *Bonifacio* (17 April).[22] They were probably taken by road to Catalonia in May, for the French frontier was opened by Blum's and Daladier's governments from 17 March to 13 June 1938 (see p. 233). These were the only arms that Asúa succeeded in procuring for the Republic during the twenty-two months of his mission to Czechoslovakia.

The financial arrangement was that the full price of £922,000 would be paid by the Soviet government, which would, of course, deduct the sum from the Spanish gold in Moscow. The Spaniards had already paid £582,000 to the ZB company, who agreed that when the instalments from Russia reached this amount, they would repay it to the Spanish government. However, the ZB director, Outrata, found reasons to delay until the whole £922,000 had been received by March 1938 and then flatly refused to refund the £582,000. Throughout the spring and summer Asúa tried every means, through the Czechoslovakian government and courts, to recover the money, in vain. On 15 July he was told by Premier Negrín that he was to be transferred to Geneva to represent Spain at the League of Nations and on the 18th received a letter of farewell and felicitation from Antonin Hampl, the president of the Social Democrat (i.e. Socialist) Party of Czechoslovakia. In reply, Asúa courteously thanked him but went on to say that in view of Hampl's ardent promises of support when Asúa had first arrived in October 1936, the Spanish Socialists now had the right to ask if the Czechoslovakian Party could point to one single thing that it had done to help its fellow party in Spain during these years of peril, whether it be in helping to procure arms, to raise volunteers or now, in the present crisis, to force the ZB company to return the money it was trying to steal.

Hampl had great influence among the factory workers at Brno; the sinister Outrata had been ordered by the government time and again to repay the money by instalments, orders which he had met with excuses, put-offs and outright disobedience; surely the Social Democrats could find means to bring pressure to bear upon him. Yet, at the very time when the same forces of Nazi Germany, which had brought so much suffering upon Spain, were threatening to invade Czechoslovakia itself, he had been told that the Czechoslovakian government had sent a commercial representative to Franco – what could he achieve, when Germany and Italy had control over Nationalist trade? The Czechs were about to give official recognition to Sanz y Tovar, whose conduct in stealing the records and money from the legation and the money from the Spanish government account in the bank in October 1936 had been openly criminal. Yet not a single Socialist in the government had raised a whisper of protest.[23]

In August President Beneš, although almost wholly preoccupied by the looming Sudetenland crisis, found time to intervene and oblige Outrata to commence paying the instalments, the last being received by the Soviet bank in Paris, on behalf of the Spanish government, on 29 September 1938, two days after the signing of the Munich agreement. Asúa, meanwhile, had departed for Geneva on 26 August, leaving Martínez de Aragón and two others at the legation as a skeleton staff, with instructions to keep a car near by in which to escape if danger threatened. They continued to look for ways to obtain arms, despite the new pro-Fascist government, and did indeed succeed in one matter. In 1936 a Dr Guimet, sent by Negrín (who was then finance minister), had bought 11 million cartridges from Sellier and Bellott but had been unable to arrange transport for them. They had been lying in the factory warehouse ever since and by some means Martínez de Aragón managed to get them out of the country on 17 November, although it was almost certainly too late by then for them to reach Spain.[24] I have been unable to discover whether or not he and his colleagues got away safely when Hitler invaded what was left of Czechoslovakia on 15 March 1939.

From 14 October 1936 to the end of July 1937 Asúa included in his dispatches (many of which he typed himself late at night since he was often without a shorthand-typist he dared trust) quite informative accounts of the negotiations to buy arms and the complex and intersecting rings of intrigue that swirled about them. Sent with the dispatches were the 'hard' documents – the contracts, lists of weapons, prices, proposed routes by which it was intended to transport the material to Spain and the exact sums that had been spent on bribes and commissions and to whom – which Alvarez del Vayo was to pass on to Prieto at the ministry of marine and air (and, after May 1937, of defence). In January 1937 Asúa discovered to his consternation that Vayo had not done so and that Prieto had not heard a word about Pastor's activities since Asúa had arrived in Prague in October. This must have been quickly rectified, for these papers are not in the archives of the Spanish foreign ministry in Madrid, where they would be if Vayo had continued to hang on to them. By April 1937, however, Asúa had even greater cause for exasperation with Vayo.

In November 1936 Leopold Kulczar, an Austrian journalist and Socialist living in Czechoslovakia, had been taken on by Asúa to create an espionage network in Germany and central Europe.* In April 1937 his agents reported signs that the Condor Legion in Spain was being re-equipped with modern aircraft and that a number of bombers, departing from airfields at Hannover and Staaken, were believed to be flying to Spain directly across France at high altitude by night. (This was untrue, for we now know that the aircraft were shipped by sea.) On 15 April Asúa telegraphed the information, for immediate relay to Prieto as 'top secret',[25] to Vayo, who, thinking it would make wonderful propaganda with which to shake up the Non-Intervention Committee in London, released it to the press. With the Gestapo now alerted and converging on Hannover and Staaken, the agents had to be dispersed, the network dismantled and months of patient and dangerous work abandoned, as Asúa pointed out in an icy letter to Vayo.[26]

This incident was to have repercussions in England and France (see below, pp. 232–3). Meanwhile, Asúa decided to send all sensitive information, especially about arms procurement, directly to Prieto by separate courier. From May 1937 his sections on 'Armamentos' therefore become briefer and briefer and after July consist only of a single paragraph stating that all reports relating thereto have been sent to the ministry of defence.

---

* Kulczar appears – thin, tense, arrogant and utterly dedicated to the Cause – in Arturo Barea's *The Clash* (Flamingo edn, 1984, pp. 346–58). His wife, Ilsa, went to Spain in November 1936 and worked in the foreign press office under Hidalgo Rubio. There she met Arturo Barea, became his lover and later married him. In the Republican Archivo de Barcelona in the Archivo del Ministerio de Asuntos Exteriores (AMAE), Madrid, there is an unsigned denunciation by a Communist of Ilsa Kulczar as an immoral woman, a social climber and a spy in touch with Germany and the 'Fascist Zone' of Spain who ought to be arrested (RE 98 c. 4 pl. 6). Leopold Kulczar died of uraemia on 24 January 1938, though some suspected, such was the atmosphere of those times, that the Russians had poisoned him. After the civil war Arturo and Ilsa Barea escaped to France and thence to England, where they subsequently became well known in literary society.

It seems that all the records (at least those concerned with arms buying) of the ministries of marine and air and of defence were destroyed at the end of, or after, the civil war, for none, apart from a few fragments that happened to be in other archives, have as yet been found. Most were probably burnt by the Republicans themselves, though I have been told that one or two train-wagonloads of such documents were captured and kept by the Nationalists for some years until an order came down to burn the lot.* 'What they contain is shameful', so the general giving the order is reported to have said, 'and although many of the people implicated were Reds, they were also Spaniards and it will not do to have Spaniards shown up as fools or knaves. There are also their families to think about.'[27]

At the Prague legation, however, a complete set of all correspondence relating to purchases, attempted purchases, bribes, etc. in Czechoslovakia and central and eastern Europe was kept, for business continued until Asúa arranged from Geneva for the whole of his 'secret archive', as he called it, to be sent from Prague in the Soviet diplomatic bag to the Spanish embassy in Moscow on 15 September 1938.[28] At some time in 1939, perhaps in March after the end of the Spanish Civil War or certainly after the signing of the Nazi-Soviet pact in August, all the records in the Spanish embassy in Moscow were destroyed, including, presumably, the 'secret archive' from Prague and, possibly, the records from the Warsaw legation which the chargé d'affaires, Manuel Martínez Pedroso y Macías, might have brought with him when he was transferred to Moscow in the summer of 1938.

It is possible, however, that instead of delivering Asúa's 'secret archive' to the Spanish embassy, the NKVD, knowing that the wealth of detailed information it contained would be invaluable to their purposes, sequestered it when it crossed the frontier. If that did happen, then it might be worth a search to see if it is still lying forgotten in one of the immense archives in Russia.

---

* These, however, may not have been defence ministry records. On 10 December 1973, José Calviño told Francisco Olaya, during an interview, that at the end of the civil war the records of the arms-buying commissions in Paris were transferred to a building in the Avenue Marceau occupied by a Basque Republican group. When the Germans occupied Paris in 1940, the building was taken over by Spanish police agents on the orders of José Félix Lequeria Erquiza, the Basque Falangist whom Franco appointed as Spanish ambassador in France. It was he, for instance, who helped the Gestapo to round up exiled Republican leaders, including Companys and Zugazagoita, and send them back to Spain for execution (see pp. 180 and 226). After the Second World War the records were never found in France and may have been those in the goods wagons. Alternatively, if they were not destroyed on some other occasion, they may still be in the Spanish archives, uncatalogued. (The interview with Calviño is mentioned in Olaya, *El oro de Negrín*, pp. 47–8, n. 47.)

22

'A Prospect of Unlimited Opportunities'

IN THE SUMMER of 1936 Americans were still preoccupied with the effects of the Depression, and the prevailing mood among them was isolationist. Two Neutrality Acts, for instance, made it a felony to export so much as a single .22 cartridge to any foreign country at war with another. They omitted, however, to mention civil wars, and since the fighting in Spain broke out at a time when Congress was not sitting, President Franklin D. Roosevelt found that he had no powers to prevent the sale of arms to the Spanish government or, for that matter, to the rebels.

The war in Spain divided opinion in the USA as it did in other democracies, with big business, finance, conservatives and Catholics generally supporting the 'Insurgents' (Nationalists) and labour, liberals, Jews and others who had cause to fear Fascism supporting the 'Loyalists' (Republicans). The American Republican and Democrat parties were each split fairly equally, but it happened that most Catholics voted Democrat and, since Roosevelt needed their votes for his coming re-election in November, he had to devise a policy which would placate them without losing the votes of the pro-Loyalists among his supporters. Somewhat hesitantly, he settled for what he called a 'moral embargo', which amounted to little more than a threat that whoever sold arms to either side in Spain would incur the grave displeasure of the State Department.[1]

Neither the Spanish Republicans nor would-be vendors were seriously alarmed by this, for they suspected that the American authorities would not enforce the embargo too strictly. During the Gran Chaco War the American Armaments Corporation had sold arms to Bolivia. When prosecuted under the Neutrality Acts, Alfred and Ignacio Miranda, the directors, had claimed that the Acts were unconstitutional and had been upheld by a federal court. The case had gone to the Supreme Court, which so far seemed in no hurry to give its ruling.[2] Moreover, Texaco and other oil companies were supplying petroleum openly to General Franco, and the

State Department, on the flimsy pretext that petroleum was not a vital war material, had made no effort to stop them. If large and wealthy corporations were willing to ignore the 'moral embargo', smaller companies, especially the perennially unstable aviation companies, would be even more so in this time of economic hardship.

At the Spanish embassy in Washington, Luis Calderón, the ambassador, Major Ramón Franco (General Franco's brother), who was air attaché, and others, while pretending loyalty, were feeding misinformation to their government and inventing reasons for being unable to carry out instructions to procure war material. Ramón Franco was rumbled and, after being dismissed on 14 August, began a slow journey back to Spain.[3] Calderón resigned at the end of the month and with Juan de Cárdenas, the former ambassador in Paris (see above, p. 23), who had recently arrived in New York, set up an alternative 'embassy' for the Nationalists in the Ritz Carlton Hotel.

It seemed a stroke of good fortune to the Republicans therefore that don Félix Gordón Ordás, the Spanish ambassador in Mexico, was one of the few Spanish diplomats who did not, as soon as the civil war broke out, desert his government and join the rebels. On the contrary, he threw himself body and soul into the task of procuring the arms and aircraft his government so sorely needed. Mexico, besides being the immediate neighbour of the United States to the south, was the only country in the world whose government had, from the first day, unequivocally declared its support of the Spanish Republic, for President General Lázaro Cárdenas and his ministers saw the struggle in Spain as similar to the revolution that Mexico herself had endured in the 1920s. Their position, however, was both lonely and precarious, in that every other Latin American government sympathized with the rebels to a greater or lesser degree, while large and influential sections of Mexican society loathed Cárdenas and his regime and devoutly prayed for the triumph of General Franco. Cárdenas nevertheless instructed his ministers and consuls abroad to provide 'cover' for arms bought by the Republicans and sent as a gift, though the Republicans insisted on paying for them (see above, p. 103), 20,000 ex-army rifles and 20 million cartridges on the *Magellanes* at the end of August. She was a Spanish ship, for Cárdenas ordered that, as a precaution against possible international incidents, no arms should be transported across the Atlantic on Mexican ships. The Mexicans would have sold their whole air force as well, but its fifty or so decrepit Vought and Douglas biplanes were not considered worth the expense of crating and shipping. The only possible source of substantial supplies in the Americas, therefore, could be the United States, which indeed – so Gordón excitedly assured his chief, Alvarez del Vayo, the Republican foreign minister – presented 'a prospect of unlimited opportunities'.[4]

By the third week of September and with the help of Mexican ministers and service chiefs, Gordón had received from the United States, despite the 'moral embargo', offers of at least 128 aircraft, including 50 bombers, as many mountain-guns and trench-mortars as desired, 5,400 machine-guns (many of them 'Tommy Guns') 450,000 rifles and nearly a billion cartridges, with more offers coming in daily.[5]* He telegraphed the details to Vayo, on the assumption that they would be passed for decision to Largo Caballero, who was war minister as well as premier, and to Indalecio Prieto, the naval and air minister. Vayo's replies were infrequent and, when they came, mostly non-committal or critical. On 11 September Prieto telegraphed to say that although he had been told that there had been some very interesting offers from vendors in the United States, he had no details and requested Gordon to send them in full and at once. Gordón did so and received a cable from Vayo to say that he must not send so many details, for they might be decoded by pro-Nationalist spies at the telegraph offices.[6]

Then, on 25 September, Gordón received a telegram from Captain Agustín Sanz Sainz in New York, of whose existence he had known nothing, to say that he had bought a number of American aircraft for the Spanish government and hoped that they could be exported via Mexico. Suspecting a trick by a Nationalist *provocateur*, Gordón cabled Vayo, who replied that he had never heard of such a person. Three days later Vayo cabled again to say that apparently this Sanz had been sent to New York from Paris on the orders of Lt.-Col. Angel Pastor Velasco.[7] This was an extraordinary thing to say. In the archives of the Spanish foreign ministry, of which Vayo was then chief, are fifteen telegrams between Sañz and Madrid, all relating to aircraft-buying, all sent between 21 July and 9 October 1936 and some signed by Vayo himself.[8] Indeed, since Sanz, as an air force officer, was under Prieto's authority, there must have been many more sent directly to Prieto which have now vanished. It appears, therefore, that Vayo was failing not only to keep Gordón informed but to pass Gordón's reports to Largo Caballero and Prieto, just as he was failing to

---

* The '50 bombers', with bombs, 5,000 Thompson sub-machine-guns, 400 Hotchkiss machine-guns and ammunition were offered by Henry Green & Co. Inc., investment brokers of 165 Broadway, New York, which had previously been the address of Armand Hammer's American Allied Trading Corporation. Three hundred and fifty thousand of the rifles were to be bought through an un-named Canadian, though the only arms dealer in North America able to supply such a huge number would have been Frank Bannerman of Philadelphia, whose main depot was a fortified island on the Hudson River. Among the other offers was one of twenty-eight Sikorsky amphibian flying boats, almost certainly S-43s. This seems odd, for Igor Sikorsky, who had fled Russia during the revolution, was denounced by the Communist *Daily Worker* [New York] (16 Nov 1936) as a 'White Guard Russian' who paid low wages.

pass the reports of Asúa and Pastor Velasco from Prague (see above, p. 162). Whether this was incompetence, an obsession with 'security', the deliberate act of a Communist fellow-traveller who wanted the Soviets to be the sole purveyors of armaments or a combination of all three is impossible to know.

Captain Agustín Sanz Sainz, a Socialist since youth, had been in the Spanish air force under the monarchy. In 1930 some officers – including Queipo de Llano, Hidalgo de Cisneros and Ramón Franco (who had then been on the left) – had attempted an anti-monarchist coup. It misfired and Sanz, who had no part in it, was ordered to take off and shoot down Ramón Franco, who was showering Madrid with leaflets from a Breguet Bre 19. He refused and was court-martialled and imprisoned. He was reinstated by the Republic but in October 1934 escaped abroad rather than obey the orders of General Francisco Franco to bomb miners' villages during the Asturian revolt. He served in the Venezuelan air force for six months, but when his contract expired his colonel, hoping to avoid the obligation of paying him his last three months' salary, ordered him to test an aged biplane that nobody had dared to fly for more than a year. Sanz flew it, performed several loops and rolls and on landing invited the colonel to accompany him on a second flight. The colonel declined and Sanz left with his pay.[9] Taking an apartment in Harlem, New York City,[10] Sanz spent the next year as a flying instructor and aircraft dealer and, as soon as the war broke out in Spain, sent a telegram to Lt.-Col. Angel Pastor, who was then the sub-secretary for air, in Madrid: 'As an aviation officer and co-religionist of yourselves I place myself at the disposition of the Republic.'[11] He was re-enrolled as a captain of the Aviación Militar, though several weeks passed before he received his first wages,[12] and ordered to stay in the United States and buy aircraft. (This perhaps explains why Vayo, whose enquiries could not have been very thorough, supposed that Pastor had sent him to New York.)

Sanz promptly got in touch with Charlie (Charles Harding) Babb, a one-eyed, one-armed ex-pilot whose business as 'The World's Largest Exporter of Used, Re-Conditioned Airplanes and Engines' was based at Grand Central Air Terminal, Glendale, Los Angeles, and, on the east coast, at Floyd Bennett Field (the present naval air station), Brooklyn. 'Babb's Bargains' were a regular feature of the aviation press, and his friends included not only Hollywood moguls and film stars, many of whom were his personal friends, but also professional record-breakers such as Amelia Earheart and Wiley Post. Much of his business came from Latin America and it is possible that Sanz, as a Spanish-speaking flying instructor and aircraft dealer, had served him in some capacity before.

When Sanz told him that he had been empowered by the Paris agency the Office Générale de l'Air to find modern aircraft for a new airline in

French West Africa, Babb, who was not deceived by this explanation, remarked that he could hardly have come at a better time. A recent safety regulation had made it mandatory for all commercial passenger-carrying aircraft to have at least two engines[13] and had thus obliged operating companies to put their single-engined Lockheed Orions, Northrop Deltas and Vultee V1-As up for sale; but, since these machines, though fast and modern, were rather too large and expensive to run to be attractive to sports pilots, buyers had béen few. American Airlines, for example, had nine Vultee V1-As, which had cost $30,000 each when new only two years before, on offer for $20,000 each, which included complete refurbishment and complete sets of spare parts, all brand new from the factory. After an inspection Sanz agreed to buy them for $22,000 each, to include Babb's commission and the cost of crating and embarking.[14] This made a refreshing contrast to the shabby treatment that the Republicans had received in Europe; indeed, Cyrus Smith, the president of American Airlines, appears as one of the very few people who did not overcharge or otherwise cheat the Spanish Republicans in their dealings with them. Smith, a tough Texan, is remembered as the man who transformed American Airways, as it was called when he joined it in 1934, from a small and struggling company into one of the great airlines of the world. Politics that did not concern his airline were of no concern to him and, regardless of who the buyers were, to have raised the declared price was not to his mind good business.[15]

A plan to ship the Vultees from New York, on board the SS *Paris*, to France through the London agents T. H. Chamberlain and J. D. Hewett[16] had to be dropped because Sanz had as yet received no money from Madrid to pay for them. Shortly after Sanz sent his telegram to Gordón on 25 September there arrived in New York a Republican buying commission – Colonel Francisco León Trejo, its chief, Major José Melendreras, a pilot whose left arm was paralysed as the result of a flying accident, and Sergeant Francisco Corral, an aero-engine expert – and on 6 October Professor Fernando de los Rios passed through on his way to Washington to take up his post as the new ambassador. In a series of telegrams to Vayo, Gordón argued that to have two independent commissions, one in New York and one directed from Mexico, both trying to buy material in the United States and inevitably colliding and bidding against each other,*

---

* Gordón's fear was justified. On 25 September, the day Sanz wrote to Gordón, a Mr Haas, representing the Buda Company of Harvey, Illinois, telephoned the State Department concerning the export of nine Vultees to France. Since he had not known that the aircraft were already sold to Babb, the enquiry almost certainly originated from Mexico. Sanz and Gordón both received offers, probably specious, of Martin 139W bombers (see below, p. 188) and others, doubtless well-intentioned, of twenty Curtiss Condors and twenty-eight Sikorskys (probably S-43s) being built for Latin America, from the Spanish anti-Fascist committee and 'Antonio Cornudella' (or

could lead only to disaster.[18] In the very same week that Asúa was sending identical warnings from Prague, Gordón explained that the difficulty lay not in buying arms but in getting them out of the country to Spain. Since the ships the Republicans were using had been commandeered by the government, it was risky for them to dock at American ports, for the pro-Nationalist shipping agency in New York, García and Díaz, and the Nationalist 'embassy' at the Ritz Carlton Hotel would institute legal proceedings to hold them on the claim that they rightfully belonged to their previous owners. Rios could do little in the way of procuring arms lest he upset relations with the US government, and communication between Gordón and the embassy in Washington was hazardous because the telephones were probably tapped. On the other hand, a single commission in Mexico supervised by Gordón would avoid duplication of effort, not prejudice Rios's position, and be able besides to check out the offers Gordón had received and send the material to Mexico for loading on to Spanish ships at Veracruz. Vayo rejected this, however, and said that since Rios and Gordón must have equal authority, it was for them to work out some arrangement between them.[19] A far more serious problem, however, was that the money that Juan Negrín, the Republican finance minister, had sent to Gordón and Rios to pay for the material had still not arrived.

In September Gordón has asked for $3 million which, as more offers came in, he increased to $9 million (£1,800,000) and on 9 October Prieto cabled to say that this sum had been sent in one remittance of $3 million and a second of $6 million. Rios in Washington had likewise asked for $7 million and this too had been authorized.[20] As usual, there being no direct route, the money was to go through the Chase National Bank in Paris and the Midland Bank in London before reaching the Bank of Mexico. After a fortnight of silence, Gordón discovered that the Midland Bank was refusing to transfer the $3 million because it was credited to 'Félix Gordón Ordax' instead of 'Félix Gordón Ordás'. Several days were lost while officials in Madrid pointed out that 'Ordax', the Catalan and more common spelling, and 'Ordás', the Castillian, were equally correct and that in any case 'Ordax' was the spelling on their diplomatic register. Moreover, 'Ordás' was merely his matronym and of minor importance since Gordón was the Spanish ambassador and could not be confused with anybody else. The Midland Bank did not budge and the order had to be made out once more and sent again, this time to the 'correct' name and to three other people at the embassy who could accept it should Gordón be absent, for

Cormidella), both of New York. The last is probably Anthony Cornudella, who with his wife, Martha, ran a print shop at 23 East 10th Street. Sanz's telegram was wrongly decoded as '200 Curtiss', a quantity so improbable that Prieto rejected it out of hand.[17]

Gordón had telegraphed Vayo to say that, although many of the deals had fallen through for lack of money, he still had the chance to buy considerable quantities of rifles, machine-guns, artillery pieces and aircraft, including 'fifty modern fighters,* if money arrived quickly. Vayo replied, 'This seizing on the detail of "Ordax" instead of "Ordás" is a typical example of how most European banks are now sabotaging our war effort', and Negrín sent a telegram to say that 'sabotage and boycott have now reached almost unimaginable limits'.[21] The Nationalist attack on Madrid and the consequent flight of the Republican government to Valencia during the night of 6 November caused further delay, which was extended by the silence of the Midland Bank in response to Republican enquiries as to why the money had not reached its destination, and it was not until 21 November that Gordón learnt that the Midland Bank was claiming that it could not send the money because the Bank of Mexico had refused to accept an order for so large a sum while it was made out to more than one person. Yet when Gordón asked the directors of the Bank of Mexico for an explanation, they told him that they most definitely had not refused; nor could they have done, for the Midland Bank had never been in touch with them. Seven weeks had now passed since the $3 million should have arrived, and five weeks since the $6 million: there was nothing for it but to start all over again. This time the money was sent through the BCEN (Banque Commerciale de l'Europe du Nord), the Soviet bank in Paris, with the result that the $3 million arrived on 25 November and the $6 million on the 30th.[22]

Similarly in Washington, Rios, who had been waiting for money almost since his arrival on 6 October, received the first half of his $7 million on 16 November and the second on the 25th. His troubles did not end there, however. Joseph P. Larkin, the vice-president in charge of European affairs at the Chase National Bank, which was owned by Rockefeller and was later renamed the Chase Manhattan Bank, refused to allow Rios to open an account and tried to force the Spanish government to withdraw its account from the Paris branch. After many heated arguments, Rios was able to place the money in Riggs's National Bank in Washington and immediately authorized the transfer of $2 million to Rafael Méndez, an official of the Republican finance ministry whom Negrín had sent, with

---

* There not being any, let alone fifty, modern fighters available in the USA at this time, Gordón was probably referring to the fifty as yet unbuilt Grumman GE-23s for which secret negotiations between Sanz and the Canadian Car and Foundry Company of Montreal had begun in September (see below, p. 222). They were not fighters but were advertised as such. The other material included 24 3 in. artillery pieces 'complete with park and reserves', 16 anti-aircraft machine-guns, 70 Lewis machine-guns, 20,000 new Springfield rifles (.300) and 100 million cartridges, none of which were bought for lack of money. (The list is in Gordón, p. 711.)

Luis Prieto (Indalecio Prieto's son), to America as advisers to the embassy. Riggs's Bank, however, sent the money to the Wall Street branch of the Chase Bank, which refused to allow Méndez to transfer it into a current account on which he could draw. The cashiers explained that 'for political reasons' they could do no more than give him a receipt. With the help of American supporters of the Spanish Republic he was able two days later to open an account at the Amalgamated Bank, which handled the accounts of the New York labour unions. Next morning, however, the bank told him with profuse apologies that it would have to close the account again and asked him to return his cheque books, for the Chase Bank had blocked the money, which it still held. Eventually, he was able to obtain cash only by buying US treasury bonds, which the Chase could not refuse to allow him to do, then selling them and storing the cash in a safe deposit box, but this, of course, meant that he had to spend part of the money in the process. Thus it was not until 15 December that he was in possession of cash which should have been available eight weeks before and was now rather less than had been calculated to meet the contracts.[23]

23

The Manhattan Purchases

WHEN IT APPEARED that the Vultee aircraft might have to be abandoned for lack of money, Gordón turned for help to Lt.-Col. Roberto Fierro Villalobos, the recent director-general of Mexican Aviation, who was the most enthusiastic of the Mexican officers that were helping him[1] and, since a record-breaking flight from New York to Mexico City in June 1930 in the white-painted Lockheed Sirius *Anahuac* (Aztec for 'Land of Herons'), a national hero.[2]*

In Mexico, a country of primitive roads and few railways, there were already numerous small airlines serving as bus routes to take miners and such to and from their places of work over otherwise impassable mountain ranges, deserts and jungles; indeed, the proportion of the population that travelled daily by air was probably higher in Mexico than in any country in Europe or even in the United States itself.[3] Many of those who managed or flew these routes, such as Francisco Sarabia, Carlos Panini or 'Pancho Pistolas' ('Pistol Pete', or Charles Baughn) were extraordinary characters who, had they been sailing yachts or paddle-steamers or riding pack-horses instead of flying aeroplanes, could have stepped from a novel by Joseph Conrad.

Fierro put Gordón in touch with Antonio Díaz Lombardo, who had recently bought Aeronaves de México, today the great airline Aeroméxico, to fly parties of wealthy American holiday-makers from Mexico City to the new Pacific coast resort at Acapulco, which he was helping to develop and which was then just beginning to become fashionable. In order to break the monopoly on air routes between the United

---

* The *Anahuac* was indeed one of three Lockheed aircraft, the other two being a Vega and an Orion, which Fierro, who had mortgaged his house to raise the money, bought and resold without profit to the Republicans. They were embarked on the Spanish ship *Sil*, which docked at Santander on 13 January 1937. In the same cargo were 2,000 Mexican Mauser 7 mm rifles, 8 million cartridges, 100 Mendoza machine-rifles and 24 guns, types unspecified, with 15,000 shells.

States and Mexico then held by Pan American Airways and its subsidiaries, Lombardo wanted to fly tourists directly in from Laredo, Texas, and to do this needed something more substantial than the eight small air taxis of his present fleet. Gordón therefore proposed that, if Aeronaves would act as the nominal buyer of the aircraft that the Republicans wanted, Lombardo would be given the two or three modern aircraft he required for the new service. This would also leave Aeronaves with more money for its coming struggle with Pan American and once again the forces of socialism and free-booting capitalism would join in pragmatic alliance to the benefit of both. Lombardo agreed and D. Morgan Hackman, an American trader living in Mexico, sent a telegram to Frank Ambrose, a Long Island aircraft dealer, instructing him to buy not only the Vultees but all the aircraft possible, preferably in lots of twenty so that wholesale prices could be negotiated. Ambrose would receive a $5,000 flat-rate commission on every aeroplane plus the $500 fee he would need to register as an arms exporter* and would therefore earn $100,000 on each deal of twenty planes. 'A million dollars gives a man a thick skin', he declared, 'and for this kind of money I'd risk everything short of going to jail.'[4] His zeal, however, was not put to the test.

In the State Department, as in the British Foreign Office, there existed precisely among the officials that were most directly concerned with Spanish affairs a bias against the Spanish Republic in general and the Popular Front in particular. This was true especially of James Dunn, chief adviser on European affairs, who supplied Cordell Hull, the Secretary of State, with the information upon which Hull himself based his advice to the President. It cannot be said, therefore, that the picture of Spain that Roosevelt received was impartial. Indeed, Dunn remained on close terms with Calderón, the Spanish ex-ambassador who had joined the Nationalists, and held weekly secret meetings with Juan de Cárdenas at the Ritz Carlton Hotel in New York.[5] Joseph C. Green, whose job as the chief of the Office of Arms and Munitions Control in the State Department was to see that the Neutrality Acts were enforced, was a friend of Dunn's and no admirer of the Spanish Republic but nevertheless a professional bureaucrat who played by the book. When Babb had applied for a licence to export the Vultees via T. H. Chamberlain in London to the Office Général de l'Air in Paris, Green had, despite information that the OGA had already supplied aircraft to the Republicans, been unable to find legal grounds for refusal.[6] This time, however, the country was

---

* Under the Neutrality Acts all arms dealers were required to register at the newly established Office of Arms and Munitions Control at the State Department, pay a fee of $500 and submit detailed lists of their sales to foreign buyers, with valuations, before they could receive export licences.

Mexico, not France, and when Ambrose applied for licences to sell to Aeronaves Green objected that it was impossible that a small Mexican airline could need or afford aircraft in such profusion and insisted that the company sign a guarantee that the machines would not soon be resold. Lombardo, sensing a conspiracy between Pan American and the State Department, refused, saying that no one had the right to tell a commercial airline when it should replace its equipment. Before the matter went any further, however, Ambrose's secretary accidentally enclosed, with a letter to Cyrus Smith at American Airlines, a carbon copy of an offer of aircraft to the Spanish Republican buying commission at 515 Madison Avenue, New York, and Smith had no choice but to break off negotiations for the time being.[7] Ambrose continued to look for aircraft, however.

Across the Atlantic the buying commission in Paris was making its own efforts, of which a few traces can be seen in the records, to obtain 'cover' for these and other aircraft. For instance, C. E. Paisley, a timber merchant in Gibraltar with companies registered in Casablanca, Cairo and Bucharest, wrote to Marcel Rosenberg, the Soviet ambassador at Madrid, to say that he could supply '10 A.D.C. Monoplanes' (i.e. Vultees, which were made by the Aircraft Development Corporation at Downey, Los Angeles) to the Spanish government. Since no one had briefed him, Rosenberg suspected Paisley to be a Fascist agent provocateur or, worse still, a Trotskyite wrecker, and decided to spike this plot by informing George Ogilvie Forbes, the British chargé d'affaires, who informed both the Foreign Office and the authorities at Gibraltar. Paisley, 'who carries a Canadian passport but is believed to be an Armenian or Greek whose real name is unknown', took the first boat to Tangier.[8] At about the same time W. E. Fitzgerald, a Birmingham arms dealer with an office in Mayfair, London, and a Dutchman named 'Peek'* called at the Greek war ministry in Athens and proposed a scheme by which the Greek air force would order one hundred aircraft from the USA, Britain and the Netherlands, transfer ninety of them to the Spanish government and keep ten as a gift. They too were disbelieved and reported to the British.[9]

When Rios received the second part of his $7 million on 25 November, he telegraphed Paris to suggest that as Babb had procured ten aircraft in addition to the Vultees, a new approach should be tried to a different group, and asked for his friend Dr Otero to be sent to America to create an agency similar to SFTA in France through which the buying commission could deal with vendors indirectly and thus more safely. It happened that the Paris commission had recently engaged, with the approval of Prieto, the services of Daniel Wolf, the owner of the N.V. Hunzedal shipping

---

* This was Hans Christiaan ('Han') Pieck, a Dutch–Swiss artist and Soviet agent based at The Hague, who is mentioned in most books about the Cambridge spies.

company at The Hague, as an intermediary in procuring foodstuffs and such and transporting them to Spain.* He had a brother, Rudolf Wolf, in New York, a commission agent and broker in burlap who ran a small 'one-girl' office on the eleventh floor of 80 Wall Street, owned an apartment on Manhattan and spent the weekends with his family at their home in Larchmont, which overlooked Long Island Sound. It was therefore arranged that Rudolf Wolf would buy the aircraft on behalf of his nephew Daniel for speculative resale in France. Otero then left for New York, accompanied by Martin Licht, as financial adviser, and Dr Leo Katz (see below, p. 222), and arrived on about 5 December (see addendum, p. 338).

The ten additional aircraft, seven Lockheed Orions and three Northrop Deltas, had been bought from various owners by Major R. G. Ervin, president of the P & E Corporation at 420 Lexington Avenue. Ervin had known Babb since his days as chief of the aviation division of Shell (US) in the early 1930s and their mutual friend James Haizlip, a former Shell company pilot, was already in Europe trying to sell Beechcrafts to Spain (see above, p. 71). Shell was partly a Dutch company and Daniel Wolf had contacts within it. On 23 November Ervin called on Joseph Green at the office of arms control to say that he was in a deal with Babb to sell ten aircraft in Europe, but when he admitted that their destination might be Spain, 'Green read him the law etc.'[10] A week later Green received a visit from Brigadier Richard Coke Marshall, a retired army construction officer (but, despite having the same unusual middle name, Coke, no relation to General George C. Marshall), and his attorney, Julius Rosenbaum, and was told that Ervin had sold the aircraft to Rudolf Wolf, who needed licences to export them to the Hunzedal company at The Hague. Green became suspicious, however, when Rosenbaum said that the planes would be shipped direct to Le Havre instead of Rotterdam, since they were to be resold in France; but while Rosenbaum was reading aloud a sworn affidavit from the Hunzedal agent in New York, which guaranteed that the planes were going only to France, Green received a telephone call from Sumner Welles, the Assistant Secretary of State, who said that he had just been called by Hall Roosevelt, the President's brother-in-law, to say that Wolf was a friend of long standing, that he was certain that the true destination of the aircraft was France (Hall Roosevelt was well known in

---

* Hunzedal specialized in shipping timber. C. E. Paisley was a timber-merchant. Pieck, with connections in England, was based at The Hague, as was Krivitsky; indeed, the two knew each other and worked together. Fitzgerald, Paisley, T. H. Chamberlain (mentioned in British aeronautical magazines of the time as a 'flying commercial traveller') and J. D. Hewett, the London agents through whom the OGA was to have bought the Vultees, all met in the Hotel Majestic, Paris, on 29 December 1936 to discuss the supply to Spain of 500 Fordson trucks via Iran (FO 351/20831 E 81, 161, 318, 435 to 3211).

the French aviation world) and hoped that Mr Wolf would be extended every courtesy, adding that 'he also had great confidence in the Dutch airplane manufacturer Mr Fokker.'[11] Green was at a loss to understand what Anthony Fokker had to do with any of this.

The story went back to 1934, when Fokker, having secured the European concession to sell Douglas DC-2s, had involved Elliott Roosevelt, the President's son, in a shady deal to sell fifty to the USSR. The deal had collapsed when a congressional inquiry tried to discredit the President as a profiteer and relations between Fokker and the Roosevelt family had become strained.[12] Fokker's European sales of DC-2s had included five to the Spanish airline LAPE (which, he told a shocked Nye Committee, had required a certain amount of bribery[13]), of which the last had been delivered illegally in September 1936 after the outbreak of the civil war, and in October 1936 he had secretly contracted to build twenty-five Fokker G.1s for the Spanish government and granted licences for the Republicans to build fifty fighters and twenty-five light bombers in Spain (see below, p. 209). In November he had returned to America, where he now spent most of each year. Fokker knew everyone in the small Dutch aviation world, where Daniel Wolf was well known, and was probably alerted to the Rudolf Wolf transaction by the Hunzedal agent in New York, A. H. Couwenhaven. Seeing a chance to reopen friendship with the Roosevelts, he approached Hall Roosevelt, Elliott's uncle and Eleanor Roosevelt's younger brother. Hall, though unstable and an alcoholic, had the same generous heart as his sister, who had always protected him, and shared her passionate conviction that the Spanish Republic was the victim of a tragic injustice.

On 4 December Marshall,* Rosenbaum and Wolf called at the office of arms control to apply to export the nineteen aircraft. Green pointed out that in recent months several parties had tried to buy the Vultees and in each case the Spanish government had obviously been behind the attempt. Wolf produced another sworn affidavit from Hunzedal, a company

---

* In October 1938 Hall Roosevelt, who in June had tried a frankly hare-brained scheme to supply a hundred aircraft to Republican Spain, and Brigadier Marshall applied yet again for licences to export twenty-two Bellanca 28B light bombers recently completed and being held at Wilmington, NC (Howson, p. 52). On being told that previous attempts to sell these and other machines to Spain had been blocked and the persons concerned were liable to prosecution, Marshall suddenly exploded in a show of indignation: he had had no idea that even the Wolf shipment aircraft had had a Spanish connection and he certainly had no intention of breaking the law. Protesting that he had been deceived by Hall Roosevelt, he stormed out of the room (Cordell Hull Papers, 'The Morgan-Green Report', p. 143, in the Library of Congress). Yet the Castillo report shows a Republican payment to 'M. R. C. Marscha. J' of $105,000 (£21,000), presumably his commission on the Wolf and Bellanca deals (Archivo del Ministerio del Aire, Villavicios a de Odón, Exp. 196, p. 2).

which, he said, was part of his family business. The aircraft were to be sold in France to the highest bidder, and if that should turn out to be an agent for the Spanish Reds, the French authorities would take care of it. More impressed by this reasoning than by Hall Roosevelt, Green granted the licences next day. Hall Roosevelt rang again to thank him. That night Wolf celebrated with Babb in a restaurant, but on the way home, as a British Foreign Office memorandum rather heartlessly put it, 'fell down dead in the street, to the great delight of the State Department'.[14] On the Monday Babb asked Green to cancel the licences so that the planes could be put straight back on to the market. There followed a rather unseemly scramble as various aircraft dealers tried to snap up the machines in order to sell them to the Spaniards at higher prices (see addendum, p. 338).

While attending to her husband's funeral and all the other matters arising from the sudden death of the head of a large and fairly wealthy family, Janet Wolf energetically formed another company, Rudolf Wolf Inc., registered as an arms exporter and retrieved all but three of the aircraft: a Lockheed Orion, bought from TWA, which had crashed on its way to New York, and two Deltas bought by Robert Cuse, who reappears in the next chapter. Babb replaced them with three Consolidated Fleetsters, high-wing 'parasol' monoplanes, which TWA gladly sold in order to get rid of their last single-engined passenger planes. As it happened, however, TWA had already promised them to Condor Airlines, a small company founded in August by Frank Flynn to carry freight up and down the California coast. Without these Fleetsters, Condor Airlines promptly folded and Flynn sent a furious telegram to Green denouncing Babb as a Communist agent. For the first time, too, the newspapers, probably alerted by Flynn himself, became interested and began to print stories of how scores of modern aircraft, convertible into bombers, were being smuggled out of America to 'Red Spain'.[15]

Janet Wolf's nineteen aircraft were loaded aboard three ships by Christmas Eve – in the nick of time, for on Monday 28th the New York dockers went on strike. Moreover, next day almost every newspaper carried a story on its front page that Robert Cuse, a 'new Jersey junk dealer', had been granted licences to export 18 aircraft and 411 aeroengines, valued at $2,777,000, directly and openly to the Spanish loyalists. With all attention focused on this scandal, the three ships sailed from New York unnoticed by the press.*

---

* The three ships were chartered by the Barr Shipping Corporation. The *Waalhaven*, carrying seventeen aircraft, and the *American Traveller*, carrying two Vultees, sailed on 29 December. The *President Harding* sailed on the 31st. On board were the wings of the Northrop Delta, and among her passengers were Clell Ernest Powell, a test pilot, Jack A. Martin, a Vultee engineer, and Mr Couwenhoven, the Hunzedal representative.

24

'These Deadly Weapons of War'

WITH LITTLE INFORMATION and no photographs to go on, newspaper reporters rushed to interview Robert Cuse at his Vimalert Company address, which turned out to be not a scrapyard but an ugly factory in the dingiest part of Jersey City. A youth opened the door a few inches, held up a wooden bar menacingly and shouted, 'Whatever you ask, I'm goin' to say "No" to it, see? So go ahead and ask questions!' His boss, who was 'always flyin' away someplace', would be back in a day or two and they'd know him because he was 'short, fat, bald and clean-shaven'.[1]

In fact, Cuse was over six feet tall, broad-shouldered, square-faced, thick-haired and wore a moustache and was thus able to enter and leave his factory undetected during the next few days. According to the pro-Franco Hearst newspapers, he was really Alexander Sjasin, a Latvian who had never legally changed his name since arriving in the USA in 1914 and had been engaged in questionable deals with the Soviets since 1925.[2] According to Cuse himself during an interview in 1973, his real surname had been Kuze (pronounced 'Koozah'), but the immigration officer had mistranscribed the Cyrillic on his passport, Latvia then being part of the Russian empire, and he had been stuck with it ever since. His father had been a wealthy Latvian, his mother a Baltic German and, after some trouble with the Czar's police, she had sent him to live with her relatives in Berlin. Soon tiring of their 'strutting about, toasting the Emperor and smashing glasses in the fireplace etc.', he emigrated to the United States and during the Great War made a good living from the then new technique of electric welding. A gifted though self-taught engineer, he founded the Vimalert Company in 1925, specializing in converting surplus Liberty aero-engines for marine use, his chief customers being the US Coast Guards, who installed them on their fast launches for anti-rum-running patrols during Prohibition, the rum-runners themselves and Amtorg, the Soviet trading agency in New York.[3]

At that time Amtorg was staffed largely by White Russian emigrés who had been appointed by the Soviets on the assumption that such 'bourgeois riff-raff' would know more about American business practices then Communists. It soon became evident that they knew little about American or any other business practice, but when the young zealots sent from Moscow to reform the agency proved to be even less knowledgeable, the White Russians were left in place. The president's secretary, for instance, was a reactionary Russian countess drawing a salary, astonishing in those days, of $15,000 a year.[4] Cuse steered through these shoals of intrigue with skill and gained the trust of the Soviet government by never pretending ideological sympathy with Marxism, by never offering bribes and by always delivering on time. He regarded the Soviet system as 'the most outrageous and inefficient example of state capitalism the world has ever seen'. However, when talking in 1973, he defended without qualification Stalin's massacre of the Red Army high command. He had known Marshal Tukachevsky and several officers in his entourage well and grown to like them; nevertheless, he believed that they were becoming a law unto themselves and that if Stalin had not eliminated them, they would have eliminated him and set up a military dictatorship.[5]

During a visit to Paris in September 1936, Cuse ran into Basil W. Delgass, a former president of Amtorg who in 1930 had given a wealth of information about its activities to a congressional committee investigating Communism in America and had gone into hiding to escape the vengeance of the NKVD. Now, having become a French citizen with a new name, 'Benjamin Mirott', he was inexplicably restored to favour by the Soviets and was helping to organize the supply of arms to Spain. The Republicans, Mirott said, needed planes badly and Cuse was in a position to buy them in America.[6] The proposal was sent to Prieto and, as soon as it was approved,[7] Cuse returned to New York at the beginning of October with a letter authorizing Amtorg to furnish him with the necessary cash. As this was in British bank notes, Cuse was instructed to go to a Los Angeles bank to change them into dollars. On the way he visited Cyrus Smith at the American Airlines headquarters in Chicago and offered to buy the Vultees for a price higher than Babb's, but when he admitted that the aircraft might be sent to Spain from Mexico, Smith said he was not interested. Cuse then laid a large wad of notes on the desk, but Smith said that as American Airlines traded only in dollars, there was no point in further discussion.[8] While waiting in Los Angeles for the money to be changed, Cuse was attacked in his hotel room by a gunman, whose detailed knowledge of the money suggested that he was either an Amtorg functionary or an NKVD agent who had decided to settle in the United States and needed capital in untraceable cash with which to establish a business. While they were talking, Cuse managed to jump up, disarm the gunman and throw him out.[9] From Los Angeles he flew to Mexico City, where he told Gordón that the Spanish government had granted him exclusive rights to buy aircraft in the United States and that he hoped to send them out through Mexico. Gordón asked for proof and, when Cuse was unable to show any, said that in any case nothing could be done until funds arrived from Madrid. Cuse thereupon offered to lend him $2 million on the spot, at which Gordón, suspecting a Fascist provocation, politely ended the meeting.[10]

On 19 October Cuse called at the office of arms control in Washington and told Green of a plan to export US aircraft to Mexico, which would enable the Mexicans to send an equivalent number to Spain. Green warned him of the 'moral embargo' and of the possible consequences to Cuse's business should the American aircraft subsequently be sold to the Spanish government.[11] Six weeks later, on 27 November, he visited Green again. He had had no luck with the Mexicans, who had no aircraft to sell apart from three civil machines found by Lt.-Col. Fierro and shipped off, with some arms, by the Spanish ambassador (see above, p. 172). The Spanish consul-general in New York had $5 million to spend on aircraft and had been instructed from Paris to deal exclusively through Cuse. He had heard that Cordell Hull, the Secretary of State, had told Rios, the Republican ambassador, that the government would have no objection to the purchase of arms in the USA by the loyalist government. Cuse intended to buy, therefore, a large number of civil aircraft, all second-hand and most in such a condition as to be almost useless to anyone but the Spanish loyalists. If he did not buy these machines for them, others would. What would be the attitude of the US government, therefore, if he applied for licences to export them directly to Spain or indirectly through a third country, which could easily be arranged? Green assured him that Rios must have misunderstood, the policy had not changed, and the 'moral embargo' applied equally to direct and indirect exports.[12]

By the middle of December Cuse had bought eighteen second-hand civil aircraft in various parts of the United States[13] and on Thursday the 24th applied for licences to export them, and the 411 engines, directly to Bilbao, the consignee being named as Francisco Cruz Salido, Prieto's private secretary.* There being no grounds for refusal as the law stood, Green said that the licences would be ready on Monday 28 December. This left Roosevelt and the State Department four days in which to consider a course of action. On the Monday, Green issued a statement to the press that the US government would propose a change in the law to

---

* Salido was the editor of Prieto's newspaper *El Socialista*. He took refuge in France at the end of the civil war but after the German Occupation he was arrested with other Republican leaders (including Luis Companys, Julián Zugazagoita and Juan Peiro) and handed over to the Franco government. They were all executed.

prevent the shipment as soon as Congress reconvened on 5 January. At his morning press conference President Roosevelt deplored Cuse's 'perfectly legal but thoroughly unpatriotic act' and R. Walton Moore, the Acting Secretary of State (Hull was abroad), compared Cuse to Mammon in Milton's *Paradise Lost*: 'the least erected Spirit that fell/From Heaven'.

Unaware of the copious quantities of arms and aircraft that the Spanish Republicans had been secretly offered in the United States since August (see above, p. 166, and below, pp. 189–91), Moore expatiated on the contrast between 'this shoestring scrap dealer' and the aircraft manufacturers, every one of whom had 'patriotically resisted the temptation to profit from the tragic events in Spain',[14] and later that day Leighton Rogers, the president of the Aeronautical Chamber of Commerce, told the press that 'American aircraft manufacturers are co-operating one hundred per cent in seeing that their products are not exported abroad contrary to the spirit of neutrality.'[15] Next morning Green received a file from Turner Battle, the Acting Secretary of Labour, as well as a letter from the American Legion, denouncing Cuse as a professed Communist who had once *worn red suspenders*, had dodged the draft during the Great War by claiming to be a Russian and was probably still a Red agent.[16]

Keeping out of sight, Cuse sent statements to the press defending his right as an American to do business with anybody, explaining that the aircraft were old civil machines unsuitable for conversion to military use and denying that he was unpatriotic. To replace the aircraft he had sold he would have to buy others, and reconditioning them would keep 1,500 men employed for a full year in a time of high unemployment. Such was the world situation that America would soon need skilled technicians like those to whom his company would provide training and experience.[17]

Behind the scenes he was being very active, for he had decided to ship the planes away, if possible, before the new law came into effect in six days' time. It happened that a Spanish Republican cargo vessel, the *Mar Cantábrico*, lay at Pier 35, at the bottom of Coffey Street, Brooklyn, where she had been taking on food and clothing donated by Save Spain committees in America. The loading had been halted by the strike, which grew more serious as violent clashes at the dock gates and in the neighbouring streets broke out between the dockers and gangs of strike-breakers hired from organized crime by the boss of the dockers' own International Longshoremen's Association, Joe Ryan, who was accused of taking bribes from the dock owners and port authorities, and most of the supplies were still piled on the quay. The captain of the *Mar Cantábrico*, José Santamaría, agreed to embark the aircraft, and accordingly the eighteen planes were flown in from their various places – a twin-engined Lockheed Electra, bought from the May Co. department store chain in San Francisco, allegedly breaking the transcontinental speed record in the process, though the feat was not officially recorded – and landed at North Beach airport, Queens (the present La Guardia airport). Calls went out for volunteers and soon several score, including a party of New York anarchists, joined the dockers that had been granted a special dispensation to load this one ship, and began to work round the clock. By Tuesday 5 January, a cold and drizzly morning, two planes had been stowed safely in the hold and six others, in huge pinewood crates, were waiting on Merritt-Chapman lighters alongside to be hoisted aboard.[18]

In Washington, the 75th Congress reconvened and Roosevelt asked the Senate to add a joint resolution to the Neutrality Act to cover 'the unfortunate civil strife in Spain', this being judged the quickest way to force through the legislation. The rest of the day was spent in debating what form the resolution should take and the next day in debating the resolution itself. The Senate passed it quickly, by eighty votes to none. In the House of Representatives, chairman Sam McReynolds warned that this was 'a race between Congress and the people who want to send these deadly weapons of war to Spain'. Only one Representative, John T. Bernard of Minnesota, opposed the resolution and, hoping to prolong the debate until the Mar Cantábrico was outside territorial waters, kept it going by raising technical objections and then speaking without a stop.

By the end of the morning eight aircraft had been loaded, four in the holds and four lashed down crosswise on the decks.* Since dawn stevedores and volunteers had formed a human chain up the gangplanks to pass cartons of tinned food, bandages and bags of flour from hand to hand while customs officials had done what they could to hinder them by opening boxes in search of contraband and demanding that this or that stencilled marking should be obliterated. A group of reporters climbed aboard and were forced off again by angry Spanish sailors, who shouted, 'You have no right on Spanish territory! You all have full bellies, like Morgan and Rockefeller! Get off this deck!'[19] Shortly after noon Captain Santamaría, seeing that no more aircraft could be loaded without rearranging the cargo, gave orders to cast off. Tugs pulled the Mar Cantábrico out into the harbour and she headed for the open sea. Ten aircraft and all but one of the aero-engines were left behind.[20] She had hardly reached the Buttermilk Channel, however, when she was ordered to stop. A coast guard cutter drew alongside and two aircraft of the coast guards and New York City police circled low overhead, soon joined by half-a-dozen more, carrying reporters and photographers. Two American pilots, Bert Acosta

---

* A Lockheed Electra and a Fairchild 91 at $60,000 each; two Northrop Deltas at $30,000 each; three Vultee V1-As, second-hand, at $35,000 each, and one new Vultee V1-A at $40,000. The prices, especially for the Vultees, were high and it is not certain that the sums actually paid were not higher.

and Gordon Berry, who had served briefly in the Republican air force and were now in Paris, had telephoned a New York attorney to issue a writ of damages against the Spanish government, which, they claimed falsely, owed them back pay, and the attorney had seen that this might be a way of detaining the ship until the resolution became law. After an hour or so Harry Durning, the port controller, ruled the writ inapplicable and the *Mar Cantábrico* weighed anchor and made for the three-mile limit as fast as her engines could drive her. She was clear by 4.30 p.m., the news was telephoned to Washington, Representative Bernard stopped in mid-sentence and the resolution was passed 411–1. By then, Vice-President John Garner had gone home and the Spanish Embargo Act consequently did not become law until 8 January. Captain Santamaría would thus have had ample time to load all the aircraft and the rest of the cargo besides.

The *Mar Cantábrico* sailed to Veracruz, where Gordón had her loaded with an additional cargo of assorted Mexican arms and munitions. Since, however, her departure from Veracruz had been reported by local Nationalist sympathizers, the Portuguese navy was able to track her course across the Atlantic and pass the information to the Nationalists. It is possible too that there was an attempted mutiny by some of the crew, which was put down, for as she approached the Cantabrian coast she broke radio silence by sending incomprehensible messages.[21] The cruiser *Canarias* intercepted her, put a prize crew on board and escorted her to El Ferrol, the Nationalist naval base and General Franco's birthplace in Galicia. Despite a plea for clemency from the Portuguese government, which probably was sent too late, Captain Santamaría, ten members of the crew and five Mexican passengers were executed and the rest of those on board sentenced to life imprisonment with hard labour.[22] In July and August 1936, before leaving for America, the *Mar Cantábrico* had been used as one of the prison-ships in Valencia harbour and, in view of the number of naval officers who had been shot for pro-rebel sympathies while held on these ships, she had been marked down for retribution should she ever fall into Nationalist hands.

The Spanish Embargo Act was welcomed by the British and French governments, while General Franco declared that Roosevelt had 'behaved like a true gentleman'. Praise came too from Mussolini, who at that moment was busy preparing the dispatch to Spain of the 250 aircraft of the Aviazione Legionaria and several infantry and motorized divisions. The Germans expressed their appreciation in a more restrained manner:

> Cuse's scheme has understandably aroused indignation all over America. It is noticeable how the US government has not endeavoured to hush the matter up, but has laid it openly before the public and asked them for their decision . . . This sequel stands in contrast to the methods of certain other countries, where lip service is paid to Non-Intervention, but actually intervention continues.[23]

25

Nine Million Dollars

AT THE END of October 1936 Major Melendreras and Sergeant
Corral were transferred to Mexico City to establish a liaison
between Gordón and the Spanish Republican purchasing commission at 515 Madison Avenue, New York. As soon as Gordón received his $9
million, therefore, they set off on a tour of American airfields and airports
to buy every machine available and pay in cash as they went. By the end of
December, they had bought twenty-eight civil aircraft, of which nineteen
had been flown to Mexico.[1] Since there was no time, or because it was
inadvisable, to apply for export licences or even tourist permits, the majority were flown over surreptitiously by Fritz Bieler, a German adventurer
and friend of Lt.-Col. Roberto Fierro, or by Cloyd Clevenger, an American
who had worked in Mexico for years and recently become Gordón's personal pilot. Other pilots were hired from among those who could always be
found hanging about the airfields looking for employment. The points of
departure were San Antonio, Texas, and Calexico, California.

Meanwhile, Gordón tried to revive some of the deals that had fallen into
abeyance for lack of money and was already excited by the chance to
obtain nearly a hundred aircraft altogether, as well as tanks, artillery,
machine-guns, rifles and ammunition. He intended, and had received permission, to go to Washington, when he had a free moment, in order to
confer with Rios and to see to one or two projects requiring his personal
attention. The most impressive of these was a proposal by Richard Dinely,
an ex-major of the Marines who ran Consolidated Industries Inc., a
'dummy' company in San Francisco through which arms and munitions
manufacturers conducted sales with which they did not want their names
to be publicly associated. Dinely offered 47 aircraft, 1,000 machine-guns,
7,000 rifles and 40 million cartridges. The aircraft included six Vultee V11-
GB attack bombers built for China which, he said, the Chinese were
willing to relinquish at the right price. Melendreras inspected the bombers
at the factory at Downey, Los Angeles, and gave his enthusiastic

approval.[2] When Dinely said that he intended to apply for export licences declaring the destination of the material to be Republican Spain, however, Gordón refused to agree, pointing out that this would only provoke the US government to introduce new legislation which would jeopardize all the other deals he had in hand. Dinely backed down, a contract was signed on 28 December and Gordón paid him $5,000 in cash to cover immediate expenses. An hour or so after Dinely left to return to San Francisco and begin to collect the arms and aircraft, Gordón heard on a news bulletin of the Cuse affair and, aghast at what it portended, decided to go to Washington at once. Before leaving, he sent telegrams to Vayo and Prieto reporting his meeting with Cuse two months previously and asking for more information about this man, whose crude and insensitive action threatened to wreck all the Republican buying operations in the Americas.[3]

He left on 1 January in one of the aircraft smuggled across by Bieler, a Lockheed Electra, and hastily provided with a new Mexican registration, for he wanted to travel secretly and hoped that the landing of a Mexican-registered Electra, of which there were several, on an American airport would attract less notice than an ordinary commercial airliner. As an added precaution he took along his wife and young daughter, so that he could pretend they were on holiday for the New Year. Unfortunately, the airport at Brownsville, Texas, their first refuelling stage, was covered in fog, and Clevenger, preoccupied by the problem of landing in such conditions with a woman and child on board, forgot to lower the retractable undercarriage. The Electra was damaged, word of the accident reached the local newspapers and Gordón was obliged to continue the journey by train, surrounded by reporters firing questions at him. He was particularly worried by the fact that they all knew that he had received $9 million from Spain. Who had told them?[4]

After two days in Washington he flew to New York, where a cable from Vayo awaited him to say that apparently Cuse was employed by the Russians to handle an offer made to the Soviet government.[5] Then Rios telephoned to say that Dinely had followed Cuse's example and applied to export aircraft and arms valued at $4.5 million openly to the Spanish Republic. The information, Rios said, had come from the State Department and been phrased to imply that Dinely was not to be trusted. Indeed he was not. Having returned to the United States, Dinely had not begun to prepare the material but had gone to Washington and told Joseph Green at the arms control office that he had a contract to export $9 million worth of arms and aircraft to the Spanish Republic and that he would receive the full amount as soon as the licences were granted. Why, he asked, could Green not sign the licences and revoke them after the money had been paid? In that way, no one would do anything illegal and he would be the richer by $9 million.

Green, notwithstanding his low opinion of the Spanish Republic, was shocked and accused Dinely of trying to swindle a friendly government. Dinely replied that all he wanted was the $9 million not to violate United States policy, but if the State Department was so squeamish he would go ahead and ship the material anyway, and that was surely not what the State Department wanted. Green said that the licences would be ready on 5 January, the day when Congress was to reconvene and debate the change in the law to prevent the sale of war material to Spain. Meanwhile, his aeronautical advisers told him that some of the aircraft on Dinely's application did not exist and that it was unlikely that he had any of those that did exist in his possession. His prices, moreover, were ludicrously high. Green remembered that at an earlier date Dinely had been accused of swindling some Cuban revolutionaries, who had been planning to over-throw Batista's dictatorship, of $77,000 and accordingly sent his warning to Rios in the hope that it would at least dissuade the Spaniards from paying any money to Dinely.

While senators and representatives denounced Cuse and Dinely as 'unpatriotic merchants of death', Dinely spoke to the newspapers:

> What right does anyone have to call *me* unpatriotic? We got this business away from foreign nations and got nine million dollars into this country, where there is need of it. After we've been working on this deal for months, the President starts shooting off and the thing gets screwed up.

Asked why he spoke of $9 million when his licences covered only $4.5 million, Dinely said that $9 million was sitting in a New York bank that very moment to cover the costs of another deal he was working on. As for the forty-seven airplanes, if only Gordón were here in Washington, where he should be, so that payment could be made, they would all be in Mexico by tomorrow morning. 'I don't know why he's stalling now. Seems like a fine running around after all the work I've done on this deal.'[6]

On his way back to Mexico, Gordón had a last conference with Rios and his advisers Rafael Méndez and Luis Prieto, cancelled all pending deals and asked Dinely to return the $5,000. Dinely indignantly refused, saying that he had spent far more than that getting the airplanes ready and was now grievously out of pocket. In his memoirs Gordón lists Dinely's $5,000 as the only sum he had actually lost. It had been due to inexperi-ence, and he had never paid advances again.[7] Yet it does not seem that he ever realized the full scale of Dinely's imposture – 'one of the boldest swindles ever attempted by an American citizen upon a foreign govern-ment' was how Green put it – or how narrowly he escaped losing half the entire sum entrusted to him for the purpose of buying war material in the Americas.

Nor was Gordón ever able to obtain a clear explanation of why Cuse had acted as he did, though he suspected from the evasive replies of Méndez and Luis Prieto that there had been some kind of conspiracy and told them to their faces that if only they had kept him informed, he could have co-ordinated his plans with Cuse and the disaster would have been averted. Now, everything would have to be abandoned and the chances, once so promising, of procuring arms in the United States in future were negligible.[8]

When asked about this in 1973, Cuse replied that he had always regarded the *Mar Cantábrico* shipment as a one-off deal and that was all there was to it. A probable explanation is that Cuse had his company to consider and had no intention of antagonizing the US government, with whom he did most of his business and on whose goodwill he depended if he was to continue as an exporter of machinery. The government could not later accuse him of trying to play games with them if he stated openly that the aircraft were for Spain, and if that brought unfortunate repercussions on the Spaniards, that was their problem, not his. Meanwhile, at the Spanish embassy Rafael Méndez, a militant and aggressive character who later transferred to the security police, was becoming increasingly irritated by the civilized and gentle Rios, and in a letter to Negrín on 8 December, at which date he had only just heard of Cuse but had not met him, he wrote:

> Gordón works well, but don Fernando is the same as always, timid and ineffective. It strikes me that the only things that concern him are his personal relationships and not making an unfavourable impression so that, should we lose the war, he can stay on here as a professor in some university. He refuses to accredit me as a diplomat because (and this really takes the biscuit!) he says my activities might land him in trouble![9]

Between such temperaments as those of Méndez and Rios there is an unbridgeable gulf. Rios knew America and well understood the reasons for Roosevelt's 'moral embargo', but hoped that the president and the American people would sooner or later come to see the Spanish Civil War in its true light and change their attitude. Until then, as the ambassador of the legitimate government of Spain, he should do nothing to prejudice this outcome and certainly not countenance any crass behaviour from the likes of Méndez. To Méndez such caution seemed cowardice, and it is not impossible that, ignorant of America and exasperated by inaction, he privately advised Cuse to challenge the 'moral embargo' head-on and then, when the consequences of this blunder later became only too apparent, disclaimed all knowledge of the matter.[10]

Yet some of the deals whose loss Gordón lamented appear so dubious that perhaps it was fortunate for the Republicans that they were cancelled. It may be remembered, for instance, that six months before the civil war the Spanish government ordered eight Martin 139W bombers and acquired a licence to build forty-two in Spain, an order which the Germans alleged had been secured by bribery (see above, p. 31). The overall unit price worked out at a rather high $96,000, for it is always more expensive to build foreign aircraft under licence than to import them outright.[11] The Spaniards preferred to meet the extra cost, nonetheless, because production would provide the training and facilities needed to expand the Spanish aviation industry. In the spring of 1936, however, the Spanish government refused, for some reason, to make payment in dollars in New York and the order was cancelled. Then, after the outbreak of the civil war, Madrid cabled the Martin company to ask if the eight bombers might still be purchased and to offer to pay in cash if they could be delivered immediately, but the company, on the advice of the State Department, said it was impossible.[12] On 7 October Melendreras was told by 'an arms exporter named Humbert' that the Martin company would, after all, be willing to sell not eight but eighteen of these bombers. A Dutch commission now in America had made a bid for them but was haggling over the asking price and if the Spaniards acted quickly they could buy them for $110,000 each. Melendreras strongly urged Ríos and Méndez to accept, only to be told that nothing could be done until money arrived from Spain.[13] Had the deal gone further, however, the Spaniards would have discovered that the Martins had been ordered by the Dutch government in February and May, that the Dutch commission had come not to buy but to collect them and to propose a contract for twenty-seven more (eventually, they were to buy a total of 140, to the value of $8.5 million).[14] Since it is unlikely that the Glenn Martin company, an important supplier of aircraft to the US army and navy, would have been willing to jeopardize all this as well as entangle itself in deep trouble with both the Dutch and US governments, it is safe to assume that someone was attempting a confidence trick. There is no record of a 'Humbert' employed by the company or registered as an arms exporter at that time.[15]

Humbert's price of $110,000 each is curious, however, for it was also the price that the Soviets charged the Republicans for an SB Katiuska, which the Nationalists and almost everyone else called 'Martin Bomber'. As the Dutch were buying the Martins outright, the unit price was only $78,947.[16] It has been shown in a previous chapter that the $110,000 for an SB Katiuska represented a fraudulent overcharge of $27,925, that is to say 34% on each aircraft (see above, p. 149). The Russians did not work out their bills to the Republicans until December 1936. Could it be that when Melendreras gave the details to the Spanish embassy in October, someone passed them to the Soviet embassy, which passed them to Moscow, where it was decided that if the Spaniards were willing to pay $110,000 for a Martin bomber, they might as well pay the same for an SB Katiuska?

In November Gordón was visited by a 'world-famous gangster' who offered to supply fifty Martin bombers as well as large numbers of tanks, artillery pieces and other weapons. The deal would cost $6 million but no payment would be required until everything was safely aboard ship at Veracruz. Gordón was unable to conclude anything for lack of money, but when he visited New York in January, by which time the gangster was in prison for lottery fraud, he was sent word that the deal was still on so far as the gangster was concerned, for it could be organized just as easily from inside jail as from outside.[17] Gordón and Melendreras took the scheme very seriously, but it is hard to see how even the most powerful gangster could have had the resources to smuggle such quantities of material – the aircraft alone would have been packed in a hundred enormous crates of which fifty would have measured 50 ft × 30 ft × 12 ft – down to Mexico and to Veracruz undetected. The gangster could not have been Capone or Luciano, as both had been in prison since before the Spanish Civil War.

There were also two propositions to set up factories in Spain for the production of 300 modern military aircraft, though it should be noted that the agent for both was the American Armaments Corporation, whose ambiguous repute has already been mentioned. The first was made by a short-lived outfit called the Military Aircraft Corporation (MAC), a subsidiary of American Armaments, which was trying to raise finance to develop in more saleable form the celebrated Gee-Bee racers of the early 1930s. The plan was to produce in Spain fifty fighters, called 'VPs', and fifty observation aircraft, called 'VOs', but all that was really on offer were sets of drawings for experimental prototypes which had not yet been built, let alone tested, and Prieto rejected it out of hand.[18] Indeed, when a prototype, the MAC HM-2, eventually took to the air in 1938, it crashed on an early test flight, killing its pilot, and the company folded.[19]

The second offer came from the Seversky Aircraft Corporation at Farmingdale, Long Island, for whom American Armaments were the sales agents. Major Alexander Prokofieff de Seversky, like Igor Sikorsky a refugee from the Russian Revolution, had founded his company in 1931. His first product, the SEV-3 'Amphibian', was of advanced and innovative design, attracted much attention and broke several records, of which one still stands, and from it were descended the Seversky P-35 of the US Army Air Corps and a succession of fighters, of which the most famous was the Republic P-47 Thunderbolt of the Second World War.* In October 1936

---

* Seversky Aircraft changed to the Republic Aviation Corporation in October 1940. Alexander de Seversky was a tireless publicist for 'air-mindedness' and a prolific journalist, a role into which he was forced by his poor business sense and the consequent financial troubles of his company. He had no financial say in the affairs of Republic Aviation. In 1943 he wrote and took part in the Walt Disney propaganda film *Victory Through Air Power* and published a book of the same title.

American Armaments offered to divert to Spain three SEV-3WW amphibians destined for Colombia, but the offer was declined for lack of funds. This, however, inspired Seversky with the idea of building a factory in Catalonia for the production of a hundred single-seat fighters similar to the P-35 and a hundred two-seat observation aircraft, probably similar to the Seversky 2PA.[20] On 8 December Captain Agustín Sanz Sainz, having been recalled to active service, left for Spain with a party of American volunteers, among whom was Charles Koch, a Seversky engineer, who took with him plans and data to show to Prieto, the minister of marine and air. While awaiting a decision from his technical advisers, Prieto instructed Gordón to buy the original SEV-3 prototype, which flew to Mexico on 7 January 1937. Koch stayed on as a fighter pilot in the Republican air force. Sanz, who had achieved more than anyone else in the procuring of aircraft in the United States, was killed on 23 March during a Nationalist air attack on the airfield of Alcalá de Henares.

By then the Spanish government had been obliged to cancel the Seversky project, for it had become obvious that many of the vital components, such as engines, retractable undercarriages and variable-pitch propellers, would not be obtainable in the required numbers. Gordón was particularly disappointed by this, for, he said, had the project been carried through it would have broken the monopoly of the USSR as the sole purveyor of military aircraft to the Republicans and thereby checked the overweening ambitions of the Spanish Communists. Melendreras, who was unaware of the difficulties that the Republicans had experienced in transferring money as a result of the tactics of the banks and whose technical knowledge, although he was a pilot, was slight, wrote scathingly in his report of the failure of the government to send money on time and of the incompetence shown by its decisions to cancel these operations, which he attributed to the sloth, negative attitude and probable bad faith of Prieto and his advisers. His comments were taken up by the CNT Anarchists in the reports that they compiled in 1938 on the mismanagement and corruption of the arms-buying commissions, and used after the war to support their case that Negrín and Prieto had been guilty of nothing less than high treason, a charge repeated to this very day.[21]

Yet one wonders if even Seversky himself really believed that his scheme was practicable. The terms of the contract are not reassuring. The aircraft were not to be cheap, as Gordón and Melendreras had believed, for each single-seater was to cost $51,000, enough to buy a Spitfire two years later, and each two-seater $61,000. A total of $4 million was required in advance, which would not have been recoverable in the event of failure. The factories would have to be built, the work-force recruited and trained (Seversky boasted that the aircraft were designed to be constructable by illiterate peasants, which was utter nonsense) and all the materials and components smuggled in through the Nationalist blockade and the Non-Intervention controls that came into force in April 1937. Had everything gone smoothly, which it would not have done, it is unlikely that any aircraft would have been in service before the beginning of 1939, by which time they would have been obsolescent and easy prey to the newly arrived Messerschmitt Bf 109Es of the Condor Legion.[22]

There remained in North America only a project, initiated by Sanz, to build fifty Grumman biplanes in Canada, and another to build twenty-two light bombers, under the pretence that they were mailplanes for Air France, at the Bellanca factory in Wilmington, North Carolina. To Gordón in Mexico, there remained the twenty-eight assorted civil aircraft that had been brought across from the United States and were now crowded onto the airport at Veracruz, in expectation of a ship to carry them to France, from where, with luck, they could be flown to Spain.

26

Buying from the Enemy

O N 22 SEPTEMBER 1936 the *Bramhill*, a cargo steamer belonging to
Angel-Dalling of Cardiff, Wales, sailed from Hamburg carrying
several hundred tons of rifles, machine-guns, pistols and cartridges marked for delivery to the CNT, the Anarchist trade union, at
Alicante.* The shipping agent was Lessing AG of Cologne, Hamburg and
Lübeck. Her arrival and unloading at Alicante on 1 October were
immediately reported by HMS *Woolwich*, which happened to be in
harbour at the time, to London, where it caused astonishment at the
Foreign Office. As Walter Roberts minuted next day, this cargo had been
insured at Lloyd's with Foreign Office approval on 17 September for
delivery to Saudi Arabia and the Yemen; the declaration at Hamburg must
therefore have been false and the German government 'completely taken
in, since it can hardly have wished arms to go to the Spanish government!'[1]

The German government, to show that it had not been taken in,
reminded the British government that Hamburg had a Free Port area
outside German trade jurisdiction. The arms were not German but
Czechoslovakian, had been brought to the Free Port by a Swiss businessman before the outbreak of war in Spain and put in storage when his customer had been unable to pay for them. The German government
therefore had no powers to stop anyone who had bought them later from
exporting them wherever he wished.[2]

The Welsh anarchist Albert Meltzer describes in his autobiography
how a group of anarchists in London, assisted by a member of the CNT
from Barcelona, procured a quantity of rifles and machine-guns from a
Czechoslovakian manufacturer and sent them out from Hamburg to the
CNT. He was writing from memory forty years later, and according to his

---

* 19,000 rifles, 101 machine-guns, 28,650,000 cartridges, all 7.92 mm; 4,000 pistols,
500,000 pistol cartridges. The British reports put the total weight at 1,500 tons. The
real weight would have been about 840 tons, including the boxes.

story the ship was Irish, the consignee was 'General Franco', the destination was Bilbao and three shipments were sent before the Czechs tumbled to what was going on, informed the Non-Intervention committee and stopped further sales. Nevertheless, he would appear to have been thinking of the *Bramhill* incident, for I have found no trace of any other that fits. According to Meltzer, the Anarchists used the address of a huge international corporation in the attic of whose building in Soho Square Alf Rosenbaum, a Jewish tailor, had a workshop. When this violation of Non-Intervention was discovered, a Special Branch officer called at the workshop and, after a search, exclaimed, 'It looks as if a little Jew tailor has been making fools of us!' Rosenbaum, Meltzer and the others were threatened with prosecution, but heard no more. Some months later Rosenbaum received a 'substantial' cheque from Prague as his commission, plus a bonus for having enabled the company to top some preset export target. It happened that bailiffs were in his shop that very moment, but he refused to touch the money and gave it to finance the showing of the film *Storm Over Spain*.[3]

Yet the pride of the Anarchists at having fooled the British and German governments, both of whom were objects of nearly equal anathema to them, may have been mistaken. So too may have been the NKVD defector Walter Krivitsky, who, when relating his activities as an organizer of arms supplies to the Republicans, wrote, 'Such is the nature of the munitions trade that we even bought some arms in Nazi Germany ... The director of the German firm [in Hamburg] was interested in nothing but the price, the bank references and the papers of consignment.'[4]

It is true that in the Weimar years Hamburg Free Port had been a favourite transit base for arms manufacturers and dealers of all nationalities, as the Nye Committee hearings in Washington testify,[5] but since the advent of Hitler the practices of freedom, regardless of the legal status of the Free Port, had become increasingly hazardous. Moreover, since the end of July the aircraft, arms, equipment and men of *Unternehmen Feuerzauber* had been embarking for Spain, under the most elaborate precuations of secrecy, from quays that were only a few docks away. Abwehr and Gestapo agents were everywhere in the Free Port and not a pistol or cartridge, let alone a howitzer or shell, entered or left without their knowledge and the tacit consent of their superiors. It may be remembered that in August Lt.-Col. Riaño had been sent on a futile errand to buy arms and aircraft for the Republic in Germany and that at his first meeting with German officers in Berlin Admiral Canaris, the chief of the Abwehr, had been present. Usually, writers of history should not guess, but here the circumstantial evidence is so strong that I shall do so without apology. Canaris had spent years in Spain and had a better knowledge of Spanish politics than any other senior German commander. He was also wily and manipulative and I suggest that after Riaño's departure he, foreseeing an eventual clash between the Spanish Communists and Anarchists, decided that a limited supply of small arms to the CNT could help to push things in the desired direction, especially when it became known, as it did, that the arms had come from Nazi Germany. When the clash did occur in Barcelona in May 1937, one of the charges that the Communists reiterated against the Anarchists and the POUM, whom they accused of putting the interests of their own extremist social revolution before the interests of the Republic as a whole, was that their leaders had been in a conspiracy with the Fascists.

My conjecture is to some extent borne out by what happened next. Early in September, when Otero was looking for ships to bring the first consignments of arms sold by SEPEWE in Poland, Dr Marcovici-Kleja of the Société Européenne proposed, among other vessels, the *Philomelia*. After enquiring, Otero objected that the ship and her captain, Spiro Katepodis, had been at the centre of several scandals.[6] In 1932 the OGPU had hired Katepodis to assist in the kidnapping of Georges Agabekov, who had defected from the OGPU in the 1920s and revealed many of its secrets to the world. Agabekov had been lured to the port of Constanta, Romania, where Katepodis and his crew were to seize him, carry him aboard the *Philomelia* and take him to Odessa. The plot had been exposed, Katepodis had been imprisoned in Romania for six months and, when he had been released, the Russians had refused to pay him. In revenge, he had stolen a cargo of Soviet timber and tried to sell it in Egypt, only to be hauled before a Cairo court, deprived of the timber and fined.[7] No matter, Otero was assured, the *Philomelia* now had a different captain and was under completely new ownership, that of Pandelis, a highly respected Anglo-Greek firm in the City of London whose representative, Mr Newman, was the chief of the British chamber of commerce in Antwerp and would be handling the arrangements. With the position on the Madrid front rapidly deteriorating and no time for further delay, Otero accepted. A long chain of intermediaries, as insisted upon by Colonel Beck, the Polish foreign minister, was set up: PAM (Polska Agencja Morska, the marine counterpart to SEPEWE) in Gdynia, Willy Daugs in Berlin, Michel Rosenfeldt (a Soviet agent working under Krivitsky) at The Hague, Edgard Grimard in Liège, and Auxite (the shipping branch of the Société Européenne) and Edgar Brandt, the trench-mortar manufacturer and dealer, in Paris. The ostensible buyers were the government of Mexico, the provincial government of Szechuan, China, and Brandt himself. Brandt had been prohibited from selling modern trench-mortars directly to the Spaniards but had recently sold several hundred to the Poles. He therefore arranged that SEPEWE would sell one hundred of these to the Republicans, which he would replace immediately. All the material was to be delivered to Cartagena.[8]

There were sinister signs from the beginning. When the *Philomelia*, now renamed *Silvia*, arrived at Danzig on 16 September she did not load in four days, as agreed in the contract, but made a quick voyage to Gdynia. On her return, one of her holds was seen to be full of large crates, which the captain, who turned out to be Katepodis after all, explained were an ordinary commercial cargo to be dropped off on the way to 'Veracruz', his ostensible destination.[9] None of the SEPEWE material arrived at Danzig until 30 September except the trench-mortars, which M. Peyrethon, a French trade union official sent from Paris to enquire what was happening, found to be not the modern (M 1928) ones promised but 1917 models, many badly worn and all without their stands and aiming devices. This 'oversight' by SEPEWE was rectified and the *Silvia* set sail at last on 7 October, seventeen days late. Fearing the worst, the Spanish embassy in Paris – the buying commission was not yet functioning – ordered Katepodis to go to Bilbao instead of Cartagena. Ignoring this instruction, he sailed south until the *Silvia* was 'captured' by Nationalist ships in the Straits of Gibraltar.

After this calamity, the Republicans put a trustworthy 'cargo supervisor' on board every ship to prevent recurrences, but on 26 November the Swedish ship *Rona*, carrying ammunition, was 'captured' in the Bay of Biscay.[10] The third 'capture', in March 1937, was that of the *Allegro*, whose cargo was found to be bricks and rubble under a top layer of bales of cartridges.[11] During this period another ship belonging to Angel-Dalling, the *Yorkbrook*, made three trips from the Baltic to Bilbao and on two of them nearly all the arms were found, when unloaded, to be useless or sabotaged: cartridges without percussion-caps or the wrong size for the rifles, machine-guns without firing-pins or springs, aircraft-bombs without fuses, shell-cases filled with rags instead of explosives and field-guns with their carriage-axles broken. The weapons had been paid for by public subscription and the last occasion, on 12 March 1937, had therefore been particularly harrowing, for the *Yorkbrook* had been intercepted off the Biscay coast by the Nationalist cruiser *Canarias*. Three Basque armed trawlers in the vicinity had bravely gone to rescue her and, although they had succeeded, during the unequal battle two had been sunk.[12]

Of the various documents about these incidents, the most informative are an unpublished report on the *Silvia* in the archives of the Spanish foreign ministry and an Anarchist report on the *Silvia* and *Rona*, likewise unpublished, in the archives of the CNT.[13] The Anarchists identified the chief culprit in both cases as Captain Manuel Escudero, the first secretary at the Mexican legation in Paris, who had been sent to Poland at the request of Otero to supervise the loading of the ships that were to embark material bought from SEPEWE. In Warsaw he had been contacted by a Nationalist agent named Quibrache, or Quibrachán, and the two were said to have held 'scandalous orgies' in the Hotel Europejski. In Danzig he had ensured that material intended for other ships was loaded on to the *Silvia* and *Rona* and in December he had visited Berlin. Yet the Anarchists did not judge Escudero too harshly, but pointed out that his salary had been only 10,000 Ffr. (£95 or $475) a year and that his family in Mexico City, unable to pay the rent, were about to be evicted from their home. Nor were they especially critical of the fact that with the proceeds of his double-dealing he had bought, while in Germany, a Wanderer automobile for 52,000 Ffr. (£495 or $2,476), in which he had been seen driving around Paris. The most interesting detail of their report is that the mysterious crates that the *Silvia* had embarked at Gdynia had been brought there from Hamburg in three ships belonging to the Russ company.[14] Indeed, none of the authors of these reports seems to have noticed that the agents in all these episodes included Daugs and Veltjens in Berlin, Grimard in Liège and probably John Ball in London, that is to say the ring of arms dealers mentioned in Chapters 12 and 15. For her last voyage in March the *Yorkbrook* had been hired by A.B. Transport in Helsinki, of which Veltjens was one of the directors.[15] The bricks on the *Allegro* had been loaded at Gdynia and the bales of cartridges to conceal them brought, via Helsinki, from Lübeck, Germany, which was not even a Free Port.[16] Finally, when the Nationalists unloaded the *Silvia* they saw that whereas much of the material, which can be identified from the SEPEWE list as the Polish material, was in bad condition, the most important items – ten Schneider 75 mm field-guns with their limbers, 250 Maxim guns and 4,971 Mauser 7.92 mm rifles and carbines, and ammunition for all of these – were in good condition,[17] which, since these were the items from Hamburg, suggests that the suppliers knew they were to be diverted to Franco.

I would suggest the following hypothesis, therefore: that Canaris allowed the first lot of arms at Hamburg to go on the *Bramhill* to the Anarchists, for reasons already explained, and the second on the *Silvia* in the knowledge that it would go to the Nationalists; indeed, the rifles and machine-guns may have been those referred to by Krivitsky, for the dates fit and his agent Rosenfeldt is named as an intermediary in Araquistaín's unpublished report. Krivitsky may not have known what happened subsequently or, if he did, preferred not to mention it.*

---

* There may have been as well a connection with agents in England through Rosenfeldt or Han Pieck, another Soviet agent based at The Hague (see above, p. 174, and below, p. 216). When Rosenfeldt was tried in France for violating Non-Intervention (see below, p. 211), one of his associates was named as Podsnikov, the White Russian who, with Dickie Metcalfe, ran an arms-dealing business in Regent Street, London (see p. 317, n. 4). On 18 September 1936 the Marqués del Moral, a member of the Nationalist Junta in London, gave Special Branch a report in which 'A. Postiukon', a White Russian, was said to be leaving for Germany to negotiate an arms

The *Allegro* and *Yorkbrook* deceptions were almost certainly engineered by Veltjens, since they had Helsinki as a common transit point, and were planned acts of sabotage that would extract foreign currency from the Republicans in addition. The agent who bought the *Yorkbrook* cargoes was Captain Lezo Urrestieta, a brave and honourable Basque patriot who was, unfortunately, impulsive and not very astute.

We hear little more of Willy Daugs or Edgard Grimard after January 1937, when the Republicans handed over all Baltic purchasing to Daniel Wolf (see below, p. 223). Veltjens continued as a supplementary supplier to the Nationalists, sometimes through ROWAK, the official German company, and sometimes through hidden channels,[18] much of the material going out through Antwerp with no serious interference from the Belgian authorities. This allowed room for a certain amount of double-dealing. For example, the Spanish ship *Axpe Mendi*, having sailed from Antwerp on 2 April 1937, transhipped half her cargo of 10,500 rifles, in crates marked 'Dried Fruit', and 23,000 pistols, or 'Condensed Milk', on to the Greman ship *Carl Lords*, which delivered her half to Lisbon, where the arms were taken across the Portuguese frontier to Nationalist Spain.[19] More intriguing, however, is the supply of German arms to the Republicans through Greece.

On 4 August 1936, inspired perhaps by the example of General Franco, General Metaxas, the Greek premier, dissolved parliament, banned all political parties and established a dictatorship on the pretext of forestalling a 'Communist coup'. Being a monarchist, he allowed King George II to continue his precarious occupation of the throne and, as a Germanophile, Metaxas encouraged German investment, with the result that within three years Germany controlled 38% of Greek foreign trade. He had nothing but praise for Hitler's intervention on behalf of Franco's crusade to save Christian civilization and prohibited any reporting of the Spanish war, by press or radio, that suggested the slightest sympathy for the Spanish 'Reds'. He was not so enthusiastic, however, about Mussolini's intervention in Spain, where a resounding success might tempt the erratic Duce to embark on adventures elsewhere, such as an invasion of Albania. He had no wish, therefore, to see the Italians oust the British as the dominant naval power in the Mediterranean, for the most promising asset that Greece possessed was her large and rapidly growing

---

deal for the Republicans. An associate of his was named as another Russian, 'A. Ignatieff', who had an office in Shell Mex House in the Strand (PRO, FO 371/20577 W 11975). According to Metcalfe, 'Postiukon' was an alias used by Podsnikov who, he told me, would never have sold arms to the Republicans unless it were to cheat them. MI6 or SIS, the British intelligence service, had an office in Shell Mex House, which may explain how Special Branch traced Alf Rosenbaum so quickly. Moral would hardly have been on the 'need to know' list.

merchant marine. A considerable proportion of this, however, was jointly based in Piraeus and London and, to reassure the British, Metaxas saw to it that Greece signed the Non-Intervention agreement on 27 August.

Nevertheless, the Metaxas regime faced the same problem as that facing the *Sanacja* regime in Poland, that is to say, a constant shortage of foreign currency reserves. Just as the sale of the Fokkers by British Airways alerted the Poles, so the use of ships, owned by Greek firms in London, to carry arms from the Baltic to Republican Spain alerted the Greeks to the opportunities opened by the Spanish fighting. In contrast to Franco, the 'Reds' had the cash to enable the Greek companies to raise their freight charges until the cost of a single cargo of arms would equal the value of the ship herself.[20] The answer to the question of where the arms would come from was provided by Podromos Bodosakis Athanaidis, one of those buc-caneering traders of genius who appear so frequently in the history of the eastern Mediterranean. Born of Greek parents in about 1885 he had, like Sir Basil Zaharoff before him, ascended out of the poverty and ignorance of a mud-walled Turkish village to achieve wealth, culture and an aristo-cratic German wife by the age of thirty-five. Ruined by Ataturk's expul-sion of the Greeks from Turkey in 1921, he gained a second fortune in Athens by short-selling drachmas until the collapse of one of his shadier operations made him as notorious as Stavisky in France or, in recent times, Nick Leeson in London. Tougher than either of these, however, he was neither murdered nor gaoled but, despite the enmity of the king, survived by keeping a low profile.

Shortly after the signing of the Non-Intervention agreement he sug-gested to someone in the government that the state buy the Rheinmetall Fabric Borsig, an old gunpowder factory near Piraeus which was owned by the giant Rheinmetall group of arms-makers in Germany, and that the government appoint him as managing director and major shareholder, despite the fact that he had no experience of industrial production or the arms trade. The idea was accepted, perhaps in exchange for a bribe, and while this was being done Bodosakis went to Paris in September and secured a contract to supply 5 million cartridges of the much needed 7 mm calibre to the Spanish government. Meanwhile, the factory was renamed the Poudrérie et Cartoucherie Hellénique ('Greek Powder and Cartridge Company'). On 22 September a royal decree prohibited the export of arms or munitions to Spain. At the same time the Greek government pro-vided the funds for Bodosakis to import modern ammunition-making machinery from Germany, which enabled him to accept a second order for 20 million cartridges from the Republicans.[21] It is inconceivable that any of this could have been done without the active, though covert, support of General Metaxas, who could always counter an accusation of greed by explaining that he was patriotically defending Greece against Italian domination, or an accusation of political hypocrisy by pointing to the empty coffers of the Greek treasury, which required filling by any means to hand.

The story of Greek arms shipments to the Republicans has been barely hinted at in histories of the Spanish Civil War, but since Dr Thanasis Sfikas, who had done some pioneering research in the Greek archives, is preparing a book about the subject I shall leave the telling of it to him. Suffice it to say that although, as I write, the exact quantity of ammunition and some other material sold to the Republicans is not known, the profit to the Greek treasury is estimated to have been about £1,200,000, or $6 million.[22] What is less clear is how much material was actually delivered, for some of the cargoes were disembarked at Marseille in July 1937 and may not have been allowed to cross into Spain until the opening of the frontier between 17 March and 13 June 1938. The use of Greek ships to carry arms from Greece to Republican Spain was well known by the summer of 1937 and gave rise to a long memorandum from the Foreign Office to the Greek and French governments (see below, p. 337).[23] This, however, raises the question of why Franco's headquarters in Salamanca waited a full year before making any serious protest to Metaxas. The occasion indeed seems to have been the discovery that a number of rifles recently captured from the Republicans – they had probably crossed into Spain shortly after 17 March – were modern Mausers made at Augsburg in Germany. What on earth, they wanted to know, was going on?

Quiñones de León, the Nationalists' intelligence chief in Paris, and the Marqués de Magaz, their ambassador in Berlin, made their investigations and reported back in August 1938.[24] Magaz wrote that he had long ago heard rumours that German arms were to be smuggled to 'Red Spain' and in February had asked Reichsmarschall Goering about it, who had promised to deal with the matter. Since then 'persons close to the Reichsmarschall' had given him information that pointed to the involvement of Goering himself. An agent for the Poudrérie et Cartoucherie Hellénique, L. Catsouropolos, had placed orders for no fewer than 750,000 Mauser rifles on behalf of Fritz Mandl's Hirtenberg arms company in Austria, which was reselling them to Bodosakis, ostensibly for supplying the Greek army or for export. However, it happened that employed by the Poudrérie et Cartoucherie at Piraeus, recently a Rheinmetall factory, were numerous German technicians to supervise the conversion to modern production. All of them had been personally appointed by Goering, and on this pretext Goering was to receive a commission of £1 per rifle for the whole 750,000. There was no doubt, however, that most of the rifles were not destined for the Greek army but for 'Red Spain' and would go via Marseille through the usual camouflaging chain of intermediaries. Magaz had also heard reports of a large order placed with Krupp by agents acting for Dr Otero, who by then was the Republican sub-secretary for armaments and had made a special journey to Paris to oversee the contract.[25]

The implication of Fritz Mandl, the owner of the Hirtenberg company, in this affair deserves mention. If he is remembered today it is because, while married to Hedy Lamarr, he had tried to buy up all copies of the film *Extase*, in which she had appeared scampering naked through woodland. I have already suggested that since Stefan Czarnecki was in his employ, Mandl may have owned the mining firm that was supposedly buying the British Airways Fokkers (see above, p. 63). In November 1936 he sent one of his agents, a 'Baron Pfyffer' or 'Pfeiffer' (who may have been the 'Pfeiffer' who turned up in Prague, see above, p. 157), to England to buy two Airspeed Envoys from Mrs Bruce, an offer she refused because she was in enough trouble already. Later, Erich Hoffmann did buy two Envoys from the Airspeed company, one of which was supposed to be for Mandl's personal use. William T. Middleton, an American in Paris connected with Quiñones de León, informed the Foreign Office of a transfer of £90,000 to the Midland Bank in London to pay for these and other British aircraft, but the British authorities allowed the Envoys to sail on the SS *Cheshire* on 22 January 1937 for Antwerp before informing the Belgians, who impounded them. They were then sold to another Austrian, Reynders, and transferred to the Netherlands, where they still were in the summer of 1940, commandeered by the Luftwaffe. Hoffman was one of the Gestapo agents whom Mandl, a Jew, employed to maintain relations with Nazi Germany and was still infiltrating Republican arms-buying efforts in September 1937. Mandl eventually escaped to Argentina. In his report from Paris, Quiñones de León traced the Hirtenberg connection through to a Dr Berner, the Austrian chargé d'affaires in Republican Spain.[26]

In his dispatch Magaz pointed out that he could not pursue his enquiries further, for, although he had contact with the Abwehr, by which he presumably meant Canaris, he had none with the Gestapo. As a matter of fact, Magaz was a devout Catholic and monarchist and had no sympathy with Nazis, whose quasi-pagan superstitions and underlying nihilism placed them, in his view, no higher on the moral plane than the Bolsheviks, and he probably derived some secret satisfaction from passing on these extraordinary allegations. Were they true?

In 1948 the Franco government, which by then was trying to conceal how close it had been to the Nazi government in Germany, published a pamphlet on Communist intervention in the civil war in which this story appears in censored form.[27] There is no attempt to deny Goering's role, however, which is implied rather than stated outright, but an interesting detail is the mention of Fuat Baban, like Bodosakis a Turkish-born Greek, as the head of one of the companies concerned (Mavrocortado), for what the authors seem to hint at is that Fuat Baban, a dealer in arms and drugs based in Istanbul and Paris, was using his share of the money to finance a drug ring connected to Goering. Fuat Baban, however, was the representative in Turkey and eastern Europe for the Schneider, Skoda and Hotchkiss arms companies, as well as for the Lockheed Aircraft Corporation, one of whose agents, Frank Ambrose of Long Island, was to bring Turkey in as the cover for the Grumman deal in Canada (see below, p. 222).

27

Prieto

INDALECIO PRIETO, THE leader of the moderate Socialists and in overall charge of arms procurement for the Republicans from late November 1936 to April 1938, was one of the most charismatic of the prominent figures on either side in the Spanish Civil War. Though not a large man, he gave an impression of vast bulk, his great domed head on top of a rotund body irresistibly suggesting Humpty Dumpty. His ovoid shape and sleepy demeanour, perhaps effects of his diabetes, belied an active and well-informed mind, however, and an energy that often exhausted his colleagues and subordinates. He it was, for instance, who originally conceived and supervised the plan for the great irrigation schemes in Extremadura that the Franco government carried out and claimed credit for thirty years later. Unfriendly historians have argued, on the other hand, that at critical moments in his career, as when he refused the premiership in May 1936, he retreated into passivity, as though lacking self-confidence.[1] Yet his reason on that occasion seems sound enough: he was not willing to head a government while Largo Caballero, the leader of the left wing of the Socialist Party, was rampaging around the country calling for revolution and could not be trusted to support him. Indeed, he regarded Largo as a 'political imbecile' whose naïve rhetoric had – by splitting the Socialists, the largest political party in Spain, down the middle – done as much as anything else to bring on the civil war, for it had given the rebels the chance, as well as the political ammunition, to stage their coup while the labour movement was divided and weak. For all that, Prieto believed in party discipline and when Largo Caballero, on becoming premier and war minister in September 1936, had offered him the newly created ministry of marine and air, he had accepted.

Prieto was thus responsible for procuring material for the navy and air force while Largo, as war minister, was responsible for the army and militias. The effect of this, however, was to place the arms-buying commission in Paris under two competing authorities and the question of who could claim precedence, when sending requests to Paris for material, therefore became delicate.[2] Moreover, Dr Otero and the buying commission were rarely able to buy what was asked for, but usually had to accept what was offered by dealers who frequently included diverse items for the three services in the same package. To obtain anything the buyers had to act quickly lest the dealers should take advantage of delays and find pretexts to raise their prices. While offers and negotiations were thus changing from day to day and messages and queries continually passing back and forth between the government and the Paris embassy, and all in the greatest hurry since the need for arms was desperate, it was almost impossible for Dr Juan Negrín, the finance minister, to allocate funds for specific purposes, in case valuable material should be lost as a result. In September and October 1936 he sent a total of 660 million Ffr. (£6.3 million, or $31.4 million), the last remittance being on 9 November.[3] Then he called a halt, for the bulk of the gold reserve had just been shipped to Russia on 25 October and there was in addition the problem of the money, totalling $17 million, whose transfer to the United States and Mexico was being obstructed by the Chase and Midland banks, and the finances of the Republic had to be reassessed before more money could be sent anywhere.

There was also the matter of the 'commissions' that some of the buying agents awarded themselves, which were calculated as a percentage of the value of the materials they had succeeded in buying. Although there are numerous, mostly indignant, references to this practice, there is no information as to whether it was officially approved, or merely tacitly condoned, by the government or as to how or why it started. It was clearly pernicious, for the buyer and vendor had only to agree between themselves to raise the prices of the goods in order to enrich themselves at the expense of the state. The practice has become widespread since the Spanish Civil War and has been at the bottom of every major arms scandal since the 1950s.*

---

* A typical example today would be when some ministers in the government of A, a country with no aviation industry of its own, find themselves personally in need of money. They therefore decide to order ten advanced military aircraft, which the country neither needs nor can afford, from a leading company in Europe or the United States. Through the company agent in A they agree a price of £200 million. When the time comes for payment, £250 million is paid into the bank account that the company holds in A, from which the agent deducts his cut and remits the agreed £200 million to the company. The remainder, after suitable laundering, finds its way back to the ministers. They in turn, however, have to pay off numerous officers and officials who administered the practicalities but receive such wretched salaries themselves that without these occasional windfalls they might stage a coup and overthrow the government. Some time later an increase in taxes is announced to meet the cost of national defence. The same procedure is followed when ordering spare parts etc. to maintain the aircraft in service. My thanks to the person who gave me this information, which is based on a long experience of such transactions.

Certainly it aggravated tensions within the Paris buying commission, made up as it was of delegates from all the political parties and groups within the Republic in accordance with democratic principles. As a result, Dr Alejandro Otero in particular became the target of ferocious denunciation by the Anarchist FAI/CNT throughout and after the civil war, one report asserting that to appoint him as sub-secretary for armaments, as he was appointed in 1937, was tantamount to appointing Al Capone to be governor of the Bank of Spain.[4] However, Julián Zugazagoita, a Socialist minister in Negrín's government, writes that of all the people engaged in arms-buying abroad, Otero was not only one of the most skilful and dedicated but also the most honest, and that he was regarded by both Negrín and Prieto as irreplaceable. He refused commissions and even a salary and lived on his private capital until, by the end of the war, he was almost destitute, 'going into exile with the poorest refugees'.[5] He had to wine and dine the heads of arms companies, dealers and government officials and to dress his part to deflect their ridicule and it was this which affronted the Anarchists, struggling to exist as they were on pittances in cockroach-infested *pensiones*.[6]

Throughout this period Negrín and Prieto tried to persuade Largo to put all arms buying under one control, which he refused to do on the grounds that unless he were war minister as well as premier he would be a mere figurehead. At the beginning of November he then made two mistakes. He entrusted, against all advice, jewellery to the value of 20 million Ffr. (£192,307, or $961,535) to Captain Antonio Rexach and Pablo Rada, who had assured him that with the money earned from the sale thereof they could buy some modern French fighter aircraft. In France, however, they tried to set up as free-lance arms traders, failed, submerged themselves into the criminal underworld and eventually absconded with the remains of the money to Cuba (see below, p. 227). Meanwhile, when Franco's armies were coming within artillery range of Madrid, members of the cabinet debated whether the government should move to the safety of Valencia. Prieto opposed this and, when outvoted, said that the move should at least be made in an open and orderly manner and the public informed of its practical necessity. Instead, everything was left to the last minute, and when the government did move during the night of 6–7 November it appeared to be fleeing in panic and incompetently organized secrecy. A day or two before, Largo suggested that the war ministry and the ministry of marine and air be combined into a single ministry of defence under Prieto. Prieto refused, which some have again taken as proof of his underlying weakness of character.[7] Yet here too his response seems reasonable, for Largo's sudden proposal looked to be no more than a politician's ploy to shuffle off the responsibility for defeat on to somebody else. 'If we have to abandon Madrid', Prieto explained, 'the blame would be entirely mine, and if we save it, the syndicalists [i.e., militia] will take the credit.'[8]

Once in Valencia Largo decided to retain the war ministry after all, but towards the end of November he did agree to the creation, within Prieto's ministry of marine and air, of a commissariat of armaments and munitions, which would be responsible for all matters concerning war material, including its procurement. Prieto then proposed that the buying commission in Paris be disbanded and replaced with a new body of military officers appointed by his ministry. This would simplify the process of buying, remove the potential causes of friction between the different political groups represented on the commission and, although he does not mention it, end the practice of self-awarded commissions, for the military officers would be drawing their regular salaries. The cabinet agreed and the instruction was sent to Luis Araquistaín, the Republican ambassador in Paris, on 23 December 1936. It added that, Otero being in America, Calviño and Estevé were to stay on to settle current business, including the legal dispute with the Société Européenne. Deals in progress could be completed but no new offers accepted. All money left over was to be placed in a single account and used only for purchases authorized by Prieto himself.

Since Araquistaín had long been Largo's adviser on Socialist doctrine, his relations with Prieto were less than cordial and on 1 January he telegraphed Prieto to say that although the buying commission was now dissolved, certain offers were too important to be dropped 'just because they come from some gangster arms dealer.'[9] Prieto's reply, which I have not found, must have angered him, for on 12 January he circulated a paper to all ministries in which he retold the history of the buying commission and defended the integrity of its members. Coming from peaceful occupations far removed from the unforgiving world of arms traffickers, they had, at the beginning, made some mistakes but by the time the closure was ordered they had cured all the worst teething troubles. Now, however, war materials – including aircraft, tanks, artillery and 73,000 new rifles – to the value of £9.5 million ($47.5 million) were in danger of being lost and all arrangements for shipping were at a standstill. The accusation of inefficiency implied by the closure could be levelled more justly at the government than at the commission, for requests for material had come with no indications of priority and money with no indication of what it was for (the reasons for which, however, have been explained earlier in this chapter).[10]

The military organization, under General Francisco Matz, was in place by the end of January 1937[11] and was called the Comisión Técnica or, more commonly, Oficina Técnica. Some of the military officers on the old commission, including Lt.-Col. Monreal of the artillery section, were transferred to it, as was Calviño later, despite being a civilian. An aviation section was established at 61 Avenue Victor Emmanuel II (the present Avenue Franklin Roosevelt) under Lt.-Col. Riaño, who was replaced by Lt.-Col. Angel Pastor when he arrived from Prague at the end of February. The Comisión Técnica, benefiting from the fact that its finances were now handled in security by the BCEN (the Soviet bank in Paris), continued to function until the end of the civil war.

It was in February, however, that Prieto discovered to his fury that much of the remaining money of the old commission had not been put into a single fund as he and Negrín had instructed, for during November and early December 1936 Largo himself had secretly ordered large sums, including 100 million Ffr. (£952,381, or $4,762,000) intended for use by Riaño, to be transferred to the Anarchists for the purchase of aircraft and arms.[12] Largo's motive is not recorded, but the most likely explanation for his conduct is that in November, when he had finally persuaded the Anarchists to 'overcome their priestly scruples' and join his government in order to make it fully representative of the Popular Front, he had promised in return to ensure 'a fair distribution of arms, so that the Communists, your great fear, do not begin to monopolize everything with the blackmail of Russian aid.'[13] No sooner did the first Russian aid arrive, however, than ugly rumours began to spread that all the best weapons were going straight to Communist units. From what we have seen in Chapter 19 regarding the quality of the Soviet army material, apart from the tanks, sent in 1936, there can have been little to quarrel about in reality, but the story was believed and has been repeated ever since. It is likely, therefore, that Largo, knowing Prieto's lack of sympathy for the Anarchists and seeing that he himself was about to lose control of arms procurement, authorized the transfer to show that his promise to the CNT had been sincere.

Whatever Largo's reasons, Prieto's anger is understandable, for the Oficina Técnica had had to cancel important orders for material and suffer embarrassment as a result. By March, Largo had quarrelled with the Soviets over their interfering demands that he replace certain military officers who were not Communists with others who were, and in response the Communists, with Soviet backing, had started a conspiracy to oust him, accompanied by a press campaign to portray the former 'Spanish Lenin' as a senile dodderer.[14] In May open violence between the Anarchists and Communists broke out in Barcelona and Republican troops were sent to restore peace. Behind them Orlov and his acolytes moved in and murdered or arrested scores, some say thousands, of members of the CNT and POUM, whose leader, Andrés Nin, was kidnapped and never seen again: according to one report, the poor man, who had once been Trotsky's secretary, was flayed alive.[15] During the ensuing hugger-mugger which forced Largo Caballero from office, Prieto temporarily allied himself with the Communists. Negrín became premier and appointed Prieto minister of defence, a post he held until 31 March 1938, when, largely owing to Communist manoeuvring against him on the grounds that he was 'pessimistic', he too was forced to resign.

This account has been based on what is admittedly very scant and unclear information – no explanation by Prieto himself of his reasons for closing the commission seems to have survived, for example – and I would not claim that it is accurate in all details, only that it fits the known facts. According to Calviño, whom two French authors interviewed in the 1970s, the Republicans needed the co-operation of the French Communist Party if arms were to be transported across France to Spain, and to this end they allowed one or two French CP members to sit on the buying commission. However, Calviño went on, even more vital was the continued supply, which might stop at any moment, of Russian aircraft, tanks and men, and Largo reluctantly agreed to close the commission as a concession to the Soviets. Calviño did not explain why the Soviets should have wanted the commission closed and the French authors thoroughly confuse the matter by saying that the decision was finally taken as a result of the *Allegro* incident, which it could not have been since that did not occur until March 1937.[16]

It is unlikely that the Soviets or the Comintern wanted to take control of Republican arms-buying outside the USSR, but if they did they failed, for the Comisión Técnica was staffed largely by non-Communist officers such as Pastor and Monreal; indeed, in 1938 it even employed the American mercenary Colonel Charles Sweeny, who was as anti-Communist as a man could be.[17] Besides, to what purpose? Almost all, if not all, the major arms purchases of the Republicans were initiated in the autumn and winter of 1936–7, and the rest of the war was spent in trying to get them carried through, more often than not in vain. Emile Dutilleul and other senior French Communists may, as the French authors assert, have tried to convince Prieto and Largo Caballero that they were the only efficient people to organize the clandestine procurement of arms for Spain,[18] but in fact after July 1937 very little material of real military use reached the Republic from countries outside the USSR, and neither the French Communist Party nor the Comintern took part in the buying of any of it.

Some historians have nevertheless criticized as 'unforgivable' Prieto's turning against the Communists after having co-operated with them, and others have criticized his ever being in alliance with the Communists at all. Both groups, therefore, have tended to dismiss his accusation, made in 1957, that the Soviets, in supplying arms, were guilty of 'colossal fraud and embezzlement'[19] as merely the self-serving fantasy of an embittered old man.

28

Krivitsky and Company

MANY OF THE accusations that Walter Krivitsky, the Soviet defector, hurled against Stalin and all his works in 1939 have turned out to be true or nearly true,[1] despite campaigns by Communist parties all over the world to discredit him as an imposter. Some of the things that he wrote about his activities as an organizer of arms supplies to the Spanish Republicans, however, are clearly untrue, though whether the blame should lie with Krivitsky or his ghost-writer, Isaac Don Levine, is hard to say. His book has been republished at least twice recently,[2] and these untruths should be indicated in case there are any future editions.

Krivitsky states, for example, that within ten days of being ordered by Moscow to move from The Hague, where he was the NKVD *rezident*, to Paris to create a system of procuring arms for Spain, he and his colleagues established a chain of brand new import–export firms across Europe, each with its own NKVD agent as a silent partner who provided the funds, controlled all transactions and 'in case of a mistake, paid with his life.'[3]

Of the various firms and agencies that appear in the records as intermediaries in these operations, all but one, or possibly two, were in existence before the Spanish Civil War began or were not created until 1937 or 1938, most of these last being ephemeral shipping lines. Nor is it likely that the agencies or individuals that we have so far encountered – such as SEPEWE, Daugs, Grimard, or Ball – would have allowed an NKVD agent near their premises, let alone to 'control' their transactions. As for providing funds, only two instances, those of 'Tomson' and 'Argus', appear in the 'Operation "X"' records in the Russian State Military Archive (see below, p. 216, and Appendix III).

The company that most nearly resembles Krivitsky's description is the Société Française des Transports Aériens (SFTA). On 12 September 1936 Alfred Pilain, a French pilot, bought a Fokker F.XII airliner from KLM on behalf of 'Air Tropique', which seems to be the same non-existent airline, said to be opening a new service between Dakar and Gao, near Timbuktu, in French West Africa, that was supposedly buying the Vultees from American Airlines. On the 23rd Pilain bought three more Fokker airliners and on the 27th he announced the foundation of SFTA, whose head office was at 78 Avenue des Champs Elysées, Paris. Its declared market value was 12 million Ffr. (£114,286, or $571,429) and its capital 100,000 Ffr. (£952, or $4,762).[4] The four Fokkers staged at Le Bourget, Paris, on 23 October, raising an outcry from the French right-wing newspapers and their arrival being reported to the Foreign Office in London. Eden considered asking the French government to detain the aircraft, but before he could do so they had flown to Barcelona.[5]

On 2 December Pilain was replaced as director by Edouard Godillot, who, with his brother Jean, had flown with distinction in the Great War, for both had won the Croix de Guerre and the Médaille Militaire. Both were still on the register of French pilots in 1930.[6] Jean Godillot too worked for SFTA, acting as Edouard's deputy, until at least April 1937.[7] The Godillots may have been wealthy, for in May 1937 Edouard was enrolled into the exclusive Aéro Club Roland Garros.[8] Edouard Godillot, however, was a Communist, which suggests that the French Communist Party and, through the Comintern, the Soviet agents in Paris, had something to do with the creation of the company.[9] By prudently keeping itself small, the company was able to keep its day-to-day transactions remarkably secret, even though its role as a supplier of aviation material in general soon became well known. Between 120 and 140 aircraft can be identified as having been exported to Republican Spain by SFTA during the Civil War,[10] but the majority were civil or training machines unadaptable to military use. The most effective were six, but only six, of the Vultee V1-As (see below, p. 235), which were converted into light high-speed day-bombers.

All attempts by SFTA to procure modern military aircraft ended in failure owing either to the blocking of delivery by governments or to the trickery of the vendors. For example, in 1936 the Fokker company in Amsterdam built the prototype G.1, a twin-engined fighter still remembered as a formidable warplane for its time. Anthony Fokker wanted an order from the Dutch government but, as the aircraft was of highly unorthodox design, realized that this might be difficult to obtain until the machine had proved its qualities by prolonged testing, which would put a financial strain on the company. In October, therefore, he invited some Spanish Republican air force officers, said to be South Americans and probably led by Lt.-Col. Riaño, to inspect the G.1 in secret before he showed it to the Dutch air staff. The Spaniards ordered twenty-six and, when the G.1 exceeded predictions during its trials in March and April 1937, confirmed the contract through SFTA. Now that the Republicans were paying for the setting-up of the production lines, Fokker was able to

secure the contract he wanted from his own government by offering a
price lower than he could have offered previously. The two series were put
into production, the Dutch aircraft having Bristol Mercury engines. To
avoid problems with the British, the Spanish series had Pratt & Whitney
Twin Wasp engines imported from the USA. There remained the problem
of 'cover', for it was evident that if the contract with SFTA became
known, the British and French, not to mention the Germans, would put
pressure on the Dutch government to stop the export. On 1 January 1938,
therefore, Godillot agreed a contract with the Estonian war ministry,
although the contract itself, signed by an Estonian official named Tiivel,
made no bones of the fact that the real buyer was still the Spanish government. In the meantime, however, as soon as Fokker had obtained the
Dutch contract, production of the Dutch series had taken precedence over
the Spanish, with the result that by the time the civil war ended on 31
March 1939, only six of the Spanish G.1s had been completed and none
delivered. Sixteen of the Spanish G.1s were eventually built and were
bought by the Royal Netherlands Air Force in December 1939 to reinforce the Bristol-engined G.1s already in service. The Fokker company
was therefore not only part-subsidized by the Spanish Republicans in
meeting production costs but paid for the same aircraft twice. After the
Second World War it was taken to court and obliged to pay to the Franco
government the money it had received from the Republicans, which
amounted to £484,699 ($2,423,495).[11]

In addition, Fokker sold licences for the Republicans to build two types
of aircraft, the D.XXI fighter and the C.X reconnaissance biplane, at fac-
tories in and near Alicante, a pattern example of each being sent to Spain.
Production was to be accelerated by the creation of a new company at
Haren, Belgium, called Les Ateliers de Construction des Brevets
Aéronautiques (LACEBA), which was to supply parts and accessories.
This it did not do and by the end of the civil war only one D.XXI and one
C.X were completed.[12] LACEBA was also contracted to build twenty-six
French Romano R.83 fighter–trainers, of which only six were completed
and (reputedly) delivered via SFTA in 1938. These failures by LACEBA,
to which the Republicans had paid at least £160,000 ($800,000),[13] may be
partly explained by a note which its director, Jean Bastin, sent to Ernesto
de Zulueta, Franco's representative in Brussels, on 20 April 1937, to say
that his true sympathies were with the Nationalists and that he would
keep them informed of all developments.[14]

Krivitsky nowhere mentions the Republican arms-buying commission
in Paris, with which he was in touch daily. One would assume that this was
to protect people, were it not that both his presence and even his name
were known not only to the authorities but to the French newspapers:
'Rosenfeldt's immediate chief is K....y, whose relations with the Spanish

ambassador, under whom he holds the post of engineering adviser, are close at the present time.'[15] Since Krivitsky was supposed to be a secret agent long experienced in the 'trade-craft' of espionage, this is odd, to say the least, and raises the question of whether previous accounts of his career before his defection in September 1937 should be revised.* 'Rosenfeldt' was Michel Rosenfeldt, born in Smolensk of Jewish parents. During the 1930s in Paris, where he ran a property development and finance company, he met, probably through artistic friends, Philippe Berthelot, Alexis Léger's predecessor at the foreign ministry and a pillar of the French civil service. To Berthelot he introduced Suzanne Linder, a young relative said also to be his mistress. Suzanne then became Berthelot's mistress and after his retirement stayed on in the foreign ministry as a shorthand typist. During the first months of the Spanish Civil War Rosenfeldt's name appears in connection with various transactions, including the *Silvia* affair and the orders for aircraft in the Netherlands (for his connection with Podsnikov, the White Russian arms dealer in London, see above, p. 196), while Suzanne Linder, using French foreign ministry stationery, typed out false export clearances for aircraft intended for Spain. Both were arrested on 12 December 1936. This the right-wing press hailed as proof that Blum's government was riddled with Communists, Jews, Freemasons and traitors and, during a parliamentary debate in January 1937, deputies of the extreme right accused Blum and Cot of having already exported 400–500 aircraft, mostly military, to 'Red Spain'. In May 1938 Rosenfeldt was sentenced to eighteen months imprisonment. At the trial, his business partner, Emile Joly, said that Rosenfeldt represented many Franco-Belgian firms in Europe and Russia and the question of whether Rosenfeldt was a Soviet agent, a Communist or merely another Robert Cuse remains open.[16] In Spanish Nationalist comments on the affair Rosenfeldt was said to have been the first to approach the Estonians with a proposal that they provide 'cover' for fifty Czech fighter aircraft ordered by the Republicans. He was turned down, but shortly afterwards one Mikhail Bondarenko, a former minor agent of Sir

---

* Regarding the reference to Krivitsky as engineering adviser to Araquistaín, I should mention that in his tribute to Krivitsky (*The Commonweal*, 27 Feb 1941) Dr Paul Wohl, who had hidden Krivitsky in France after his defection in 1937 and organized his escape to the USA in December 1938, described him as 'a skilled mechanic'. During the 1970s I came to know Dr Wohl well, my family and I even staying with him in New York in 1973. When I asked him whether Krivitsky would have been technically competent to choose and order aircraft and armaments for a foreign government in time of war, he told me that Krivitsky, like many of his fellow commissars, had been so unmechanical that he couldn't drive a car, ride a bicycle or use a typewriter, or only with great difficulty, an assurance he repeated a year or two later in a letter. Unfortunately, at that time I knew too little about this subject to pursue the question, and I doubt that there is anyone alive now who could resolve this contradiction.

Basil Zaharoff, went to the Estonian war ministry with the same offer, this time explaining that on each plane the war ministry could make a profit of £1,000. His proposal was accepted.[17] In common with Latvia and Lithuania, Estonia was later accused by the Nationalists of having sold vast quantities of arms and munitions to the Republicans during the first nine months of the war, but now that we have the Polish and Soviet records it is evident that of the dozen or so ships that brought arms from the Baltic in 1936 only one seems to have come from Lithuania, one from Latvia and none from Estonia. In the first three months of 1937, when the traffic was said to have been at its most intense, only one ship, or at most two, sailed from Estonia but none from Latvia or Lithuania. All the cargoes were small, which is hardly surprising since none of the Baltic countries had 'vast' quantities of serviceable arms to spare. According to Asúa, the scheme by which Estonia was to provide 'cover' for Czechoslovakian aircraft was arranged by Max Brussovanski, the sales agent for the Czech state-owned aircraft factory Letov, and Marcelino Aguirrezabala, one of the Basques who, under Captain Lezo Urrestieta (see above, p. 197), were touring eastern Europe in search of arms and planes.[18]

The aircraft consisted of about a hundred obsolete or obsolescent machines which the Czech air force had withdrawn or was withdrawing from service. Lt.-Col. Pastor rejected at least fifteen of these as being so antiquated that to send valuable airmen in them against the enemy would be an act of murder. For this decision he was accused by the Anarchists of treason, in that, as a covert monarchist, he was obviously trying to prevent the Republic from obtaining vitally needed warplanes.[19] Of the remainder, only forty-three obsolescent and fairly useless military aircraft and two Avia 51 airliners, rejected by the Czech airline CLS as unsafe to fly, reached the Republicans, delivered in small lots during 1937 and 1938.[20]

The first consignment of these, twenty-three Aero A-101 biplanes, arrived in crates at Gdynia on 27 February 1937 and were stacked along the quay to await a ship on which to embark them. Since the crates were large, numerous and occupied a great deal of space for which the port authorities would charge high fees, an urgent enquiry was sent to Asúa in Prague. No sooner had it arrived than Lezo came to the legation in a state of anxiety to say that he had just heard that the aircraft had been bought by the Nationalists. This was the time when the 'Turkish deal' was collapsing, General Čižek was demanding another million francs to set things straight, Aguirrezabala was not in Prague and Pastor had left for Paris to avoid a second arrest. Perhaps Adler (see above, p. 156) or some other dubious dealer had got back into the deal and sold the planes to the enemy. With no one to consult, Asúa sent cables to Paris and Valencia for clarification. In Paris the new Oficina Técnica denied all knowledge of the Aeros, as in Valencia did Prieto, who had just discovered Largo's transfer of large sums of money for unauthorized purchases of which, for all Prieto knew, these aircraft might be one. What had happened was that so many inter-mediaries were involved in, or had tried to insinuate themselves into, this transaction and the channels through which the money was passing had become so convoluted in order to evade snoopers and informers in the banks that the aircraft themselves had been lost track of altogether, and nineteen days passed before the question was eventually settled: the buyers were the Republicans after all and the Aeros were to be embarked on the *Hordena* (ex-*Horden*), which had been bought from Norwegian owners by the Scotia line, a firm recently created in Panama with Republican money. The *Hordena*, however, was also scheduled to take on a cargo of arms bought from SEPEWE, but as these did not arrive at Gdynia until the end of March, the ship could not sail until 8 April. By then not only had the storage fees become enormous but everyone in Gdynia knew all about the Aeros and their destination, with the result that it was an easy matter for the Nationalist cruiser *Almirante Cervera* to intercept the *Hordena* in the Bay of Biscay on 16 April and escort her to El Ferrol. The aircraft were put into service with the Nationalist air force.[21]

In return for providing 'cover' for the Czech aircraft the Estonian government persuaded, or obliged, the Republicans to buy eight of their old Bristol Bulldog fighters and eight even more ancient Potez 25As which together represented half the first-line strength of the Estonian air force. The sixteen machines, hidden beneath sacks of potatoes, were shipped to Musel, the port of Gijón in the Asturias, on the *Viiu* at the end of June 1937. In relating this to Group Captain West, the British air attaché to Finland and the Baltic States, who had been instructed to keep a watch-out for violations of Non-Intervention, the Estonian air chief, Colonel Tomberg, explained that the Republicans had made an offer he could not refuse, for with the money earned, Estonia would be able to buy a squadron of Supermarine Spitfires. Twelve Spitfires were duly ordered, the order was approved by the British Air Ministry, which knew perfectly well where the money had come from, and their delivery was prevented at the last moment only by the outbreak of the Second World War in September 1939.[22] Whereas the Bulldogs and Potez 25As would have been worth about £100 each for scrap, an export Spitfire cost about £10,000 ($50,000). The Republicans thus spent at least £120,000 on this venture alone in the expectation of obtaining high-class war material in Czechoslovakia, an expectation in which, as we have seen, they were dis-appointed.

Despite many reports to the contrary, no aircraft reached the Republicans from Romania. Eight Potez 543 heavy bombers had been delivered to Romania in April and March 1936 and in August, through the intercession of Max Litvinov, the Soviet foreign minister, Pierre Cot agreed with Nicolas Titulescu, the Romanian foreign minister who was then convalescing in the south of France, that these and other Romanian aircraft, which the French would replace, could be sold to the Spanish Republic. Cardel Dorman, a White Russian arms dealer in Paris, was then sent to Bucharest to confer with the Romanian air minister, Gheorghe Caranfil. King Carol used this as an excuse to get rid of Titulescu, whom he feared as one of the most respected of European statesmen and disliked for his anti-German, pro-French and pro-British attitudes. Caranfil then resigned, protesting that with the money earned Romania could have bought a squadron of Hawker Hurricanes. No explanation for Titulescu's dismissal was published, which caused much speculation among Western commentators, who predicted that it would greatly strengthen the hand of the extreme right and especially the Fascist Iron Guard in Romania, as indeed it did.

At the end of October, King Carol paid a state visit to Czechoslovakia accompanied by Queen Helena, his mistress Madame Lupescu and a military staff, the secret purpose of the visit being to discuss the possibility that, should Czechoslovakia be attacked by Nazi Germany, Carol would allow Soviet troops and planes to cross Romanian territory to come to her assistance. The king refused to agree to this but, during the visit, Lt.-Col. Pastor received a confidential message from Madame Lupescu to say that the transit of Czechoslovakian arms and aircraft across Romania to a Black Sea port for shipment to Spain might be arranged after all. The proviso was that Madame Lupescu, and by implication the king, would receive a 25% 'commission' on the value of the articles transported. Almost on the same day, Pastor received an identical proposal, at the same rate of commission, from the lover of Queen Helena, a Romanian general who was with the party (see above, p. 155). Pastor and Asúa, considering the terms extortionate and the promise untrustworthy, politely declined both offers. Cardel Dorman, whom the Romanian authorities had allowed to stay in Bucharest in case the Spaniards should accept the proposition, was then arrested and deported for attempting to violate Non-Intervention, to which Romania was a signatory.[23]

It was at this time too that Swissair sold off four American passenger aircraft to the Republicans, a Douglas DC-2, two Lockheed Orions and a Clark GA-43A. These crossed France to Spain at the end of October, the Douglas by air and the others in creates by train and lorries. The agency was SFTA, represented by 'Antonio Spina' (probably the Spanish novelist Antonio Espina, a friend of Corpus Barga and Araquistaín) and the agent in Switzerland was Vladimir Rosenbaum-Ducommun, a distinguished Zurich attorney of Lithuanian–Jewish origin whose father, formerly a member of the Russian Duma, was then the president of the Jewish court at Tel Aviv, and whose wife, Aline, was the daughter of the Nobel Prize laureate Elie Ducommun. Rosenbaum was an active anti-Nazi, and it was in his office that Thomas Mann heard Dr Grigorovitch, Dmitrov's lawyer, describe the grotesque proceedings of the Reichstag fire trial. On 11 March 1937 the Zurich police broke down the doors of his apartment and arrested him on a charge of violating Swiss neutrality laws, and in May he and Max Brunner, a brother of the leader of the tiny Swiss Communist Party, were brought to trial, accused of the Swissair sale and of master-minding a 'large shipment' of 60,000 rifles and their ammunition from Lithuania in October 1936. The shipment cannot have been so large, however, for its weight was stated in court to have been 59 tons, which would have been that of only 2,000 rifles with 2,000 cartridges each (60,000 rifles and 60 million cartridges would have weighed 1,200 tons). Rosenbaum was sentenced to four months' imprisonment and a 400 Sfr. fine (£18, or $90), and Brunner to one month and a 100 Sfr. fine (£5, or $25). The anti-Semitic and pro-Franco Swiss newspapers, such as the *Neue Zürcher Zeitung*, were furious at such leniency and complained that 'this crafty Jew' had gained thousands of US dollars by the deal. Yet a list in the RGVA shows that the agent, 'Argus', bought the aircraft, with money lent by the Soviets, for $138,250* and a Spanish Republican list shows that the Spaniards repaid the Soviets 1,712,472 pesetas ($139,225.36),[24] a small difference ($975) probably resulting from the exchanges between pesetas, French francs, Swiss francs and US dollars. Rosenbaum therefore could not have taken any commission at all. Swissair meanwhile denied any prior knowledge of a Spanish connection since it had thought the buyer to be Air France, but José-María Carreras, the LAPE pilot who flew the Douglas from Paris to Barcelona, told me that Swissair had insisted that if the Spaniards wanted the DC-2, which they did, they would have to buy the other three aircraft, which they did not want, as well. Nor could Swissair have believed for a minute that Air France would have wanted three such small, elderly and nearly worn-out single-engined machines at a time when it was re-equipping with modern, new-generation airliners.[25]

The only specific operation that Krivitsky describes in any detail is the purchase of fifty obsolescent fighters of French design from an eastern European country. The negotiations were entrusted to 'a Dutch blue-blood' who was a committed anti-Fascist and the ostensible buyer was China. As the ship carrying the fifty aircraft approached Barcelona, however, Moscow ordered her captain to change course and unload them

---

* The Douglas DC-2 cost $86,000, the Lockheed Orions $14,250 each and the Clark GA-43A $23,750. The Republicans thought these prices reasonable. The DC-2, which was pretty well worn, seems high and the Clark seems excessive.

at Alicante. This could not be done owing to the Nationalist blockade and for several days the ship sailed about in constant danger of being captured or sunk until she eventually managed to slip through the blockade and unload the planes at Alicante.

The point of Krivitsky's story was to illustrate the mentality of Stalin, who did not want the planes to go to Barcelona lest the Anarchists should 'get hold of' them and so gain prestige by winning a victory over the Nationalists with them.[26] In her memoir *Our Own People*, Elizabeth Poretsky writes that in fact Krivitsky had had nothing to do with that particular operation, but had merely heard of it from her husband, 'Ludwik', the NKVD agent Ignace Reiss, whose defection and murder in 1937 provoked Krivitsky's own defection.[27] It would be more accurate to say, however, that that particular operation, at least as described by Krivitsky, could never have happened at all, for the shipments of aircraft from eastern and central Europe, which are those described in this chapter, are now known exactly and Krivitsky's story does not correspond remotely to any of them. The idea that the CNT might have won a victory by getting hold of fifty obsolescent fighters unloaded at Barcelona is, besides, merely silly. Fighters are of little use in ensuring a victory on the ground and, in any case, the Anarchists had no trained air crews, air bases or facilities for putting the machines into service. One might add that the only cargo of arms known to have been consigned to the CNT, that on the *Bramhill* in September 1936, was delivered not to Barcelona but direct to Alicante from Hamburg (see above, p. 192). Some such episode, probably involving small arms, evidently did occur, however, for Poretsky writes that the 'Dutch blue-blood', whom she knew well, later survived five years in Buchenwald, which identifies him as Han Pieck, the Swiss-Dutch Soviet agent.[28]

'Argus', then, may have been Rosenbaum or Pieck, but whoever he was I suspect that he was the same who, in Switzerland in 1935, negotiated the sale of the three Focke-Wulf Stösser aircraft to Captain John Ball on behalf of Haile Selassie (see above, p. 83). The code-name Argus, as opposed to Argos, is an unusual spelling and may have been suggested by the fact that the Stösser were powered by Argus engines. 'Tomson', who used Russian money to buy the Czech material on the *Hillfern*, may have been Rosenfeldt, Rosenbaum, or possibly Lt.-Col. Hugo Tamsar, the son-in-law of the Estonian war minister, for he acted as a go-between in attempts, almost all unsuccessful, at arms sales to the Republicans in Czechoslovakia and the Baltic states in 1936 and 1937, though the NKVD usually chose code names as different as possible from the real names of their agents.[29]

Finally, Krivitsky writes that one day in Moscow in May 1937 he was crossing the huge Red Square with an NKVD officer who had been one of those who had disembarked the Spanish gold at Odessa. 'If all the boxes of gold we piled up in Odessa', the officer said, 'were laid side by side here in the Red Square, they would cover it from end to end!' As this anecdote has been quoted by some historians, including the distinguished Burnett Bolloten, it should be mentioned that there were 7,800 boxes, each 48.2 cm in length and 30.5 cm in width,[30] which, laid side by side, would have covered an area of 48.2 m by 21.62 m, about the size of two small suburban gardens in London. Of course, considering the value of gold at the time, it was still an enormous quantity.

29

Nether World

THE NUMBER OF arms traffickers who flit in and out of the records is very great, but their misdeeds were, for the most part, tediously similar, so a few may stand in for the rest.

When the fifth Marquis of Bristol died in March 1985, several of those who wrote the press notices remembered him as, among other things, 'the man who sold arms to both sides in the Spanish Civil War'. Certainly he would not have been the only man, or woman, to have done that, but there is good reason to doubt that he ever succeeded, despite many attempts, in selling any arms to either side. In September 1936, at the age of twenty-one, the Hon. Victor Hervey, as he then was, offered the services of his newly founded Hervey Finance Corporation to lend General Franco £250,000 for the procurement of weaponry.[1] The offer was declined, perhaps because of Hervey's notoriety as 'London Playboy Number One' or perhaps because the ex-queen of Spain was his godmother. According to a story he wrote for the *Sunday Dispatch* in July 1939, after he had been gaoled for robbery in connection with the 'Mayfair Men' case, he had met a 'drunken Spaniard' in Cannes in July 1936 who was looking for aircraft for the Republic. Hervey had offered five at £5,000 each. The Spaniard had insisted on paying £10,000 each. By going to and fro between the Spaniard and other agents or vendors and selling the planes one at a time, Hervey had earned, he claimed, a commission of £1,300 per plane, out of which he had paid five pilots £40 each to fly them to Barcelona.[2] He was, looking back, clearly proud of his acumen, doubtless unaware that to earn even his £6,300 clear profit, the result of one afternoon's work, the average Spanish peasant, for whose benefit these militarily useless machines were being bought, would have had to work from dawn to dusk, seven days a week, twelve months a year, for 173 years. His tale, however, seems a fantasy, for no group of five French civil aircraft crossed to Spain at this period.

In December 1936, through introductions by K. D. Vacha of St Mary Axe in the City of London, whom he had met in Florida, Hervey was entrusted by the Republicans, through a London brokerage firm named Scaramanga, with a credit of about £3 million to buy 140,000 rifles and 740 million cartridges. The first 35,000 rifles and 35 million cartridges, plus 555 Maxim guns and 130,000 grenades, he procured in England (Hull), Belgium, Estonia and Finland, and in January 1937 he went to Helskini with John Lonsdale, a young 'man-about-town' who had just won £500 in a slander action against a Miss Paula Blake, and the Marquis of Donegall, the gossip columnist of the *Sunday Dispatch*. There they promised a 7.5% commission on the net profits of their deal to Major Kuuesale of the Finnish war office, who introduced them to 'a swarthy, Oriental-looking Finnish arms baron' whom they called 'Jusu' and whom the records in Madrid show to have been Captain Jusu Juselius. Juselius, who was said to have made £500,000 out of arms trading in the previous six months, organized the concealment of such material as had so far arrived in shops, garages and the like around the city and 'cover' was procured from someone at the Brazilian consulate for £5,000. On 24 February Edouard Godillot, who told them he was representing Vacha, arrived to organize sea transport by one of the shipping companies affiliated to SFTA.[3]

Trouble began on 22 March 1937, when Hervey's creditors, who presumably included Vacha and the arms vendors in Hull and Liège (Ball?), met at the London bankruptcy buildings, only to be told by the official receiver that Hervey had just sold arms to General Franco and that, when he received his commission of £30,000 in three weeks' time, they would all be satisfied. On 18 April the *Sunday Dispatch*, whose coverage of the war in Spain had always been favourable to Franco, printed a front-page story in which the Marquis of Donegall 'exposed the racket' of smuggling arms to the 'Spanish Reds' and accused Hervey and Lonsdale of planning to betray the Republicans, for as soon as the arms were embarked Hervey would inform Franco's agents in London so that the ship could be intercepted at sea. For this service he would receive the £30,000 mentioned by the official receiver in addition to the £243,125 profit he was to make from the Republican part of the deal.[4] Neither then nor later did Hervey or Donegall mention the likelihood that, since the *Mar Cantábrico* incident, the Nationalists would probably shoot any Spaniards they found on the arms-carrying ships they captured. Hervey then fled to the British consulate in Copenhagen and from there to Paris, where the Spanish 'Reds' not only refused to believe his protestations of innocence but, so he claimed, tried on several occasions to murder him. His defence, apparently, was that the weapons had turned out to be not what he had expected;[5] indeed, there is no record of what happened to them afterwards and one wonders if some of them were the junk that Veltjens shipped to the Basques on the *Allegro* and *Yorkbrook* (see above, p. 196). Another possibility is that they became part of the cargo of the *Vena* (ex-*Jaron*, see

Appendix II), for these were arms which Juselius sold to the former Zaharoff dealer Mikhail Bondarenko and his partner Boris Linde. These two cut-throats fell to quarrelling and the arms, after being stored for months at Paldiski, Estonia, were eventually taken by the *Diana* (ex-*Scotia*) in April and May 1938 to Le Havre, France, from where they may or may not have crossed into Catalonia (see below, p. 240).

On 31 May, in answer to a question by Captain Cazelet MP, Eden told the House of Commons that Donegall had gone to Helsinki purely as a journalist and that there was no evidence that Finnish officers had given any assistance to Hervey or Lonsdale.[6] When Hervey published his own account in the *Sunday Dispatch* in July 1939* and accused Donegall of lying, Donegall replied that he stood by every word he had written in 1937.[7] Since Hervey was bankrupt and in gaol there was no question of either suing the other for libel. Besides, whom could they call as witnesses?

Possibly acquainted with Hervey was Serge Rubinstein, the Cambridge-educated son of a St Petersburg banker who had emigrated to England. After settling in France in the 1930s Serge had made a fortune by what is now called 'asset-stripping' and by transferring to France worthless shares from China, where his brother André had bought the Chosen Mining Corporation from Martin Coles Harmon of Lundy Island (see above, p. 83). Meanwhile, learning that Daladier's mistress, the

---

* In his 23 July article Hervey reproduced a photograph of a page of his company file listing material on offer to '55 Ave George V' in about Nov–Dec 1936. There are four types of aircraft: Fiat C.R.32 (the main Italian fighter in Spain), Caproni Ca 133 and Ca 135 and the Czech Avia 534/II. When I asked the Marquis how he came to offer Italian aircraft to the Republicans, he replied (25 March 1979) that there were always generals anxious to keep their wives and mistresses bejewelled and in fur coats and that 'British of the old school type if well skilled' is always the best intermediary in such affairs. At that time, it is true that eight 'Capronis' were offered by an Italian to the Republicans in Paris, but Carlos Rosselli warned that it was a set-up by the OVRA and the French Fascist *Cagoulards* (J. S. Vidarte, *Todos fuimos culpables*, vol. 2, p. 566). When I mentioned that several early pro-Nationalist writers (Belforte, José Gomá) had averred the presence of Avia 534 fighters in the Republican air force, Bristol replied (25 March 1979 and 30 April 1980) that 'several squadrons of Avia 534/IIs did indeed reach Spain in crates . . . I personally saw to their unloading . . . Ostensibly they disappeared. I then led a Red Cross convoy containing these right through the lines and after a little hubbub waving white flags etc. got them through the lines to Seville. They were then assembled and flown by my pilots which contributed to the final knockout of the Communists.' Leaving aside the absurdity of the notion that a convoy of large crates crossed the lines without being inspected, the facts are that thirty-six Avia 534/IIs were part of the Turkish deal of November 1936. When 'cover' was switched to Estonia, the Czech government prevented delivery. On 20 May 1938 Asúa and the director of the Avia factory appealed to Alexandrovsky for help, which was not forthcoming. On 7 June 1938 Negrín cancelled the operation (Fundación de Pablo Iglesias, Madrid, Archivo de Luis Jiménez de Asúa, *Inf.* 65°, p. 273, 67°, p. 372).

Marquise de Crussol, whose soirées were frequented by Parisian *haute bourgeoisie*, was in financial difficulties, Serge Rubinstein offered to pay the costs of the soirées in exchange for a standing invitation and any scraps of stock market information that might be useful.[8] Then in December 1936 he appeared at the Republican legation in Prague with a note of introduction from Araquistaín and a scheme for procuring arms and aircraft from England, Czechoslovakia, Poland and Austria with 'cover' already provided.[9] The commission for procuring 'cover' would be 20% of the net prices of the goods set by the manufacturers, which was to be paid into a reputable bank in Prague before negotiations began, as a guarantee that the legation had the money available.[10] Asúa, suspicious, sent to Paris for clear instructions, adding that he would negotiate with Rubinstein only if compelled to do so by an explicit order from Paris and Valencia.[11]

Neither Asúa's dispatch nor Rubinstein's written proposal explains how the scheme was to work, but fortunately the outline can be found in the dispatches of J. F. Brenan, the British consul-general in Shanghai, which show that through the Banque-Franco-Asiatique, which was the fiscal bank of the Kuomintang and happened to be owned by Serge Rubinstein, and Sassoon's Bank in Shanghai, not to mention Trevor's Bank in Paris, of which Duff Cooper, the British war minister, was a director and in which Zaharoff and the Rothschilds were partners, certain generals in Chiang Kai-shek's entourage were to receive a 4% commission on £4 million worth of arms and aircraft ordered in Europe by China and diverted at sea to Republican Spain. One of Brenan's informants, a Shanghai businessman named Carl Haas, even claimed to have received his instructions in person from Edouard Daladier, the French war minister, and that other members of the French government had financial interests in the plan as well. The false export certificates etc. were to be provided by a Dr Fischer, 'an expert in finding loopholes through Non-Intervention'. Sensing the whole thing to be a confidence trick, Brenan warned his informants off the scheme, though even by December 1936 several of them already feared that they would lose the money they had invested.[12] Prieto met Rubinstein and afterwards instructed the embassies and legations that the man was not to be spoken to, though Rubinstein continued to pester them until July 1938, when Daladier had him deported from France for 'speculating on the franc'. Shortly after, André Rubinstein's Chosen Mining Corporation collapsed amid a scandal in which shareholders were robbed and the two brothers settled in America, where they perpetrated the notorious Panhandle Swindle. In 1953, by which time he was a 'financial adviser' (i.e., money-launderer) to the Mafia, Serge Rubinstein was murdered in New York, which occasioned a quip by the police officer on the case that has since become proverbial.

'Certain clues', he said, 'have narrowed the list of suspects down to ten thousand.'

Dr Leo Katz, another Jew from eastern Europe or Russia, appears by contrast to have been brave, absolutely honest in his dealings with the Republicans, and, according to Asúa (who himself was not without a streak of anti-Semitism), highly intelligent.[13] In November 1936, despairing at the lack of cohesion among Republican arms buyers in Europe, Katz went with Otero and Martin Licht, a financial adviser, to New York (see above, p. 175). There they set up the Hanover Sales Corporation under the direction of Miles Sherover, ordered military aircraft from the Bellanca company – none of which were delivered to Spain, however, owing to government prohibition – and carried through the famous Grumman deal initiated by Sanz Sainz in Canada.[14] The orders from the Turkish government received by the Canadian Car and Foundry Co. at Montreal for fifty Grumman GE-23s, obsolescent naval biplanes, were forged. The forgery was discovered only by accident after the first thirty-four had been shipped to France, the remainder being impounded by the Canadian authorities. General Ozalp, the Turkish war minister who, in view of the Turkish deal in Prague, had obviously been implicated in the 'Spanish trade' since the beginning of the civil war, resigned 'in order that the investigation of the scandal might be carried out in an atmosphere of complete freedom'. An associate of Fuat Baban and Bodosakis, Ekram Konig, who had forged the orders and confirmations, escaped to France and Ruhi Bozcali, a clerk in the Turkish ministry of protocol who had supplied the stationery, was arrested. The case was not heard until 1940 and Bozcali, who insisted that everything he had done had been with the knowledge of his superiors, was given a light sentence of three months in gaol for 'neglect of duties'. The connection between America and Turkey was made through Frank Ambrose, the Long Island aircraft salesman[15] and his opposite number in the Balkans and Turkey, Fuat Baban, and perhaps it is significant that, according to the Gestapo, Fuat Baban, Leo Katz and an NKVD agent all rented apartments in the same building in Paris. The brain behind this elaborate conspiracy, however, was Leo Katz's, and it would be interesting to know what eventually became of him.[16]

Another who was involved in the Turkish-Spanish traffic was Viscount Victor Churchill, a cousin of Sir Winston Churchill. He writes in his autobiography of the moral imperatives that moved him and his colleagues to answer the calls for 'Arms for Spain!' and thereby to do something positive to counter the miserable and cowardly attitude of the British government and ruling classes towards the Spanish Civil War, which he calls one of the pivotal events of this century.[17] However, such evidence as I have been able to find regarding what he actually did is, to put it mildly, conflicting. Two who knew him well – Nan Green, a Communist who worked in Barcelona with the Spanish Medical Aid organization (of which Victor Churchill was a treasurer), and Patrick Burke – assured me of his integrity and courage as a gun-runner in the eastern Mediterranean for the Republicans. On the other hand, S. J. Noel-Brown, the pacifist secretary of the General Aircraft Company and an official of the International Red Cross, published an article in 1985 in which he described with some resentment how Victor Churchill had tried to use him as a front for procuring fifty Hawker Fury II fighters for the Republicans via an order from the Turkish government.[18] There is also a letter, dated 25 January 1938, from a J. W. Walton to Manuel Begoña, the Republican chargé d'affaires at Ankara, to say that he and some Turks had smuggled arms in the spring of 1937 and that Victor Churchill had not yet paid them; then on 12 April 1938 Pablo de Azcárate, the Republican ambassador in London, informed his government that Victor Churchill had absconded with money and was henceforth a person of no confidence. According to a Nationalist report, the Hawker Fury scheme was blocked by the Turkish prime minister, who was evidently unaware of the activities of the war ministry, and that all that Victor Churchill managed to achieve was to carry on small boats to a Spanish tanker, the *Campillo* or *Campomanes*, a single lot of 1,200 machine-guns which had been rejected by the Turkish army and sold to a Greek dealer (who sounds like Bodosakis).[19] When I showed all this to Patrick Burke, after Nan Green's death, he refused to believe it and insisted that Churchill must have been framed and used as a fall guy by the Turks or Greeks.

In their book *Les brigades de la mer* Dominique Grisoni and Gilles Hertzog have described Daniel Wolf as the most efficient of all the foreigners who procured arms and other supplies for the Republicans.[20] His Hunzedal company at The Hague, with its Belgian subsidiary SOCDECO (Société Belge d'Entreprises Commerciales) at Antwerp, had been founded by his brother, Nathan Wolf, its largest trade being in shipping timber. In the autumn of 1936, with the help of the Italian Communist Giulio Cerreti and Emile Dutilleul, the treasurer of the French Communist Party, he persuaded the Republican government to employ him as a provider of materials of all kinds, including dried vegetables (of whose processing he held the patent), and at about the same time his relatives in New York took over the purchase of the Vultee and other aircraft, as already described. At this time too he sent his brother Marcel Wolf to Warsaw to found the Gokkes company (possibly named after a relation) and to buy the Polski Bank Komercyjny for handling the SEPEWE material, and to found the Bandera company in Gdynia for organizing the shipping, an arrangement that held until the end of the war.[21] According to Grisoni and Hertzog, it was Wolf who introduced the system of using code words for various types of arms, such as 'apples' for rifles and 'citrus fruit' for machine-guns. Cerreti portrayed Daniel Wolf as an extraordinary figure, 'tall, athletic, bald as a pear', who would conduct business by telephone from his bed, often with a girl or even two girls beside him, in his suite at the Ritz Hotel in Paris and would spend every night in a night club or brothel. Calviño too could never make him out and suspected that he was a Soviet agent since, like Krivitsky, Rosenfeldt and Pieck, he was based at The Hague. It may be remembered, however, that it was Wolf's chief agent in Warsaw, Stefan Katelbach, who boasted that by selling junk to the Republicans they were able to restore their bank to solvency (see above, p. 113). In Prague, Asúa was furious to learn, for example, that Wolf had bought the Renault FT-17 tanks from SEPEWE, which had been rejected by the Poles 'for their absolute uselessness', as well as some batteries of ancient Italian 75 mm field-guns, as is confirmed by the SEPEWE list (Appendix II).[22] What happened to Daniel and Marcel Wolf after the German conquest of Europe is not clear. According to one author, in 1940 Goering bought two Dutch paintings from Daniel, 'whose brother had unfortunately given financial aid to the Republicans during the Spanish Civil War'.[23] According to others, in 1940 Daniel escaped to America, where he died a year later[24] (see addendum, p. 338).

One of the most baffling and intriguing of these stories would require several chapters to do it justice and only the barest outline can be given here. Lt.-Col. Juan Ortiz Muñoz of the Republican air force had served bravely in the Moroccan wars, had been imprisoned for anti-monarchist activities under the Primo de Rivera dictatorship, had been responsible, at the time of the Nationalist uprising, for saving the air bases at San Javier and Los Alcázares, near Cartagena, for the Republicans and in December 1936 was chief of the second air region, which covered south-eastern Spain and had within its area Albacete, where the Soviets had established their air headquarters. It happened, however, that Major Romero Basart, a fellow African veteran and one of Ortiz's senior officers, wrote an article in a local newspaper in which he expressed sympathy for the Anarchists and criticized the Communists. The Russians demanded his dismissal and Ortiz, not a man to tolerate outside interference in his administration, leapt to his defence. The Russians then warned Prieto that they had evidence that Ortiz was a homosexual and that they would produce it if he were not dismissed as well. Prieto's humane solution was to send Ortiz to Paris to buy aircraft. Shortly afterwards, however, the buying commission was closed and, to save Ortiz from returning permanently to Spain, Prieto told him to stay on and set up an aircraft-buying commission of his own.

According to two informants whose parents had known Ortiz well, Prieto never intended that Ortiz should take his new job too seriously, but join the Comisión Técnica when it was formed and in the meantime keep busy by inspecting the airfields in France where Spanish pilots were being trained in secret.[25] Ortiz, however, did take it very seriously, rashly enrolled his brother Captain José Ortiz, Daniel Ovalle, the one-time mayor of Getafe (see above, pp. 85–6) and a few others and within a week or two placed contracts for fifty Potez 540 bombers, twenty-six Dewoitine D.371 fighters and various other machines, all of which came to nothing when he was refused the money to complete the contracts.[26]

In a rage and further embarrassed by the fact that several of the dealers with whom he had negotiated had turned out to be crooks, Ortiz flew to Valencia and accused the minister of treason in that he was deliberately sabotaging the purchase of aircraft in order to help Franco. Prieto wrote a letter to Ortiz explaining that Ortiz had, after all, taken on staff, such as his own brother, without authorization and agreeing with Ortiz's own admission that 'you have no head for business'.[27]

Ortiz went into hiding at an FAI safehouse in Barcelona, where he wrote a long report on the whole affair, which the Anarchists copied, together with all the contracts and other related correspondence.[28] After the May events in Barcelona, Ortiz escaped to France. By then Prieto had had no choice but to dismiss him from the air force.

Later in the year the Nationalists obtained copies of Ortiz's report, the contracts and the rest of the papers; according to their own account they did this by tracking him down to his refuge in the pine forests near Arcachon, south of Bordeaux, befriending him and, during a visit to Paris, photographing them while he was asleep in his hotel, a story it is hard to believe. They then used the documents as the basis of a *note verbale* which they circulated to all the foreign ministries, including the British, as proof of the moral turpitude that prevailed in the Republican buying agencies and among members of the French government who were conniving at the traffic.[29] Meanwhile, Ortiz and the equally embittered José Melendreras, who had likewise written a report for the Anarchists on his misadventures in the United States, emigrated to Mexico. Ortiz, who took with him a large car, was accompanied by a girlfriend, which throws into question his alleged homosexuality, and Melendreras was accompanied by his wife. Gordón declined to meet them but resisted attempts to have them returned to Spain because, he said, he was convinced that they were still fundamentally loyal to the Republic. Melendreras remained in Mexico, where he ran a chemist's shop. Ortiz, I believe, returned to Spain in the 1960s under a general amnesty.

There is, however, a file in the Araquistaín archive containing a report that throws new light on this affair and points to a connection with the death of the distinguished Anarchist philosopher Camillo Berneri (see above, p. 45). Berneri's mysterious murder during the May events in

Barcelona has ever since been a subject of speculation, the consensus of informed opinion nowadays attributing it to the Communists, who had many reasons for wishing him eliminated.

Before we come to this document, however, it should be explained that after the bulk of the gold reserve had departed for Russia, the Republican government decided to raise additional money for the purchase of arms by sending abroad jewellery and valuables confiscated from the estates of aristocrats and other wealthy people who had fled, or been imprisoned or executed. Among those employed to take such articles into France was Georges Agabekov, the OGPU defector who had escaped the kidnap attempt in 1932 (see above, p. 194), though he was murdered in 1937, according to one source while crossing the Pyrenees and according to another in Brussels by the NKVD, whose agents seem to have taken charge of at least some of these operations.[30] There was also a group of men – the names of Charles Kennett (real name, Kenneth Apjohn-Carter), Robert Bannister-Pickett and Michael Corrigan are on record – who brought the jewellery by plane to the airfields at Abridge (north of London, alongside the present M11 motorway) and West Malling, in Kent.[31] Among the 'fences' was the young Porfirio Rubirosa, whose marriages to millionairesses, affairs with film stars and reputation as a latter-day Casanova in later life made him the most famous of post-war playboys until he was killed in a car crash in 1965. In 1936–7, as the son-in-law of the Dominican dictator General Rafael Trujillo, he was an attaché at the Dominican legation in Paris and it was by selling such jewellery to his friends in Parisian society that he made his first fortune.[32]*

The report referred to above asserts that Angel Galarza, the minister of the interior in Largo Caballero's government and a former chief-of-police, had taken to profiteering personally from this traffic.[33] Among those involved were: Major Navacerrado, the chief of security at the Paris embassy; Justiniano García, a secret policeman of sinister repute who ran the notorious prison at the convent of Santa Ursula in Barcelona, where prisoners under interrogation were subjected to a form of torture by being enclosed in weirdly painted wooden spheres and boxes; a Catalan named Metziat, an old friend of Galarza's and said by the author of the

---

* In 1940–1, during the German occupation of France, Rubirosa sold Dominican visas to Spanish Republican refugees trying to escape arrest and deportation to Franco's Spain by the Gestapo. His fees varied between $500 and $5,000 each (Mariano Asnó, *Yo fui ministro de Negrín*, p. 258). As mentioned elsewhere, among Republican leaders who were returned to Spain and executed were Companys and Zugazagoita. After the Liberation, Rubirosa claimed that he had been in the Resistance. During the post-war years, among the better known of his many lovers were, or are said to have been, Ava Gardner, Janet Leigh and Zza Zza Gabor and among his wives Danielle Darrieux, Doris Duke ('the richest woman in the world') and Barbara Hutton.

report to be a British agent;[34] Daniel Ovalle; a group of Italians, including several Anarchists or former Anarchists, who had broken with the Rosselli brothers and Giustizia e Libertá and turned to crime; and, finally, Captain Antonio Rexach and Pablo Rada who, it may be remembered, had been entrusted by Largo Caballero with 20 million Ffr. worth of jewellery for buying French fighter aircraft which they claimed they had been offered. Instead, they had embezzled the money and eventually escaped to Cuba (see above, p. 204). The report relates how part of this money had been distributed amongst the gang, with Galarza's connivance, how the Italians had conspired against one another and how one of them, Demetrio Londero, was murdered in a car near the frontier by another, named Bellver, while taking a suitcase full of jewellery from Spain to Paris.

It was among these dangerous people that Ortiz and his brother sought refuge for a time and, according to the report, it was during the confused fighting in Barcelona in May 1937 that Camillo Berneri and his fellow anarchist Barbieri were arrested and then murdered on the orders of Galarza, who feared that Berneri was in possession of evidence that would reveal his 'dirty transactions' in connection with the export of confiscated jewellery. Although these allegations probably cannot be proved or disproved by now, the report does have a nasty ring of truth to it. The identities and characters of those named and some of their actions are corroborated by other independent sources.[35] It does not appear to have a Communist motivation or to have been written by a member of the Communist-controlled secret police, the hated SIM.

Michael ('Mick') Corrigan, who had been involved in the bringing of jewellery to England, later played a role in another unpleasant affair. He had been born Kenneth Edward Cassidy in the workhouse at Youghal, southern Ireland, and in 1929 had changed his name by deed poll to Michael Dennis Corrigan. In 1930 he had been sentenced to five years in prison for fraud, but in 1936 was rich enough to afford a flat at 4 Park Lane, one of the more expensive addresses in London. During the first year of the Spanish Civil War, he took part not only in jewellery-running but also in trying to supply aircraft to the Republicans, for which he was fined £30, plus £30 costs. I was told by several people, including the Marquis of Bristol and Oloff de Wet,[36] that he swindled the Republicans out of £250,000 by a fake scheme to transfer a squadron of RAF Hawker Demon two-seat fighters to Spain, though this tale may well be a fantasy based on a confusion with the Hawker Fury affair, with which he was involved in some capacity,[37] and another scheme to sell to the Republicans eighteen ex-RAF Armstrong-Whitworth Atlases, none in flying condition and all awaiting the scrap merchant. Whether or not he made any money from the attempt I do not know, but its exposure resulted in his being *persona non grata* at the Comisión Técnica in Paris. Nevertheless, in 1938 he still managed to cheat them in a most damaging manner.

Aero-Marine Engines Ltd, a manufacturing company and sales agency, had been registered in February 1937 with addresses at Kent House, 7 Telegraph Street, EC2 and 28 Pall Mall in London and at 52 Avenue des Champs Elysées in Paris. Its declared capital was £70,000, its chairman a Colonel C. F. Hitchins and on the board of directors was Claude Grahame-White, one of the foremost pioneers of aviation in Britain, indeed in Europe. The company secretary was Simon Epstein, who had previously had an office in Kent House, and his assistant was Edouard Weissblatt, who lived at the same address as Corrigan, 4 Park Lane. About fifteen months later, on 8 May 1938, the Franco government sent the Foreign Office a *note verbale*, with a foreword by Sir Robert Hodgson, the recently appointed British representative at Burgos, to say that Aero-Marine Engines was building twelve extremely modern torpedo boats, faster and more powerful than any in the British or French navies, ostensibly for China but in reality for the Spanish Republicans: two were being built at Looe in Cornwall, two in Scotland and eight in France under licence by the Romano company (see below, p. 232). The scheme had been exposed when 550 cases supposedly containing the anti-aircraft machine-guns and ammunition for the torpedo boats had been unloaded at Marseille and found to contain nothing but bricks, rubble and old tyres.[38]

CNT reports and a probably exaggerated article in the extreme right-wing French newspaper *Gringoire* relate that Lt.-Col. Luis Monreal of the Comisión Técnica and a Theodore Lafitte, who had been involved in several arms deals, almost all unsuccessful, with the Republicans since the beginning of the war, had gone to Marseille on 18 April to receive the guns, which had been brought on the *SS Merkland* from Denmark, via Tilbury and Lisbon. After the deception had been discovered, Lt.-Col. Monreal had been seized in the street, hustled into a car and put on a plane for Barcelona, where he had been arrested on a charge of having arranged with Fascist agents for the guns to be switched for rubble at Lisbon, after which he disappeared into the Santa Ursula prison and was never heard of again. *Gringoire*, with its usual slavering anti-Semitism, stated that Epstein and Weissblatt were both 'OGPU' agents who had set up Aero-Marine Engines as a Communist front, that the respectable directors must have been duped, and that after Monreal's arrest two Russian agents had broken into the flat at 4 Park Lane with the intention of shooting Weissblatt, who had, however, escaped with Epstein to France.[39] This story must have had, in France at least, a degree of credibility, for during the past year, when Stalin's purge had extended to the NKVD itself, Russians, Red and White, had been hunting down and killing one another all over western Europe, thus adding a new dimension to the problems of the Spanish Republicans in Paris, to whose Comisión Técnica were attached not only Russian and other Communist advisers etc., but also White Russian interpreters, drivers and runners of errands. Meanwhile, in the opinion of the Anarchists, the swindle had been perpetrated by the Communists as a part of their lunatic determination to destroy non-Communist officers and officials of the Republic.[40]

In November 1938, however, Corrigan was brought to trial by Lafitte at the Mansion House Justice Room in London, charged with robbery and fraud. During the trial it emerged that Corrigan had been introduced to Chu Tin Hsu, an agent for the Chinese government, by Captain John Ball. Instead of ordering the guns, Corrigan had used the advance money to buy a derelict Wesleyan chapel in Tottenham, north London, had hired some workmen to knock it down and pack the rubble in the 550 boxes, which had been made by a local carpentry firm, and had embarked the boxes, labelled 'machine-tools and parts for cars', valued at £15,000, on the *Merkland* at Tilbury for shipping to Marseille. Ball had died in September 1938 and could not be charged, while Chu Tin Hsu had gone to America. Corrigan was sentenced to six months' imprisonment or a fine of £500, which he paid.[41] A year or two later he was arrested again for defrauding a lady of a large sum of money by means of a confidence trick involving jewellery once belonging to an Indian maharajah. He hanged himself in Brixton Prison.

30

Blockade

THROUGH THE WINTER of 1936–7, the Non-Intervention Committee discussed schemes to prevent the passage of arms into Spain, but progress was slow because any plan proposed by one delegate was immediately blocked by another. Eventually, however, a system of naval patrols and frontier posts was agreed which, it was hoped, would be operative by 6 March. This created difficulties for the Republicans, who, apprehensive of losing material in the pipeline, modified their orders to specify that everything must be delivered by that date. This merely enabled the less honest vendors to hold up delivery on various pretexts until the day had passed and then refuse to deliver the material unless the prices were increased or to return the initial down-payments on the grounds that the contracts were no longer binding. In the event, the scheme did not come into force until 20 April. The British and French navies patrolled the Biscay and Galician coasts and, in the south, from the Portuguese frontier to the Cabo de Gata in the Mediterranean. From there up to the French frontier, the coast, entirely Republican, was patrolled by the Germans and Italians. The scheme lasted but two months, until, as a result of the inadvertent bombing by Russians of the pocket-battleship *Deutschland*, to which the German navy responded by shelling Almería, and a probably false claim that a 'Red' submarine had fired a torpedo in the direction of the cruiser *Leipzig*, Hitler and Mussolini withdrew their navies from the patrols. The French lost interest and left the Royal Navy to carry on as best it could.*

---

* This it did on occasions with a punctiliousness verging on the sadistic. On 14 October 1937, having boarded a vessel belonging to the McAndrews Shipping Company and seen that the cargo was harmless, the Observing Officer noticed in one hold 'an armoured motorcycle and sidecar, with a label "From the workers of the de Havilland Aircraft Company, Hatfield, England, to the workers of Spain in their fight against Fascism".' He warned the captain that he 'would be committing an offence if he allowed the "armoured vehicle" to land' at Cartagena. 'The cycle was dismantled

The patrols really achieved nothing. Since only ships registered in countries which had signed the Non-Intervention agreement could be inspected, the German ships flew Panamanian or Liberian flags. The Italians did not trouble to do even that, but stared down the Royal Navy by close-escorting their transports with warships. As for the frontier observers, in France their only success was, on two occasions, to detain some squadrons of Republican Chatos and Natachas which, trying to reach the Basque zone from the main zone, landed on French airfields, and, having confiscated their armaments, to send them back to Catalonia. Along the frontier of Portugal, the Portuguese allowed as observers only British officers, who, having no authority to stop or inspect anything, were treated with little respect. On one occasion, for instance, the Spanish Falangist drivers of two lorries crossing through Elvas into Spain shouted at the British Observing Officers, who were unaware that the lorries were carrying 250 Bergmann machine-rifles, the word *Mamanachos!* ('Cock-suckers!'), which was tactfully translated to them as 'Down-and-outs!' That evening they were told by the Portuguese military governor of the town that had they been there only a few days before, they would have seen a trainload of gun-tractors and lorries, made by a British firm and sent out from England, pass through to Nationalist Spain.[1]

In London the Foreign Office received monthly reports from the War Office on the aid being supplied to the two sides in Spain and was aware that from December 1936 to February 1937 Italy alone had sent to Franco between 40,000 and 50,000 troops complete with light tanks, artillery and motorized transport, as well as about 130 aircraft, in addition to the 100 or so before that, and that the Germans were re-equipping their air force in Spain, believed to be about 100 aircraft strong, with their latest types of bombers and fighters.[2] This information, at least its general gist, was known by other governments and was repeated, with varying degrees of exaggeration, by the liberal and left-wing newspapers; yet in the House of Commons Eden or his deputy, Lord Cranborne (the future Lord Salisbury), answered questions from an increasingly indignant opposition by denying that the government had any reliable information on the matter, a tactic which was continued, after Eden's resignation in February 1938, by Lord Halifax's deputy, R. A. Butler, until the end of the war.[3] Nor was the Foreign Office forthcoming in its dealings with the other ministries.

In April 1937, the British minister in Prague, having read in the newspapers the reports of German aircraft movements to Spain that Vayo had

and the armour thrown overboard in the presence of the Observing Officer' (PRO, FO 371/21349 W 20972).

foolishly released to the press (see above, p. 162), sent a 'Most Secret' letter to London, as though the information had come direct from spies. An extract of it was passed to Wing Commander (later Air Marshal Sir) Victor Goddard at Air Ministry intelligence, among whose responsibilities was that of estimating the growing strength of the Luftwaffe. Goddard accordingly wrote to Owen O'Malley, soon to become known as a determined advocate of appeasement, at the Foreign Office to ask if more detailed information could be obtained; for, although we had fairly good data on the Italian and even the Russian aircraft in Spain, our knowledge of the German was still inadequate. It was not much use knowing the types without knowing how many were employed, more accurate figures of which would make it possible to assess their quality and discover how many the Germans were able to spare. Not until seventeen days later did an answer, drafted by Walter Roberts, arrive to say 'We do not feel that because the Spanish minister at Prague happens to claim to have given information on aircraft departures from Hannover there is any particular reason why the British minister there should have such information.' Indeed, so annoyed was the Foreign Office at Goddard for referring to the presence of German aircraft in Spain at all that it could not even get his name right, addressing the letter to 'Wing Commander Odbert'.[4]

About two weeks later Group Captain Colyer, the British air attaché at Paris, told the Foreign Office that he had had a conversation with Captain Bartlett, the Bristol Aircraft Company representative, who had just completed his annual tour of the French aviation industry. Bartlett had told him that during his tour he had not only heard that Cot was conniving at the supply of large numbers of Potez 54 bombers and other military aircraft to the Spanish Republicans and allowing Dutch aircraft to cross France to Spain, but that the French manufacturer Etienne Romano had even asked him if the Bristol company could supply ninety aero-engines for aircraft he was building in Belgium and France for the Spanish government. This letter sped upwards through the Foreign Office, gathering comments as it went on 'the shifty and disingenuous behaviour' of the French delegates on the Non-Intervention Committee. 'A shameless breach of faith and honour by the French govt. in the person of this young crook' (i.e., Cot), wrote Walter Roberts, for instance, to which Sir Alexander Cadogan added that a representation to the French government would have to be made which, he hoped, 'would cook Mr Cot's goose – he seems a proper little ruffian'.[5] A representation was indeed made, Romano was dismissed as director of the SNCASE, the group of nationalized aircraft companies in south-eastern France, the sub-contractor building the aircraft, Jean Biche, went bankrupt when the production of the aircraft in France was ordered to be stopped and the Spanish government lost another 6 million Ffr. (£57,143, or $285,715) when it was unable to dispose of the wings and fuselages so far completed.[6]

It was at this time, in July 1937, that Dr Otero, who was about to be appointed sub-secretary for armaments by Prieto, visited the Zborojovka factory at Pilsen, Czechoslovakia, in an effort to salvage at least something from the ruins of the Bolivian deal (see above, p. 160). When Outrata, the director, caustically asked why the Republicans bothered any more, unless of course they were mad, Otero replied, 'We would be mad if we stayed on here without the hope of getting what we need, and soon, for in another month the catastrophe will be complete. After all, wouldn't we rather keep the money for ourselves? I might add, by the way, that in the end the blame for all this lies with the English!'[7]

In Britain the Labour opposition became split between those who demanded, ineffectually since the Conservative majority was decisive, that Non-Intervention be enforced impartially and those who demanded that it be abandoned. Although feelings were high – 'Save Spain' offices, the majority organized by the Communist Party, to collect money for clothes and medicines, appeared in every town – there was not much resolve, the most visible manifestations being occasional marches by university students carrying banners on which 'ARMS FOR SPAIN!' was painted in large black letters.

In France, Blum's government fell on 22 June 1937 and was replaced by that of Camille Chautemps, who had opposed aid to the Spanish government from the beginning. To retain some support from the left, however, Chautemps invited Blum to become vice-premier, to which Blum agreed on condition that Pierre Cot stay on as air minister, Daladier as war minister and Marx Dormoy, a Socialist and strong supporter of aid to the Republicans, as interior minister in order that the policy of *non-intervention relâchée* ('relaxed Non-Intervention'), that is to say the discreet smuggling to Spain of small quantities of war material and of civil aircraft by ones and twos, could continue. In January 1938 Blum and the Socialists resigned from the government, whereupon Chautemps had the frontier closed completely. Within two months, however, his position as premier had become untenable and the remains of his government resigned on 13 March, the day after Hitler had ordered the German army into Austria and four days after the Spanish Nationalists had begun the massive offensive in Aragón that, by April, carried them to the Mediterranean coast, cut the Republic in two and left Catalonia separated from the main zone by a corridor eighty miles wide. Blum became premier once more and, when his suggestion that France intervene militarily to save the Spanish Republic from defeat was rejected with horror by the cabinet, ordered nevertheless that the frontier with Spain be opened on 17 March to allow material that had been accumulating in France since January or earlier to cross into Catalonia unhindered. Blum's government, however, fell on 20 April and was replaced by that of Edouard Daladier, who kept the frontier open until pressure from the British obliged him to close it on 13 June.

Throughout the twelve months between 22 June 1937 and 13 June 1938 the Spanish Nationalists, their German and Italian allies and their supporters all over the world claimed that armaments were flowing into 'Red Spain' almost without interruption and that after 17 March 1938 the flow became a torrent. This was supported to some extent forty years later when various French and Italian Communists and Socialists published their memoirs or gave interviews to historians in which they claimed that although no French arms were delivered to the Republicans, everything else that arrived in France from other countries was delivered, regardless of who was in power and whether or not the frontier was closed. From a careful reading of what they actually say, however, it is evident that, with a single exception (the ninety Mosca fighters brought by the last three deliveries from the USSR in June, July and August 1938), all the episodes they cite as examples occurred between mid-March and mid-June 1938, when the frontier was open. Indeed, the records show only two confirmed deliveries to France during the second half of 1937, both of SEPEWE material from Poland and neither of them large (see Appendix II, the *Al Racou* and *Ploubazlanec*).[*8] Nor is it certain whether the material crossed into Spain then or after 17 March 1938. As for Spain itself, apart from the last three deliveries from the USSR in June, July and August 1937 (voyages 35, 36 and 37) the only deliveries during the second half of that year seem to have been about six, of ammunition, by Greek ships in June and July, but because they all called at Marseille first and the reports are rather vague, it is impossible to say how much material, if any, remained in France or was taken on to Barcelona.[9] I do not count the three ships that carried material to the northern zone during this period – the sixteen ancient aeroplanes from Estonia on the *Viiu*, the 400 Lewis guns from SEPEWE on the *Heine* and some marine mines on the *Reyna* – for the Nationalists completed their conquest of the enclave on 20 October and the material, such as it was, became theirs. The *Reyna* was found sunk, by

---

* On 15 January 1937 Thorvald Erich, the Latin American partner of Willy Daugs in Berlin, bought a quantity of war material, much of it captured from the Bolivians during the Gran Chaco War and consequently worn out, on behalf of the Spanish Republic. It was shipped to Buenos Aires, where it was transhipped onto the *Herakles* and taken to an unnamed consignee in Gdynia, Poland. From there the arms went to Helsinki 'for reconditioning' and sending back to Paraguay. According to a dispatch from Ferrer Sicars, the Nationalist agent in Estonia, the Paraguayan arms were brought to Tallinn and there loaded onto the *Ploubazlanec* at the end of September 1937 (PRO, FO 371/ 21395 W 6774 and 10184; AMAE Madrid, DR R 1047 c. 34). The arms are listed in Appendix II, *Ploubazlanec*.

bombing, in Gijón harbour. Of the forty-four aircraft from countries other than Russia that reached the main zone between 22 June and 31 December 1937, only fourteen (ten Dewoitine D.371s and four Potez 540s; see Appendix I) were military.*

There were three reasons, then, why so little war material reached Republican Spain itself during the whole year from June 1937 to June 1938: at the supplying end all the deals had fallen through or were being renegotiated; as the northern zone dwindled and the Basques and Asturians, who had no money left, ceased to be customers, it became impossible to send ships from the Baltic round to the Mediterranean, for the Nationalists controlled the Straits of Gibraltar; delivery to Republican ports from across the Mediterranean became impossible after August 1937.

At the end of July 1937 General Franco, receiving erroneous reports that an enormous new supply of Soviet arms, including 300 aircraft and 2,600 tanks, was on its way from the Black Sea, appealed to Mussolini for help in preventing its arrival. Italian submarines accordingly attacked more than thirty ships, of which eleven, including four British and two Soviet, were sunk in the Mediterranean. Despite the reluctance of Neville Chamberlain, who had replaced Baldwin as prime minister on 20 May and hoped to reach an understanding with Mussolini, the British and French governments called an international conference at Nyon, Switzerland, and on 14 September warned that henceforth any 'unidentified' submarines appearing to threaten merchant ships would be sunk. For the rest of the year there were increased naval patrols, which Italy was invited, and agreed, to join.

Thus when the Soviets began to plan the next phase of 'Operation "X"', due to commence in December, it was obvious that the Mediterranean was no longer viable as a route to Spain and that the only alternative was to send the arms from Murmansk, by a wide curve through the Atlantic to avoid the English Channel, to Bordeaux. Between 14 December 1937 and 11 August 1938 there were twelve such voyages, all carried out by ships of France Navigation. This company was founded on 15 April 1937 for transporting supplies to the Spanish Republic. It was financed by Republican money, its director, Georges Gosnat, was a Communist and it was under Communist control. Its president, Joseph Fritsch, an elderly engineer who knew nothing of maritime affairs, was appointed precisely because he was not a Communist and would make a presentable figure-head. (The RGVA list in Appendix III, however, shows one additional delivery to a Mediterranean port, perhaps to Marseille or Barcelona, but it

---

* Of the twelve Vultees bought altogether, seven reached Republican Spain, of which six were converted into light bombers in 1938 (Howson, pp. 288–9).

is so small as to be negligible.) The details of the negotiations are not as yet known, but it seems that, since Blum and his fellow Republican supporters were still in the cabinet when the agreement was made, the transport of the goods from Bordeaux to the Spanish frontier would be allowed by the French authorities. The cargo of the *Guilvinec* (formerly the *Stanmore*, sold to the Republicans by Jack Billmeir) was the first to arrive at Bordeaux, on 25 December, and may have been taken on to Spain before the frontier closed on 18 January, but the cargoes of the next three, which arrived in February and March, were held in France until after 17 March. So too was the cargo on the *Ibai* from Mexico, of which something should be said here.

When the United States Congress had passed the Spanish Embargo Act on 7 January 1937, the government had strengthened it with a regulation demanding newly devised 'end-user certificates' for all exports of war material, including civil aircraft, a measure which has been adopted by all governments since the Second World War to prevent, at least in theory, the re-export of weapons by the buying country to a proscribed third country. This meant that the vendors of the twenty-eight American civil aircraft that Félix Gordón Ordás had collected at Veracruz would now be liable not only to prosecution and fines, since few of the aircraft had received export permits and nine had crossed the frontier after the passing of the act, but imprisonment too should any of the aircraft be shipped on to Spain. The same would apply to the buying agents in Mexico, should any of them set foot in the United States. In addition, Josephus Daniels, the United States ambassador to Mexico, left President Cárdenas in no doubt of the economic retribution that would follow upon such an eventuality. Gordón, therefore, saw that if he were to fulfil his duties to his government, he had no choice but to ship the planes out by means of deception, even though this would bring his own diplomatic career to an end and damage Cárdenas's already difficult relations with the US government.

For a time Gordón tried to throw journalists off the scent by having the planes flown from airfield to airfield across Mexico, during which one of them, the Breese Racer, was lost in an accident. He abandoned this when he learnt that FBI agents had already stolen into the hangars at Veracruz by night and listed the construction numbers and registrations of all the machines.[10]

On 20 February 1937 the Bolivian ambassador to Mexico told Gordón that he was willing to arrange for his government to provide 'cover' for all the aircraft and let it be known, in the course of the conversation that followed, that the personal gratuity that he would expect in return for such a service would be very low, that is to say $5,000 per aeroplane, or $140,000 (£28,000) altogether. Although this would raise the cost of the twenty-eight aircraft (*c.* $505,550) by nearly 30%, Vayo approved it on 22 February, for the Turkish deal in Czechoslovakia had just collaped and it appeared that Bolivia might open a way to saving the arms.[11]

Gordón's main problem through the whole of 1937 was therefore to find a ship to take the aircraft to France or Spain and by August it seemed that the only possibility was that offered by the *Motomar*, a Spanish cargo ship recently arrived at Veracruz. Before she could cross the Atlantic again, however, repairs were needed to her hull and, since to send her to the dry dock at Galveston, Texas, where García and Díaz, the Nationalist shipping agency in New York, would immediately try to claim her, was too risky, application was made to the Admiralty in London to use the dry dock at Bermuda. This was granted and the *Motomar*, loaded with food, clothing and three civil aircraft, reached Bermuda on 1 September. There, however, her captain, Fernando Dicentas (the son of the Spanish dramatist Joaquín Dicentas), was told, with apologies, that the dry dock would not after all be available until 24 September, that before the ship could go into dry dock the cargo would have to be unloaded and that, once unloaded, it could not be reloaded because the three civil aircraft shown on the cargo manifest constituted war material. An inspector from García and Díaz arrived from New York and made a formal application to detain the ship, but before this could be granted Dicentas took her out of territorial waters and returned to Veracruz.[12]

By then the Bolivian arms and munitions (see above, p. 160) had arrived by rail at Mollendo, Peru, where they had to wait until 19 October, when the Japanese ship *Florida Maru*, which was already carrying a few thousand Japanese rifles which Gordón had managed to buy through an agent, arrived to take them on board. She sailed on 2 November, but next day the Japanese legation, warned by the right-wing newspapers that the arms were intended for Republican Spain, ordered her to return. The cargo was unloaded and, after three weeks, transferred to two trains, which left for Veracruz on the 23rd.*[13] In December Gordón was at last able to embark

---

* According to Gordón Ordás (p. 769), the Bolivian arms loaded onto the *Ibai* were: 15,000 Mauser rifles, 111 Vickers machine-guns and 40 million cartridges, all 7.65 mm; 80 Bergman and Schneider [*sic*] light machine-guns, 9 mm; four Schneider 75 mm model M.P.C. field-guns and 3,721 shells; four Schneider 75 mm L.D. field-guns and 2,729 shells; six Krupp 7.65 cm M16 field-guns and 1,792 shrapnel shells; four Krupp 60 mm [*sic*] guns and 1,208 shells; thirty 105 mm trench-mortars and 6,000 mortar-grenades; fourteen 47 mm trench-mortars and 6,000 mortar-grenades; six Spanish naval guns transferred from the *Motomar* and fifty Mauser rifles bought from an individual. As usual, the artillery ammunition was woefully insufficient. The list by Juan de Cárdenas, Franco's agent in New York (Archivo del Servicio Histórico Militar, Madrid, Microfilm 23, Armario 4, L. 266, *c.* 4, 8 June 1937), corresponds almost exactly, which means that someone on Gordón's staff was passing information to the other side.

nine of the aircraft and the arms from Bolivia on board the motorship *Cabo Quilates*, which, renamed *Ibai*, sailed on the 27th and reached Le Havre on 13 January 1938, too late to cross the frontier before it was closed.

There is a puzzle, however, concerning the Bolivian rifles, 15,000 Mauser 7.65 mm, which were packed on the *Ibai* in 603 boxes. During the spring and summer of 1938, the Nationalists noticed that 7.65 mm rifles were being used by the Republicans. This was an unusual calibre, and after the civil war their recuperation service estimated from captured weapons that the number of these Bolivian rifles could not have been more than 1,500.[14] What happened, then, to the other 13,500 or, for that matter, to the 7,119 Mausers of the same calibre bought in Paraguay by Thorvald Erich and said to have been shipped on the *Ploubazlanec*?

31

'This Question is no Longer Important'

ON 9 MAY 1938 William Bullitt, the United States ambassador in Paris, sent a telegram to Cordell Hull, the Secretary of State, to recount a conversation he had held with Edouard Daladier. Asked about the war material reported to be crossing into Spain from France,

Daladier said that he had opened the French frontier to Spain as completely as possible. He had done even more. After the recent successful offensive of General Franco the Russians had indicated their willingness to send 300 planes if France would make arrangements for their transhipment across France to Spain. He had transported the 300 planes across France successfully in the largest trucks available, although he had had to cut down many miles of trees along the sides of the roads in order that the large bombers might pass.[1]

Daladier added that he had recently told Chamberlain that he would ship through France anything any country wished to send to Spain and would continue to do so until the German and Italian aircraft were withdrawn from Spain. Some months later Pierre Flandin, a new minister in Daladier's cabinet, declared in public that 25,000 tons of war material had crossed the frontier in April and May 1938 alone, a figure which has since found its way into general histories of the Spanish Civil War.[2]

First, it should be said that the second phase of 'Operation "X"' voyages began in December 1937, three months before the Nationalist offensive in Aragón. Secondly, the total number of Soviet aircraft sent between 14 December 1937 and 11 August 1938 was not 300 but 152 (31 SB Katiuskas, and 121 I-16 Moscas) of which only 62 (31 Katiuskas and 31 Moscas) had arrived at Bordeaux from Murmansk by 9 May, when Daladier had his conversation with Bullitt (Appendix III). Flandin's figures of 25,000 tons was another political exaggeration. Since we know the quantities and types of arms and munitions that the Soviets sent in 1938, their total weight can be calculated to have been about 13,000 tons at the most.* To this we should add the *Ibai* shipment (about 1,820 tons), the thirty-four Grummans (about 70 tons) and two shipments of about 500 tons each from Estonia brought by the *Diana* (ex-*Scotia*) in April and May, which bring the total to about 17,190 tons. Even if we add the cargoes of the *Al Racou* (656 tons) and *Ploubazlanec* (266–373 tons), assuming that they crossed at this time and not in the autumn of 1937, we still have only 18,219 tons for the whole period between 17 March and 13 June, of which 8,000–10,000 tons were sent across in April and May. This illustrates some of the problems that have faced historians of the Spanish Civil War for sixty years.

Daladier's story that he had ordered many miles of trees to be cut down along the sides of the roads was yet another exaggeration and seems to have originated from a story in a right-wing newspaper. This says that on 26–27 April eleven aircraft, which at that date would have been Katiuska bombers, and four tanks crossed the frontier. The aircraft crates, however, were so high that at one place near Millas, a small town west of Perpignan, some of the roadside trees had to be pruned to allow the crates to pass beneath. 'The pruning was carried out by the Communist Gendre himself.' 'Gendre' was André Gendre, a Communist militant employed in guiding such convoys from Millas, a favourite assembly point, along the narrow roads to the Pyrenean frontier.[3]

On 15 June 1938 Emilio Togliatti (alias 'Ercoli'), the Italian Communist leader and the senior Comintern representative in Spain, sent a telegram to Georgi Dmitrov, the general secretary of the Comintern in Moscow. He begged Dmitrov to draw the attention of the Soviet Instantsia (which might be roughly translated as 'Establishment') to the fact that the Spanish Republicans were in truly desperate need of much more effective help than they were receiving. Admittedly, they were for the moment better armed than they had been recently, but the officer corps was extremely weak and Communist officers in particular, who now played a major role on all fronts, were proving to be inept commanders in the field.

> Negrín emphatically requests that we send more competent people who, more-over, have experience in the field. Since the Party is doing all it can to help

---

* Since a rifle cartridge weighed 25 grams, a million weighed 25 metric tons. An average rifle weighed about 5 kg, a Maxim gun 45 kg (74 kg with its Sokolov wheel-mounting), a light machine-gun 10–12 kg, a 75 mm or 76.2 mm field-gun or howitzer between 1.5 and 1.7 metric tons, and so on. Ammunition was always the heaviest component of any arms cargo. The 13,000 tons of Soviet material includes the ninety Moscas unloaded at Bordeaux in June, July and August after the frontier was closed for the second time, for they crossed into Spain nonetheless. This also includes their spare parts, engines, and arms. If the usual amounts of petrol oil and coolants were delivered as well, they would add another 870 tons to the overall total, raising it to 14,000 tons between 17 March and 11 August.

Negrín, surely it is possible to send better personnel to the General Staff, over which Negrín now exercises considerable control in operational matters . . . Therefore we respectfully implore you to intercede on our behalf as soon as possible. I repeat, we are all asking for your help as a matter of the utmost urgency.[4]

The telegram was delivered to Stalin, who, regarding the Comintern – *lavochka* ('market stall') was his name for it – as irrelevant to important policy, may or may not have passed it on to Dmitrov.

On 25 July the Republicans opened a major attack across the River Ebro, along the northern front of the corridor separating the two-parts of the Republic, and within a week pushed forward some twenty-five miles on a narrow sector. Their intention was to catch Franco off balance, relieve Nationalist pressure against Valencia by threatening their forces in the Mediterranean end of the corridor and, by throwing them on to the defensive, keep the war going until a general European war, as was now expected in view of the crisis over Czechoslovakia, should break out; then Britain and France would become allies of the Republic, with important naval and air bases on the Mediterranean coast at their disposal and large German and Italian forces trapped in Spain. However, Nationalist superiority in manpower and material, especially in artillery and aircraft, brought the attack to a stop. The fighting, the fiercest of the civil war and accompanied by the largest air battles seen in warfare up to that time and not to be equalled until the Battle of Britain, continued until 18 November, when the last Republican units withdrew to the north bank of the river.

By then the Republicans had received no material of any kind since August, when the last group of Mosca fighters had been unloaded from the *Bougaroni* at Bordeaux on the 11th, and no army material since May. The 188 artillery pieces from the USSR – as usual, they were old and foreign and included twenty ancient Japanese Arisaka 107 mm – had come with about 1,500 shells each. There had been delivered only twenty-five T-26 tanks and four of the modern 45 mm anti-tank guns, only eighty Maxim machine-guns and 3,850 light machine-guns, of which 2,000 had in any case come from Czechoslovakia as part of the atrocious Bolivian deal. Perhaps the most useful were the 250 light (37 mm) Gochkisa anti-tank guns, which at least came with 20,512 rounds apiece. It should be mentioned too that the I-16 Moscas were equipped with ShKAS M 35 machine-guns, at the time perhaps the best aircraft machine-guns in the world. However, although their extraordinarily rapid rate of fire of 1,800–2,000 rounds per minute wore out the barrels after only a few actions, throughout the whole war each air regiment of thirty-one Moscas was supplied with only six spare guns, and there is no record of any additional spares being sent separately.

In August 1938 the Soviets informed Negrín that only 1.5 tons of the gold reserve remained in Spanish possession. Marcelino Pascua, the former ambassador in Moscow and now the ambassador in Paris, was sent to Moscow to ask for a loan of $60 million. Apparently it was granted, although no details are known.[5] However, the heavy losses suffered during the Battle of the Ebro and the disappointing outcome at Munich convinced Negrín that only a massive transfusion of material aid would enable the Republic to continue resistance for much longer and, accordingly, General Hidalgo de Cisneros, the air chief who was by now an unquestioning Communist, was sent to Moscow with a request for, among other things, 250 aircraft, 250 tanks, 650 artillery pieces and 4,000 machine-guns, a catalogue which appeared to him a pure fantasy, despite the fact that, so he implies, it consisted largely of requests that had been made in vain during the previous year. There has been uncertainty over the dates and manner of his journey, for the letter from Negrín that he took with him is dated 11 November, while he himself states that he left a few days before the Nationalist offensive against Catalonia, which began on 23 December.[6] A letter from Voroshilov to Stalin shows, however, that he was in Moscow on 27 November and had arrived that day or a day or two before.[7] Most probably, therefore, he flew from Spain in the Douglas DC-2 EC-AGA (the DC-2 bought from Swissair; see above, p. 215), which took a party of Republican ministers and generals to Ankara to attend the funeral of Kemal Ataturk on the 21st, there being a photograph of this aeroplane at Malta on the 20th,[8] and went on from Ankara to Moscow by train.

Hidalgo de Cisneros told Marshal Voroshilov that the Republican army now lacked even the most basic equipment. Entire battalions and regiments at the front had no rifles; and the army lacked artillery, munitions and aviation material, for what little remained was mostly worn out. 'Except for your country, no one has sold us anything. The truth is that we have paid money to various swindlers and crooks and received practically nothing in return. If for some reason you cannot supply all we ask, at least help us to obtain arms from other countries.' Voroshilov promised to pass the letters that Hidalgo de Cisneros had brought with him to Stalin and that there would be an answer soon. 'I think it essential that we give him some kind of reply'.[9]

Hidalgo de Cisneros was astonished when Stalin, who saw him next day, agreed to all the requests without demur and was even more astonished, when discussing payment with Anastas Mikoyan, the trade minister, that the Soviet government would lend the full amount, $103 million and that all he need do was to sign a paper recording the fact. He goes on to say that all the material was promptly carried by seven Soviet ships to France, where the French authorities delayed their transit to Spain until the beginning of February, by which time most of Catalonia had been overrun by the Nationalists. The material was therefore returned to France, the Nationalists laid claim to it and the French government would have complied had not the Soviet government insisted that it had not been paid for and, as Soviet property, must be returned to the USSR.[10] Hidalgo de Cisneros, who was after all a patrician familiar since youth with the emollient ways of courtiers, emphasizes that in Moscow he and his wife (Constancia de la Mora), who had been invited to supper after the meeting, had been deeply moved by the unaffected simplicity of Stalin and his entourage. Here was living proof, if any more were needed, of the disinterested generosity with which the whole people of the Soviet Union had supported the cause of the people of Spain and, whatever might have been said later about the dark side of Stalin's strange character, this greatness of spirit should always be remembered.[11]

Lists in the RGVA (Appendix III) show, however, that the material sent fell short of the material promised: 168 aircraft instead of 250, 40 tanks instead of 250, 539 pieces of artillery instead of 650, and again many of them old and foreign, and 2,770 machine-guns instead of 4,000. Moreover, the practice of overcharging by fiddling the exchange rates was not only continued but on some items, such as the Vickers 115 mm howitzers, was exacerbated, for the rouble prices were lowered while the dollar prices remained the same as they had been in 1936.[12]

Lacalle writes that on 1 February he was ordered to inspect a number of crates that had been brought over the frontier and dumped in a field. They contained, he discovered, Mosca fighters and Katiuska bombers, but there being no airfields left where they could be assembled and no suitable aircrews to fly them, he ordered them to be sent back to France.[13] Appendix III shows how much material was shipped to France – not in Soviet ships, as Hidalgo de Cisneros believed, but in those of France Navigation – and how much crossed into Spain: thirty I-15bis Superchatos, which took no part in the fighting before escaping to France on 6 February, three 45 mm anti-tank guns, 35,000 rifles, 2,000 light machine-guns, 777 Maxims and large amounts of ammunition and aircraft parts and equipment.

By 9 February the Nationalists had conquered the whole of Catalonia and 400,000 Republican troops and refugees, including the government, had crossed into France. So too, among many other treasures, had the paintings from the Prado: as the lorries carrying them approached the frontier, the crowds of refugees had moved apart, pulling aside their carts and prams and donkeys loaded with clothes and pots and pans and children, to let them pass. President Azaña, whose aesthetic sense was strong, observed to Negrín, as they watched them go by, that all the notions of monarchy and republic were not worth a single Velázquez.[14] It is said that neither really believed this, though one cannot be certain.

Negrín and a few of the ministers returned by air to the main zone on 10 February, establishing a temporary seat of government at the small town of Elda, west of Alicante, and declared that the Republic should resist to the end, as the Spanish Communists and the Comintern were urging them to do. On 16 February Voroshilov wrote a short memorandum of which only two copies were made, one for Stalin and the second for the Politburo. He said that according to information from the Soviet embassy in Paris, Negrín was trying, through Pascua, to obtain a reply to several letters regarding the promised supply of arms to the Republic army.

In case Pascua or someone else continues to press this matter, it might be appropriate to reply as follows:
1) The USSR has always paid close attention to the necessities of the Spanish government and complied, as far as possible, with all its demands for arms and military assistance;
2) The last demand, made through Cisneros, has been complied with for the most part. If the Spanish government cannot reach an agreement with the French government over the transit of arms to Spain, we are sorry to hear it;
3) For them to demand now that the material we have already sent, the greater part of which is still on French territory, be sent on to Spain, where it will become a prize for the Fascists, is at the very least inopportune. I request your thoughts.

Voroshilov's letter is countersigned by Malenkov. Stalin's thoughts are expressed by a scribble on the left margin of the page: 'This question is no longer important.'[15]

Eleven days later the British and French governments formally recognized Franco's regime as the legitimate government of Spain and they were quickly followed by most of the governments of the world except those of the USSR, Mexico and, be it noted, the United States. Negrín, now with no international status or hope of receiving help from anywhere, nevertheless appealed to the people to continue the fight by claiming that ample supplies of new armaments, including hundreds of the latest Russian and American aircraft, would soon arrive from France.[16] Colonel Casado, the commander at Madrid, denounced further resistance as futile, declared his intention to negotiate peace terms with the Nationalists and, when the Communist regiments in the capital tried to remove him, crushed them with Anarchist help and executed their commanders. Franco, however, was interested only in unconditional surrender and the implementation of his new 'Law of Political Responsibilities' by which anyone who had actively or passively supported the Republic would be liable to arrest, trial and, if found guilty, punishment by imprisonment or death. Casado, his approaches rebuffed, fled to Gandía, near Valencia, whence he was taken by a British ship to England. Thereafter, La Pasionaria and other Communist leaders who escaped to the Soviet Union anathematized him and his colleagues as the worst of traitors, who bore 'the mark of Cain' on their foreheads. Scores of thousands of people, terrified by rumours of mass executions in Barcelona, converged on Alicante and Valencia in the expectation that ships would arrive to carry them to safety, only to see the ships, whose captains were alarmed at the sight of the crowds crammed on the quays, turn and sail away. Negrín and such senior Republican and Comintern functionaries as had been able to obtain aircraft for themselves flew to France or Algeria and the Republic surrendered on 31 March.

32

Conclusions

I N FEBRUARY 1939 Ernest Hemingway, whose support of the Republic had always been unequivocal, wrote to a friend:

> There is only one thing to do when you are in a war and that is to win it. When you have been betrayed and sold out in a dozen different ways you shouldn't object to being lied about in addition. The British were the real villains. All the way through from the very start.[1]

This could be shrugged off as just another piece of Hemingway's habitual Britain-baiting were it not that many people in Britain, including those whose views had previously been neither one way or the other, were saying much the same. One of the most unexpected was Captain W. E. Johns, the creator of Biggles, who wrote in the editorial to the March 1939 issue of his magazine *Popular Flying*, 'Of all the foul and craven hypocrisy of which those in power in Britain had been guilty during the past decade – and nowhere in history will you find such a sequence of faint-hearted perfidiousness – this Spanish business is the worst.' His point was that he had no personal interest in party politics and that it should have made no difference to those in Britain, supposedly a democracy, that the Spanish government had been left-wing. It had been elected by the vote of the people and was as democratic as a government could be.

> The soul of democracy lies in the simple fact that the people are always right. But our government, being right-wing, does not hold that view. So it prefers to see Spain slaughtered by its own worst enemies rather than lift a finger to help it. There you have the truth of the affair.[2]

In 1998 few people, certainly not historians or even left-wing historians, still believe that there we have the truth of the affair. During the Second World War and for about twenty years after it, Baldwin,

246

Chamberlain, Halifax and others were labelled the 'guilty men' of appeasement, and their conduct towards Spain was seen as but a part of this policy. They were excoriated for their myopic stubbornness and class arrogance, which had nearly brought about the triumph of those two bellicose and illiberal tyrants, Hitler and Mussolini, and the end of everything that was civilized and decent in life. By the 1970s, however, a number of conservatively minded historians, not working together and certainly not in conspiracy, had begun to argue for what they regarded as a more fair-minded view. They claimed that Chamberlain in particular had not been the conceited, ignorant, bowler-hatted, umbrella-wielding incarnation of the 'Establishment' portrayed by caricaturists, but a far-sighted practitioner of *realpolitik* who, by skilfully conciliating the dictators, had gained for Britain the opportunity to rearm for the confrontation in September 1939. 'Appeasement', wrote Robert (today Lord) Skidelsky in 1972, 'is now increasingly seen as an attempt to buy time rather than to buy off Germany.'[3] Twelve years later, during a TV programme to mark the fiftieth anniversary of Munich, Lord Home (who as Lord Dunglass had been secretary to Chamberlain), Lord Hailsham and a retired senior official from the Foreign Office all insisted that Chamberlain had been right to sacrifice Czechoslovakia. Had Britain gone to war in September 1938 instead of a year later, they said, so great was German superiority of strength that Britain would have been defeated, an assertion which Hailsham qualified at the last moment by adding, 'At least that's what the chiefs-of-staff told us.'[4]

The story of Non-Intervention in the Spanish war had meanwhile been brought in to support this general thesis. In another TV programme, specifically about the Spanish Civil War, Lord Home had defended Non-Intervention by saying that conciliating the dictators was the only possible policy at the time and was, moreover, agreed to by all the other political parties. In consideration of the dangers in Europe, the Mediterranean and from Japan in the Far East, non-involvement in Spain 'was geared to British interests. We needed all the arms we could get, in fact we didn't have enough when war with Hitler started in 1939. Any arms sent to Spain would have been arms lost to our forces'.[5] In 1992 another former Conservative prime minister, Sir Edward Heath, applied the same reasoning during a debate in the House of Commons over what Britain should do about the civil war in Yugoslavia. British forces, he said, should not be sent to Bosnia. He asked the House to consider history, particularly that of the Spanish Civil War, which had been in his time. 'I was against Franco. I was on the other side. I went to Spain during the Civil War. But then we had had Non-Intervention. Anthony Eden had been absolutely right to keep British forces out of that war. If we had gone into it, it would have precipitated the Second World War before we were prepared for it. That is a fact.'[6] Yet it is also a fact that no one in the Republican government had ever asked Britain to 'go into' the war or expected her to send the Brigade of Guards or squadrons of the RAF to fight the rebels, only that the Republicans be allowed to buy arms on the open market. During the days, at the beginning of the fighting in Spain, when Non-Intervention was being discussed, the need to rearm against the growing threat from Germany is nowhere mentioned in any government correspondence, nor are the larger strategic concerns until well after the Non-Intervention agreement had been drafted and circulated to foreign governments. If the British government had decided in July and August 1936 that Britain needed all the arms she could get for herself, as Lord Home says, one is entitled to ask why British arms exports to everywhere except Spain not only continued but actually increased from 1936 until shortly after the beginning of the Second World War.[7]

In a letter to the American Armaments Corporation earlier in 1936, Captain John Ball stated that his Soley Arms Company had between 700,000 and 800,000 rifles, more than 50,000 machine-guns, a considerable number of artillery pieces and enormous quantities of the appropriate ammunition and spares, all ready for immediate delivery; so much material, in fact, he said, that if it were sold to a single country it would change the balance of power in the whole region.[8] This was enough to equip the British peacetime army, at home and in the empire, several times over, and the number of rifles alone was greater that that obtained by the Spanish Republicans during the entire civil war. But for the Foreign Office, the Spanish government could have bought the lot, at market prices, in July and August 1936. As for aircraft, fifty Bristol Blenheims were sold to Turkey, and numerous Hawker Hurricanes to half-a-dozen countries. Twelve Spitfires, the most vitally needed and secret of British warplanes, were even sold to Estonia when that country was in imminent danger of invasion by the Soviet Union or Nazi Germany or both, and when the Air Ministry knew that Estonia was able to pay for the aircraft only because of the extortionate profits it had made from selling sixteen old crocks from its own tiny air force to the Spanish Republicans (see above, p. 213).

How true, then was the assumption by the left that Non-Intervention was the principal cause of the Republican defeat, in that its one-sided application denied arms to the Republicans but allowed enough to reach Franco to ensure his victory? In 1952 Lord Halifax wrote apropos of the Non-Intervention Committee that 'I doubt whether a single man or gun less reached either side in the war as a result of its activities',[9] but he stressed that the Committee had nonetheless served its purpose by keeping down the temperature in Europe. Histories of the Spanish Civil War in which impartiality was attempted did not begin to appear, and then only outside Spain, until the early 1960s, and by the time these questions about the Spanish war had been subsumed within the larger questions about appeasement, much had been written about the politics behind the Non-Intervention policy but very little about its effects in practice. This was not because the historians were unwilling to discuss the subject but because, with most archives still closed and with the people who had been involved in the clandestine traffic still unwilling to talk, useful information was impossible to find.

Meanwhile in Franco's Spain, since the 1950s historians had been publishing books and articles, accompanied by detailed charts and tables, to show that the story that Non-Intervention had deprived the Republicans of arms was a myth invented by the Communists and liberals. Captured Republican documents, on which the figures in the tables were said to be based, revealed that the Republicans had obtained huge quantities of arms, aircraft, munitions and war material of every kind from the USSR and through the black market from all over the world, more indeed than the Nationalists had ever received from Germany and Italy.[10] As the years passed, some of these claims were revealed to be exaggerated and their authors toned them down a little, but many of the figures, for lack of any others, passed into histories of the Spanish Civil War and from them into works of reference, encyclopaedias and general histories of the 20th century, where they still are and where students consulting them today would have no reason to doubt their accuracy.

Thus, when reviewing a new edition of Hugh Thomas's great history of the war in *The Times* (10 Feb 1977), Laurence Cotterell wrote, 'Foreign intervention was largely haphazard. The republicans got more planes and tanks from abroad, the insurgents more men and artillery pieces.' (Thomas says no such thing.) The gist of Cotterell's article is that by 1977 everything that could be said about this rather tiresome event of the past had been said and all its myths could now be laid to rest. More recently, in the 1996 edition of Paul Johnson's *Modern Times*, described on its back cover as having 'established itself as the global handbook to twentieth-century history', there is a long and in many respects accurate account of the war. However, Johnson writes that 'the outcome of the war was not... determined by great power intervention, which cancelled itself out, nor by the non-intervention policy of Britain and France, since arms could always be obtained for gold or hard currency...' and he goes on to say that 'In quantity, the Republicans received as much *matériel* from abroad as the Nationalists' and concludes that 'Foreign aid and intervention did not tip the military balance either way.'[11]

This, I believe, is the prevailing view now and is coming to be accepted generally as the historical truth. Certainly, when I was in Madrid in 1991 and 1992, the Spanish friends with whom I discussed this and from whom

I received valuable specialist help, were convinced, despite their fundamental sympathy for the Republic, that the Republicans had obtained abundant supplies of arms but had not known how to use them properly. Nevertheless, they had admitted that, being busy people with jobs and families, they had had little time to do any serious research in the archives, which was one of the reasons, apart from their natural Spanish disposition to kindness, why they were so generous to me.*

It would follow, then, if the two sides in the war were equally balanced, that Non-Intervention never worked, that there would be no point in waxing indignant over its 'heaped-up iniquities', as Thomas Mann called them, and that yet another charge against the 'guilty men' of appeasement should now be dropped. It would follow too that an explanation for the Republicans' defeat should be sought elsewhere, for example in their political disunity and the disorganization and incompetence that resulted from it, or, as some have claimed, in Franco's superior judgement.

The validity of the whole case, however, stands upon the assumption that the data and figures generally accepted now are true. I have not been able to compile an exact inventory, down to the last pistol and cartridge, of all the weaponry and munitions that the Republicans acquired during the war, but the facts presented in this book are sufficient to prove, once and for all, that the figures are *not* true, and that the material strengths of the two sides were balanced so unequally against the Republicans that a great deal of what has been published about the history of the Spanish Civil War in general and of the various battles in particular will have to be rewritten.

Arms could *not* 'always be obtained for gold or hard currency': on the contrary, the Republicans rarely obtained more than a fraction of what they needed and even then only after long delays and at a terrible cost, physical and moral. As the records published here show, they were faced by a wall of blackmail wherever they turned: by ministers of government, chiefs-of-staff and other officers and officials in more than thirty countries** who demanded bribes of between £5,000 ($25,000) and £45,000 ($275,000) a time, in 1937 money, for their signatures on dubious export licences and 'clearance' papers. Below them were officials down to harbour- and station-masters who not only demanded bribes but found

---

* This was a group of young men who, in their spare time, were compiling a scholarly catalogue of a collection of weapons, most of them from the civil war period, for the Museo del Aire at Getafe, Madrid. When I arrived for my second visit, I found that, since they regarded the *pensión* where I had stayed before as unsatisfactory, they had booked me into a more expensive hotel where I would have peace, seclusion, a larger room and a writing desk, and that they had arranged to pay half my bills. Such is Spain.
** In 1940 Colonel Alfonso Barra of the Nationalist Servicio de Recuperación, which had examined and classified weapons captured from the Republicans, stated that as a result of having had to purchase from so many different sources, the Republican army

pretexts to delay transportation in order to charge accumulating 'storage fees', of which one, it may be remembered, rose to as much as £10,000 ($50,000). How often, too, the ministers and officials changed their minds, found ways to withhold delivery of the material and to refuse to return the money! And below them again were the arms dealers, brokers and other go-betweens. Yet such behaviour appears trivial beside that of the Soviets, whose defrauding of the Spanish government of millions of dollars, by secretly manipulating the exchange rates when setting the prices for the goods they were supplying, belied everything they professed to stand for.

If people continue to make moral judgements about the Spanish Civil War, as they do, and to make political capital out of it, as they do, then first they must be sure that their history is accurate. This book has dealt with one part, and a very important part, of the Spanish Civil War that historians have still to get right. Until they do, we cannot consider properly why the Republicans lost the war.

---

had had forty-nine different types of repeating rifle, forty-one different types of automatic weapon and no fewer than sixty different types of artillery piece. Normally an army would have one type of rifle (and perhaps a carbine), three or four types of machine-gun (heavy, light and sub-) and perhaps ten different types of artillery piece from light to coastal defence and siege guns (*Ejército*, June 1940).

Appendices

APPENDIX I

A. French military aircraft in the Spanish Civil War

Les Archives de la Haute-Garonne, Toulouse: Liasse No 1912/55, folder no. 14, contains telegrams, 8–9 August 1936, reporting the departures of the thirteen Dewoitines and six Potez for Barcelona. The key document, however, is no. 389, the *compte rendu*, dated 26 Aug 1936, sent by the airport inspector at Toulouse-Francazal to the prefect of police, which lists the arrivals of the aircraft from 4–8 August and their departures from 7–9 August. The 'No.' column refers to the production series numbers stencilled under the cockpits of the Dewoitine D.372s. This document has not been previously published.

ARRIVALS

Date	Time	Type	No.	Pilot	Remarks
4.8	17.00	D.372	4	Doumerc	Test pilot
"	17.05	"	5	Roulland	"
"	18.00	"	6	Lepreux	"
"	19.05	"	7	Abel Guidez	Reservist
"	19.55	"	8	Bois	"
5.8	19.48	"	11	Roulland	
"	19.51	"	10	Schnee or Scheer	Reservist
"	20.20	"	13	Guidez	
6.8	11.30	"	1	Brefford	?
"	16.10	"	3	Lepreux	
"	16.10	"	14	Totem	Reservist
"	16.27	Potex 54		Descamp	Test pilot
"	16.27	"		Micolf	?
"	20.07	D.372	2	Dary	Reservist
"	20.07	"	12	Guidez	
7.8	20.00	Potex 54		?	
8.8	06.00	"		?	
"	17.15	"		Corniglion-Molinier	The Malraux as passengers
"	17.20	"		?	

Dewoitine no. 9, flown by the reservist Réné Halotier, came down *en route* near the village of Maubourguet, north of Tarbes, on 4 August. It was repaired and flown to Barcelona by Roger Nouvel on 5 November (*Le Figaro*, 10 Nov 1936).

DEPARTURES

Date	Time	Type	No.	Pilot
7.8	18.30	D.372	7	Bois
8.8	07.30	"	11	Halotier

Date	Time	Type	No.	Pilot
"	09.15	"	2	Dary
"	09.15	"	12	Issart
"	09.15	"	1	Tardy
"	11.30	Potez 54		Gontcharoff
"	11.40	"		Grand
"	11.45	"		Guidez
"	17.25	D.372	10	Bois
"	17.37	"	5	Halotier
"	17.50	"	13	Nouvel
"	18.30	"	14	Gontcharoff
"	18.40	"	3	Issart
"	18.45	Potez 54		
"	18.45	"		
"	18.45	"		
"	18.47	D.372	6	Dary
"	19.07	"	4	Guidez
9.8	09.45	"	8	Bois

The number of aircraft is confirmed by Major Juan Aboal's report to Madrid, 6 Sept 1936 (Archivo del Ministerio de Asuntos Exteriores, Madrid, Archivo de Barcelona, RE 135 c. 5 pl. 3), the radio message from the USS *Quincy* (see above, p. 55) and a Nationalist intelligence report, 14 Aug 1936, quoted in Ismael Saz, *Mussolini contra la Segunda República* (p. 246) and *Le Figaro* (10 Nov 1936), where Maurice Pujo, a very pro-Franco journalist, summarizes all known deliveries to the Spanish Republicans to that date. Indeed, none of the French newspapers of the time claims that more than twelve or thirteen Dewoitine and six Potez were sent on or about 8 August; the exaggerations began later, probably during the parliamentary debates in December.

These aircraft were followed on 26 August by a Potez 544 and a Bloch MB 210, both bombers, and on 5–7 September by five Loire 46 fighters. These were likewise unarmed and the arms were never delivered. From 18 to 20 October there arrived two pre-production Dewoitine D.371s and seven Potez 542s (i.e. with Lorraine Petrel instead of Hispano 12X engines). They too were probably without arms, but this is not certain. At the end of October three Bloch MB 210s were delivered in crates, though they may not have been assembled until the following February (Internationaal Institut voor Sociale Gerchiedenis [IISG], Amsterdam, CNT Microfilm 153, A 7, report to Mariano Vázquez of a meeting between Prieto, two Russians, Colonel Camacho, deputy chief of the Republican air forces, and others on 8 Feb 1937, which refers to some Blochs and Potez still not assembled or repaired). A Breguet 460, a rejected prototype, was flown to Barcelona on 20 November, but stayed in Catalonia until it crashed or was shot down by anti-aircraft fire on 7 March 1937. Two Dewoitine D.510s, built for Turkey but rejected, were delivered at the end of December 1936. It may be remembered that when Cot had sold a D.510 to the Russians in September, the right-wing deputies in the chamber had raised a storm because it had been fitted with a 'secret' motor-cannon. The two sent to Spain were unarmed, but the right-wing deputies again raised such an uproar that Cot was obliged to insist that the engines of both were removed and returned to France, lest the Russians should see the layout of the engines that would have enclosed them! As a result, the two fighters were immobilized until they were fitted with M-100 engines taken from a written-off Katiuska in October 1937.

Of the aircraft delivered in 1936, none was armed and the arms for them were never delivered, with the faintly possible exception of the seven Potez 54s in October. The delivery dates for all these aircraft are taken from the French newspapers. My argument (*Aircraft of the Spanish Civil War*) that ten Dewoitine D.371s were delivered not in the summer of 1936 but in the autumn of 1937 is based on long correspondence with Jean Cuny, co-author with Raymond Danel of *Les avions Dewoitines* (Paris, 1982), a solid and authoritative monograph, on references to these aircraft in the Ortiz report and its derivatives (Chapter 29 above) and on Angelo Emiliani's *Italiani nell'aviazione repubblicana spagnola* (Florence, 1981), pp. 66–7. Here it says that Giuseppe Krizai returned to Spain in October 1937 to take command of the new 1ª Escuadrilla of Grupo 71, equipped with these fighters, and shows a photograph of his personal aircraft, with '13' under the wing. Another photograph, showing the same machine from the other side, with 'R–9' under the wing, which Krizai gave to William Green, clinches the matter, for, as Cuny confirmed, 'R–913' was a French air force registration and the D.371s did not enter French service until the spring and summer of 1937.

My argument in the same book that only four more Potez 54s were delivered in October 1937, which brought the total for the whole war to eighteen and not the forty-nine often asserted, was based on the Ortiz report etc., on numerous reports in the Italian, German and French newspapers throughout 1937 and on one of the letters from 'C' (Celestino Alvarez) to Negrín, dated 10 Nov 1937, in which he emphatically states that after 'endless' negotiations, only four were bought 'last month' (IISG, Amsterdam, Kleine Iberische Archiv FAI/Olaya, letter no. 14, reprinted in F. Olaya, *El oro de Negrín*, pp. 421–2). 'C' was not always truthful, particularly when spreading scandal about other people,* but there seems no reason why he should have lied about this, since it was a fact already known to Negrín.

Of the obsolete French military aircraft little need be said since they took no significant part in the war. They included two Blériot SPAD 51s, a Blériot SPAD 91/6, a Lioré et Olivier 20 and a 213 and fifteen or twenty Gourdou-Leseurre GL-32s (delivered to the Basques). Regarding the six GL-633 dive-bombers, I now have reason to believe that only one was delivered, but that is insufficiently important and too complicated a matter to go into here.

B. Malraux

Exaggerated stories about Malraux in Spain first appeared in April 1937, while he was on a fund-raising tour of the United States and Canada. Ted Farah, a Canadian journal-

---

* In this same letter 'C' accused Prieto of reserving to himself a commission of 1 million Ffr. on the purchase of these aircraft, with which his son Luis, who was then an adviser to Gordón in Mexico, had bought one of the best villas in Chapultapec, Mexico. It was not right, wrote 'C', that a man in Prieto's position should use public money to provide himself with a bolt-hole abroad in the event of a Republican defeat. Since Olaya has published this letter without comment, it should be dealt with. The rumour originated from a story in the *Diario de Yucatán* (4 April 1937), one of the anti-Cárdenas and pro-Nationalist newspapers conducting a smear campaign against Gordón Ordás and the Spanish Republicans. It said that Luis Prieto had signed a contract in Los Angeles with Engineer Luis L. León to buy this villa from the former director of *La Nación* for $120,000. The report was relayed to the CNT in Barcelona (IISG, Amsterdam, FAI/CNT Microfilm 327, CNT 005, B. 12, Dossier Luis Prieto). There seems to have been no truth in the story whatever. $120,000 would have been 2,520,000 Ffr. When Prieto settled in Mexico in 1939, he did not move into a large villa that he already owned, but rented an apartment.

ist, wrote that Malraux had told him that during a visit to Spain before the civil war he had advised Largo Caballero to buy American transport planes that could be converted into bombers in the event of a coup, that eight were immediately bought and that they formed the 'backbone of the Red aviation at the start of the war' (R. S. Thornberry, *André Malraux et l'Espagne*, p. 35). In reality, five Douglas DC-2s were ordered by LAPE in November 1934 as a result of the fine performance of one in the England–Australia air race in October. Malraux visited Spain in May 1936, at a time when Largo was neither in government nor in a position to order anything, let alone large and expensive airliners. In 1940 Louis Fischer wrote that during the Spanish Civil War Malraux had 'applied the inventiveness of a great novelist to buying arms and gunrunning' and that he had bought aircraft in Czechoslovakia, Belgium and France (*Men and Politics*, p. 334).

After the Second World War, as Malraux's fame as a writer on art grew, so did legends about him as a rare artist-cum-man-of-action in our time. By 1950, for instance, it was believed by everyone that I knew, and by me, that he had himself created and led the Republican air force and fought battles in the sky as a pilot. Articles about him appeared in the *New Yorker*, *Life*, *Time* and *Collier's* magazines and in such newspapers as *The Observer* under distinguished by-lines, the climax being reached during Malraux's visit to Washington as de Gaulle's minister of culture, when President Kennedy welcomed him with a fulsome speech in which some of these tales were repeated. Communists, of course, had been hostile to him since his breaking with them after the Nazi–Soviet pact of August 1939, alleging that he was a cowardly fraud who, when the going in Spain had got tough, had deserted his men for the comforts and applauses of a publicity tour.

The real backlash began in 1963, when General Hidalgo de Cisneros, the former Republican air chief and a simple-minded Communist, devoted a few pages of his autobiography to lambasting Malraux as a Byronic poseur who knew nothing about military aviation. Thereafter the debunking continued until Malraux's death in 1976, a strong contribution being Jean Lacouture's good but rather unflattering biography which had appeared the year before. Moreover, by then it was apparent that Malraux's novel *L'Espoir*, whatever its great merits, was of no use to historians in trying to sort out the muddle of the history of the early months of the air war in Spain.

Nevertheless, Victor Veniel notwithstanding (see above, p. 84), others who served in the international squadron continued to speak well of him. In 1991 Vincent (formerly Sanzio) Piatti, who had been a mechanic and sometimes an observer in the squadron, told me that Malraux had been an excellent commander who had gone on numerous missions, not merely a few as some alleged, and that he was courteous as well as brave, an opinion shared, I believe, by other mechanics of the squadron to whom Malraux's biographer, Professor Walter G. Langlois, had spoken. There is also the long tribute to Malraux's conduct and courage (In *Icare*, no. 118, 1983, 'La guerre d'Espagne', vol. 1) by Paul Bernier, who had been the political commissar to the squadron. From a Communist one would have expected a very different judgement. Finally, Republican leaders, too, trusted him. On 16 January 1937 Jiménez de Asúa wrote in his dispatch from Prague to Alvarez del Vayo that 'Palacios' (Lt.-Col. Angel Pastor Velasco), having some urgent queries about the transportation arrangements for the 'Turkish' armaments, had decided to send the message not by telegram, in case the Germans decoded it, but by courier to Paris, from where Corniglion-Molinier would take it to Valencia, 'where Malraux is by Prieto's side'. Prieto would then allot the funds and arrange the shipping (Fundación de Pablo Iglesias, Madrid, Archivo Luis Jiménez de Asúa, 442–13, *Informe* 11°, p. 81).

Although Malraux bought no arms, ran no guns, was only one of many intermediaries in the complicated business of buying aircraft, and then only briefly, and was certainly not a pilot or knowledgeable about aviation, his role in the Spanish Civil War does not deserve the extreme denigration it has received during the past twenty-five years. His hyperactive dashing about and badgering of French ministers in August 1936 got things done that might otherwise never have been done at all. Nevertheless, he should have destroyed the legend, even if he had originally been responsible for some of it himself. One has only to think of what would have been the response of George Orwell, the author of another classic book about the war, had journalists begun to concoct similar fantasies about him.

APPENDIX II

A. Polish arms shipments to Spain, 9 September 1936–25 September 1937

The following is based on the list compiled by Professor Marian Zgorniak of Kraków University, and published in *Studia Historyczne*, vol. 26 (1983). My thanks, therefore, to Professor Zgorniak for his kind permission to use this list, to alter it where I feel it necessary and to add comments, for which I take full responsibility.

'Cover'	Agent	Port of Sail	Date of Sail	Ship	Material	Quantity	Price in zlotys (25 ztys = £1, 5 ztys = $1)	Remarks
Mexican legation, Paris	E. Grimard, Liège	Danzig (Gdansk), Westerplatte	9.9.36	*Azteca* (ex-*Sebastián*)	Hand-grenades GR-31	300,000	944,250	
					PWU 28	200	250,000	Polish-made Browning Automatic Rifles (BAR).
"					PWU 29 kbk	10,000	1,070,000	Polish-made Mauser M98 carbines.
"					Mauser cartridges, old	10,600,000	299,041,50	
"					Mauser cartridges, new	2,000,000	231,400	
Mexican legation, Paris	W. Daugs, Berlin				PWU 29 kbk	9,300	995,100	Polish-made Mauser.

Source	Supplier	Date	Ship	Item			Notes
Szechuan provincial govt, China				Gunpowder	30,000 kg	414,300	
				Hand-grenades GR-31	100,000	314,750	
France	E. Brandt, Paris			Hand-grenades GR31	600,000	1,888,500	
Mexican legation, Paris	E. Grimard	7.10.36	*Silvia* (*ex-Philomelia* or *-Filomila*)	PWU 28	100	125,000	Polish-made BARs.
"				Shells, 75 mm	35,000	2,340,672	
"				Mauser cartridges, new	500,000	57,850	
"				Chauchat machine-rifles, old	5,000	1,000,000	
"				French cartridges 8 mm old	15,000,000	1,575,000	
Szechuan provincial govt, China	W. Daugs, Berlin			Bergmann light machine-guns, old	1,481	370,250	Bergmann 15 na, since they are described as 'rkm'. The more famous Bergmann MP 18/I and MP 18/II, known as 'Schmeissers', of which the Republicans obtained numbers, would have been classified as 'lkm' or 'sub-machine-guns'.
"				Mauser cartridges, old	3,000,000	94,200	

'Cover'	Agent	Port of Sail	Date of Sail	Ship	Material	Quantity	Price in zlotys (25 ztys = £1, 5 zyts = $1)	Remarks
E. Brandt, Paris	E. Brandt, Paris				Stokes mortars Stokes mortar grenades	100 20,000	175,000 670,000	Spiro Katepodis, the captain of the *Silvia*, arranged for the ship and her cargo to be 'captured' by the Nationalists in the Straits of Gibraltar (see above, p. 195).
E. Brandt, Paris	W. Daugs, Berlin		9.10.36	*Vincencia* (ex-*Rollom*)	Gunpowder	50,000 kg	690,700	These were part of the *Silvia* cargo. The *Vincenzia* sailed to Riga and took on 4 Krupp 77 mm M16 field-guns, with 6,000 shells and 8 Krupp-Putilow 76.2 mm guns, with 15,000 shells, supplied by A. Klaguine of Paris. The loading was supervised by an officer of the Latvian war ministry (PRO, London, FO 371/20984 W 15171). Sailed from Riga, 17 Oct 1936.

Destination	Supplier	Date, ship	Item	Number	Quantity/Value	Notes
"	"		Stokes mortar grenades	24,000	804,000	
"	"		Electric relays	130,000		
Hungary	W. Daugs, Berlin	29.10.36 *Hillfern*	Männlicher M95 carbines	10,000	420,000	£1 6s. each on this list; £3 each on the Soviet list (Appendix III).
"	"		Bayonets for above	9,400	61,000	
"	"		Cartridges 8 mm for above	12,000,000	504,000	
Szechuan provincial govt, China	"		Schwarzlose M 1912 heavy machine-guns	92	41,400	£18 each on this list; £82 each on the Soviet list (Appendix III).
"	"		'Austrian sub-machine-guns, old, 08/18'	167	74,340	An error somewhere. The MG 08/18 was a Maxim; the sub-machine gun an MP 18, or 'Schmeisser'; neither was Austrian though both may have been used by the Austro-Hungarian army.
"	"		Mauser cartridges, new	800,000	99,960	
"	"		Mauser cartridges, old	1,200,000	37,680	The Soviet list for this cargo also has 171 Maxim guns at £40 or $200, each.

'Cover'	Agent	Port of Sail	Date of Sail	Ship	Material	Quantity	Price in zlotys (25 ztys = £1, 5 zyts = $1)	Remarks
Mexican legation, Paris	A. Klaguine, Paris				Russian-made Schneider 76.2 mm M 1904/09 mountain-guns	8	160,000	(See Appendix III, voyage 10, and Chapters 15, 19 and 28.)
"	"				Shells for above	15,000	675,000	
"	"				Detonators '3 lusek'	1,500	3,000	
Latvian war ministry	A. Klaguine, Paris		30.10.36	Turmont	Fuses, old	18,600	97,650	
Uruguayan consul-general, Warsaw	Aljurgo, Warsaw		8.11.36	Rambon (ex-Tyne)	Army boots	10,000 prs	236,000	
					Renault FT-17 tanks	1 company of 16	3,000,000	
"	"				Schneider 75 mm S.B. field-guns	4	680,000	S.B. = 'Short-barrelled'.
"	"				Shells for above	971	153,418	
"	"				Hand-grenades GR 31	100,000	380,256	
China	W. Daugs, Berlin				Mauser cartridges, old	800,000	25,120	
Mexico	E. Grimard, Liège		16.11.36	Rona	Shells, 75 mm	60,000	4,330,000	This cargo, bought by the Republicans, was taken to the Nationalist port of El Ferrol.
"	"				Trotyl	100,000 kg	550,000	

Consignor	Agent	Port	Date	Ship	Item	Quantity	Value	Remarks
Portuguese consulate, Warsaw	J. Herse, Warsaw	Gdynia	24.11.35 2.12.36	*Bordseo* and *Tczew*	Gunpowder	54,500 kg	54,000	Bought by and delivered to the Nationalists, via Hamburg.
"	"				P.W.S. 10 fighters	20	1,009,371.50	
"	"				R.W.D. 13 cabin monoplanes	2	72,000	
"	"	Danzig	2.12.36	*Warmond* (ex-*Lodewyk*)	Vickers aircraft machine-guns ·303"	100	380,000	Delivery at Alicante, 17.12.36, confirmed by ASHM, Madrid, Armario 47. Legajo 71. c.7, on microfilm 55/532/5/18. This and some other deliveries are published in R. Salas, *La historia del ejercito popular*, vol. 3, pp. 2584 ff.
"	"				Cartridges for above	200,000	⎫ 144,000 ⎬	
"	"				Spare parts for above		⎭	
Uruguayan consulate, Warsaw	Hunzedal (i.e. D. Wolf) The Hague				Synchronization mechanisms SS 33 bis for the Vickers	50	125,000	There are several discrepancies between the Polish and Spanish lists, noted below. To this cargo (p. 2584), Salas adds '30 Bergson machine guns' (*sic*).

'Cover'	Agent	Port of Sail	Date of Sail	Ship	Material	Quantity	Price in zlotys (25 ztys = £1, 5 zyts = $1)	Remarks
Hungary	W. Daugs, Berlin				Männlicher M95 rifles, old	3,000	126,000	
"	"				Cartridge, 8 mm for above	3,000,000	126,000	
Szechuan provincial govt					8 mm rifles (Lebel?)	10,000	720,000	Salas says 'Mauser'.
"	"				Cartridges for above	4,000,000	208,000	i.e. 400 rounds per rifle. Salas gives the number as 9 million.
Brazil	J. Herse, Warsaw	Gdynia	5.12.36	?	R.W.D. 13 cabin monoplanes	4	144,000	To the Nationalists.
Uruguayan consulate, Warsaw	M. Wolf	Gdynia	15.1.37	*Saroamid* (i.e. *Sarkani*)	Mine-throwers 76 mm, old	126		Salas, p. 2586. Arrived Alicante 2.2.37. Adds to this cargo 10 Gnome-Rhône aero-engines, with accessories, and 90,000 gas-masks.
"	"				Mines, 76 mm, for above	6,290	378,000	
"	"				Männlicher M95 rifles, old	7,000	294,000	
"	"				Cartridges for above, old	7,000,000	294,000	

Buyer	Date	Ship	Port	Supplier	Item	Quantity	Value	Notes
"					Skoda 100 mm M 14/19 howitzers	4	550,000	Ex Austro-Hungarian Army.
"					Shells for above	10,000	1,000,000	
"					Mauser cartridges, old	2,000,000	310,000	
"					Hand-grenades GR 31	250,000	1,050,000	
"					Maxim M 10/28 machine-guns, old	580	1,234,240	
"					Cartridge powder	200 tons	3,800,000	
"					Shell powder	50 tons	600,000	
"					Cartridge powder	105.5 tons	1,529,750	
Mexico				E. Grimard, Liège	Mauser muskets	2,000	144,000	Salas gives '2,600' rifles. They were M 90 muskets made at Erfut.
China				W. Daugs, Berlin				
Uruguayan consulate	17.1.37	Rambon	Gdynia	M. Wolf, Gokkes Co., Warsaw	Shells 77 mm, old	12,973	1,080,372	Salas, p.2586, which gives a long list of materials but does not mention these shells (see Section B below).
"	21.2.37	Janu (ex-Kenwood)			Shells, 80 mm for artillery (Austrian)	40,000	1,400,000	
"					Artillery powder	100 tons	1,200,000	
"					Mauser cartridges, old	10,000,000	1,550,000	

'Cover'	Agent	Port of Sail	Date of Sail	Ship	Material	Quantity	Price in zlotys (25 ztys = £1, 5 zyts = $1)	Remarks
"	"		22.2.37	Autom (ex-Berta)	Renault FT-17 tanks	1 company of 16	2,800,000	The price of £7,000 ($35,000) per tank is astonishing, since the tanks had been rejected by the Polish army as useless. A Soviet T-26 cost only $21,500. See also above, Chapter 20, p. 147. The Autom arrived Santander, 3.3.37.
"	"				Krupp-Erhardt 77 mm M 96 n.a. field-guns	20	600,000	Salas, p. 2587, adds 4 Krupp 77 mm (long-barrelled), and gives shells as 42,084. Also 10 lorries and 1 mobile workshop.
"	"				Shells, 37 mm for tanks	10,000	420,000	Salas has '10,194' shells.
"	"				Shell powder	75 tons	900,000	
"	"		21.2.37	Andra	Renault FT-17 tanks	2 companies (32 tanks)	5,600,000	F. Belforte: La guerra civile in Spagna, vol. 2,

		Port	Ship	Date	Cargo	Quantity		Notes
"					Shells, 37 mm for above	20,000	840,000	p. 193, gives a detailed list of the cargo and says that the *Andra* reached Santander on 31.3.37.
"			*Warmond*	6.2.37	Skoda 76.5 mm M 1905, M 05/08, M 17 and M 18 field-guns	56	168,000	Ex-Austro-Hungarian army.
"					Shells for above	23,000	805,000	i.e. 410 shells each.
"					Artillery powder	75 tons	900,000	Salas, p. 2587, adds 51,000 cartridges of 17.92 mm.
Portuguese consulate, Warsaw	J. Herse, Warsaw				Synchronization mechanisms for aircraft	10	22,500	The *Warmond*, docked at Alicante, 14.2.37.
German govt.	J. Veltjens, Berlin	Gdynia	*Tczew*	10.2.37	Lebel cartridges	8,000,000	840,000	To the Nationalists, at £4.89 ($21) per thousand. It would appear that Veltjens charged the Nationalists at a rate of £5.87 ($27) per thousand for Mauser and £7 ($35) per thousand for Lebel cartridges. (Archivo Histórico

'Cover'	Agent	Port of Sail	Date of Sail	Ship	Material	Quantity	Price in zlotys (25 ztys = £1, 5 zyts = $1)	Remarks
Uruguayan consulate, Warsaw	M. Wolf, The Hague		9.2.37	Rambon	Maxim guns M10/28	1,272	2,706,816	Nacional, Madrid, Archivo del Presidente del Gobierno, D.G. de Adquisiciones, Legajo 191, 8.5.37, and invoice from Veltjens). Presumably these too came from Poland.
	"				Shell charges (80 mm)	17,000	595,000	
	"				Mauser cartridges, old	1,550,000		
	"		4.3.37	Morna	Shell powder	75 tons		
					Krupp 77 mm M16 field-guns	14	420,000	Arrived Santander 13.3.37. Salas p. 289: 5 guns.
	"				Italian 75 mm field-guns	12	749,000	Probably Krupp M 1906.
	"				Shell charges 75 mm	12,000	720,000	
	"				Mauser cartridges, old	5,000,000	975,000	Salas: 4,100,000.

	Date	Place	Item	Quantity	Value	Notes
"			Artillery powder	120 tons	1,440,000	
"			French Berthier rifles, 8 mm	14,479		Salas: 14,460.
"			Cartridges for above	10,447,890		Salas: 11,280,000.
"	9.3.37	*Sarkani*	Italian 75 mm field-guns	24	1,488,000	Arrived Santander 13.3.37.
"			Shells for above	21,963	1,317,780	Salas: at top of list are 8 large crates of dismantled aircraft. These must have been the 8 Letov S 231 fighters bought in Czechoslovakia.
"			Mauser cartridges, old	4,550,000	706,250	
"			Berthier rifles, 8 mm	14,881	} 3,214,296	
"			Cartridges for above	16,955,203		
"			Trotyl	50 tons	285,000	
Finnish war ministry — W. Daugs, Berlin	9.1.37	*Cieszyn*	Russian rifles and spare parts, old	2,930	58,731	Probably sold by Captain Jusu Juselius.
Uruguayan consulate, Warsaw — M. Wolf	14.4.37	*Tinge*	Italian 75 mm field-guns	32	1,984,000	Krupp M 1906.
"			Shells for above	18,491	1,109,400	
"			Männlicher rifles 8 mm, M 88/90 M 95	7,000	294,000	

'Cover'	Agent	Port of Sail	Date of Sail	Ship	Material	Quantity	Price in zlotys (25 zltys = £1, 5 zyts = $1)	Remarks
"	"				Cartridges for above, old	7,000,000	294,000	
"	"				Berthier rifles, 8 mm	8,040	1,806,240	
"	"				Cartridges for above	10,596,957		
"	"				Mauser cartridges	9,458,000	1,405,990	
"	"				Hand-grenades GR 31	223,200	1,153,412	
"	"				Powder	109 tons	1,260,000	
"	"				Trotyl	50 tons	285,000	
"	"		8.4.37	Hordena (ex-Horden)	Mauser cartridges, old	8,992,000	1,393,760	Captured at sea by Nationalists, 16.4.37. On board too were 22 Aero A-101 light day-bombers (see above, Chapter 28, p. 212).
"	"				Shells, 75 mm	15,546	932,760	
"	"				Männlicher rifles M88/90, M90	5,000	210,000	
"	"				Cartridges for above	5,000,000	210,000	
"	"				Spares for Bergmann light	5,846 kg	70,912	

		Date	Ship	Item			Notes
German govt.	W. Daugs and J. Veltjens, Berlin	10.4.37	*Hans*	machine-guns Shells, 155 mm	3,000	846,000	To which side these were sold is not certain.
Portuguese consulate, Paris	S. Czarnecki, Paris	24.5.37	*Scotia* (ex-*Ring*)	Whitehead torpedoes	20	491,530	
Greek consulate, Gdynia	M. Wolf	16.6.37	*Lola*	Chauchat machine rifles	3,690	2,100,000 ⎫	*France-Navigation* charter. Never delivered. The *Lola* was detained at Constanta, Romania, until the end of the Spanish Civil War, and the Chauchats and ammunition were still there in 1940, subjects of a legal wrangle (Polish Institute and Sikorski Museum Archive, London, B.I. 113/D/19, p.1).
	"			Cartridges for above	10,000,000 ⎬		
	"	20.8.37	*Ploubazlanec*	Shells, 75 mm	15,000	1,140,000	France Navigation ship. Arrived Bassens, Bordeaux, at end of September, after taking on additional arms at Tallinn on Paldiski,

'Cover'	Agent	Port of Sail	Date of Sail	Ship	Material	Quantity	Price in zlotys (25 ztys = £1, 5 zyts = $1)	Remarks
"	"				Mauser cartridges, old	1,000,000	35,000	Estonia (see Section B below).
"	"				Shells, 75 mm	25,000	1,100,000	
"	"				Shell powder	100,000 kg	1,100,000	
"	"		31.7.37	*Al Racou*	PWU 30 medium machine-guns	48	166,368	Polish-made Browning M 1917s.
"	"				PWU 28	225	216,075	Polish-made BARs.
"	"				PWU 29	5,800	733,700	Polish-made Mausers.
"	"				Shells, 37 mm	36,000	1,512,000	The *Al Racou*, of France Navigation, docked at Bassens, Bordeaux, on 8.8.37 (for details see Grisoni and Hertzog, *Les brigades de la mer*, pp. 81–4, 419, 423, 426–7, 430).
"	"				Shells, 155 mm	4,500	1,269,000	
"	"				Shells, 77 mm	35,000	1,650,000	
Haitian legation,	E. Grimard, Liège		3.3.37	*Heine*	Lewis light machine-guns,	400	160,000	Delivered to Bordeaux or

Paris				.303″, old			
"				Cartridges for above, old	7,000,000	546,000	perhaps Gijón, in Asturias.
Greek consul-general, London	M. Wolf, The Hague	21.9.37	*Jaron* (ex-*Nikolina Natovic*)	37 mm guns	26	540,000	Type unspecified.
"	"			Krupp 77 mm M 96 n.a. field-guns	25	1,373,000	
"				Krupp 105 mm M 1898/1909 howitzers	15	1,350,000	
"				Italian Krupp 75 mm M 1906 field-guns	54	3,348,000	
"				Shells, 75 mm for above	54,000	3,240,000	
"				Shells, 105 mm for the howitzers	28,000	3,220,000	
"				J.D. mine-throwers 75 mm	127	266,700	It seems that as the result of a plot to divert this cargo to the Nationalists, none of these arms reached France until April and May 1938 (see Section B below).

B. Supplementary information

All the materials on the above list were sold by or through SEPEWE, the arms-trading organization of the Polish government. Since, however, several ships took on additional cargo at other Baltic ports, the following should be noted:

1) Danish ship *Bess*, or *Bass*, at Gdynia reported to have embarked 5,000 × .303" rifles and 5 million cartridges on 1 Oct 1936 and to have transhipped these at Trompeloup, France, to a Spanish vessel, which took them to Bilbao. The dates of this incident vary in different reports ('A Barrister', *I Accuse France*, p. 4; Archivo del Ministerio de Asuntos Exteriores, Madrid, DR. R. 1048 c. 22.).

2) Norwegian ship *Bjornoy*, or *Bjornboy*, embarked 21,000 rifles and 29 million cartridges, all .303", on 6 Oct 1936 at Memel (Klaipeda), Lithuania. Said to have sailed to Onega, White Sea, USSR, and taken on cargo (probably foodstuffs) on 10 Oct 1936. At Cartagena, 21 Oct 1936. After this journey, renamed *Reyna* (see below, n. 5; PRO, FO 371/20580 W13628; 20581 W13852; *Lloyd's List*, 6 Oct 1936).

3) *Dobesa*, ex-*Walborg*, ex-*Miranda*, at Gdynia, 19 Dec 1936. Cargo: 91 machine-guns, 5 million cartridges 7.92 mm and 5 million 7 mm (R. Salas, *La historia...*, p. 2585). At Alicante, 14 Jan 1937.

4) *Elaie* or *Elsie*, at Alicante, 18 Jan 1936, delivered: 10,500 cartridges, 7.62 mm; 362 Colt machine-guns, 76.2 mm, 44,000 shells; 6 ex-Russian anti-aircraft guns, 75mm; 9 gun-platforms, 7,000 shells, range-finders, 2 lorries with 'auxiliary guns'. Apparently from Baltic. (Salas, p. 2586; FO 371/2131 W1698).

5) *Reyna* (1,436 tons) and *Scotia* (770 tons), both of the new Scotia Line, spent most of 1937 at Riga, Latvia, and Tallinn, Estonia, waiting for cargoes, which were several times loaded and taken off again. *Reyna* sailed on 26 Sept 1937 with a small cargo of naval mines. When the Nationalists captured Gijón, Asturias, on 22 Oct 1937, they found the *Reyna* among the ships sunk in the harbour.

6) *Ploubazlanec* arrived Tallinn, c. 25 Sept 1937, to take on arms left over from earlier deals. She was already carrying the cargo listed above. How much additional material was embarked is uncertain, but it was said to include five old Rosenberg 37 mm M 15 infantry-guns, presumably for use as makeshift anti-tank guns. They had probably been captured from the Russians in 1919. The cargo may also have included some of the weapons bought in Paraguay by Thorvald Erich, which were: 7 Krupp 75 mm M 1907 mountain-guns; 1 Vickers tank, with machine-gun (76.5 mm) and 1 cannon (47 mm); 10 Vickers machine-guns, 7.65 mm; 75 Maxim machine-guns, 7.65 mm; 233 Vickers Berthier machine-rifles, 7.65 mm; 2,000 75 mm shells; 175,500 Chilean Mauser cartridges, 7 mm; 7,119 Mauser rifles, 7.65 mm, 'mostly in bad condition'. The *Ploubazlanec* sailed for Bordeaux on 27 Sept 1937 (FO 371/21395 W6774 and 10184 etc; AMAE, Madrid, DR R 1047 c. 34, dispatch 8 Oct 1937).

7) On c. 1 Oct 1937 the *Jaron* (see list above), renamed *Vena* and flying a Greek flag, arrived at Paldiski, Estonia, where the Estonian army had its main munitions depot. Why she did so instead of sailing to France is not clear, but it had something to do with a plot concocted by the two captains, John Williams and Nicolas Vassilakis, to divert her cargo to the Nationalists. Perhaps there was a mutiny. Be that as it may, her cargo (see list) was unloaded and stored, while she remained, first at Paldiski and then at Tallinn, as the object of complicated law suits throughout the winter and following spring. I have no knowledge of her final fate. Meanwhile, other materials, including probably the arms left by the Victor Hervey affair, were added to the *Jaron/Vena* cargo at Paldiski and were likewise squabbled over by the numerous dealers

– Juselius, Bondarenko, Linde, Löötsmann, Veltjens and others – who were trying to divide the spoils amongst themselves. It is said that some were taken to France by two Finnish ships, the *Virumaa* and *Jarumaa*, in December, but I have found no reports of two such ships sailing to France with arms on board. In April and May 1938 the *Scotia*, renamed *Diana*, made two arms-carrying voyages to France: there is a photograph of her on one of them, taken while she was slipping through a Dutch canal on the way to the North Sea (R. González Echegaray, *La marina mercante...*, opp. p. 209). Since her tonnage was only 770, her cargoes cannot have been large, but may have included most of the artillery pieces that had been on the *Jaron*. Nationalist reports speak of 49 guns unloaded at Le Havre on 14 April and 12 loaded at Gdynia (?) on 10 May 1938.

VALUATION: At 25 zlotys to £1 and 5 to $1, SEPEWE sales up to 25 Sept 1937 came to about £4,740,000, or $23,700,000 to the Republicans and £110,695, or $553,475, to the Nationalists. However, the cargoes of the *Silvia*, *Rona*, and *Hordena* were captured by the Nationalists, the *Lola* was held in Romania, and it is uncertain how much of the cargo of the *Jaron* was eventually delivered.

Although SEPEWE sold more arms to Spain after September 1937, not many could have been delivered, there being no record of which ships carried them or to where, while Bandera company correspondence of June–August 1938 mentions quantities of arms still held on trains in Poland or on the Czech–Polish frontier (AMAE, Madrid, DR. R 1048, c. 24, *passim*). According to the French armaments historian Stephane Ferrard (*Les matériels de l'armée de terre française*, vol. 1, p. 53), 3,250 Erma MPE sub-machine-guns were surrendered at Le Perthus by Republican troops crossing into France in February 1939. These had probably come from Poland, since the Poles had imported them from Germany during the early 1930s.

Since both Col. Sokołowski and Col. Witkowski wrote in their depositions that SEPEWE had made 200 million zlotys out of the Spanish Civil War, the total of 121,673,605 zlotys up to 25 Sept 1937 further supports the suspicion that the prices on the SEPEWE list are not those actually paid by the Spaniards, especially since Sokołowski said that sales stopped at the beginning of March 1938 (see above, Chapter 15, p. 110).

APPENDIX III

Soviet arms shipments to the Spanish Republic, September 1936–February 1939, as shown by lists in the Russian State Military Archives (RGVA)

Photocopies of these and other complementary documents were given to me by TV-3 de Catalunya (for further details, see Acknowledgements). The lists are headed: 'Report on the number of voyages effected to transport special cargoes to "X"' and are marked *Sov. Sekretno* ('absolutely secret') throughout. No archive references are visible on the photocopies of the voyage lists, but those of the first three series of voyages, from 26 September 1936 to 13 March 1937, are probably those of the Appendix attached to General Uritsky's letter to Marshal Voroshilov of 8 May 1937 (F. 33987, O. 3, D. 893, L. 231–7). Of the voyages of the first four series (26 September 1936 to 10 August 1937), the *Andreev* (no. 7) and *Hillfern* (no. 10) went from the Baltic to Bilbao, the *Linhaug* (no. 11) from the Baltic to Cartagena and Marseille, and the route of the *Vaga* (no. 26) is not recorded. All the rest went from the Black Sea to Cartagena. All subsequent voyages were from Murmansk to Bassens, Bordeaux, France, via the Atlantic to avoid the Channel. 'Displacement': the top figures are those on the Russian lists, which do not seem to be always accurate. I have therefore added below, where possible, 'Gross Register' (GR) and 'Deadweight' (DW) tonnages taken from such sources as *Lloyd's Shipping Register* and especially R. González Echegaray, *La marina mercante y el tráfico marítimo en la guerra civil* (Madrid, 1977).

Voyage No.	Dossier No.	Name of Ship	Displacement and tonnage	Departure	Arrival	Material carried	Quantity	Remarks
First Series: 26 September 1936 to 30 November 1936								
1	Y-1	*Campeche* (sailed from Feodosia, Crimea)	6,300	26.9.36	4.10.36	Rifles (old, foreign)	20,350	Vetterlis, Arisakas, Lebels, Gras-Kropotcheks, etc.
						Heavy machine-guns	350	Saint-Etiennes, Colts, Vickers, etc.
						Light machine-guns	200	Probably Maxim MG 08s and Hotchkiss M 09s.

No.	Code	Ship	Date	Tonnage	Date	Cargo	Quantity	Notes
						Cartridges for above	16.5 million	
						German grenade-throwers	240	Primitive trench mortars.
						Grenades for above	100,000	
						Vickers 115 mm (4.5") Mk. I Howitzers	6	Exported to Russia pre-1914.
						Shells for above	6,000	
2	Y-2	*Komosomol*	4.10.36	7,500	12.10.36	T-26 Tanks with complete supplies of spares, fuel and ammunition	50	
3	Y-3	*Stari Bolshevik*	7.10.36	6,200	15.10.36	Tupolev SB bombers with complete supplies of spares, fuel and ammunition	10	
4	Y-4	*KIM*	13.10.36	7,500	19.10.36	same as above	10	On her return journey, the *KIM* was one of the four ships that transported the gold to the USSR.
5	Y-5	*Volgoles*	13.10.36	5,900	21.10.36	same as above	10	
6	Y-6	*Lepin* (from Sevastopol)	20.10.36	5,900	28.10.36	Polikarpov I-15 fighters with complete supplies of spares, fuel and ammunition	25	Russian list says '15 aircraft' which is an error.
						Armoured cars, with complete supplies of spares, fuel and ammunition	30	$16 \times$ BA-6, $1 \times$ BA-3 (radio), $3 \times$ BA-3, $10 \times$ FA-1.
7	Y-5	*Andreev* (from Leningrad to Bilbao)	22.10.36	3,600	1.11.36	Polikarpov I-15 fighters with complete supplied spares, fuel and ammunition	15	

Voyage No.	Dossier No.	Name of Ship	Displacement and tonnage	Departure	Arrival	Material carried	Quantity	Remarks
						Armoured cars, with complete supplies of spares, fuel and ammunition	30	
						Maklen infantry-support guns, 37 mm.	15	Intended as makeshift anti-tank guns.
						Shells for above	25,000	
						Grenade-throwers	50	
						Grenades for above	40,000	
						Lewis light machine-guns	200	
						.303" cartridges for above	9.5 million	
						Armstrong 127 mm field guns	6	This was the BL 60-pdr. M 1912 Mk. I field-gun, of which 52 were exported to Russia before the First World War.
						Shells for above	7,000	
						Old foreign rifles	15,655	These are not on the voyage list but are on F.33987.O.3.D.83 2. L.117–118. Nine thousand of these rifles were Winchesters, and the rest included Gras, Gras-Kropotchek (both 11 mm), Lebel (8 mm)
						Cartridges for above	9.15 million	

					Item	Quantity	Notes
8	Y-7	*Kursk* (from Sevastopol)	5,900	25.10.36	3.11.36	Polikarpov I-16 fighters with complete supplies of spares, fuel and ammunition	15	and perhaps a few Vetterlis (11 mm).
						Armstrong 127 mm field guns	6	
						Shells for above	40,000	
						Winchester 7.62 mm rifles	9,000	
						Degtyarev DP light machine-guns	150	
						Cartridges 7.62 mm for above	11 million	
9	Y-8	*Blagoev*	4,500	26.10.36	4.11.36	Polikarpov I-16 fighters with complete supplies of spares, fuel and ammunition	16	
						Maklen 37 mm infantry-support guns	15	
						Shells for above	25,000	
						Maxim machine-guns	200	
						Cartridges for above, 7.62 mm	19 million	
						Lewis light machine-guns	200	
						Cartridges for above, .303"	4 million	
						Cartridge powder	100 tons	
10		*Hillfern*	2,500 1,535 GR	30.10.36	7.11.36	Schneider 7.62 mm, M 04 and M 09 mountain-guns	8	Russian-made, from Czech army.

Voyage No.	Dossier No.	Name of Ship	Displacement and tonnage	Departure	Arrival	Material carried	Quantity	Remarks
						Panoramic sights for above	8	The only panoramic sights supplied by SEPEWE for artillery pieces.
						Shells for above	15,000	
						Heavy machine-guns	253	Eighty-two of these were Schwarzelose 8 mm M 07/12s, originally from Austro-Hungarian army.
						Männlicher 8 mm rifles Cartridges for above For additional cargo see Appendix IIA – Hillfern.	10,000 10 million	The Hillfern sailed from Danzig to Bilbao. All material bought by agent 'Tomson' from Technoarma, Prague, via SEPEWE, Warsaw (see Chapter 28 and Appendix II, Russian ref: F,33987.O.3.D.8930 L.1).
11		Linhaug	3,500	26.10.36	10.11.36	77 mm Field-guns	22	Probably Krupp 77 mm M16.
						Shells for above	40,000	
						105 mm howitzers	8	Probably Rheinmetall 105 mm M 16.
						Shells for above	13,000	Cargo bought by agent 'Argus' in Baltic States

No.	Ship	Code	Tonnage	Date	Date	Item	Quantity	Notes
12	*Sergo Ordzonikidze*		10,000	1.11.36	12.11.36	Benzine from Baku	2,221 tons	via Switzerland (see Chapter 18, esp. n. 29).
						Benzine top grade	1,689 tons	
13	*Artza Mendi*		2,500 GR 2,955 GR 3,800 DW	6.11.36	16.11.36	Vickers 115 mm howitzers	4	
						Shells for above	10,000	
						Colt M 1895/1914 heavy machine-guns	300	
						Cartridges for above	6 million	
						Lee-Enfield rifles .303"	1,000	
						Cartridges for above	1.5 million	
						Lebel 8 mm rifles	900	
						Cartridges for above	1.5 million	
						F-1 grenades	50,000	
14	*Aldecoa*	Y-9	5,800 GR 3,088 GR 6,100 LW	11.11.36	19.11.36	R-5sss with complete supplies of spares, fuel and ammunition	31	Two-seat ground attack biplanes.
15	*Cabo Palos*	Y-10	6,300 7,500 DW	15.11.36	25.11.36	Rifles (assorted)	1,920	
						Cartridges for above	4 million	
						Heavy machine-guns	1,500	Including 900 Colts.
						Cartridges for above	20 million	
						Chauchat machine-rifles	400	
						Cartridges for above	3.5 million	

Voyage No.	Dossier No.	Name of Ship	Displacement and tonnage	Departure	Arrival	Material carried	Quantity	Remarks
						Hand-grenades	70,000	
						Vickers 115 mm howitzers	84	
						Shells for above	90,522	
						T-26 Tanks	37	
						Pistols	1,010	
						Cartridges for above	505,000	
						45 mm shells for the tanks	100,000	
16		Chicherin	1,500	17.11.36	26.11.36	Personnel of the 'Tank Group Pavlov'		
17	'Docs Lost'	Mar Caribe	5,500 5,192 GR 6,100 DW	20.11.36	30.11.36	T-26 tanks	19	
						Incendiary cartridges	1,035,000	
						Shells, 115 mm	84,000	

SECOND SERIES: 23 DECEMBER 1936 TO 14 FEBRUARY 1937

Voyage No.	Dossier No.	Name of Ship	Displacement and tonnage	Departure	Arrival	Material carried	Quantity	Remarks
18	Y-14	Darro	2,600 2,610 GR 2,200 DW	23.12.36	30.12.36	Polikarpov I-15 fighters with complete supplies of spares, fuel and ammunition	10	
						Aviation bombs	17,500	
						II-AK Radios	2	
						Hucks starters	5	
						Autocompressors	2	

No.	Ship	Code			Tonnage	Item	Quantity	Notes
19	Sac-2	Y-15	16.1.3	4.1.3	2,900 2,959 GR 5,000 DW	Polikarpov I-15 fighters with complete supplies of spares, fuel and ammunition	20	The first Russian rifles to arrive in Spain.
						Mosin-Nagant M 1891 rifles, 7.62 mm	25,500	
						Cartridges for above	20 million	
						Hucks starters	11	
						Petrol trucks	3	
						Mobile workshop	1	
20	Mar Blanco	Y-16	16.1.37	6.1.37	5,100 5,512 GR 6,100 DW	Polikarpov I-15 fighters with complete supplies of spares, fuel and ammunition	30	
						Mosin-Nagant rifles	24,580	
						Cartridges for above	30 million	
						76.2 M 31 anti-aircraft guns	32	
						Shells for above	32,600	
21	Aldecoa	Y-17	14.2.37	5.2.37	5,800 3,088 GR 6,100 DW	R-Z light bombers with complete supplies of spares, fuel and ammunition	31	
						Hucks starters	4	
						Petrol trucks	3	
						ShKAS cartridges	3.5 million	
						PV-1 cartridges	1,891,000	
						Aviation bombs	12,500	
						Vickers 115 mm howitzers	20	
						Shells for above	40,798	

Voyage No.	Dossier No.	Name of Ship	Displacement and tonnage	Departure	Arrival	Material carried	Quantity	Remarks
						76 mm shells	17,600	
						37 mm shells	50,000	
						Special cartridges	1,948,000	
						Reflectors (searchlights?)	16	
						Deep penetration bombs	200	
						47 mm shells	7,010	
						Ammunition wagons	54	
22		Turksib	5,400	16.2.37	26.2.37	Personnel		
THIRD SERIES: 28 FEBRUARY 1937 TO 13 MARCH 1937								
23	Y-18	Cabo Santo Tomé	12,500 12,589 GR 10,000 DW 16,900 DP	28.2.37	6.3.37	T-26 tanks with complete supplies of spares, fuel and ammunition	60	
						Rifle cartridges	65 million	
						45 mm shells	353,000	
						115 mm shells	28,222	
24	Y-19	Darro	2,600 2,610 GR 2,200 DW	27.2.37	3.37	T-26 tanks with complete supplies spares, fuel and ammunition	40	
						Rifles	20,720	
						Degtyarev DP light machine-guns	1,646	
						Heavy machine-guns	277	

No.	Code	Ship	Tonnage	Date	Date	Cargo	Quantity	Remarks
25	Y-20	*Antonio de Satrústegui*	12,700 / 3,289 GR / 5,000 DW	2.3.37	13.3.37	45 mm shells	17,000	Purchased in Paris. No information received by 'X' office concerning the cargo of this ship.
						Rifle cartridges	56,022	
						45 mm shells	210,000	
						76 mm shells	49,000	
						115 mm shells	4,800	
						Mauser rifles	25,000	
26		*Vaga*	1,600			Cartridges for above	50 million	

FOURTH SERIES: 21 APRIL 1937 TO 10 AUGUST 1937

No.	Code	Ship	Tonnage	Date	Date	Cargo	Quantity	Remarks
27	Y-27	*Escolano*	4,250 GR / 3,070 DW / 5,000 DW / 5,881 Disp.	21.4.37	29.4.37	M-25 aero-engines	100	
						M-100 aero-engines	100	
						Rifle cartridges	35,032,000	33,324,245 according to note against C. *Santo Tomé* below.
						76.2 mm anti-aircraft shells	900	
						115 mm shells	17,109	
						45 mm L/46 anti-tank guns	15	
						45 mm guns for tanks	10	
						Aviation bombs	11,700	

Voyage No.	Dossier No.	Name of Ship	Displacement and tonnage	Departure	Arrival	Material carried	Quantity	Remarks
28	Y-28	Cabo Santo Tomé	12,500	25.4.37	1.5.37	R-Z light bombers	51	
						Petrol trucks	2	
						Hucks starters	2	
						Mobile workshop	1	
						Aviation bombs	10,750	3,750 × 20 kg; 6,000 × 50 kg; 1,000 × 70 kg.
						ShKAS & PV-1 cartridges	2.5 million	Included 47,000 tracers.
						76 mm field-guns	40	
						Light machine-guns	1,000	Maxim-Tokarev M 08/15.
						Heavy machine-guns	601	Maxims.
						Rifles	25,000	
						Cartridges for above	64,840,000	
						45 mm shells	200,000	
						76 mm shells	100,000	
						115 mm shells	81,377	With fuses.
						Cartridges for Maxims	67,851,775	Listed as '101,196,000, of which 33,344,245 were delivered by the Escolano above'.
						Tracer cartridges	7,000	
						Radio transmitters 135 Kz	5	
						Aerial cameras	6	
						Torpedo boats G5.9	2	

29	Y-29	*Cabo Palos*	6,300	29.4.37	7.5.37

Cargo	Quantity	Notes
Torpedoes	8	
Reid radios for above	10	
Buchka radios	5	
Mounted machine guns for torpedo boats	7	Of which 5 were brought on the *Elcano*, which otherwise carried food-stuffs.
Cartridges for above	70,000	
Polikarpov I-16 fighters with spares, fuel, ammunition	31	
Petrol trucks	2	
Hucks starters	2	
45 mm L/46 anti-tank guns	100	
Cases of spares for above	219	
45 mm guns for tanks	10	
Spare sights for above	12	
T-26 tanks with spares, fuel, ammunition	50	
Degtyarev DT machine-guns for tanks	10	
Boxes of spares for above	12	
Cartridges for above	300,000	
45 mm shells		
Spare tank engines	20	
Optical apparatus sets	12	
Maxim machine-guns	3	

Voyage No.	Dossier No.	Name of Ship	Displacement and tonnage	Departure	Arrival	Material carried	Quantity	Remarks
						Cartridges for Maxims	30,000	
						Spares for Maxims	150 boxes	
						Mosin-Nagant M 1891 rifles	15,000	
						Foreign rifles	10,000	
						7.62 mm cartridges	6,302,500	
						Foreign cartridges	44,743,000	
						Other cartridges	2,800,000	
						KTI fuses	300,000	
30	Y-30	Ciudad de Cádiz	3,600	3.5.37	11.5.37	Japanese 107 mm field-guns	40	In *Ejército* (Nov 1992, p. 101) J.-L. Infiesta-Perez calls these Schneider/Krupp M 1908/1910 guns sold to Russia before the First World War.
						Shells for above	48,000	
31	Y-31	Sac-2	2,900	8.5.37	21.5.37	R-Z light bombers with spares, fuel and ammunition	31	
						Aviation bombs 50 kg	6,000	
						Aviation bombs 70 kg	1,000	
						Radios 135 Kz	5	
						Anti-aircraft machine-guns for torpedo boats	6	

No.	Ship	Code	Tonnage	Date	Quantity	Cargo	Notes
32	Antonio de Satrústegui	Y-32	5,000	12.5.37	60,000	Cartridges for above	
					500,000	Cartridges for R-Z (for PV-1 fixed machine-guns)	
					625,000	for ShKAS machine-guns for observers	
				21.5.37	17	I-16 fighters	
					3,750	Aviation bombs 20 kg	
					10	Spare ShKAS 35 machine-guns for wings	That is, for I-16 fighters.
					1,500,000	Cartridges for ShKAS	
					1,500 (?)	Cartridges for PV-1	
					18	Spare M-17 engines	
					3	Spare M-34 engines	
					130	Propellers	
					8	Automobiles	
					51,297	107 mm shells	
					6	Machine-guns for boats or ships	
33	Jaron		5,300	21.5.37	60,000	Cartridges for above	Cargo diverted to *Artea Mendi*, which sailed under same voyage number. For the later history of the *Jaron*, see Appendix II.
					(23)	Polikarpov I-15 fighters	
					(10)	Tupolev SB bombers	
33	Artea Mendi	Y-33	3,594 GR 5,700 DW	20.5.37 31.5.37 or 1.6.37	23	Polikarpov I-15 fighters	

Voyage No.	Dossier No.	Name of Ship	Displacement and tonnage	Departure	Arrival	Material carried	Quantity	Remarks
						Tupolev SB bombers	10	See Chap. 18, p. 134.
						Aviation bombs: 50 kg	650	
						100 kg	1,000	
						250 kg FAB	20	
						ShKAS cartridges	800,280	
						Incendiary cartridges	2,000	
						Clips and links for above	660,000	
						ShKAS machine-guns for turret-mounts	10	
						Belt-fillers	6	
						Ship machine-guns	6	
						Cartridges for above	60,000	
34	Y-34	Aldecoa		31.5.37	21.6.37	Tupolev SB bombers	21	See Chap. 18, p. 134.
						Aviation bombs: 50 kg	1,350	
						100 kg	2,000	
						250 kg	40	
						500 kg F.A.B.	15	
						ShKAS cartridges	1,701,000	
						Links for above	1,360,000	
						Combs (strips)	12	
						Incendiary cartridges	4,000	
						Petrol tankers	6	

35	Y-35	Cabo Santo Tomé	24.6.37	30.6.37	12,500	Torpedo boats	2	
						Torpedoes	8	
						Depth charges	200	
						AO A2T fuses	531,250	
						152 mm shells and fuses	11,968	
						Machine-guns for ships	6	
						20 mm anti-aircraft cannons	2	
						Cartridges	60,000	
						Shells	1,000	
						Tin helmets	10,000	
						Polikarpov I-15 fighters	8	
						Polikarpov I-16 fighters with spare engines and sundries	14	
						Aviation bombs: AJ × 25 kg	500	
						20 kg	3,500	
						PV-1 cartridges (ordinary and perforating)	2,400,240	
						Incendiary	1,000,120	
						Clips and links	2,235,000	
						Belt-fillers	6	
						UTI trainers	4	
						Petrol pumps	2	
						Petrol tankers	2	
						152 mm howitzers	24	Perm M 1877; Putilov M 1909; Perm 1910.

Voyage No.	Dossier No.	Name of Ship	Displacement and tonnage	Departure	Arrival	Material carried	Quantity	Remarks
						French 155 mm field-guns	20	de Bange M 1877; Saint-Chamond M 1877.
						Shells, 152 mm and 155 mm	76,061	
						Mine-throwing guns	4	
						Field-guns	2	
						Shells for above	2,000	
						Ship's machine-guns	8	
						Cartridges for above	80,000	
						20 mm cannons	4	
						Shells for above	2,000	
Y-35		Iciar				T-26 tanks	25	At Leningrad. Loaded 1 July 1937, moved to Oranienburg, 8 July. Voyage cancelled and 'Y-36' file assigned to *Darro* (Ref: F. 33987. O.3. D.1856. L.40–41 – Berzin to Voroshilov, 11 July 1937; F. 33987. O.3. D.1056. L. 190– Voroshilov to Stalin, Nov 1937). According to a Nationalist report, this was because the crew refused to sail to any Spanish port (AMAE,
						Field-guns	32	
						Machine-guns	750	
						Rifles	25,000	
						Ammunition		

No.	Code	Ship			Tonnage	Cargo	Quantity	Notes
36	Y-36	*Darro*	29.7.37	10.8.37	2,600	Aviation petrol	404.5 (tons?)	Madrid, DR. R. 1047 c. 39, 6 July 1937).
						Aviation oil	40 (tons?)	
						Coolants	9.48 (tons?)	
						Aviation incendiary bombs	8,815	
						Machine-guns for ships	8	
						Cartridges for above	80,000	
						VEST telephones, radios, etc. Special automobiles		
37	Y-37	*Cabo San Agustín*	30.7.37	10.8.37	12,500	Polikarpov I-16 fighters with complete supplies of spares and ammunition but *not* fuel or oil	62	Cargo listed in Spanish at F.33987 O.3. D.1056. L.113–114.
						M-25 engines	15	
						Propellers	40	
						Spare wheels for SB bombers	68	
						ShKAS cartridges (ordinary)	2.6 million	
						Incendiary and armour-piercing	400,000	
						BT-5 tanks, with radios	50	
						Spare M-5 engines, for above	50	
						Spare radios, equipment, etc.		
						Mosin-Nagant M91 rifles	39,550	

Voyage No.	Dossier No.	Name of Ship	Displacement and tonnage	Departure	Arrival	Material carried	Quantity	Remarks
						Mosin-Nagant M91/30	10,450	The first modern Russian rifles to be delivered.
						Maxim-Tokarev machine-guns	2,000	
						Maxim machine-guns	1,007	
						Rifle cartridges	52,696,000	
						Armour-piercing cartridges	1,209,000	
						45 mm shells, armour-piercing	45,000	
						45 mm anti-tank guns	4	
						Shells for above	20,000	
						45 mm guns for tanks	10	
						Spare M-26 engines for T-26 tanks	30	
						Machine-guns for tanks	8	
						Cartridges for above	80,000	

The details of the cargoes of voyages 31 to 36 above, which are not shown on the 'Operation "X"' voyage lists that I have, are taken from Angel Vinas, *El oro español en la guerra civil*, pp. 274–9, where, fortunately, it is precisely these six voyages that are given in full, being taken from documents formerly in the possession of Dr Marcelino Pascua, the Spanish Republican ambassador in Moscow, October 1936 to March 1938. The original top copies are presumably in the RGVA.

FIFTH SERIES: 14 DECEMBER 1937 TO 11 AUGUST 1938

The following is taken not from the original voyage list for 1938, which was not among the documents given to me, but from a summary which appears to have been made on an electric typewriter of a kind that would not have existed in 1937–8. Despite two clear mistakes (voyages 39–40 and 46) it is probably not seriously inaccurate regarding the quantities of materials sent. All the ships belong to France Navigation (see Chapter 30, p. 235 and n.). All voyages from Murmansk to Bassens, Bordeaux.

No.	Code	Ship	Tonnage			Material	Quantity	Notes
38	Y-38	*Guilvinec*	3,222 GR	14.12.37	25.12.37	45 mm anti-tank guns	20	
						Sets of spares for 76.2 mm anti-aircraft guns	25	
						Heavy machine-guns	25	
						Light machine-guns	500	
						Ammunition and equipment		
39	Y-39	*Cabo Santo Tomé*	12,500	2.38	2.38	75 mm field-guns	8	The *Cabo Santo Tomé* could not have made this voyage, for she had been sunk on 10 October 1937.
40	Y-40	*Cabo San Agustín*	12,500			45 mm anti-tank guns	4	The *Cabo San Agustín* must have sailed to Marseille, for so large and well-known a ship cannot have reached the Spanish coast, less still have passed through the Straits of Gibraltar (p. 235). Shortly after this, she was commandeered by the Russians, though never paid for, at Feodosia, in the Crimea.
						Maxim guns	8	
						Rifles	20	
						Pistols	20	
						Ships armaments		
						Ammunition		
41	Y-41	*Bonifacio*	3,566 GR	23.1.38	7.2.38	Aero-engines	80	
						Rifles M 91/30	26,500	

Voyage No.	Dossier No.	Name of Ship	Displacement and tonnage	Departure	Arrival	Material carried	Quantity	Remarks
42	Y-42	Ain el Turk	2,477 GR	13.2.38	26.2.38	Rifles M34	8,400	
						Degtyarev DP and DT light machine-guns	1,350	
						Maxim machine-guns	50	
						Maxim-Tokarev light machine-guns	750	
						76.2 mm anti-aircraft guns M31	12	
						76 mm field-guns	91	
						Ammunition		
						Spare aero-engines (M-29) for I-15s	50	
						76.2 mm anti-aircraft guns	20	
						Vickers 115 mm howitzers	15	
						Japanese 107 mm field-guns	20	
						Shells	152,000	
						Rifles M 91/30	40,100	
						Cartridges for above	7,940,000	
43	Y-43	Gravelines	2,477 GR	1.3.38	13.3.38	French 76 mm field-guns	20	
						Shells for above	35,116	
						Czech machine-guns	1,000	Bought by Asúa in Czechoslovakia.
						Czech rifles	50,000	"

No.	Ship		Date	Item	Quantity	Notes
44	*Bougaroni*	3,050 GR	22.3.38 2.4.38	Czech cartridges	10,000,200	
				T-26 tanks	25	
				SB bombers	5	
				Equipment		
				Polikarpov I-16 fighters with equipment	31	
				Cartridges for above	1,450,000	
				37 mm *Gochkisa* anti-tank guns	250	i.e. M.30 L/45 guns, a German Rheinmetall design (PAK 35/36) built under licence.
				Shells for above	5,128,200	
				155 mm shells	5,154	
				Czech cartridges	20,495,400	Bought by Asúa in Czechoslovakia.
45	*Winnipeg*	8,379 GR	29.3.38 6.4.38	Tupolev SB bombers	16	
				Aviation bombs	7,724	
				Shells	45,049	
				Vickers 115 mm howitzers	30	
				Putilow 76.2 Mo3/30 field-guns	10	
				Rifle cartridges	35,621,672	
				Czech cartridges	16,924,400	Bought by Asúa in Czechoslovakia.
46	Y-48 *Bonifacio*	3,566,610	5.4.38 17.4.38	Tupolev 93 bombers	10	
				Czech machine-guns	1,000	Bought by Asúa in Czechoslovakia.

Voyage No.	Dossier No.	Name of Ship	Displacement and tonnage	Departure	Arrival	Material carried	Quantity	Remarks
47	Y-48	*Cabo Quilates* (*Ibai*)				French cartridges for above	30,000,000	
						Russian rifle cartridges	4,990,976	There is a note which says '*Cabo Quilates* could not deliver her Mexican cargo to Bilbao; therefore took it to Murmansk and thence to Spain'. This is nonsense; besides, the Soviets had nothing to do with this shipment (see Chapter 30, pp. 237–8).
48	Y-49	*San Malo*		27.4.38	8.5.38	'*Periotpravka grusa*'		Cargo either not disembarked and returned, or transhipped at sea to another vessel.
49	Y-50	*Cabo Quilates* (*Ibai*)				Arms and munitions		Transhipped from *San Malo*?
50	Y-51	*Ain el Turk*	2,477	13.6.38	27.6.38	Polikarpov I-16 fighters	25	
51	Y-52	*Winnipeg*	8,379	14.7.38	24.7.38	Polikarpov I-16 fighters ⎫		
52	Y-53	*Bougaroni*	3,050	11.8.38	11.8.38	Polikarpov I-16 fighters ⎭	65	

Sixth Series: mid-December 1938 to mid-February 1939

According to some sources, three voyages, according to others, seven. Perhaps Russian records exist to throw light on this. The material that crossed the frontier, or at least was not returned to the USSR.

Polikarpov I-15 bis fighters	30	out of	30
45 mm anti-tank guns	3	"	120
M 91/30 rifles	35,000	"	40,000
Degtyarev DP light machine-guns	2,000	"	2,000
Maxim machine-guns	772	"	1,000
Cartridges	38,763,000	"	50 million
Shells – anti-tank 45 mm	164,598		
Shells – anti-aircraft	41,000		
Shells – other	37,360		
Large quantities of aviation equipment			

Also sent, but returned:

Tupolev SB bombers	50	All with ammunition and equipment
Polikarpov I-16 fighters	70	
Nyeman R-10 light bombers	18	
UTI-4 trainers	6	
37 mm anti-tank guns	180	
French 76 mm field-guns	60	
F-22 76 mm field-guns	48	
Vickers 115 mm howitzers	40	
122 mm M 10/30 howitzers	20	
Armstrong 127 mm field-guns	17	
Japanese 107 mm field-guns	14	

Scheduled, but not embarked:

T-26 tanks	40
Torpedo boats	15

Summary of Material Supplied by the USSR

The significant totals are those for Oct 36–Aug 1938, since the material that arrived in Jan-Feb 1939 took no part in the war (see Table 4 above, p. 142).

	4 Oct–30 Nov 1936	1 Jan–10 Aug 1937	Mar–Aug 1938	Totals for Oct 36–Aug 1938	Jan–Feb 1939	Final Totals
Aircraft						
SB Katiuska	30	31	31	92		92
I-15 Chato	50	81		131		131
I-15 bis Super-Chato					30	30
I-16 Mosca	31	124	121	276		276
R-5sss Rasante	31			31		31
R-Z Natacha		93		93		93
UTI trainers		4		4		4
Tanks						
T-26	106	150	25	281		281
BT-5		50		50		50
Armoured Cars						
BA-6	37			37		37
BA-3	3			3		3
FAI	20			20		20
Artillery, Machine-guns and Rifles						
German grenade-throwers	240 or 340			240 or 340		240 or 340
Infantry-support guns, Puski Maklen 37 mm M 17	30			30		30
Anti-tank guns, 37 mm M 30 L/45 *Gochkisa*			250	250		250
Anti-tank guns, 45 mm M 32 L/46		119	24	143	4	147
Field-guns, unspecified		2				2
Field-guns, 75 mm			8			8

Item	(1)	(2)	(3)	USSR total	Bought outside USSR	Total
,76.2 mm	80	90			Bought outside USSR (8)	170+(8)=178
,77 mm					Bought outside USSR (22)	(22)
,107 mm	40	20				60
,127 mm	12					12
,155 mm	20					20
Howitzers, 105 mm					Bought outside USSR (8)	(8)
,115 mm	94	20	45			159
,152 mm	24					24
Erhardt mine-throwers, 170 mm and 240 mm	4					4
Anti-aircraft guns, 76.2 mm M 31	32	32				64
Heavy machine-guns	2,603	1,908	83	4,594	772	5,366
Light machine-guns	1,150	4,664	4,660	10,414	2,000	12,414
Rifles	58,825	195,800	125,020	379,645	35,000	414,645

Thirty field-guns, 8 howitzers, 2,420 machine-guns and 85,000 rifles were bought in Europe, but for various reasons were included on the 'Operation "X"' lists. The same is true of the 4 Swissair aircraft and 8 other aircraft, perhaps those shipped on the *Mar Cantábrico* and captured by the Nationalists at sea. I have not included ammunition because the lists are incomplete. Of the cartridges, 656,865,723 are listed; of the shells, 6,614,504. Of the shells, however, about 5.4 million were for 37 mm and 45 mm, leaving about 1.2 million for field artillery, or about 2,700 per gun for the whole war. The quantities were not equally distributed and deliveries were irregular, however, (see above, Chapter 19). Note that the total number of military aircraft on the list is 623. Valuation up to 10 Aug 37: $131,567,580.70; for 1938: $39,871,209. Total: $171,438,789.70, but see above, pp. 150–2.

APPENDIX IV

A. Sweden and Switzerland

At their exhibition of captured Republican war material held in the Grand Kursaal, San Sebastián, in the autumn of 1938, the Nationalists included a Bofors 37 mm M 35 anti-tank gun, one of four, they claimed, taken on the Castellón front north of Valencia. Manuel Tagüeña Lacorta writes (*Testimonios de dos guerras*, p. 205) that twelve such guns and sixteen Bofors 40 mm M 38 rapid-firing anti-aircraft cannons, all short of ammunition, were brought to the Flix-Vinebre sector to support the Republican attack across the Ebro on 25 July 1938. How many of these modern Swedish guns the Republicans managed to obtain, or through whom, is not clear, but the evidence points to a Swiss connection, through Rosenfeldt, Rosenbaum and the Baltic states. Fernando Valdés, Franco's agent in Stockholm, told his government that he suspected that George Branting, the Swedish Socialist leader, was using money, collected for the relief of Spanish children, for buying artillery instead. In fact, the Bofors were yet another of those many purchases which the Republicans made in the autumn of 1936 and then spent the next year-and-a-half, more often than not in vain, trying to get delivered. The anti-tank guns may have been bought through SEPEWE, for the cargo of the *Jaron* (Appendix II, 25 Sept 1937) included twenty-six 37 mm guns, type unspecified, whose unit price was £830 ($4,150), which was about right for a Bofors M 35. It should be remembered, however, that none of her cargo arrived even in France until brought by the *Diana* in April and May 1938.

In a letter to me (23 June 1983), Dickie Metcalfe (see below, p. 317) referred to 'an abortive attempt in Paris in 1940, just before the fall of France, to locate on behalf of HM Government some Bofors 40 mm *en route* from Spain to Finland'. In conversation, however, he said that he had found the owner, 'a Captain Calvinio', and 'forced' him to embark the guns on a British steamer at Le Havre. Whatever the truth, the name 'Calviño' suggests that these guns were not in transit, having been sold by the Franco government to Finland, but had been bought by the Republicans and were still in France when the civil war ended and that Calviño had been trying to sell them to anyone he could find. I doubt that the British offered him money or a safe passage to England. If the guns did indeed cross the Channel, presumably they were used to defend RAF airfields during the Battle of Britain, a detail that could be checked.

After Michel Rosenfeldt was arrested on 12 December 1936, an attempt to buy Bofors guns was among the many deals with which he was said to have been connected, as well as the deals in Switzerland. It may indeed have been his arrest which led to the arrest of Victor Fisse, the former deputy for Geneva in the Swiss parliament, early in January 1937. From Republican records we know that on 18 December 1936 the Republicans had opened a credit on Fisse's behalf in a Paris bank for 157,488,255 Ffr. (a little over £1.5 million, or $7.5 million; Angel Viñas, *El oro español en la guerra civil*, p. 87). According to a Nationalist report, this was to cover the purchase of 100,000 Polish Mauser rifles and 1,000 cartridges and a bayonet each at £12.50 ($62.50). He was released on bail of 2,000 Sfr., but I have seen no reports of his trial. The deal came to nothing, and in any case would have been a purchase from SEPEWE, perhaps the same huge offer that the Polish chief-of-staff made to Pastor at about that time (see above, p. 112). The only Swiss small arms known to have reached the Republicans were a few machine-rifles, one of which was exhibited at San Sebastián and is now in the Museo del Ejército, Alcalá de Henares. It is described as a 'Neuhausen made in 1922', but in fact is a SIG KE-7, which was not produced until the early 1930s (for a photograph, see the Urbión edition of Hugh Thomas, vol. 2, p. 359).

In *Ejército* (Nov 1992, p. 105), J.-L. Infiesta Pérez writes that a hundred Swiss-designed Oerlikon 20 mm rapid-firing anti-aircraft cannons, made in the USSR under licence, were sent to the Republicans from Russia. Only six such guns appear on the Soviet lists (two brought on the *Aldecoa*, voyage 34, on 21 June 1937, and four on the *Cabo Santo Tomé*, voyage 35, on 30 June 1937). It may be remembered, however, that fifty were said to have been taken by the Mexican ship *Jalisco* from Marseille to Alicante on 21 August 1936 (see above, p. 103). Shortly after Fisse's arrest, Bernabé Foca, Franco's agent in Berne, reported that Dr Emile Bührle, the director of the Werkzeug Maschinenfabrik Oerlikon, was conniving at the sale of these weapons, several lots of which were being exported to 'Red Spain' via the Baltic and Marseille. Accordingly, he asked the Italian and German chargés d'affaires in Berne to make discreet inquiries. Sr. Fantoni, the Italian, told him that Bührle was 'a man of dubious moral reputation'. The German, Baron Bibra, assured him, however, that Bührle was a German national who had long been an active member of the German Nazi Party and would never knowingly sell his products to Communists. Indeed, he had already refused offers from agents, supposedly acting for Iraq, Iran and Turkey, whom he regarded as suspect and had taken steps to ensure that no more Oerlikon cannons would reach 'Red Spain' in future. Among the agents named was Vladimir Rosenbaum-Ducommon, whose case has already been described (see above, p. 214; AMAE, Madrid, DR R 1048 c 39, *passim*). It was no coincidence, therefore, that at this time the counsellor at the Iraqi legation in Berlin was recalled to Baghdad and arrested on a charge of trying to sell arms, via Switzerland and Czechoslovakia, to the Spanish Republic. His counterpart in Paris, Abdul Aziz al-Mudhaffar, who was said to have earned £50,000 already in supplying false export certificates for arms to Spain, was likewise recalled, but took refuge in Syria. The Syrian authorities rejected a demand from the Iraqi government for his extradition. Syria was then under a French mandate and Iraq, though theoretically independent and ruled by King Ghasi, under strong British influence. The embarrassing crisis that ensued between the British and French was further complicated by the fact that al-Mudhaffar was being protected by a group hostile to the Iraqi monarch (FO 371/20797 E 1876). The British reports do not explain the political dimensions to the affair or how it ended, but I suspect that it had something to do with conflicts arising from nascent Arab nationalism, the recent massacre of the Assyrians north of Mosul and the like, and was not merely a piece of cynical profiteering. Some Oerlikons, however, did reach the Republicans thereafter. Bührle's Paris agent, Raymond Sancery, was living in the rue de la Tour in 1937, for instance, but by 1938 had changed his address to 55 Avenue George V, which was that of the Republican buying commission (*Interavia*, 1939). It was through him and Ferdinand Gros, an associate of the Gourdou-Leseurre aircraft company, that a number of Oerlikons adapted for aircraft were acquired. Four were fitted onto two of the Dewoitine D.371s that arrived in October 1937, though I have found no reports of their use in action (Howson, p. 114; IISG, Amsterdam, FAI/CNT Microfilm 153, A 7, 8 Feb 1937).

As for Dr Emile Bührle, he is remembered today for his large collection of French Impressionist and Post-Impressionist paintings, which went on a world tour from 1989 to 1991. The catalogue prepared by the Royal Academy of Art, where the collection was shown in London, describes him as having been 'a machine-tool manufacturer'.

B. Yugoslavia

Several lots of arms were ordered, including a large one from the French Batignolles company, by the Republicans from Yugoslavia but, despite persistent efforts to get them out, none was delivered, owing to the pro-Franco stance of the regent, Prince Paul (FO 371/20575 W 10554 and 20381 R 5842; IISG, Amsterdam, FAI/CNT Microfilm 153, 63-A-7; also numerous references in Asúa's dispatches from Prague).

C. The P.Z.L. P.37 Łos

The story of this mysterious affair, to which I have briefly referred on p. 113 above, is too complicated to retell in detail here. This very advanced and top secret bomber was first offered to the Spanish Republicans on 26 July 1937, ten months before its very existence was revealed to the world, and the offer, made discreetly to Manuel Martínez Pedroso, the Republican chargé in Warsaw, through a Mexican named Oscar Ossorio, could not have been made without the approval of the Polish government (AMAE, Madrid, Arch. Barcelona, RE 11 c. 44 pl. 11). In September 1937 the visit to Barcelona under false names by three Polish air force officers, including Major Ziembinski (see above, p. 107), may have been in connection with this offer (ASHM, Madrid, microfilm 23, A. 4, L. 267, c. 13, Doc. 5), as may have been the arrival in Barcelona on 20 October 1937 of 'General' Zymierski and a German named 'Fancella', both using Spanish names (AMAE, Arch. Barcelona, RE 11 c. 80 pl. 5). Zymierski, incidentally, was to become the notorious General Rola-Zymierski who, as head of state security after the Communist take-over of Poland, was responsible for some of the worst cruelties of the Stalinist repression during the 1940s and '50s.

According to possibly reliable Nationalist intelligence reports, a contract for fifty of these bombers was signed by Lt.-Col. Angel Pastor Velasco and Olivier Jury, a resident of Clermont-Ferrand and the Socialist mayor of Langeac, France. Jury, the reports claimed, was a Freemason, the Grand Master of Lodge 33 in Alliers, and hence a personal friend of Prieto. The unit price of the aircraft was £21,400 ($167,300) and half the total value of the contract (£1,800,000, or $9,000,000) was paid to the Poles through the Federal Industrial Development Bank, 14 Mincing Lane, EC4, in the City of London. However, the directors of another intermediary company (Dominion Trading Co. Ltd, of Laurence Pountney Lane), Edward King and Louiza, were both in prison, King in Barcelona and Louiza in Paris (AMAE, DR R 1048 c. 22 pl. 'Aviones'). Indeed, on 22 February 1938 Pablo de Azcárate, the Republican ambassador in London, warned his government that his enquiries revealed that the Dominion Trading Co. had 'no credit whatsoever' (AMAE, Arch. Barcelona, RE 4 c. 6 pl. 19).

On 10 August 1938 Franco's representatives in Warsaw and London presented reports on this offer to the Polish and British governments. The Poles shrugged, protested ignorance and promised to pass the details to Marshal Smigly-Rydz 'next week'. From London, now that the Czechoslovakian crisis was approaching its climax, the Foreign Office sent a note to the Duque de Alba on 20 September, six weeks after receiving the report, to say that there was no evidence of such a deal in London and that therefore it was of no concern to HM Government, a reply very different from any that would have been given six months before (FO 371/22652 W 10707).

In November 1938 Negrín sent two leading fighter pilots, José Bravo and Manuel Zarauza, to Paris 'to buy aircraft' (Lacalle, p. 428, and F. Tarazona, *Yo fui piloto de caza rojo*, pp. 278–9). José Bravo told me (March 1992), however, that their main duty had been to 'chase up a contract for a Polish bomber', but, he said 'no podíamos colocarlo' ('we couldn't finalize it').

These are the essential facts and they defy rational explanation. King, it is true, was a confidence trickster of the Corrigan type and he appears as a prisoner ('a cheerful little Cockney') in Barcelona in E. C. Lucas Phillips, *The Spanish Pimpernel*, a book about Captain Christopher Lance, who organized the escape of several Nationalists from Republican Spain. King is mentioned in some of the Polish depositions cited in Chapter 15 above and his company also appears in a suspect offer to buy petrol for the

Republicans in Galveston, Texas, in April 1937 (RE 4 c. 6 pl. 15). In November 1937 the *Daily Mail* carried a story about Charles Way, who had committed suicide, apparently after being cheated out of the ownership of his invention, a 'death ray' which could stop aero-engines at 1,000 metres' distance and which he and King had demonstrated in Barcelona the previous spring. After being released from prison at the end of the Spanish Civil War, King returned to Britain, was arrested on a warrant issued two years earlier, tried and gaoled for fraud. Nevertheless, the sending of the two airmen to Paris suggests that Negrín had eliminated the confidence-trickery from the deal by November 1937.

The P.Z.L. P.37 Los is well known to aviation historians as a remarkable aeroplane for its time. For example, despite its high performance (maximum speed, 280 m.p.h., or 448 km/h), it could lift a disposable load equal to its own tare (i.e. empty, equipped) weight, an unprecedented achievement for a military aircraft before the Second World War, and when it was first shown at the Belgrade air show in May 1938 it created enormous international interest. Poland was once again in the front rank of producers of military aircraft, as it had been in the early 1930s.

The essence of the puzzle is, therefore, that Colonel Beck, who insisted on approving all offers of exports of war material to Spain before they could be expedited, approved this offer to the Republicans in July 1937 and continued to approve it through the next year, at the very time when he was supposedly trying for friendlier relations with Hitler. It is hard to conceive of anything more likely to provoke Hitler's fury and, when his fury had abated, contempt.

Notes

1. CONTRASTS

1. Antonio Primo de Rivera, *Discursos frente al parlamento*, p. 224, quoted in Burnett Bolloten, *The Spanish Civil War*, p. 3.
2. Gerald Howson, *Aircraft of the Spanish Civil War* (hereafter 'Howson'), p. 145, and Ignacio Hidalgo de Cisneros, *Cambio de rumbo*, pp. 132–3. That the two F.VIIs were numbered 20–5 and 20–6 is evident from a photograph in *Aeroplano*, no. 3 (Nov 1988), p. 99.

2. 'THE TIME OF CHAOS'

1. Andrés García Lacalle, *Mitos y verdades* (hereafter 'Lacalle'), pp. 71–82, quoting the eye-witness account by the veteran mechanic Lieutenant José Macías Ruíz, corroborated by other sources. Not surprisingly, his version disagrees on many points with accounts published by Nationalist historians.
2. *ABC de Sevilla* (23 July 1936).
3. Manuel Rubio Cabeza, *Diccionario de la Guerra Civil Española*, vol. 2, p. 675.

3. 'AIR-MINDEDNESS'

1. H. Montgomery Hyde, *British Air Policy between the Wars*, p. 284; *Hansard*, vol. 270, 10 Nov 1932, c. 632.
2. The Dragon Rapide was hired from Olley Air Service, Croydon, on 11 July. Luis Bolín's own account is in *Spain: The Vital Years*, Chapters 1–5. See also: Hugh Thomas, *The Spanish Civil War* (hereafter 'Thomas'), Chapter 13; Paul Preston, *Franco*, pp. 140–43; and Antonio González Betes, *Franco y el Dragón Rapide* (1987), the most complete account of the affair.
3. Luis Bolín, op. cit., p. 53.
4. PRO Foreign Office General Correspondence (hereafter the document class ref. 'FO') FO 371/20533 W6758 and W6996.
5. Klaus Maier, *Guernica 24.6.1937* (hereafter 'Maier'), p. 22; Angel Viñas, *La Alemania Nazi y el 18 de julio*, p. 460 (2nd edn, p. 383). Both sources are based on 'Das Unternehmen Feuerzauber', f. 22, a report in the Bundesarchiv-Militärische, Freiburg, at RL 2/V 3187.
6. Ismael Saz, *Mussolini contra la Republica*, p. 183.
7. Ibid.
8. Howson, pp. 304–5. The Luftwaffe strength figures are taken from Anthony Adamthwaite, *France and the Coming of the Second World War*, p. 161. See also R. J. Overy, 'German Air Strength', in *Historical Journal*, vol. 27 (1984).

9. *Daily Mail* (23 and 27 July 1936).
10. Jean Cassou, *La mémoire courte*, p. 9.
11. Louis Fischer, *Men and Politics*, p. 340.
12. Julián Zugazagoita, *Guerra y vicisitudes de los españoles*, vol. 1, p. 102.

4. PARIS

1. *Les événements survenus . . .* annexe I, p. 215, deposition by Léon Blum, 23 July 1947. For an explanation of this reference, see Sources: Printed Documents.
2. *L'Echo de Paris* (6 July 1936), article by Henri de Kerillis.
3. Peter Wright, *Spycatcher*, pp. 239–41. Also named as spies are Admiral Muselier and André Labarthe, an air ministry official who will appear in the narrative later.
4. Juan Simeon Vidarte, *Todos fuimos culpables*, vol. 1, pp. 505–6; Thomas, pp. 343, 344 and n.; information given to the author by José Warleta, the son of Major Ismael Warleta de la Quintana, one of the two officers who arrived in Paris on 21 July. He had been Director General de Aeronáutica, 1934–5.
5. *Documents diplomatiques français*, Series II (hereafter *DDF*), vol. 3, p. 52, n. 3, and p. 61, Doc. 34.
6. *L'Action Française* and *Le Jour* (23 and 24 July 1936); *L'Intransigeant* (25 July 1936).
7. *Les événements survenus . . .*, Blum's deposition, p. 216.
8. *L'Action Française* (22 July 1936).
9. José Fernández Castro, *Alejandro Otero: el médico y el político*, p. 174.
10. Pierre Renouvin, 'La politique extérieure du premier ministre Léon Blum', in Edouard Bonnefous, *Histoire politique de la Troisième République*, vol. 6, p. 394. This essay is also in *Léon Blum, chef de gouvernement, 1936–1937*, a collection of lectures and testimonies presented at a conference in 1965 in honour of Léon Blum.
11. Jules Moch, *Rencontres avec Léon Blum*, p. 194, and his *Le Front Populaire: Grande espérance . . .*, p. 233. Although the Dewoitines are not specifically mentioned, Lithuania is, for the first time, and it must have been at this meeting, therefore, that Cot pointed out that these fourteen fighters were available.
12. This is in the letter Rios sent to Giral next evening (25 July), see n. 15 below. See also Jean Lacouture, *Léon Blum*, p. 311.
13. Angel Viñas, *El oro de Moscú*, pp. 29 and 56, n. 9. Delbos's original statement is in Renouvin, p. 396, and can also be read in the French newspapers (Monday 27 and Tuesday 28 July 1936).
14. *DDF*, vol. 3, p. 60, Doc. 33, 26 July 36, and Renouvin, p. 396. Translations of this and the above statement (n. 13) are in Lacouture, p. 315.
15. Rios to Giral, 25 July 1936. A copy of this letter was later stolen in Switzerland, probably by an agent of the OVRA, and published in the Italian *Il Messagero* (10 Dec 1936). See also *DDF*, vol. 4, pp. 194 and 201. A translation of the whole letter is in William Foss and Cecil Geraghty, *The Spanish Arena*, pp. 372–5, and in the pro-Nationalist pamphlet *I Accuse France* by 'A Barrister' (1937).
16. Details of Rios's conversation with Warleta kindly sent to me by José Warleta.

5. MEN AND ARMAMENTS

1. Michael Alpert, *El ejército republicano en la guerra civil*, Chapter 2. Paul Preston, *Franco*, p. 152, estimates a figure of 130,000 men in the army on the Peninsular and Thomas, p. 328, gives *c.* 100,000, of which a third was on leave. I have decided to accept Dr Alpert's figures until proved wrong.

2. While the literature of the Spanish Moroccan war of 1909–27 is extensive, there is not much for the non-Spanish reader, who for the time being may be entrusted to Raymond Carr, *Spain, 1808–1975* and Preston, op. cit., Chapters 1 and 2.

3. My thanks to don Rafael Varo Estacio for detailed information on Spanish army weaponry and for supplying technical literature, some of it hard to obtain (e.g. J. Genova, *Armas de guerra*, 1910, various instruction manuals printed for the Republican army during the civil war and an official manual printed by the Nationalist army in 1939, *Armamentos de infantería*), without which I should hardly have been able to undertake this book.

4. These figures are from José-Luis Alcofar Nassaes, 'Las armas de ambos bandos' in *Historia 16: la guerra civil*, no. 10 of the series.

5. Ibid., and F. C. Albert, *Carros de combate...*, pp. 13–14.

6. Michael Alpert, *La guerra civil española en el mar*, Chapter 4; and Juan García Durán, 'Supremacía en el mar: La marina de los dos bandos', in Hugh Thomas, *La guerra civil española* (Urbion edn, 1975), vol. 6, pp. 177–203.

7. Howson, under the aircraft type headings, and pp. 6–8, 20, 301–2.

8. Ibid., under Douglas DC-2, Junkers F.13.

9. Angel Viñas, *La Alemania nazi...*, pp. 126–7 (p. 102, 2nd edn). Von Welczeck's dispatch was written in October 1936, before the decision had been made public.

10. Carmen Díaz, *Mi vida con Ramón Franco*, pp. 86–93 and 185–90.

11. Howson, p. 10.

12. Information from Dr Richard K. Smith, who interviewed Lacalle in Mexico City, 1970.

6. 'NON-INTERVENTION'

1. FO 371/19858 C5702, enclosed with dispatch from the British ambassador in Paris, Sir George Clerk, to Eden, a report of the debate in the Chamber of Deputies, 31 July 1936. This is fuller than the extracts quoted by Renouvin (see above, Chapter 4, n. 10) and Lacouture, *Léon Blum*, p. 316.

2. *L'Intransigeant* (21 July 1936).

3. *Le Figaro* (29 July 1936) reported that the rescue flights began the day before, 28 July. The gold flights are listed in Angel Viñas, *El oro de Moscú*, pp. 30–39, and Jesús Salas Larrazábal, *La intervención extranjera en la guerra de España*, pp. 505–6, taken from the log-book of José Macías Ruíz, who provided the eye-witness account of events at Tablada on 18 July (see above, Chapter 2, n. 1).

4. FO 371/20475 W11340, 20 July 1936, memorandum by Sir Maurice Hankey, Secretary to the Cabinet and the Committee of Imperial Defence (since 1912) and Clerk to the Privy Council. He added 'and the greater our detachment (from France) the better'.

5. Thomas Jones, *Diary with Letters*, p. 231, recording a conversation with Baldwin on 27 July 1936. He continues, 'I reminded him of Bullitt's prophecy made to me two months ago that Moscow looked forward to a Communist government in Spain in 3 months.' William Bullitt had been US ambassador in Moscow and was about to become ambassador in Paris. He was forever making alarmist remarks of this kind, which were later shown to have no foundation in fact. It is possible that some fool of a Russian had bragged in this way at a reception, but Stalin's policy at that time (May 1936) had been to avoid such provocation, promote the Popular Front and soothe the Western democracies, particularly as the first show trials, which might arouse suspicion and fear even on the left in the West, were about to begin in Moscow. The outbreak of the civil war in Spain and the lack of any serious protest from the left against the show trials were to change things by the autumn.

6. Italian foreign ministry archives, Spagna Fondo di Guerra, b. 3, R. 2441/640, Vitetti to Ciano, 29 July 1936. Quoted in Ismael Saz, *Mussolini contra la República*, pp. 204–5, and by Enrique Moradiellos, *Neutralidad benévola*, p. 172.
7. FO 371/20527 W7781, quoted by Jill Edwards, *The British Government and the Spanish Civil War*, p. 23.
8. *Hansard*, 29 July 1936, col. 1498.
9. *New Republic* [New York] (19 Aug 1936); J. M. Martínez Bande, *La campaña de Andalucía*, p. 44.
10. Gabriel Jackson, *The Spanish Republic and the Civil War*, p. 248, from an interview with General Kindelán in 1960.
11. Hugh Dalton, *The Fateful Years*, p. 95.
12. Lacouture, *Leon Blum*, p. 312.

7. MALRAUX AND HIS MEN

1. Walter G. Langlois, 'Aux sources de *L'Espoir*: Malraux et le début de la guerre civile en Espagne' in *Revue des Lettres Modernes*, nos 355–9 (1973), p. 98.
2. Howson, p. 128.
3. Ibid. pp. 9, 221–2; Langlois, pp. 100–02.
4. Ibid. Much of what follows is similarly based on Langlois, 'Before *L'Espoir*; Malraux's Pilots for Republican Spain', in *Witnessing André Malraux: Visions and Revisions*, ed. Brian Thompson and Carl A. Viggiani, pp. 91–2, and notes, pp. 201–5.
5. *Rundschau über Politik* (30 July 1936). Interview quoted in full by Günther Schmigalle, *André Malraux und der spanischer Bürgerkrieg*, pp. 90–92; also in part by Langlois, 'Before *L'Espoir*', p. 100.
6. According to information kindly given to me by Professor Langlois, Malraux was introduced to Barga in Paris by Fernando de los Rios. Barga was cousin to the writer Ramón Gómez de la Serna, whom Malraux had met during his visit to Spain in May 1936. Julio Gómez de la Serna, another relative, translated several of Malraux's novels into Spanish. There is a brief sketch of Corpus Barga's life in the foreword to his early novel *Pasión y muerte* (1930 edn).
7. Howson, pp. 302–3.
8. Richard Rumbold and Lady Margaret Stewart, *A Winged Life*, pp. 120–21; Curtis Cate, *Antoine de Saint-Exupéry*, pp. 212–14.
9. Archives du Service Historique de l'Armée de l'Air (hereafter ASHAA), 'Témoignage du Colonel Victor Veniel', 28 March 1973, p. 1. Photocopy kindly given to me by Professor Langlois.
10. Franco Fucci, *Ali contro Mussolini*, contains valuable information about Italian anti-Fascists in the 1930s. My thanks too to Dorothy Warren, Ruth Draper's biographer.
11. Fucci, pp. 109–10.
12. *Les Ailes* (23 July 1936, 13 Aug 1936, 7 Jan 1937). Also Langlois, 'Before *L'Espoir*', p. 107.
13. Victor Veniel, *L'aviation française et la guerre d'Espagne*', in *Icare*, no. 118, pp. 135–6; Patrick Laureau, *L'aviation républicaine espagnole*, p. 143.
14. Lacalle, pp. 144, 150, 173, 181. Dary is also praised in Vincent Doherty's report to Wing Commander Medhurst at the Air Ministry, FO 371/20547 W15491. During the Great War Dary had won the Croix de Guerre and Médaille Militaire and been made a Chevalier de la Légion d'Honneur. For his car-stealing enterprise, see *L'Intransigeant* (11 Jan 1936), p. 1.
15. FO 371/21284 W2999, two reports, 8 Oct 1936 (13 pp.) and 21 Nov 1936 (11 pp.), written for Jean Moulin and Pierre Cot. In December 1936 and January 1937 Flight Lieutenant H. M. Pearson, assistant air attaché at the British embassy in Paris, was temporarily detached to the British embassy, Valencia, from which he

made at least one visit to the Malraux squadron, which was then at nearby La Señera. On returning to Paris, Medhurst wrote a report for Wing Commander Victor Goddard, of Air Ministry Intelligence, enclosing Dary's reports with it. He does not explain why Dary gave it to him.

16. Lacalle, p. 150.
17. Not an entirely fantastical conjecture. Dary gave his reports to Moulin, who passed them to Cot, who may have mentioned their interest to a Russian at the Soviet embassy without intending any harm. The Russian would then have been obliged to act on the information lest he be accused of failing to root out 'traitors and spies' and end his career in a labour camp. Finally, Dary wrote an article for *Revue de l'Armée de l'Air*, no. 96 (July 1938), which contained some of the information from his reports. Some writers have insisted that his name was 'Darry'. In his reports he calls himself 'Dary', however, and that is the name given at his trial for car-stealing.
18. ASHAA, Carton B, 178, 'Enseignements à tirer des opérations aérieenes d'Espagne', 19 Dec 1936 (15 pp.); 'Note sur enseignements . . .', 16 Jan 1937 (9 pp.) and see n. 9 above. Also 'Témoignage de M. Pierre Cot, 21 juin 1973'.
19. William Green, *Warplanes of the Second World War*, vol. 7, pp. 93–8 for the history of the Bloch MB 131; Raymond Danel and Jean Cuny, *L'aviation française de bombardement et renseignement*, see index, Bloch MB 130, MB 131, MB 132, MB 133. The MB 131 eventually went into production and service but proved unsatisfactory. The MB 132 prototype variant was cancelled before construction had begun and the MB 133 prototype rejected after brief testing.
20. *Le Figaro* (27 July 1936), *L'Action Française* (6 Aug 1936), *L'Express du Midi* (8 Aug 1936) and many other newspapers.
21. *Le Figaro* (27 July, 26 Dec 1936); Howson, pp. 224–6.
22. *L'Action Française* (31 Jan 1937), p. 3.
23. Information to author from Langlois, who had interviewed du Perron and the Belgian Paul Bernier, the political commissar of the Malraux squadron.
24. Archives Départementales de la Haute Garonne, Toulouse: liasse 1912/55, Doc. no. 348, 6 Aug 1936, Corpus Barga's request for an importation permit. For market prices of the Dewoitine D.371, D.372 and D.373 (478,000 Ffr., or $31,447.37 each), see Jean Cuny and Raymond Danel, *Les avions Dewoitine*, pp. 142–4. For the price of the Potez 540 to the French air force (945,000 Ffr., or $62,295.29 each), see the history of the Potez company in *Aviation Magazine de l'Espace*, no. 320, p. 49. For the price of a new Douglas DC-2, see Nye Committee hearings (see Sources: Printed Documents), pp. 13503 and 13510.

8. SETBACKS

1. Howson, pp. 110–14.
2. The arrivals and departures from Toulouse-Francazal, with the names of the pilots and aircraft serial numbers, are in the Archives Départementales de la Haute-Garonne, Toulouse, liasse 1912/55, Doc. 389, 26 Aug 1936. The three test pilots of the Lioré et Olivier company were Doumerc, who also worked for the CEMA at Villacoublay, Lepreux and Roulland.
3. *L'Express du Midi* (6 Aug 1936).
4. David Wingeate Pike, *Les français et la guerre d'Espagne*, pp. 103–4.
5. *DDF*, vol. 3, p. 119, Doc. 76, Albornoz to Delbos, 4 Aug 1936.
6. Archivo Histórico Nacional, Archivo de Araquistaín (hereafter AHN, Arch. Araq.), 35/026, Ossorio to Araquistaín, 12 Nov 1936; Lacouture, *Léon Blum*, p. 311. Jiménez de Asúa's testimony is also in *Léon Blum: chef du gouvernement, 1936–1937* (see n. 13 below). The affair was reported in all the local newspapers, and see also *Journal des Débats* (26 Aug 1936), when Alfonso Otero was replaced

by Eladio Anquino Murillo (see Archivo del Ministerio de Asuntos Exteriores, Madrid, Archivo de Barcelona [hereafter AMAE, Arch. Barcelona], RE 154, c. 26, telegrams Y 474 and B 463).

7. AMAE, Arch. Barcelona, RE 123, c. 3, pl. 1, 30 July 1936; RE 159, c. 3, pl. 3, 29 July 1936; FO 371 20527 W777; *Le Figaro* (5 and 7 Aug 1936); *L'Intransigeant*, *L'Action Française* and *The Aeroplane* (12 Aug 1936). The newspapers reported three and in *Aircraft of the Spanish Civil War* I conjectured they were F-AJPJ *Tornado*, -PC *Sirocco* and -VB *Alizé*. The documents, however, mention only two, F-AJYM and F-AJXX, and a Fokker F.VIIb3m, F-AJBJ. A note in the Archivo del Servicio Histórico Militar, Madrid, (hereafter ASHM) on Microfilm 25, Armario 4, Legajo 270, c. 6, f. 40 (I regret the length of this reference, but the film contains thousands of items), undated, mentions F-AJVB *Alizé* in Republican Spain, apparently around December 1936.

8. Justo Martínez Amutio, *Chantaje de un pueblo*, pp. 22–7. The machine was probably the Latécoère 28 F-AJVI.

9. Edwards, pp. 25–6.

10. Langlois, 'Before *L'Espoir*', p. 104. These were the points argued about at the cabinet meeting on 1 August and it is inconceivable that they were not argued through again on 7 August.

11. *L'Action Française* (12 and 13 Aug 1936); Langlois, pp. 110–12.

12. Jiménez de Asúa's deposition, in *Léon Blum: chef du gouvernement, 1936–1937*, pp. 409–11; Lacouture, *Léon Blum*, pp. 311–12. Asúa dates this as 25 July, but as the *Atxuri Mendi* did not reach Bordeaux until 3 August, and the loading did not begin until a day or two after, his meeting with Blum must have taken place at night on 7 August, after the cabinet meeting, and the tearing up of the cheque early next morning.

13. Ibid.

14. Clara Malraux-Goldschmidt, *Le bruit de nos pas*, vol. 5, *La fin et le commencement* (1976), pp. 16–18.

15. Pierre Galante, *Malraux*, p. 148.

16. Mikhail Koltzov, *Diario de la guerra de España*, pp. 8–9.

17. *Foreign Relations of the United States, 1936*, vol. 3, p. 482.

18. Victor Veniel, 'L'aviation française et la guerre d'Espagne', *Icare*, no. 118, p. 132, says that the arms were bought, but did not arrive, for reasons never discovered. In an interview with the author in January 1992, Vincent Piatti, who had served as a mechanic with the squadron from August 1936 to the spring of 1937, confirmed that the Potez lacked all this essential equipment. There are also several letters in AMAE, Arch. Barcelona (RE 123, c. 3, pl. 5) concerning attempts to have bomb-racks manufactured in France, as will be seen later.

19. AHN, Arch. Araq. 30/026.

20. Howson, pp. 13, 26.

21. Angel Viñas, 'The Financing of the Spanish Civil War' in *Revolution and War in Spain*, ed. Paul Preston, p. 274. His source must be ASHM C.C.G. L. 281. c. 24 dated 26 Aug 1936, an unsigned note by a Nationalist officer.

22. Told to the author by José-María Carreras, a LAPE pilot, who was at Barajas when the Orion arrived on its ox carts.

9. THE LONDON JUNTA

1. Enrique Moradiellos, *Neutralidad benévola*, pp. 189 ff. This is the only account I know of that gives any detailed information about the Junta Nacional in London. For the light it throws on relations between the Spanish Nationalists and the 'Establishment' in Britain, it should be published in English.

2. Salvador de Madariaga, *Españoles de mi tiempo*, pp. 417–26; *The Times* (12 and 15 July 1936).

3. Moradiellos, p. 193.
4. FO 371/20569 W6893; Moradiellos, p. 165.
5. Moradiellos, p. 192. His sources are letters by Oliván and Pedro García-Conde, the embassy counsellor, who himself carried out the transfer before he resigned, rather than sign a declaration of loyalty to the Giral government on 26 July, along with several other officials. The only official at the embassy to remain loyal to the government was the commercial attaché, Daniel Fernández Shaw. In transferring the money, García-Conde was assisted by pro-Nationalist officials at the Agencia del Banco de España.
6. AMAE, Arch. Barcelona, RE 123 c. 4 pl. 2; Moradiellos, pp. 192–5; Jill Edwards, *The British Government and the Spanish Civil War*, p. 19.
7. FO 371/20534 W9295; 20576 W11131; 20582 W14539; Moradiellos, pp. 195 and 207.
8. Interview with McIntosh, Feb 1978.
9. Ibid.
10. FO 371/20526 W7503.
11. McIntosh.
12. *Daily Express* (31 July 1936).
13. FO 371/20525 W7491.
14. *Daily Telegraph* and *Le Figaro* (31 July 1936).
15. FO 371/20573 W9719; copy in PRO, air ministry file (hereafter 'AVIA') 2/1976 f 29a, report by air attaché, Paris, Group Captain Douglas Colyer on the Office Génerale de l'Air (21 Aug 1936).
16. AVIA 2/1976 f 4A.
17. FO 371/20526 W7503.
18. *El Norte de Castilla* (19 Aug 1936). Descriptions of the crash are in the *Daily Telegraph*, *Manchester Guardian* and *New York Times* (17 Aug 1936).
19. FO 371/2033 W9096; *Daily Telegraph* (17 Aug 1936).
20. Ibid.
21. FO 371/20573 W9719; AVIA 2/1976 pt I. f 29a.
22. *Bulletin Fokker* (Dec 1930).

10. 'LITTLE MEN IN BLACK SUITS WITH BAGS OF GOLD'

1. FO 371/20527 W7911.
2. AVIA 2/1976, pt. I, f 26a.
3. Alex Henshaw, *The Flight of the Mew Gull*, p. 101.
4. FO 371/20527 W7911.
5. Mary de Bunsen, *Mount up with Wings*, p. 49.
6. Interview with Mr G. C. Ames at Southend airport, 1984. In 1936–7, as an apprentice just out of school, he was in no position to make any comments about this to his employers.
7. FO 371/20527 W7911.
8. FO 371/20530 W8584.
9. FO 371/20526 W7702. The flying boat was a Savoia-Marchetti S.62, no. S-12 (Howson, p. 269).
10. Howson, pp. 49–51. Histories of all Beechcraft 17s built can be found in Robert T. Smith, *Staggerwing!* The title comes from the fact that the wings of the Beechcraft 17 were staggered backwards, i.e., the upper wing was rearwards of the lower, the reverse of conventional layout, to give the pilot in his cabin a better view.
11. Fundación de Pablo Iglesias, Madrid (hereafter FPI), AJLA 422–12, 11° *Informe*, pp. 82 and 90. AHN, Arch. Araquistaín, 70/91A and 103A.
12. FO 371/ 20576 W10255. For further information about Campbell Black, Cathcart-Jones and other British, Commonwealth and American pilots who took part in the

Spanish Civil War, see Brian Bridgeman's valuable study *The Flyers* and Sterling Seagrave, *Soldiers of Fortune*, one of the Time-Life series The Epic of Flight.

13. *Foreign Relations of the United States*, 1936 vol., pp. 663–6.
14. FO 371/20530 W8630.
15. AMAE, Arch. Barcelona, RE 4 c. 6 pl. 19, ff. 650–60; Gibernau to Alvarez del Vayo, 10 April 1937.
16. Thomas, p. 417, n. 2; Robert Whealey, 'How Franco Financed his War – Reconsidered', in *Journal of Contemporary History*, vol. 12 (1977), p. 146. Further information is in Ramón Garriga, *Las relaciones secretas entre Franco y Hitler.*

11. THE CARAVANSERAI

1. AMAE, Arch. Barcelona, RE 154, c. 33, pl. 3, Tel. B 326, 25 July 1936.
2. Angel Viñas, *El oro de Moscú*, pp. 43–4.
3. Pablo de Azcárate, *Mi embajada en Londres*, p. 21.
4. Dolores Ibarruri, *El único camino*, p. 295.
5. Indalecio Prieto, *Convulsiones de España*, vol. 2, p. 280.
6. FO 371/20437 R2162 summarizes the history and status of the company.
7. David H. Weinburg, *A Community on Trial: The Jews of Paris in the 1930s*, p. 205, n. 7.
8. Viñas, op. cit., p. 217. See Francisco Olaya, *El oro de Negrín*, pp. 371–2, for full text of the contract.
9. AHN, Arch. Araquistaín, L. 31/I, 16 Nov 1936.
10. Ibarruri, ibid.
11. José Fernández Castro, *Alejandro Otero: el médico y el político*, gives an account of Otero's career but says little about his wartime employments.
12. Ian Gibson, *The Assassination of Federico García Lorca*, pp. 110, 217.
13. Olaya, op. cit., p. 47, n. 47, said during an interview on 10 Dec 1973.
14. According to Olaya, p. 42, but I have not seen this title elsewhere.

12. LIEGE

1. *Royal Commission on the Private Manufacture of and Trading in Arms*, minutes in evidence, p. 648, tables B and C.
2. Ibid., p. 501; also Michel Vincour, 'Les exportations belges des armes' in *Revue Belge d'Histoire Contemporaine*, vol. XIII (1987), pt I, pp. 81–123.
3. Vincour, ibid.
4. *Royal Commission*, pp. 495, 502, evidence of Captain Ball.
5. Ibid., p. 494, evidence of Geoffrey Duke Burton, managing director of BSA.
6. Ibid., p. 496, evidence of Captain John Ball.
7. Ibid., p. 489.
8. *Daily Express* (3 June 1936). Also Gene Smith, *The Life and Death of Serge Rubinstein*, Chapters 5 and 6.
9. Howson, pp. 141–2.
10. Joaquín Arraras, *Historia de la cruzada española*, Book XIII, p. 447.
11. There are references to Veltjens's dealings with the Nationalists before the civil war in Angel Viñas, *La Alemania nazi y el 18 de julio* (see index) and José Escobar (Marqués de Valdeiglesias), *Así empezó . . . .* AHN Madrid, Archivo del Presidente del Gobierno, 'Dirección General de Adquisiciones', Legajo 191, Doc. 3: Veltjens's statement of money still owed to him (n.d., but obviously autumn 1938): £46,613 for material delivered to Nationalists before August 1937 and £93,000 thereafter; plus 920,732.50 RM (£79,032) for material supplied to ROWAK. It is interesting that the money is in sterling. For Veltjens in the Netherlands, see Eugene Davidson, *The Trial of the Germans*, pp. 474–5.

12. FO 371/C 6628/202/4. *North China Herald* [Shanghai] (11 Aug 1936), p. 11, has a useful summary of the facts, condensed from Belgian newspapers.

13. *L'Indépendant Belge*, throughout Aug 1936; *The Times* (4, 7, 8, 10, 11 Aug 1936); *Daily Telegraph* (11 Aug 1936).

14. AMAE, Arch. Barcelona, RE 159, c. 1, tel 8 Aug 1936.

15. *The Times* (10 Aug 1936).

16. Ibid., 11 Aug 1936.

17. D. Pastor Petit, *Los dossiers secretos de la guerra civil*, p. 57, quoting a report 'No. 1' dated 20 Feb 1937, which was passed to the Nationalists by the French Deuxième Bureau (secret service), who had received it from British Intelligence. The author signs himself 'V'. This may have been Armande Gavage, who was a source for the British intelligence services MI5 and MI6, since he is scathing about rival arms dealers such as Grimard and Klaguine, who were selling arms to the Republicans, and about the incompetence and alleged corruption of such Spaniards as Otero. Pastor Petit is vague about the document's location, unless he means that it is in the ASHM, Doc. Roja, Armario 5, Legajo 280. These archives have since been microfilmed on to several hundred rolls, each roll containing more than a thousand documents and, there being no itemized index or plain sequence of numbers, individual documents are hard to find. I did not find this one, but it is obviously there somewhere.

18. ASHM, microfilm roll 272, A. 47, L. 74, c. 11. My thanks to Carlos Avila for finding and giving me a copy of this letter and to Rafael Varo for deciphering Dorrién's handwriting.

19. Vincour, p. 90; *The Times* (22, 25 Sept 1936).

20. Ibid., and *The Times* (28 Sept 1936).

21. Arraras, see n. 10.

22. *L'Indépendant Belge* (2 Feb 1938); Vincour, p. 115. The registrations of the Fokkers were PH-AIK, -R and -S. Perel, who will appear again in this narrative, lived at 17 Rafëlplein, Amsterdam.

23. Vincour, ibid.

24. *Archive: Air Britain Civil Aviation Historical Quarterly*, no. 2 (1980), shows that Gavage did not cancel its registration until 1946 and that it consequently must have returned to Belgium shortly after it left on 27 August. *L'Humanité* (28 Aug 1936), supposed Gavage had sold it to the 'Fascists'. R. Danel and J. Cuny, *Les avions Dewoitine*, p. 32. Only seven D.9s were built, six for Yugoslavia and one for Belgium, in 1925. The '304' on its tailfin may have been a construction number.

25. *L'Indépendant Belge* (28 Aug 1936); *Le Journal des Débats* (29 Aug 1936); *Het Laatste Nieuws* (11 Sept, 10 Nov 1936; 2, 27 June 1938); Howson, p. 43. Autrique's own account, 'Beaucoup d'efforts pour rien' is in the French aviation journal *Icare*, no. 118 (Nov 1986).

26. The question of how the Republicans obtained these aircraft was a mystery to aviation historians until the 'Abyssinian connection' was discovered by my colleague James Carmody and published in a letter by the author to *Air Enthusiast Quarterly*, no. 12, in 1980. The story subsequently reappeared, without acknowledgement, in several foreign aeronautical magazines. For the voyages of the *Stanmore*, see *Index of Foreign Office General Correspondence*, 1936 volume, the references being too numerous to cite here. The assertion that the three aircraft, described as 'British' since they were bought in London, were taken to Alicante in two ships, the *Stanmore* and *Stanhope*, appears to be an error. For the Stösser as an aircraft, see William Green, *Warplanes of the Third Reich*, pp. 171–6. For the history of these three in Spain, see Howson, pp. 140–42, and Juan

Maluquer Wahl, *La aviación de Cataluña en los primeros meses de la guerra civil*, pp. 71–2.

27. AHN, Arch. Araq., L. 26, c. 3, Calviño to Araquistaín, 7 Feb 1940.

13. THE CONFIDENTIAL AGENT

1. FO 371/20577 W11778.
2. Enrique Moradiellos, *Neutralidad benévola*, pp. 192–3.
3. FO 371/16887 A1482; 16890 A3237; 16892 A5376.
4. Interview in 1983 with Richard ('Dickie') Metcalfe, who had served in MI5 until *c.* 1932 and again during the Second World War in another branch of the intelligence services as an agent in Portugal and occupied Europe. In 1936 he was running an arms-dealing business in Regent Street in partnership with Alexandr Podsnikov, a White Russian emigré. That such 'bugging' was technically possible in 1936 is shown by the fact that even in 1927 Georgi Chicherin, the Soviet commissar for foreign affairs, complained to a friend that his office, like that of most Soviet government offices, was wired with hidden microphones by the OGPU (Gordon A. Craig and Felix Talbot, *The Diplomats*, 1994 repr., p. 255). My thanks to Rupert Allason MP for putting me in touch with Metcalfe.
5. FO 371/20579 W13078; 20580 W13703; 20584 W15508. Barragán and Pastor also recruited a number of British airmen for the Republican air force. The most accurate account of the adventures of these airmen is in Brian Bridgeman, *The Flyers*, which contains much information not published elsewhere.
6. AVIA 2/1976 pt. 1, ff 26A ff.
7. PRO, air ministry file AIR 40/222; Howson pp. 247–8.
8. *Evening Standard* (13 Aug 1936); *Daily Telegraph* (14 Aug 1936).
9. FO 371/20531 W8570; 20533 W9152.
10. AVIA 2/1976 pt 1, f 9/A.
11. Ibid., ff 45A ff.
12. *The Times* (21 Aug 1936, 31 Dec 1936).
13. AVIA 2/1976, f 8A. Rollason sold -ACHV to Jack Rivers, who sold it to UFT on 25 August. UFT then sold it to the Fédération Populaire des Sports Aéronautiques in Paris along with the other ten aircraft. By October it was among the aircraft listed as belonging to Mrs Victor Bruce and locked under guard in a hangar at Croydon (n. 18 below).
14. AVIA 2/1976 ff 26A, 56A; FO 371/20573 W9719; *Journal des Débats* (29 Aug 1936).
15. FO 371/20573 W10097.
16. Howson, pp. 16, 38, 39.
17. AVIA 2/1976 F 66B, 66C.
18. Mildred Bruce, *Nine Lives Plus*, pp. 164–8. AVIA 2/1976 *passim*. The four aircraft that reached Spain were: Airspeed Envoy IIs G-ADBB (Air Dispatch, on hire from North Eastern Airways) and G-ACVJ (Commercial Air Hire); de Havilland D.H.84 Dragons G-ACKC (Commercial Air Hire) and -DL (Luxury Air Tours). The Envoy G-ADBB went to the Nationalists. Commercial Air Hire (Croydon) and Luxury Air Tours (Worthing) belonged to the Air Dispatch group, of which Sir Maurice Bonham Carter was chairman. North Eastern Airways (NEA), of which Lord Grimthorpe was chairman, was closely associated with the Air Dispatch group, which had at least three NEA aircraft on hire. Lord Grimthorpe was also chairman of the Airspeed company. The aircraft that were held in England were: Airspeed Envoys G-ADAZ and -BZ (both on hire from NEA) and de Havilland Dragons G-ACBW, -EK, -HV, -KB and -KU.
19. AVIA 2/1976 F 143A.

20. Juan Maluquer Wahl, *La aviación de Cataluña en los primeros meses de la guerra civil*, p. 128 and through Chapters III and IV; also Howson, p. 102, and 'Contraband Wings of the Spanish War' in *Air Enthusiast*, no. 10 (July–Sept 1979), p. 47, though some of the information in this article is now out of date.
21. Civil Aviation Authority Library, British Register of Civil Aircraft, 'G-ACVJ'.
22. Nevil Shute, *Slide Rule*, pp. 204–8, 232.
23. AVIA 2/1976 ff 28A, 115A, 128A.
24. Howson, pp. 39–40, 292.
25. Shute, p. 216. This was written in 1952 or thereabouts. However, C. G. Grey told the same story in *The Aeroplane* (19 Aug 1936), but gave the prices as £13,500–£9,000 for the Viceroy and £4,500 for the first prize. With the money Findlay and Waller bought another Envoy for the Schlesinger Trophy. On 1 October Findlay and his radio operator, A. H. Morgan, were killed when it crashed at Abercorn, Northern Rhodesia (now Mbala, Zambia).
26. Angel Viñas, *La Alemania nazi y el 18 de julio*, pp. 122, 140.
27. Enrique Moradiellos, *Neutralidad benévola*, p. 198; FO 371/20532 W9007; 20534 W9295.
28. FO 371/20569 W9209; 20575 W10568; 20577 W11778; AMAE, Arch. Barcelona, RE 123 c. 4 pl. 10. Pastor was officially recalled on 20 Sept 1936 (pencilled note on p. 910 of *Almanach de Gotha, 1936*, a copy previously belonging to the Chatham House Library, now in Westminster Public Library, reference division), but he appears to have left before then.
29. Moradiellos, p. 193 n. 7; Salvador de Madariaga, *Españoles de mi tiempo*, pp. 417–29; Pablo de Azcárate, *Mi embajada en Londres*, pp. 23–4.

14. THE ARMS-PURCHASING COMMISSION

1. Araquistaín's report to Federica Montseny, Republican minister of health, 12 Jan 1937, in Ramón Salas Larrazábal, *La historia del ejército popular de la República*, vol. 3, Doc. 27, p. 2557. Prieto and Negrín had closed down the arms-purchasing commission in Paris on 16 Dec 1936 and Araquistaín was defending the conduct of its members (see below, Chapter 27).
2. Otero was the target of many accusations of incompetence and corruption made by the Anarchists and others throughout the civil war. His honesty was defended by Negrín, Prieto and Zugazagoita, minister of the interior in Negrín's government (see below, Chapter 27).
3. *L'Action Française* (11 Sept 1936), p. 3. The Paris banks used by the Republicans were: Crédit Lyonnais, L. Dreyfus et Cie, Banque de l'Union Parisienne, Banque de Paris et des Pays Bas, Chase National, Barclays Bank, and, from 21 Oct 1936 (after the Soviet intervention had commenced and the decision to ship 510 tons of gold to Russia – see Chapters 17 to 20), the Banque Commerciale de l'Europe du Nord, the Soviet bank in Paris; see Angel Viñas, *El oro Español en la guerra civil*, pp. 90–97.
4. ASHM, microfilm roll 272, A. 47, L. 74, c. 11, Dorrién to Vidarte, 29 Aug 1936.
5. Didier-Bottin Paris street directory, 1937. SOCIMEX (Sociedad Mexicana) was actually the name of the front company channelling arms to Spain via Mexico. The Comisión de Compras itself was, like its predecessors, referred to by several different titles, e.g. Comisión de Compras de Material de Guerra, Comisión de Compras de Armamentos, Comisión Especial de Armamentos, Oficina de Servicios Exteriores de España and, again, Oficina Comercial. International Instituut voor Sociale Geschiedenis, Amsterdam (hereafter 'IISG'), CNT Archive, microfilm no. 327, no. 15, Dossier 68 (1) and (2), files on Otero.
6. D. Pastor Petit, *Los dossiers secretos de la guerra civil*, p. 59, from the report to French Intelligence by 'V' (see above, Chapter 6, n. 7).

7. Angel Viñas, *El oro de Moscú*, p. 218.
8. *Les événements survenus . . .*, no. 2344, 23 July 1947, p. 219 (see Sources: Printed Documents).
9. AMAE, Arch. Barcelona, RE 123 c. 3 pls 5, 6, 8, 13.
10. Information on this is muddled. According to T. Echevarría's report of 7 Sept 1936 (AMAE, Arch. Barcelona, RE 135, c. 5 pl. 3, p. 8), fifty Oerlikon 20 mm cannons had already been delivered by the *Jalisco* and the *Durango* and five or nine more were still in France. According to *L'Action Française* (14 Sept 1936 and 20 Nov 1936, p. 2), the *Jalisco* sailed from Marseille on 29 August, taking mortars and grenades, and made a second journey with a cargo of unspecified arms on 10 September. The Oerlikons may therefore never have been delivered.
11. T. G. Powell, *Mexico and the Spanish Civil War*, p. 71.

15. WARSAW

1. Mr Jerzy Cynk, the historian of Polish aviation, kindly prepared a brief history of SEPEWE for me in 1991. In 1995, in response to my enquiry, Andrjez Suschitz, the archivist at the Polish Institute and Sikorski Museum in Kensington, London, found a file on SEPEWE among those relating to the inquiry into the defeat of Poland in September 1939, conducted by a special committee set up by General Sikorski, the leader of the Polish government in exile. The SEPEWE file contains depositions by twenty-nine officers and others who had either been employed by the SEPEWE company or had been involved in its activities. The depositions were written between March 1940, when the committee was based at the Hotel Regina in Paris, and 1944, when the committee was in London. Hereafter the references are B. I. 113/D/1 to D/29.
2. B. I. 113/D/4 deposition of Major Witold Buchkowski, 9 Nov 1944, p. 4.
3. Ibid., D/27, deposition of Major Jan Zakrzewski, 2nd division (Intelligence) of chiefs-of-staff, Paris, 1 May 1940, p. 1.
4. Ibid., D/1, dep. of Lt.-Col. Wladyslaw Sokołowski, Director of SEPEWE, Paris, 10 March 1940, pp. 16–18.
5. Ibid., D/5, dep. of Wladyslaw Cmela, London, 4 Nov 1942, p. 5; D/19, dep. of Eng.-Col. Stanislaw Witkowski, p. 8; D/26, dep. of Sub-Col. Wladyslaw Ostrowski, London, 4 Sept 1944, pp. 1–2.
6. Ibid., D/26, Sub-Col. Ostrowski, pp. 1–2.
7. Ibid.
8. Ibid., pp. 2–3.
9. Ibid., D/5, Cmela, pp. 4 and 6. Also D/25, Teodor Dzierzgowski, p. 2.
10. William Shirer, *The Collapse of the Third Republic*, p. 313.
11. Marian Zgorniak, 'Wojna domowa w hispanii w oswietleniu polskiego . . .' in *Studia Historyczne*, vol. XXV, 1983, 3 (102), pp. 441–50. The SEPEWE list of shipments in on pp. 451–8. Examples of differences are: according to a list in the AMAE, Arch. Barcelona (RE 135 c. 5 pl. 3 p. 3), the *Azteca* was to embark 25,300 Mauser rifles and 800 machine-guns, whereas, according to the SEPEWE list, she embarked only 19,300 rifles and 200 machine-guns; according to the SEPEWE list, the *Sylvia* carried 5,000 Chauchat machine-rifles with 15 million rounds of ammunition, while, according to a Nationalist report on her capture, there were 4,541 Chauchats and 13,713,720 rounds (articles by Pierre Héricourt in *L'Action Française*, 14 July–1 Sept 1937, reprinted in P. Héricourt, *Arms for Red Spain*, p. 42, and 'A Barrister', *I Accuse France*, p. 27, both pamphlets published by Nationalist supporters in the UK).
12. B.I. 113/D/4, Buchowski, pp. 2–3, and D/5, Dzierzgowski, p. 2.
13. AMAE, Arch. Barcelona, RE 11 c. 44 pl. 11 pp. 540–43, 28 July 1937. This is an offer from SEPEWE to Manuel Martínez Pedroso, Republican chargé, Warsaw,

made through Oscar Ossorio, a Mexican citizen of Polish origin. The offer included a company of sixteen Renault FT-17 tanks, rifle-grenade-launchers, hand-grenades, Vickers, Colt and Lewis machine-guns, Mauser rifles at $45 each (!), twenty P.W.S. aircraft (possibly P.W.S. 16s, twenty of which were sold to Portugal at this time, for there are persistent rumours that a few were intended to be diverted to the Republicans, though I doubt if any were in the event) and, for the first time, the P.Z.L. P.37 Łos bombers. Regarding the low prices on the SEPEWE list, the exception is the FT-17 tank at the absurdly high price of $37,500 each; even on the offer it is only $34,375. A Russian T-26 cost $21,500, and even that was an overcharge.

14. Russian State Military Archives (hereafter RGVA), F. 33987, O. 3, D. 893, L. 1, Uritsky to Voroshilov, 13 Nov 1936. See Sources: Unpublished documents – Russia.

15. RGVA, F. 33983, O. 3, D. 853, L. 43 and 47. A list of material sent by Voroshilov to Stalin, 13 Dec 1936.

16. B. I. 113/D/12, Dep. of Stefan Katelbach, 8 Sept 1944, p. 3. The agents in the affair were Daugs and Erich. Daugs was to move to Finland in 1939. Veltjens was on the board of directors of A. B. Transatlantic, Helsinki (see p. 196).

17. FPI, ALJA 451–15, telegrams from Prague to Paris, Martínez de Aragón to Colonel Matz, Comisión Técnica, 25 March 1938, requesting £10,000 to pay storage fees for three aircraft and 20 million Austrian cartridges on the quay at Gdynia, deliberately held up by the authorities to extort money. There are further examples in the Asúa archives.

18. An advertisement for *Les Etablissements A. Klaguine* S.A.R., 37 Avenue Montaigne, Paris, and 16 rue de Sluse, Liège, states that he had agents in Estonia, Finland, Poland, Latvia, Romania, Yugoslavia, Turkey, Persia, Argentina, Brazil, Colombia, Uruguay, and Central America (*L'Armurier Liègeois*, Jan 1938).

19. Francisco Olaya, *El oro de Negrín*, p. 374; agencies for the cargoes of the *Linghaug*, *Hillfern* and *Saga* taken from a CNT list for which he gives no reference.

20. B.I. 113/D/19, Witkowski, p. 8; D/1, p. 16–17.

21. D/19, p. 8.

22. FPI, ALJA 442–9, *Informe 9*, Section 4, 'Guerra', pp. 1–2, in Asúa's handwriting, not typed. These pages are not in the Arch. Barcelona collection, AMAE, Madrid.

23. D/5, Cmela, p. 5.

24. D/12, Katelbach, p. 20 ('Odpis' 2, p. 4).

16. THE NON-INTERVENTION COMMITTEE

1. Douglas Little, 'Red Scare 1936: Anti-Bolshevism and the Origins of British Non-Intervention in the Spanish Civil War' in *Journal of Contemporary History*, vol. 23 (1988), p. 305; Michael Alpert, *A New International History of the Spanish Civil War*, p. 65; Jill Edwards, *The British Government and the Spanish Civil War*, pp. 29–30.

2. Alpert, op. cit., p. 66. It was entitled *Libro blanco* ('White Book').

3. FO 371/20578 W12363/9549/41, where there is a complete copy of the report, with enclosures.

4. Ibid.

5. FO 371/20585 W15978.

6. Ibid.

7. FO 371/20541 W12873; also AIR 40/219, 1 Oct 1936.

8. FO 371/20578 W12363 and 20579 W12839.

9. *News Chronicle* (1 Sept 1936). There is a fascinating correspondence about this in

FO 371/20539 W11527 and 20542 W13083. The whole series of letters, including one from Professor Lindemann, deserves to be published.

10. FO 371/20580 W13371 and 20581 W14000.
11. FO 371/20583 W14663, quoted by Jill Edwards, p. 133. The Admiralty report is at the same reference, dated 30 Oct 1936.
12. *Daily Herald* (5 Nov 1936); Ivan Maisky, *Spanish Notebooks*, Chapter 6, *passim*.
13. J. F. Coverdale, *Italian Intervention in the Spanish Civil War* (Princeton, 1975), pp. 393, 417.
14. FO 371/21340 W12903, 2 July 1937.
15. *Hansard*, vol. 317, 4 Nov 1936, col. 1923, quoted in Edwards, p. 133.
16. FO 371/20586 W16391, 23 Nov 1936, quoted in Edwards, p. 135.

17. STALIN

1. Documentary film *L'or de Moscú*, written and directed by María-Dolors Genovès, made by TV-3 de Catalunya and broadcast on 27 Feb 1994, opening shots (see also n. 12 below).
2. The literature on this affair is extensive: the recognized authority is Angel Viñas, *El oro español en la guerra civil* (1975) and *El oro de Moscú* (1979). See also Amaro del Rosal, *El oro del Banco de España y la historia de La Vita* (1976), the account of the president of the Syndiate of Bank Employees, who was among those in charge of evacuating the gold from Madrid to Cartagena, and Alexander Orlov, 'How Stalin Filched the Spanish Gold' in *Readers' Digest* (Dec 1966). Orlov, as head of the NKVD in Spain, organized the loading of the gold on to Soviet ships at Cartagena. There is a summary in *Revolution and War in Spain*, ed. Paul Preston (1984): Angel Viñas's essay, 'The Financing of the Spanish Civil War'. See also the discussion in Burnett Bolloten, *The Spanish Civil War* (1991), Chapters 14 and 62, with numerous references to other books and articles.
3. Indalecio Prieto, 'Un desfalco y un estafa' (8 May 1957), reprinted in his *Convulsiones de España*, vol. 3, pp. 143–9, and 'Kremlin prestigitador' (15 May 1957), pp. 151–6 in the same volume.
4. FPI, ALA 100–16, folio 116, letter from José Calviño to Araquistaín, from Weybridge, England, 14 Dec 1954. Araquistaín had apparently written to Calviño on 8 Dec 1954 for any information he might have on the quantities of war material sent by the USSR. Calviño replied that he did not have any:

> I can't say much because we in the commission [the Comisión de Compras, Paris] were never informed about deliveries from Russia. They can't have been all that large because in Spain they were in constant anguish over the shortages of material and financial resources, because, as you know, Negrín administered parsimoniously.

5. This is said at various places in both of Viñas's books and by Bolloten.
6. The mutual suspicions of the democracies and the USSR are graphically described by Sir John Wheeler-Bennett in *Munich: Prologue to Tragedy*, pp. 389–90. For further references in the enormous literature on appeasement in general and in relation to the Spanish Civil War in particular, see Bolloten, Chapters 16, 17 and 62 and their copious source-notes and quotations.
7. Hugh Thomas, *The Spanish Civil War* (Penguin edn, 1975), p. 339.
8. Michael Alpert, *A New International History of the Spanish Civil War*, p. 73.
9. Stephen Kotkin, *Magnetic Mountain*, pp. 227, 508, n. 150.
10. Walter Krivitsky, *I Was Stalin's Agent*, p. 100.
11. Lacalle, pp. 134–9. See also *Bajo la bandera republicana* (Moscow, 1967); Patrick Laureau, 'L'aviation soviétique en Espagne en 1936: l'échelon précurseur' in *Icare*, no. 130, *La guerre d'Espagne, Tome 2*, pp. 33–9.

12. For Orlov see: John Costello, *Deadly Illusions*, a biography; Gordon Brook-Shepherd, *The Storm Petrels* (1977); and Orlov's own *The Secret History of Stalin's Crimes* (1953); as well as the article in n. 2 above. On his role in the Andrés Nin affair and the crushing of the POUM in May 1937, there is a remarkable documentary film, *Operació Nikolai* (TV-3 de Catalunya, 5 Nov 1991), directed by María-Dolors Genovès, who also wrote the script in collaboration with Llibert Ferri.

13. Maxim Litvinov, *Notes for a Journal*, p. 208, quoted in Angel Viñas, *El oro de Moscú*, p. 184, n. 10.

14. Krivitsky, p. 100.

15. Robert Conquest, *The Great Terror: A Reassessment* (1990); for individuals, see his index. Berzin, Orlov and others too appear in Col. I. G. Starinov, *Over the Abyss*, the autobiography of a Soviet officer who led guerrilla operations in Spain and during the Second World War.

16. One letter requests permission to draw 5,620,000 roubles and $274,000 (RGVA, F. 33987 O. 3 D. (illegible) L. 63, Feb 1938). Another is for 2,462,000 roubles and $48,500 (F. 33987 O. 3 D.870 L. 150, 12 Nov 1936). For an explanation of these references, see Sources: Unpublished documents – Russia.

17. Krivitsky, p. 102.

18. The film *L'or de Moscú*, 27' 13". Sra. Genovès has kindly given me the source of this as a note by Voroshilov, 26 Sept 1936, stating that Stalin telephoned at 3.15 p.m. and, besides ordering the *Campeche* to sail, discussed the selling of 80–100 tanks ('Vickers' system, i.e. T-26), which must have all factory identification numbers etc. erased, and the sale via Mexico of 50–60 SB bombers. The reference given by Ribalkin is: Russian Institute of Military History, Ministry of Defence of the Russian Federation, Inventory 6408, p. 1.

19. Letter quoted in Yuri Ribalkin, 'La ayuda militar soviética a la España republicana: cifras y hechos', in *Ejército* (Jan 1992), pp. 44–5.

20. *Argumenty i fakti* (4 April 1996), p. 7, and *El País* (8 April 1996).

21. Félix Gordón Ordás, *Mi política fuera de España*, Appendix, p. 711, telegram 30 Oct 1936.

22. Orlov, 'How Stalin Filched the Russian Gold', in *Reader's Digest* (Dec 1966).

18. 'OPERATION "X"'

1. i) Donald Cameron Watt, 'Soviet Military Aid to the Spanish Republic in the Civil War, 1936–1938' in the *Slavonic Review*, vol. 38, no. 91 (June 1960), includes a list taken from the files of the German embassy at Ankara, Turkey, which has provided the basis for many subsequent estimates. The number of Soviet ships delivering war material from September to December 1936 is given as *twenty-four*.

   ii) José-Luis Alcofar Nassaes, *Los asesores soviéticos en la guerra civil española* (1971); Jesús Salas Larrazábal, *Intervención extranjera en la guerra de España* (1974), pp. 217–21, where the number is given as between twenty and thirty.

   iii) Rafael González Echegaray, *La marina mercante y el tráfico marítimo en la guerra civil* (1977), pp. 275–7, where the number is as high as *thirty-three*.

   iv) Michael Alpert, *La guerra civil española en el mar* (1987), pp. 183–92, and *A New International History of the Spanish Civil War* (1994), p. 76, suggests on the available evidence a figure of twenty-three arms-carrying voyages by Soviet ships before the end of 1936. I should add that, using the same evidence, I was in agreement with Dr Alpert's figure and therefore was extremely surprised at the mere eight revealed by the RGVA list.

2. RGVA, F.33987, O. 3, D. 853, L. 250–52. Efimov to Voroshilov, 29 Dec 1936.

3. RGVA, ibid., D. 832, L. 240; see also Appendix III, *Cabo Palos*, 15 Nov 1936.

4. Alpert, *La guerra civil en el mar*, p. 187 and n. 39, citing N. Kuznetsov, *Nakanune* (1960), p. 297, and R. Herrick, *Soviet Naval Strategy: Fifty Years of Theory and Practice* (1968), p. 25.

5. Edwin P. Harnack, *All about Ships and Shipping* (Faber and Faber, 1935), p. 109.

6. Although I do not have the page listing the equipment, fuel, spares, etc. to go with the SBs, I do have pages for the R-5sss, R-Z and I-16 aircraft. The SB was a twin-engined machine and much larger and I have therefore increased the quantities proportionately. They may still be too low, for an air regiment of R-Z Natachas required 300 tons of petrol, for example, to be delivered with the aircraft for immediate use. The references are: I-16 – F. 33987, O. 3, D. 832, L. 182; R5-sss – L. 184; R-Z – L. 183.

7. RGVA, F. 33987, O. 3, D. 893, L. 231, p. 2, Uritsky to Voroshilov, 3 May 1937.

8. *Soviet Shipping in the Spanish Civil War*, (Research Program on the USSR, mimeographed series no. 59, 1954), pp. 13–18. Also F. and S. Moreno de Regua, *La guerra en el mar* (1959), p. 129; González Echegaray, op. cit., p. 276, and Alpert, op. cit., pp. 195–6.

9. *International Solidarity with the Spanish Republic* (1974), pp. 302, 312.

10. RGVA, F. 35082, o. 1, D. 18, L. 49.

11. *Soviet Shipping in the Spanish Civil War*, passim, and Ribalkin in *Ejército* (Jan 1992), pp. 47–8.

12. Louis Fischer, *Men and Politics*, p. 385.

13. *International Solidarity*, pp. 312–13; González Echegaray, pp. 436–7.

19. SOVIET ARMS

1. *New York Times* (21 April 1937), column by Herbert Matthews, the foremost American journalist in Spain, headed 'WAR SHOWS LEAD OF U.S. AIRPLANES' and based on the premise that the Chato (by which he meant the Mosca) was built to the Boeing company's specifications. See also Frank Tinker, *Some Still Live*, pp. 51, 53–4, 61. For further information on these aircraft, see Howson, under the type headings concerned. The most complete history in English of the Tupolev SB series is by William Green, 'SB: The Radical Tupolev' in *Air International* (Jan, Feb and March 1989).

2. Lacalle, p. 26. He returns to this theme on various occasions in his book.

3. RGVA, F. 33987, o. 3, D. 832, L. 240, 'List of Goods sent by 29.10.36'. That these Vetterlis were on the *Campeche* is confirmed by a Republican report reproduced in Ramón Salas, *La historia de ejército popular*, vol. 3, Doc. 28, pp. 2570–71, which alludes to the 13,347 (*sic*) rifles made in Brescia, Italy. That Italian-made Vetterlis were sold to Turkey in the 1870s is in J. Genova, *Armas de guerra* (Manuales Soler, no. 10, 1910), p. 94. That the Vetterlis made in Brescia (others were made in Turin) in 1871 were single-shot was kindly confirmed for me by Ian V. Hogg. See also below, Chapter 21 and n. 1.

4. The cartridges for the 11 mm rifles – 2,489,000 for the Vetterlis and 4,161,000 for the Gras and Gras-Kropotcheks – are on the same list, D. 832, L. 241.

5. Joseph Gurney, *Crusade in Spain*, pp. 77–9, 103, 121.

6. Ibid.

7. RGVA, F. 33987, O. 3, D. 832, L. 240.

8. John Sommerfield, *Volunteer in Spain*, pp. 85–6.

9. Gurney, p. 103.

10. On the *Ain el Turk*, arrived 26 Feb 1938, which brought twenty 76.2 mm anti-aircraft guns, twenty Japanese 107 mm field-guns and fifteen Vickers 115 mm howitzers, with 152,000 shells between them all. How many of each calibre is not recorded.

11. 'udalos napravit...'. The same figures in Table 4 reappear in I. K. Kobylov, *USSR: For Peace against Aggression* (Moscow, 1976).
12. RGVA, F. 33987, O. 3, D. 853, L. 43 and 46.

20. SOVIET PRICES

1. Ramón Salas Larrazábal, *La historia del ejército popular*, vol. 3, p. 2568, 'Informe preliminar sobre el "cálculo del valor de material de guerra aportado por la U.R.S.S."' ('Preminary report on the "calculation of the value of the war material supplied by the USSR"', 27 Jan 1937).
2. RGVA, F. 33987, O. 3, D. 853, L. 43 and 46.
3. William Green, 'SB: The Radical Tupolev', in *Air International* (Jan 1989), pp. 50 ff., gives a full history of the technical and production problems of this machine. See also Howson, p. 277.
4. My thanks to Ian Hogg for these comparative price figures.
5. *Whitaker's Almanack* and *Keesing's Contemporary Archives* (1936–41).
6. Senior Major S. G. Gendin, deputy chief of RU-RKKA (GRU) to Voroshilov, 25 Jan 1938, letter no. 534107, no file reference number visible on photocopy as the left side of the page is bent into the binding. The letter concerns the costs of sending personnel to Spain at the 'official exchange rate of 1 dollar USA to 5 roubles and 30 kopeks', both up to that date and in the coming six months. For Gendin's sinister character as an interrogator and torturer, see Walter Laqueur, *Stalin*, p. 310, and the brutal questioning of L. A. Shatskin in September and October 1936.
7. RGVA, F. 33987, O. 3, D. 853, L. 250–53.
8. RGVA, F. 33987, O. 3, D. 1259, L. 86–95. Ten sheets, of which nos. 87–93 concern aircraft, aviation equipment and spare parts, every item calculated at a different exchange rate. Sheets 94 and 95 list small arms, artillery and ammunition, every item likewise calculated at a different exchange rate.
9. RGVA, F. 33987, O. 3, D. 870, L. 60 (15 Nov 1936), where £15,000 is encircled for alteration; D. 853, L. 48 (13 Dec 1936), where £12,000 is given as the final price; D. 1259, L. 94 (13 Dec 1938), where 40,000 roubles/$12,000 is given as the rouble–dollar exchange, at 3.33 roubles to 1 dollar.
10. The prices of $110,000 for an SB Katiuska and $40,000 for an I-16 Mosca in 1936 are on D. 853, L. 47; but see also Viñas, *El oro de Moscú*, illustration no. 24, listing the ten SBs at $110,000 each, transported by the *Artea Mendi* in May 1937 (see above, p. 134).
11. RGVA, F. 33987, O. 3, D. 870, L. 60–61 (16 Nov 1936), signed by General Efimov.
12. RGVA, F. 33987, O. 3, D. 1195(?), L. 60–62; F. 25873, O. 1, D. 123, L. 24–51.

21. PRAGUE

1. At this period Czechoslovakia produced 30% of the arms exports of the world (see *League of Nations Yearbook of the Trade and Arms and Munitions, 1938*). 'Without arms exports our country could not live a month', Dr P. Cermak, a deputy minister of the ministry of public works and acting chief of police, in conversation with Gaspar Sanz y Tovar, Franco's representative in Prague, 21 June 1938. AMAE, DR R 1047 c. 29 f. 13.
2. Or so believed Lacalle, pp. 108–111. In 1932 Pastor had had to implement Azaña's defence cuts, which included blocking the promotion of sergeant-pilots (as Lacalle then was) to officers. Early in September 1936 Lt.-Col. Hidalgo de Cisneros, the *de facto* chief of the Republican air forces, asked Lacalle his opinion of Lt.-Col. Pastor. Lacalle, whose promotion to lieutenant had been put through only in

August, replied with an expletive. A day or two later, Pastor was sent abroad because, so Lacalle was told, Hidalgo de Cisneros feared that in the present revolutionary situation Pastor might be harmed or murdered by disaffected subordinates. Lacalle bitterly regretted his unjust outburst and could never understand why he was neither punished nor even reprimanded for it.

3. The chapter is based chiefly on Asúa's dispatches (*Informes*) to the Republican foreign ministry: seventy-five from Prague from 14 Oct 1936 to 26 Aug 1938 and one from Geneva on 12 Dec 1938. There are two sets of these, one at the FPI, under 'Archivo de Luis Jiménez de Asúa, Legación de Praga' (ALJA 442–2 to 445–7) and the other at the AMAE, Arch. Barcelona, RE 59–62. Both sets are incomplete but they are often complementary. That at the FPI is fuller and contains besides various telegrams and notes that are important. Since the paginations of the two sets are different, I have given only the *Informe* number. This will not cause the student trouble, for all the information here, except for *Informes* 1–3, comes from the sections 'Guerra' and sub-sections 'Armamentos' and 'Investigaciones', none of which is long, unless otherwise stated.

4. Asúa, *Inf.* 2.

5. Ibid.

6. Ibid.

7. Asúa, *Inf.* 4, 6, 7, 10, 11, 12.

8. Asúa, *Inf.* 8, 10.

9. Asúa, *Inf.* 11, 12.

10. Asúa, *Inf.* 7, 8, 19 and others; the theme recurs often.

11. Asúa, *Inf.* 10.

12. Asúa, *Inf.* 10, 11, 12, 35.

13. Asúa, *Inf.* 12, 13, 14, 15, 16.

14. For Fesdji: Asúa, *Inf.* 10, p. 408; *Inf.* 15, p. 65. For von Lustig: Asúa, *Inf.* 14, 15, 31, 33, 34, 35. For von Lustig and China, see also PRO, FO 371/F2824/4/10.

15. Asúa, *Inf.* 11, 15, 16, 17, 18.

16. Asúa, *Inf.* 31.

17. Asúa, *Inf.* 33, 41.

18. FPI, 2163, AH-63-32, 19 and 21 July 1938, Asúa to Hampl, 19 July 1938, p. 2. AMAE, DR, R 1048, c. 27, Sanz y Tovar to Jordana (Salamanca), 21 July 1937. ASHM, microfilm 23, A. 4, L. 266, c. 11, Nat. Rep. La Paz, Bolivia, to Jordana, 13 Sept 1937.

19. Asúa, *Inf.* 28.

20. AMAE, DR R 1048. c. 27, Prat y Soutzo, at Bucharest, to Jordana, dispatches 10 Aug 1937 to 15 March 1938. In his letter to Hampl (n. 18) Asúa writes that it was the Bolivian ambassador in Paris who informed the Czechoslovakian government that the arms were for Spain. Perhaps Krofta received the information from both sources, for there was a change of government in Bolivia at this time and Añez was among those sacked.

21. ASHM, microfilm 23, A. 4, L. 26, c. 11 – 4/266/11/7/2.

22. Asúa to Hampl (n. 18 above). See also Appendix III.

23. Ibid.

24. Asúa, *Inf.* 10 (p. 418), 13 (p. 65), 76 (p. 265).

25. AMAE, Arch. Barcelona RE 4 c. 3, pl. 4.

26. Asúa, *Inf.* 23 (p. 72).

27. My informant is a Spaniard who, while serving in the Ejército del Aire, was told this by his commanding officer, who had himself, when a young officer, received the order.

28. Asúa's telegrams from Paris ordering the transfer of the archives, dated 7 and 11 September 1938, are in the FPI, file ALJA 451–15, and confirmation that they were

sent in the Soviet diplomatic bag on 15 September is in Asúa, *Inf.* 76, Section 2, pp. 321–2 (FPI set only). The money was brought to the Spanish embassy in Paris and a trunk labelled 'Maria' to the Socialist lawyer and deputy Victoria Kent, also in Paris.

22. 'A PROSPECT OF UNLIMITED OPPORTUNITIES'

1. F. Jay Taylor, *The United States and the Spanish Civil War*, and Richard P. Traina, *American Diplomacy and the Spanish Civil War*, are the main published sources for the next four chapters. All the unpublished documentary materials from the Department of State Records, Washington (hereafter 'DOSR'), were sent to me by Richard Sanders Allen and Dr Richard K. Smith, to whom I am greatly indebted.

2. Although Professor Traina (p. 160) writes that the Mirandas were convicted and imprisoned in May 1936 for having sold arms to Bolivia during the Gran Chaco War, 'The Case for the Miranda Brothers and Zelzer', a 19-page mimeographed statement prepared by their lawyers, Kaufman and Cronan, 30 Broad Street, New York City, probably in 1939 or early 1940, shows that this did not happen until March 1940. My thanks to James Maas, historian of the Brewster Aircraft Company, for hunting this out and to Richard Sanders Allen for sending it to me.

3. Carmen Díaz and J.-A. Silva, *Mi vida con Ramón Franco*, p. 190.

4. Félix Gordón Ordás, *Mi política fuera de España* (hereafter 'Gordón') p. 756, though he says this several times in his dispatches to the Republican government. This is the second volume of his memoirs, at the end of which is a hundred-page appendix devoted to his attempts to buy arms and aircraft for the Republic. He includes numerous telegrams quoted verbatim and this section has been another main source for this book.

5. Ibid., pp. 756–7.

6. Ibid., pp. 693–4.

7. Ibid., p. 693.

8. AMAE, Arch. Barcelona, RE 154 c. 33 pl. 3; RE 156 c. 12; RE 159 c. 1.

9. Julián Zugazagoita, *Madrid, Carranza 20*; the chapter 'Un militante moroso' is a tribute to Agustín Sanz Sainz. See also Lacalle (index).

10. AMAE, Arch. Barcelona, RE 154 c. 12, 22 Aug 1936.

11. Text is in Zugazagoita (n. 9 above), receipt confirmed by RE 159 c. 1, 21 July 1936.

12. RE 159 c. 1, 15 Aug 1936; RE 156 c. 12, 11 Sept 1936.

13. *Air Commerce Bulletin* (15 Oct 1934), 'Air Commerce Regulation 7-E (Amended 1 Oct 34)'. Operating companies were allowed two years' grace to make the change-over, provided flights by single-engined aircraft which started after sunset or before sunrise entailed no stops *en route* and were not over terrain unsuitable for forced landing.

14. IISG, Rudolf Rocker Archive: Memoria no. 82, p. 9, from a report by Major José Melendreras Sierra dated 25 July 1937. The text of the report has since been published in Francisco Olaya, *El oro de Negrín*, Appendix 5, pp. 409–20, with no indication of source. Henceforth, I shall cite the page numbers in Olaya, however, for convenience. The reference to the Vultees is on p. 410. Extracts from the report are in *Negrín y Prieto: culpables de alta traición*, an Anarchist pamphlet published in Buenos Aires after the civil war, of which there is a copy in the IISG Library.

15. For Cyrus Smith, see R. E. G. Davies, *Airlines of the United States since 1914* (index). In a letter to me Richard Allen, the aviation historian, described Smith as 'straight as an arrow'.

16. Princeton University Library, Joseph C. Green Papers, Carton 13, AM 17759, memo. 21 Sept 1936; FO 371/20578 W12088.

17. DOSR 711.00111, Box 3858, *Lic. Babb*, 26 Sept 1936; AMAE, Arch. Barcelona, RE 156 c. 12, 13 Aug 1936; RE 159 c. 1, pl. 3, 13 and 15 Aug 1936.
18. Gordón, p. 694–5. He returned to this subject repeatedly until January 1937.
19. Gordón, p. 694–5.
20. The sources for the rest of this chapter are Angel Viñas, *El oro de Moscú*, pp. 223–7, and Gordón, pp. 709–13.
21. Gordón, p. 711, telegrams to Gordón from Vayo and Negrín, both 30 Oct 1936.
22. Gordón, p. 711, Gordón to Vayo, 30 Nov 1936.
23. Viñas, p. 227.

23. THE MANHATTAN PURCHASES

1. Three of these Mexican officers were General Alfredo Lázaro Alvarez, General Gustavo León and Colonel Rafael Montero. Refs. are DOSR, 711.00111 Armaments Control Purport Book 711.00111/852, and FBI report, SA File 54.31 by Agent Gus T. Jones, 7 March 1938, on aircraft flown illegally to Mexico for shipment to Spain. My thanks to Richard S. Allen for sending me copies of these documents.
2. Howson, p. 220; this Sirius also went to Spain in January 1937.
3. See R. E. G. Davies, *Airlines of Latin America since 1919*, and José Villella Gómez, *Breve historia de la aviación de México* (1971).
4. Princeton University Library, Joseph C. Green Papers, Carton 13, RM 17759; also letter to Secretary of State Cordell Hull, 12 Dec 1936, 'Summation of Cases', 24 May 1938. Ambrose was based at North Beach airport, also known as municipal airport no. 2 and today as La Guardia airport.
5. Hugh Thomas, *The Spanish Civil War*, p. 434; F. Jay Taylor, *The United States and the Spanish Civil War*, p. 71; Gordón, p. 740.
6. Joseph C. Green Papers, 30 Dec 1936; DOSR 711.00111, *Lic. Vimalert Co./46–52*, p. 3; *Lic. Wolf, Rudolf/91*, Edwin Wilson, counsellor of US embassy, Paris, to Cordell Hull, 9 July 1937, p. 2; 711.00111/852/24.229/ F. Tejeda, director of Aeronaves de México.
7. Somebody must have told this later to a reporter from the right-wing New York *American*, which published the story on 2 Jan 1937.
8. FO 371/20577 W11446; 20580 W13702.
9. FO 371/20579 W12959; 20581 W14025.
10. DOSR 711.00111, *Lic. Babb, Charles Harding*, memo. 24 Nov 1936.
11. *Ibid.*, *Lic. Wolf, Rudolf/3*, memo. 1 Dec 1936.
12. *New York Times* (7–11 Oct 1936).
13. *Hearings before the Special Committee of the United States Senate Investigating the Munitions Industry* (Nye Committee hearings), p. 13506.
14. FO 371/21319 W777, report on the 'Wolf Case', 4 Jan 1937.
15. *Los Angeles Times* (11 Dec 1936); New York *World Telegram* (9 Dec 1936); DOSR 711.00111. *Lic. Babb*, Box 3858.

24. 'THESE DEADLY WEAPONS OF WAR'

1. *Washington Post* (30 Dec 1936).
2. New York *American* (2 Jan 1937).
3. Interview with Robert Cuse by Richard K. Smith, Mexico City, 14 Oct 1973. My thanks to Dr Smith for allowing me to use the account of his interview that he sent to Richard S. Allen that same evening.
4. Elizabeth Bentley, *Out of Bondage* (1951), refers to the contempt for Amtorg felt by Jacob Rasin (alias Golos), a Soviet agent in the USA. According to Cuse, ambi-

tious *apparatchiki* of the Golos type were less successful than the easy-going officials of Amtorg.

5. Interview, n. 3 above.
6. Princeton University Library, Joseph C. Green Papers, letter, 27 Nov 1936; DOSR 711.00111. *Lic. Vimalert*/852/134-5, 19 Oct 1936.
7. Gordón, p. 709, 20 Jan 1937. Gordón received a cable from Prieto confirming Cuse's bona fides three weeks too late.
8. New York *American* (2 Jan 1937).
9. Interview.
10. Gordón, p. 701, cable to Prieto 1 Jan 1937.
11. Joseph C. Green Papers, letter, 27 Nov 1936.
12. Ibid.
13. Howson, p. 296, lists the aircraft; see also under relevant type headings: they were the Douglas DC-1 prototype, two Northrop Deltas, one Lockheed Electra, one Fairchild 91 amphibian, six Boeing 247D airliners, seven Vultee V1-As. The Douglas DC-1, the progenitor of all subsequent Douglas transports, including the DC-3 Dakota, was brought from Howard Hughes. One of the Vultees was the famous *Lady Peace*, which had just broken the speed record for the two-way crossing of the North Atlantic.
14. *New York Times* (30 Dec 1936); New York *Sun* (29 Dec 1936); See also Traina, pp. 82 ff.
15. New York *Sun* (29 Dec 1936).
16. DOSR 711.00111, *Lic. Vimalert*, 852.24/178, 30 Dec 1936.
17. New York *Sun* (5 and 6 Jan 1937); see also Richard Sanders Allen, 'The Ship that Ran against Congress' in *Sea History* (Spring 1978), pp. 41–3.
18. New York *Sun* (5 Jan 1937).
19. New York *American* (5 and 6 Jan 1937).
20. Left behind were the six Boeing 247Ds and one old and two new Vultee V1-As. The Boeings had been bought from Pennsylvania Airways. Three were later bought from Cuse by the Spanish Republicans and flown to Mexico in March 1937, but none was shipped to Spain. See Howson, p. 297.
21. Gordón, pp. 744 ff.
22. Juan García Durán, *La guerra civil española: fuentes*, p. 296, quoting a telegram preserved in the archives of the Portuguese foreign ministry.
23. FO 371/21317 W73, cutting from the *Deutsches Diplomatische-politische Korrespondenz.*

25. NINE MILLION DOLLARS

1. Howson, pp. 296–7; see also under aircraft type headings. Dates of arrival are from the FBI (LA Office) Report SA File 54–31, 7 March 1938, by Agent Gus T. Jones. See also Gordón, p. 699.
2. Gordón, pp. 701–2; Melendreras report (Olaya, *El oro de Negrín*, p. 415); Traina, pp. 89–96.
3. Gordón, pp. 701–2.
4. Ibid., pp. 702–4.
5. Gordón, p. 702, see above, Chapter 24, n. 7; Prieto did not reply until 20 Jan 1937. Perhaps Vayo did not pass Gordon's telegram of 1 Jan 1937 on to him.
6. Traina, pp. 89–90, 95–6; *Washington Post* (6 and 8 Jan 1937); *US Foreign Relations, 1937*, vol. 1, p. 565.
7. Gordón, p. 770.
8. Ibid., p. 706.
9. AMAE, DR R 833, Exp. 24, p. 6, Méndez to Negrín, 8 Dec 1936. He mentions a 'mysterious agent with unknown source of funds', who is obviously Cuse.

10. Melendreras report, in Olaya, p. 415. Melendreras, who wrote his report on 25 July 1937, says that he never discovered who Cuse was working for, or his source of finance, and that the arms buying commission in New York was shocked by his action. Gordón felt that Rios too had been taken by surprise, which he could hardly admit without disloyalty to his two aides.

11. The prices are in *La Revista de Aeronáutica* (Sept 1934), p. 494, when the negotiations had begun. They were delayed because the US government would not release the Martin 139W, the B-10 of the USAC, for export until the summer of 1935. The 1935–6 prices are given by Sir Henry Chilton, the British ambassador to Spain, in his dispatch of 7 Feb 1936, FO 371/20558 W1232.

12. *Foreign Relations of the United States, 1936*, vol. 2, p. 475.

13. Melendreras report, in Olaya, pp. 411–2.

14. Gerard Casius, 'Batavia's "Big Sticks"', in *Air Enthusiast*, no. 22 (Aug–Nov 1983), pp. 2–4. The Martins were for the Dutch East Indies Air Force.

15. Information from Richard Sanders Allen.

16. Casius, p. 2. The first contracts were for nineteen aircraft, to the value of $.1.5 million. The first aircraft had been delivered on 2 September.

17. Gordón, pp. 704–5; Melendreras report, in Olaya, pp. 412–13.

18. Gordón, p. 757; Melendreras report, Olaya pp. 417–18. Gordón calls the company 'Gramville-De Leackler', a complicated misunderstanding. Donald DeLackner, the president of the MAC, had been a design consultant to Granville Brothers (Gee-Bee) until it closed in 1934. MAC, however, was little more than a couple of offices in the American Armaments building at 6 E 45th St, NY. None of the 'VP', 'VPO' or 'VPT' (advertised in *Aero Digest*, April 1936) appears to have been built.

19. *Journal of the American Aviation Historical Society*, vol. 26, no. 1 (Spring 1981), p. 93, describes this flight. The MAC HM-2 resembled a scaled-down Bellanca 28/90 (Howson, p. 52).

20. Gordón, p. 757–8. For Seversky aircraft, see 'The Seversky P-35' in *Air Enthusiast*, no. 10 (July–Sept 1979); William Green and Gordon Swanborough, *The Complete Book of Fighters*; for the SEV-3, see C. S. Ackley, 'The Spanish Seversky' in *Journal of the AAHS*, vol. 26, no. 1, pp. 60 ff; Howson, 'A Seversky in the Spanish Civil War', in *Air Enthusiast*, no. 18 (April–July 1982); Howson, *Aircraft of the Spanish Civil War*, pp. 279–81, 297.

21. Gordón, p. 757; Melendreras report, in Olaya, pp. 417–18. Extracts were published in the post-civil war pamphlet *Negrín y Prieto: culpables de alta traición* (Buenos Aires, 1939). See also José Peirats, *Le CNT en la revolución española*, vol. 3 (1971), pp. 204 ff.

22. Some details of the contract are in the IISG, CNT Archives, Microfilm 143, Paquete 60, E 4. When testing an EP-1 (export P-35) in 1939, an RAF pilot judged that it 'would have been pretty well useless in combat' (*Air Enthusiast*, no. 27, March–June 1985, p. 79, letter from Group Captain C. Clarkson). So it proved against the Japanese in 1941, for by then it was completely outdated.

26. BUYING FROM THE ENEMY

1. FO 371/20579 W12685; 20580 W13748; 20582 W14305; 20584 W15497; 20585 W15818. The arms are listed in Olaya, *El oro de Negrín*, p. 373. He gives no source, but it was probably from a report to the CNT by Manuel Mascarell, a CNT delegate to the buying commission in Paris.

2. FO 371, op. cit., n. 1.

3. Albert Meltzer, *The Anarchists in London, 1935–55* (Cienfuegos Press, 1976), pp. 13–14; and *I Couldn't Paint Golden Apples* (AIX Press and Kate Sharpe Library, 1996), pp. 57–8.

4. Walter Krivitsky, *I Was Stalin's Agent* (Right Book Club edn, 1940), p. 105.

5. Nye Committee hearings (see Sources: Printed Documents), vol. 472, pp. 1197–8.
6. AMAE, Arch. Barcelona, RE 133 c. 3, no. 3, p. 1.
7. Gordon Brook-Shepherd, *The Storm Petrels*, pp. 138–45.
8. Appendix II; AMAE, Arch. Barcelona, RE 133 c. 3, no. 1, p. 1, and no. 3, p. 6, for mention of Rosenfeldt.
9. Ibid.
10. AHN, Arch. Araquistaín, 70/24; IISG, Rudolf Rocker Papers, Exp. 26.
11. *El informe del Presidente Aguirre al gobierno de la República* (Bilbao, 1978), Docs. 9–22, pp. 461–75.
12. Ibid. and Sancho de Beurko, *Gudaris*, pp. 142–3.
13. As above, notes 6 and 10, IISG. The report by Araquistaín that is published in Ramón Salas, *La historia del ejército popular*, vol. 3, pp. 2563–7, is briefer and less informative.
14. IISG, Rudolf Rocker Papers, Exp. 26.
15. Olaya, *El oro de Negrín*, p. 155, n. 6, states that the arms were valued at 30 million Ffr. (£294,118, or $1,470,590), plus 30% commission ($441,177) and £75,000 to a colonel who inspected the arms. The commission and 'gratuity' seem very exaggerated.
16. FO 371/21326 W4675, Appendix D.
17. The material unloaded at Cádiz is listed in Pierre Héricourt, *Arms for Red Spain*, pp. 41–2, and 'A Barrister', *I Accuse France*, pp. 26–7. The material from Hamburg can be identified by comparing this list with the SEPEWE list in Appendix II.
18. AHN, Archivo del Presidente del Gobierno, D.G. de Adquisiciones, Leg. 191. An invoice from Veltjens listing payments owed to him by the German government, coming to an outstanding balance of £46,613 for material delivered prior to August 1937 (this balance still in dispute), and 926,732 RM for material sold through ROWAK, making £719,545 in all.
19. FO 371/21395 W9144.
20. Letter, 27 Nov 1996, from Dr Thanasis Sfikas and enclosures.
21. Sfikas, 'Greek Attitudes to the Spanish Civil War' in *Kampos* (Cambridge Papers in Modern Greek, no. 4, 1996, *passim*). Dr Sfikas also kindly sent me a copy of 'Devil Man' by Frank Gervasi, an article about Bodosakis in *Collier's* (8 June 1940).
22. Ibid.
23. FO 371/21344 W15733, pp. 6–9, memorandum by Shuckburg, 16 Aug 1937. My thanks to Dr Sfikas for sending me a copy of this document. There are also some Greek shipments of April 1937 in FO 371/21395 W9144.
24. AMAE, DR R 1047 c. 9, pl. 2, Magaz, 23 July, 10 Aug, 25 Aug 1938.
25. Ibid., Magaz, 10 Aug 1938.
26. Ibid., pl. 3. Quiñones de León, 12 Sept 1938. For the Airspeed Envoys, Hoffmann and the rest see: FO 371/20587, W17248–9; 20589 W18313; Lloyd's List (22 and 24 Jan 1937) (for SS *Cheshire*); Lt.-Col. Juan Ortiz's report in R. Salas, *La historia del ejército popular*, vol. 3, p. 2581, and below, p. 225; Howson, p. 39; William Green, *The Augsburg Eagle* (1987 edn), p. 71, for a photo of the two Envoys in the background behind a line of Messerschmitts in 1940. Further reference to Hoffmann is in David W. Pike, *Les français et la guerre d'Espagne*, p. 409.
27. Spanish Office of Information, Madrid, *Foreign Assistance to the Spanish Reds: The International Brigades* (1948), pp. 38–44.

27. PRIETO

1. Helen Graham, *Socialism and War*, pp. 34–6, but see n. 7 below.
2. Araquistaín's report on the buying commission, see n. 10 below.

3. Ibid., pp. 2560–61.
4. In 1938 the FAI/CNT plenary committees compiled a series of reports on the corruption and incompetence of almost everyone, except themselves, who had been engaged in procuring arms during the civil war, copies of which are in the CNT Archive in Madrid and in the microfilm copies in the IISG, Amsterdam. Extracts are in José Peirats, *La CNT en la revolución española* (Ruedo Iberico, 1971), vol. 2, pp. 108–10, and vol. 3, pp. 204–14, but the earlier Toulouse edition, contains specific accusations excised from the later, probably for fear of libel actions. There is also an Anarchist pamphlet published in Buenos Aires in June 1939, *Negrín y Prieto: culpables de alta traición*, which consists almost entirely of these reports. One of the principal sources of these however, was not an Anarchist but a man who, signing himself 'C', wrote a series of letters to Negrín from Paris through 1937, copies of which can be seen in IISG, the 'Kleine Iberische Archiv no. 5: FAI/Olaya', and there is another complete set in Turin, at the Archivo Centro Studi Piero Gobetti. The Anarchists refer to 'C' as an agent sent by Negrín to Paris to be an informer. Olaya (*El oro de Negrín*, p. 81, n. 45) identifies him, without giving his source, as Celestino Alvarez, a 'well-known militant of the Socialist Party. At the end of the war, he himself was accused of embezzling $1,000 in gold and 200,000 Ffr.' He cannot have been that well known, for he seems to be untraceable in the records of the Spanish Socialist Party.
5. Julián Zugazagoita, *Guerra y vicisitudes de los españoles*, vol. 1, pp. 103–4.
6. The main CNT denunciations of Otero are in the IISG, CNT Archives, FAI-CP, microfilm 226, B. 3. I-a-6; Microfilm 257 and 327. Also Rudolf Rocker Papers, 'Memoria sobre las indústrias de guerra', *Informes*, nos 2, 3, 4 and 5, *passim*. All accuse him of taking huge commissions of up to 20% and living luxuriously and licentiously at public expense, as well as of delaying deliveries of arms while haggling over his profits. In this way, the reports claim, Irún was lost, for example. When I first read these reports, I found them persuasive; now, many years later and after much more research, I treat them very cautiously.
7. Helen Graham, op. cit., pp. 60–61. Dr Graham's book and her essay on Negrín in *The Republic Besieged: Civil War in Spain, 1936–1939* (ed. Paul Preston and Ann L. Mackenzie) are important to students since they produce convincing new evidence to counter the argument that Negrín was merely a Communist puppet, as put forward in great detail by Burnett Bolloten. Nevertheless, and for reasons apparent in my narrative, I cannot agree with what she says about Prieto in the two passages referred to (see n. 1 above).
8. Zugazagoita, op. cit, vol. 1, p. 178.
9. AHN, Arch. Araquistaín, 70/75A.
10. In Ramón Salas Larrazábal, *La historia del ejército popular*, vol. 3, Doc. 27, pp. 2556–63. There are other copies in Arch. Araquistaín, L. 76/259 and 77/159.
11. Angel Viñas, *El oro de Moscú*, p. 231; R. Salas, op. cit., pp. 1141–2. The new commission was not in place when Araquistaín wrote his report on 12 January 1937, but two weeks later a CNT agent in Paris wrote to Mariano Vázquez, the general secretary of the CNT, saying '. . . now that military officers have taken over, the centre is full of shouting, gesticulating, quarrelling men. The other day an officer even fired the pistol of one of his companions . . .' (IISG, CNT-CP, microfilm 153, 63-A7, 27 Jan 1937).
12. Prieto's angry letter to Largo Caballero dated 4 March 1938, is published in *El informe del Presidente Aguirre al gobierno de la República*, 462–6. There is a copy in AHN, Arch. Araquistaín, 76/111.
13. Interview with Federica Montseny, the FAI/CNT leader, in *Tiempo y Historia* (June 1977), quoted in Burnett Bolloten, *The Spanish Civil War*, pp. 202 and 813, n. 45.

14. The whole of this story has been told by Burnett Bolloten in *The Spanish Civil War* and its earlier versions, *The Grand Camouflage* and *The Spanish Revolution*, and summaries can be found in all the general histories of the war. It is still a controversial subject, chiefly because Bolloten carried his arguments, which are by no means proved, too far. Nevertheless, the last version is dramatic and a mine of information not to be found elsewhere.

15. Similarly the literature on the May events in Barcelona is extensive. For British readers, the best known eye-witness account is George Orwell's classic *Homage to Catalonia*. Many readers may have seen, too, Ken Loach's film *Land and Freedom*, which to some extent draws on it. There is a valuable pamphlet, *The May Days in Barcelona, 1937*, published by the (Anarchist) Freedom Press in 1987. For the murder of Andrés Nin, there is an excellent documentary film, *Operació Nikolai*, shown by TV-3 de Catalunya in November 1992 and written and directed by María-Dolors Genovés. See also John Costello and Oleg Tsarev, *Deadly Illusions* (a biography of Orlov).

16. Dominique Grisoni and Giles Hertzog, *Les brigades de la mer*, pp. 53–8, and 86, n. 6.

17. *Il Giornale d'Italia* (11 Feb 1938), names Col. Charles Sweeny as a member of the 'Red' buying commission at 61 Avenue Victor-Emmanuel. See also Major John S. Arvidson, 'A Man For All Wars: Sweeny of the Legion' in *Soldier of Fortune* (May 1982). In 1940 Sweeny organized the Eagle Squadron of American volunteers in the RAF.

18. Grisoni and Hertzog, p. 56. In a letter to Montseny (R. Salas, op. cit., p. 2584), 17 March 1937, Prieto states that he created two organizations: the Soviet 'commercial delegation in Spain'; and that directed by 'the French Socialist deputy Dutilleul, for buying provisions apart from those we could get in Mexico and by some direct contracts'. Emile Dutilleul was not a Socialist but the treasurer to the French Communist Party. This must have been an interim arrangement, for military officers were in charge by the end of January (n. 11 above). Moreover, in May 1937 Araquistaín was replaced as ambassador by Angel Ossorio Gallardo, another who was anti-Communist and indeed, although loyal to the Republic, a monarchist.

19. Indalecio Prieto, *Convulsiones de España*, vol. 2, p. 146.

28. KRIVITSKY AND COMPANY

1. Walter Krivitsky's first writings were in *Sotzialisti cheski Vestnik* [Paris] (13, 18 March 1938); then in the *Saturday Evening Post* [New York] (15, 22, 29 April, 17 June, 4 Nov 1939). These were expanded into his book *In Stalin's Secret Service* (November 1939; published in the UK as *I Was Stalin's Agent*), and reprinted several times by the Right Book Club in 1940 and after. For studies of him, see Paul Wohl, 'Walter Krivitsky: A Study of a Man whose Life was Hidden behind his Political Significance' in *The Commonweal* (28 Feb 1941), shortly after Krivitsky's death in Washington by suicide or murder; Gordon Brook-Shepherd, *The Storm Petrels*; Jean Monds, 'Krivitsky and Stalinism in the Spanish Civil War' in *Critique*, no. 9 (Spring–Summer 1978); also long references in Bolloten, *The Spanish Civil War*, and its previous versions, and numerous references in books on the Spanish Civil War, the Cold War, the Cambridge and Oxford spies, etc.

2. *In Stalin's Secret Service* (Hyperion, Westport, Conn., 1979); the same, ed. William J. Hood (University Publications, Maryland, 1984); *I Was Stalin's Agent*, ed. Mark Almond (Ian Faulkner Publishing, Cambridge, UK, 1992).

3. Krivitksy, p. 104; subsequent citations are from Right Book Club edn, 1940.

4. *Registre du Commerce, 1936* (Paris), no. 203: SFTA; *L'Action Française* (24 Oct 1936).

5. Howson: see Fokker F.IX, F.XII, F.XVIII and F.XX; FO 371/20580 W14277; 20582 W14353.
6. *Registre du Commerce, 1936; L'Annuaire de l'Aéronautique* (1927–9).
7. AVIA 2/1976 f 201C, 201D, Jean Godillot to General Aircraft Ltd, 3 April 1937.
8. *L'Aérophile* (June 1937).
9. Archivo del Ministro del Aire, Villaviciosa de Odón, Exp. 196, ff. 34 and 48; his contract shows that his salary was 8,000 Ffr. (£76, or $300) per month plus 300 Ffr. (£2 13s., or $66.60) per day when travelling.
10. Howson (see index).
11. This account is based on three letters (July–October 1985) from the late Saul Somberg, who was in charge of foreign production at the Fokker factory from 1937 to 1940 and did some research into the affair in the 1970s. The contracts are reproduced in Archivo del Ministro del Aire, Exp. 196, ff. 30–69.
12. Howson, Fokker C.X, D.XXI, Romano R.83, etc. and p. 294.
13. Arch. del Ministro del Aire, Exp. 196, ff. 01–04.
14. ASHM, microfilm 33, A. 4, L. 266 c. 3, item 3. Bastin was then still the director as well of the Belgian aircraft factory LACAB. Zulueta had enquired about reports that the prototype LACAB GR-8, a twin-engined fighter biplane, had been sold to the Republicans: see Howson, p. 299.
15. *L'Intransigeant* (25 Dec 1936).
16. *L'Action Française* (25 Dec 1936); *L'Indépendant* [Brussels] (3 Jan 1937); *Le Journal* (4 Jan 1937); *Corriere de la Sera* (5 Jan 1937); *Gringoire* (Jan 1937, *passim*); all these newspapers (March and early May 1938); Rosenfeldt was freed on bail on 19 March 1937; he and Linder were tried March 1938 and sentenced in May 1938, though I have found no record of her sentence.
17. AMAE, DR R 1047 c. 32 and c. 38.
18. FPI, Arch. Asúa, *Informes* 13°, p. 87; 23°, p. 68; 24°, p. 154; and 44°, pp. 39–40.
19. The fifteen rejected aircraft were Aero A-320s, dating from 1927 and barely usable even as trainers. They appear in a list of material submitted to the Catalan Generalitat by F. F. Guardiola on 29 October 1936 (Spanish Office of Information, *Foreign Assistance to the Spanish Reds: The International Brigades*, 1948, p. 36). A typical denunciation of Pastor is that in José Peirats, *La CNT en la revolución española* (Ruedo Ibérico edn) vol. 3, pp. 207–8, in which he is also accused of rejecting British ex-RAF aircraft. This was probably the Armstrong-Whitworth Atlas affair, an attempted swindle by a group of English crooks (see above pp. 227). The wildest of all is an FAI letter of 23 July 1938, accusing Pastor of having sabotaged the delivery of no fewer than 435 aircraft, including 120 fighters and 80 large bombers, from America, all recently bought and paid for. The source of the information was the private secretary of Alvarez del Vayo, who by then was foreign minister again. The letter is reprinted in D. Pastor Petit, *Los dossiers secretos de la guerra civil* (1978), pp. 208–9. My thanks to Richard S. Allen for sending me a copy of the original letter, which he had received from Carl Geiser, author of *Prisoners of the Good Fight* and a veteran of the American Lincoln Brigade. The trouble with all these CNT denunciations, many of which Olaya quotes uncritically in his *El oro de Negrín*, is that their authors seem to have lacked even the most elementary technical knowledge or sense. How many ships, how many crates, would have been needed to transport so many aircraft across the Atlantic? Yet this nonsense was believed.
20. Howson: see Aero A-101, Avia 51, Letov S 231.
21. Asúa, *Informes* 16°, pp. 71–2; 17°, p. 55; and 18°, p. 60; FO371/21395 W9144.
22. FO 371/21344 W15824 ff. 11–13; 21346 W18712, Appendix D; 21347 W19683; 23605 N 4423, ff. 257–9; *Lloyd's Shipping Index* (30 June 1937); *Air Enthusiast*, no. 18, 'Estonia's Air Force'; Howson, see Bristol Bulldog and Potez 25.

23. FO 371/20575 W10554; 20587 W20381; 21187 R 848; *Les Ailes* (20 Aug 1936) (meeting of Cot and Titulescu); *The Times* (1 Sept 1936) (dismissal of Titulescu); *L'Intransigeant* (2 Sept 1936); Howson, p. 254; AHN, Arch. Araquistaín, 70/38a; FPI, Asúa *Informes* 1°, 2°, 3° and 10°, 'Armamentos' sections, for Lupescu's offer, Dorman etc. Prof. Andrei Oteta (*A Concise History of Romania*, 1985, p. 465) states that 'Romania allowed weapons and arms for the Spanish Republic to pass through Romanian ports'. In fact, none did so.

24. RGVA F 33987 O. 30 D. 893 L. 1–2; ASHM, A. 47 L. 71 c. 1–9, Docs. 1–6 (printed in Ramón Salas, *La historia del ejército popular*, vol. 3, p. 2568).

25. FO 371/20584 W15431; 21341 W13426; AMAE, DR R 1048 c. 39, letters to Salamanca from Bernabé Foca, Nationalist representative in Berne, 17 Feb 1937, p. 3, 12 March 1937, p. 2; *Neue Zürcher Zeitung* (8 July 1937); *Gazette de Lausanne* (9 July 1937); *Thomas Mann Diaries* (A. Deutsch, 1987), p. 178, 23 Oct 1933; information from José-María Carreras; Howson, under types.

26. Krivitsky, pp. 107–111.

27. Elizabeth Poretsky, *Our Own People* (Ann Arbor, University of Michigan Press, 1969), p. 211.

28. Igor Cornelisson: *GPOe oop der Overtoon* (1986?), an account of Soviet secret service activities in the Netherlands during the inter-war years, confirms Pieck as Krivitsky's 'blue-blood' and David A. Hackett, *The Buchenwald Report* (Westview Press, Boulder City, Montana, 1995) refers to his time in Buchenwald. Pieck seems to have been instrumental in discovering components of five French fighters and Hispano engines, destined for the Nationalists and hidden in a Biarritz garage (*The Times*, 27 Dec 1936) and two more in a garage in Bayonne (*Le Temps*, 27 Dec 1936), for Araquistaín noted that the discovery was 'thanks to our painter friend' (AHN, Arch. Araquistaín, 70/94B). Finally, references to Pieck's activities in the UK are in Chapman Pincher, *Too Secret Too Long*, and many other books on the Cambridge spies, Soviet defectors, etc.

29. Argus's material was shipped on the *Linhaug* (Norwegian flag), which is spelt in different documents as *Lenkgam*, *Linchang*, *Lineham*, *Lynkham* and *Lynham*. According to the Russians, the material was bought in France and Switzerland (n. 24 above and Appendix III). However, Foreign Office records (FO 371/20580 W14780 or -84 of 31 Oct 1936 and 20588 W17659 of 9 Dec 1936) and Lloyd's lists of 8 Oct 1936 and 28 Oct 1936 show that on 12 October the *Linhaug* was at Klaipeda (Memel), Lithuania, where she took on the arms from the Estonian ship *Hiiula*, which had sailed from Tallinn on 10 or 12 October. Lloyd's confirms that she sailed from Klaipeda on 20 or 26 October. She delivered her cargo to Cartagena on 9 or 10 November. From there she sailed to Marseille, where she was half-loaded with 'anti-aircraft guns' (probably Oerlikon 20 mm cannons bought in Switzerland), some of which she transhipped to the Greek ship *Carmen* at sea on 11 Dec 1936 (AHN, Arch. Araquistaín 70/47A, 59A, 61A). Afraid to sail to the frontier or Spain, the captain unloaded the cargo at Sète, France (Lloyds' List, 12 Dec 1936) and whether they reached Spain is questionable. From all this, the following may be deduced: the cargoes of three ships from Estonia, Lithuania and Poland – the *Bjornoy* (later, *Reyna*), *Hillfern* and *Linhaug* – were bought by 'Tomson' and 'Argus' (i.e. Rosenfeldt, or Bondarenko, or Boris Linde, or Pieck or whomever) on behalf of Rosenbaum, though the details of the transactions became muddled in the reports of the Gestapo, the Swiss police, the British acting consul at Kaunas, Lithuania, and Nationalist agents in these countries. For instance, the '60,000 rifles' which Rosenbaum was accused of buying were in fact the £60,000 paid for 10,000 Männlichers shipped on the *Hillfern*. Part of the money for the deals, said to £267,000 (FO 371/20580 W14780 or -84), was paid to Lithuania from an Amsterdam bank through a London bank, which suggests

Pieck, who was Dutch as well as Swiss and connected to a spy ring in England. Participating in the loading was Manuel Escudero of the *Silvia* affair, his treachery not yet being suspected. The Russians gave the price of the *Linhaug*'s cargo as £247,922 8s. and included it on the main shipping lists as though all the material had originated in the USSR.

30. The box sizes are in Amaro del Rosal, *El oro del Banco de España y la historia del Vita*, p. 30.

29. NETHER WORLD

1. Enrique Moradiellos, *Neutralidad benévola*, pp. 209–10.
2. *Sunday Dispatch* (23 July 1939). Hervey's articles began on 9 July and continued until 6 August.
3. *Sunday Dispatch* (18 April 1937). Brazil is identified in Eden's statement to the Commons. Godillot's arrival in Helsinki on 24 Feb 1937 is in AMAE, DR R 1047 c. 41, report by José Gómez Acebo, the Nationalist agent in Helsinki.
4. Ibid.
5. *Daily Express* (25 June 1937).
6. *The Times* (1 June 1937).
7. *Sunday Dispatch* (23 July 1937).
8. Gene Smith, *The Life and Death of Serge Rubinstein* (Macfadden Books, NY, 1963), p. 7 and Chapters 5 and 6.
9. FPI, Arch. Asúa, *Informes* 8°, pp. 2–3, and 9°, pp. 1–2.
10. AMAE, Arch. Barcelona, RE 38 c. 75 pl. 1 f. 508, 21 Dec 1936.
11. Asúa, *Informe* 10°, p. 409; 11°, p. 83; 33°, p. 15.
12. FO 371/21348 W20032.
13. Asúa, *Informes* 3°, pp. 14–15; 26°, p. 30.
14. Howson, pp. 161–4; Richard S. Allen, 'Order No. 9063' in *High Flight*, no. 2 (1981); William Green, 'A Grumman by Any Other Name' in *Air Enthusiast*, no. 9.
15. R. S. Allen, p. 154. At the end of 1938 Ambrose sued Canadian Car and Foundry on the grounds that he still had commission rights on the company's foreign sales.
16. Spanish Office of Information, Madrid, *Foreign Assistance to the Spanish Reds: The International Brigades* (1948), pp. 40–44.
17. Victor Churchill, *All My Sins Remembered* (1964).
18. S. J. Noel-Brown: 'The Red Cross Double-Crossed' in *Aviation News Magazine (UK)*, vol. 13, no. 1 (1–14 June 1984), pp. 30–32.
19. AMAE, DR R 1048 c. 46; Arch. Barcelona, RE 29 c. 149 pl. 1.
20. Grisoni and Hertzog, *Les brigades de la mer*, pp. 44–50, based chiefly on conversations with the Italian Communist Giulio Cerreti.
21. Bandera was frequently denounced in the German, Italian and Spanish Nationalist press.
22. FPI, Arch. Asúa, *Informe* 13°, p. 87.
23. Lynn H. Nicholas, *The Rape of Europa* (Macmillan, 1984), p. 105.
24. Grisoni and Hertzog, pp. 409–11.
25. Conversations with and a letter (15 Feb 1986) from General Jesús Salas Larrazábal; conversations with Colonel José Warleta. Ortiz did in fact inspect these flying schools (ASHM, microfilm 25, A. 3, L. 270 c. 6).
26. Ortiz's report on these affairs, dated March 1937, is printed in Ramón Salas Larrazábal, *La historia del ejército popular*, vol. 3, Doc. 29, pp. 2575–83. It is also in F. Olaya, *El oro de Negrín*, pp. 458–65. Typed copies are in the IISG, FAI/CNT Archives (microfilmed) and the Rudolf Rocker Papers, 'Memorias de industrias de guerra', Doc. 55, *Informe* 7.

27. A photograph of Prieto's letters (19 Feb 1937) is in José Bertrán y Musitú, *Las experiencias del SIFNE* (Madrid 1940), pp. 90–91.
28. See n. 33 below.
29. FO 371/22637 W2526, pp. 268–76.
30. Gordon Brook-Shepherd, *The Storm Petrels*, p. 149; Pavel Sudoplatov, *Special Tasks*, pp. 48 and 244, n.
31. Howson, p. 89; *Daily Sketch* (3 Jan 1937). For Abridge Flying Club and goings-on at West Malling, see also AVIA 2/1976 f 224 ff.
32. C. David Heymann, *Poor Little Rich Girl: The Life and Legend of Barbara Hutton* (1985), pp. 257–8. According to Prat y Soutzo, the Nationalist agent in Bucharest, another of the 'fences' was the Romanian consul in Antwerp, Henry Untermans, who bought, through agents named as Alexander Walter and Munchinsky, Polish Mausers, French field-guns and German and French ammunition with money raised by the sale of jewellery (AMAE, R 1047 c. 29, 22 March 1937, and R 1048 c. 29, 22 April 1937). The deal fell through when Prat y Soutzo reported it to the authorities and the men were arrested; see *Le Moment* [Bucharest] (23 April 1937).
33. AHN, Arch. Araquistaín, L. 70/20. The report is the last of three in a file on the Rada affair and seems to have been written for Negrín. It is dated 24 Nov 1937 and is a carbon copy.
34. If Metziat was 'an agent for the English', he may have been the 'Agente V.' who wrote the scurrilous report printed in D. Pastor Petit, *Los dossiers secretos de la guerra civil*, pp. 57–61, which was said to have been given to the Deuxième Bureau by someone in Paris working for the British intelligence service (see n. 17 to Chapter 12 above, p. 316).
35. Umberto Tommasini, *L'anarchico trestino* (Milan, 1984), especially the introductory notes by Claudio Venza. My thanks to Stuart Christie and *Arguments and Facts International* for sending me notes on the persons named in the report: A. Cimadori, G. Fontana, Giobbe Giopp and Gino Bibbi. See also Franco Fucci, *Ali contra Mussolini* (Milan, 1978), pp. 234–54, and index.
36. Bristol, letter 30 April 1980; conversations with Oloff de Wet, 1972.
37. FO 371/21340 W12893.
38. ASHM, A. 55 L. 518, c. 4, Doc. 3, (receipts for purchases in Paris, 3 April 1938–18 Jan 1939) notes wagonloads of rubbish instead of guns and ammunition for the torpedo boats.
39. *Gringoire* (17 June 1938), p. 3.
40. *Negrín y Prieto: culpables de alta traición* (Buenos Aires, June 1939), pp. 59–60: the affair as the Anarchists understood it, under the heading 'Una acción monstruosa'.
41. *Daily Mail* (2 Nov 1938); *The Times* (2, 9 and 16 Nov 1938).

30. BLOCKADE

1. FO 371/21330W 6720.
2. These are too numerous to list in full, but many can be found in FO 371/21395, throughout the whole box.
3. Again, dozens of examples can be found in *Hansard*: for instance, 12 April 1937 (Lord Cranborne), 5 July 1937 (Eden), 23 March 1938 (R. A. Butler).
4. FO 371/21395 W8465.
5. FO 371/21335 W10771; 21339 W12727.
6. The unravelling of the Romano deals is described by Lt.-Col. Angel Pastor Velasco in a letter to the legal counsellor at the Spanish embassy in Paris, 11 Nov 1937. *L'Action Française* somehow obtained a copy and published it on 10 March 1938, under the heading 'Les gangsters de l'aviation rouge à Paris'.

7. ASHM, microfilm 23, A. 4, L. 266 c. 11, item 21 July 1937, conversation reported by Outrata to Sanz y Tovar, Franco's agent in Prague.

8. Dominique Grisoni and Gilles Hertzog, *Les brigades de la mer*, Chapters II to IV, drawing heavily on interviews with Giulio Cerreti and his book *A l'hombre des deux Ts'*, pp. 163 ff.

9. FO 371/21344 W15733, memo by Evelyn Shuckburgh, 16 Aug 1937, names the ships as the *Kimon* (1,200 GR), the *Kimon* (a different ship of only 454 tons net), the *Naukratoussa* (yet another ex-*Stanmore* bought from Billmeir), the *Titan* (ex-*Morna*), the *Villamanrique*, the *Melitos Venetsianos* and the Panamanian ship *Carmen*.

10. Gordón, pp. 740 ff. The FBI report is at 'FBI Los Angeles Office SA File 54–31. Report by Agent Gus T. Jones, 7 March 1938'. My thanks to Richard S. Allen for sending me a copy.

11. Gordón, p. 759.

12. Ibid. p. 740.

13. ASHM, microfilm 23, A. 4, L. 266, c. 4. Report by Juan de Cárdenas, the Nationalist agent in New York, 8 Jan 1938; Gordón, pp. 752–3.

14. Artillery Colonel Alfonso Barra, 'Información y recuperación de material de guerra' in *Ejército* [Madrid], no. 5 (June 1940), p. 4.

31. 'THIS QUESTION IS NO LONGER IMPORTANT.'

1. *Foreign Relations of the United States, 1938*, vol. 1, pp. 192–3.

2. David Wingeate Pike, *Les Français et la guerre d'Espagne*, p. 311; Thomas, p. 823.

3. AMAE, DR R 1047 c. 46, note of 28 April 1938; Grisoni and Hertzog, pp. 166–73, where the authors describe the arrival of the *Winnipeg* at Bordeaux on 26 July 1938 and how her huge cargo of arms, tanks and I-16 Mosca aircraft were carried by a convoy of forty-two lorries to the Spanish frontier. According to the RGVA list, however the *Winnipeg* carried no arms or tanks, only the aircraft.

4. RGVA: F 33987, O. 3, D. 1149, L. 166–7.

5. Angel Viñas, 'The Financing of the Spanish Civil War', in *Revolution and War in Spain, 1931–1939*, ed. Paul Preston (1984), p. 272; Burnett Bolloten, *The Spanish Civil War*, pp. 674–6.

6. Ignacio Hidalgo de Cisneros, *Cambio de rumbo* (Bucharest, 1964), vol. 2, p. 242.

7. RGVA; the file and document numbers at the top right of the photocopy are illegible, but are probably F. 33987, O. 3, D.1259.

8. *The Times of Malta* (21 Nov 1938).

9. RGVA: ibid., n. 7 above.

10. Hidalgo de Cisneros, p. 247.

11. Ibid., p. 247.

12. RGVA: F. 33987, O. 3, D. 1259, L. 83–95 (14 sheets). The figures have already been discussed in Chapter 20.

13. Lacalle, p. 498. For the material left in Spain and that sent back to Russia, see Appendix III. The references are RGVA: F. 33987, O. 3, D. 1259, L. 7–15 (10 sheets).

14. Thomas, p. 880.

15. Again, no reference visible on the photocopy.

16. Lacalle, p. 428; Francisco Tarazona, *Yo fui piloto de caza rojo* (Madrid, 1974), pp. 278–9.

32. CONCLUSIONS

1. To Mrs Paul Pfeiffer, 6 Feb 1939, in Carlos Baker, *Ernest Hemingway: Selected Letters*, p. 467.

2. 'From the Editor's Cockpit', *Popular Flying* (March 1939). It is partly reprinted in Peter Beresford and Piers Williams, *By Jove, Biggles!* (1981), pp. 156–7, and wholly reprinted in *Spanish Front: Writers on the Civil War*, ed. Valentine Cunningham (OUP, 1986), pp. 76–7.

3. Robert Skidelsky, 'Going to War with Germany: Between Revisionism and Orthodoxy', in *Encounter* (July 1972), pp. 56–65.

4. Although I saw this programme, I cannot now remember its name or exact date, but I believe it was one of the BBC *Panorama* weekly series.

5. The documentary was broadcast as a major series by Granada TV in 1982. Home's words are quoted in the book of the series by David Mitchell, *The Spanish Civil War* (1982), p. 69.

6. House of Commons debate, 29 April 1993.

7. *Annual Statement of the Trade of the United Kingdom with the British Commonwealth and Foreign Countries: 1939 compared with the Years 1935–1938*, 4 vols, (HMSO, 1940); *Annual Abstract of Statistics, no. 84, 1935–1946* (HMSO, 1948); *League of Nations Statistical Yearbook of the Trade in Arms and Ammunition, 1938*.

8. Nye Committee hearings (see Sources: Printed Documents), vol. 465, pp. 613–16.

9. Lord Halifax, *Fullness of Days* (1972), p. 192.

10. The most influential works, in that they are the most frequently cited as authoritative, are those by General Ramón Salas Larrazábal and his younger brother General Jesús Salas Larrazábal, e.g., Ramón Salas, *Historia del ejército popular de la República* (4 vols., 1973), *Los datos exactos de la guerra civil* (1980) and numerous articles in books and magazines; Jesús Salas, *La intervención extranjera en la guerra de España* (1974); but see also *Guernica* (1987), the latter's *Aviones militares de España*, co-authored by his brother Ramón (1989), his essay 'Influencia de le aviación y las aportaciones materiales en la guerra de España' in *La guerra y la paz: cincuenta años después* (1990), Chapter 21, and many articles on the same theme in Journals, including *Aéroplano*, *Avión Revue Internacional* and the government-published *Revista de Aeronáutica y Astronáutica*. Other Spanish authors whose writings have propounded the same case include Ricardo de la Cierva, José-Luis Alcofar Nassaes, R. Hidalgo Salazar, Emilio Herrera and José Luis Infiesta Pérez, whose article in *Ejército* (November 1992) on Soviet artillery in the Spanish war has been referred to in my narrative. The earliest book that I know of is Miguel Sanchís, *Alas rojas sobre España* (1956).

11. Paul Johnson, *Modern Times: A History of the World from the 1920s to the 1990s* (1991), pp. 329–30 (originally published in 1983 as *A History of the Modern World*).

In a letter (19 May 1999) received as the book was going to press, Robert R. Wolf, Rudolph Wolf's son, provided the following new information:

p. 175, 177: By December 1936, Rudolph Wolf and his family were living in New Rochelle, New York. He did not own a Manhattan apartment, but dined at home every evening. Nor did Rudolph Wolf die in the street, but at his home in New Rochelle. At the time of his death, Rudolf Wolf, Inc., was an existing entity. Janet Wolf had acted as Director and Secretary of the corporation. At a meeting on 8 December 1936 Janet was elected President and authorized to apply to the Secretary of State for registration as an exporter of arms and to apply for an export license to replace the license previously granted for the export of certain airplanes.

p. 224: Daniel Wolf was in Brussels on the night of the invasion and escaped to England. He made his way to Lisbon and arrived in New York via the Pan American clipper in late August or early September 1940. He established a residence on Central Park West in New York City, attended by two Viennese émigré heart specialists and a cosmopolitan crowd of associates. He died in spring 1944. His wife and daughters, who did not escape from Holland, survived the war. Marcel Wolf was married to a Christian (also Austrian). He and his wife survived the war in the Netherlands.

Sources

UNPUBLISHED DOCUMENTS

Britain

Public Record Office, Kew
Foreign Office general correspondence (FO 371 series) for the years 1935–9. The files consulted are cited in the respective notes. There is a published annual index of all the correspondence that was originally in the files. I found that about 70% of the material in the index that I wanted to see was not in the files, having been 'weeded' or being still restricted. If, as is argued, much had to be sacrificed for lack of space, why are so many duplicate and triplicate copies of unimportant papers, such as Non-Intervention Committee proposals for restrictions on aircraft fuel and other suggestions which were never adopted or even taken seriously at the time, carefully preserved in box after box, when so much material that would have helped historians to discover what was really going on has been destroyed?

Air ministry files: AIR 2/3261 (Wing Commander Goddard's report on his tour of the Republican air force, March 1938); AIR 2/3289 (Wing Commander Colyer's report on his tour of the Nationalist air force, May 1938); AIR 40/222 (Air staff notes on the early weeks of the war); AVIA 2/1976 (Two files on British aircraft sold or intended to be sold to Spain).

Civil Aviation Authority Records
Registers of British Aircraft. Certificate of Airworthiness and export licence lists, 1930–36. CAA Gazeteer, 'Spain 1939–1951'.

The Polish Institute and Sikorski Museum Archive
B. I. 115 (the SEPEWE file) and A. I. 2/1 to 2/3 (Reports of Major Kedzior, the Polish military attaché, Lisbon).

France

Archives Départementales de la Haute-Garonne, Toulouse
Liasses 1912/55, 1912/60 and 1960/9.

Archives du Ministère de l'Air
Civil aircraft registrations and histories (relevant information sent).

Archives du Service Historique de l'Armée de l'Air (ASHAA)
Lt.-Col. Victor Veniel's testimonies, 1936 and 1973 (copies kindly given to me by Professor Walter Langlois; no document numbers visible).

Archives du Service Historique de l'Armée de Terre (ASHAT)
Liasse C. 129.c, 10 June 1939, report on small arms surrendered by Republican troops in France, February 1939.

The Netherlands

International Instituut voor Sociale Geschiedenis (International Institute of Social History), Amsterdam (IISG)
Microfilms of FAI/CNT Archives.
Rudolf Rocker Archive.
Kleine Iberische Archiv no. 5 – FAI/Olaya.

Private correspondence relating to records of the Fokker aircraft company, with Saul Somberg, who was head of export production, 1937–40.

Russia

About 200 photocopies of documents, 1936–9 most in the Russian State Military Archive (RGVA), kindly given to me by TV-3 de Catalunya (see Acknowledgements). Those for 1938 appear to have been typed at a later date, possibly in the 1970s, when the Academy of Sciences and the Institute of Military History of the USSR were both producing publications on the Spanish Civil War. There are also some pages compiled by Lt.-Col. Yuri Ribalkin, which I have not used in this book.

Spain

Archivo Histórico Nacional, Madrid (AHN)
Archivo de Araquistaín, Legajos 23–78. There is a printed catalogue of these papers.
Archivo del Presidente del Gobierno, Dirección General de Adquisiciones, Legajos 34, 42, 43 and 167.

Archivo del Ministerio de Asuntos Exteriores, Madrid (AMAE)
Archivo de Barcelona (Republican documents). There is a printed index of these and a large two-volume typed index in the Archive Office.
   Nationalist documents: DR (Documentación Roja) – R 883, E. 24: letters to Negrín from Araquistaín, Manuel de Irujo, Rafael Méndez and others.
   R 1047 and R 1048, Nationalist reports on and estimates of war material being purchased by the Republicans in or via thirty-six different countries. Here and there are a few captured Republican documents, such as intercepted telegrams.

Archivo del Servicio Histórico Militar, Madrid (ASHM)
The relevant papers are now on Microfilm and individual documents extremely difficult to find, there being, at least in 1991–2, no systematic index. There are some old bound volumes of typed indexes, but these are of little help since the items are not in any numerical order against the microfilm numbers written in ink beside them. Microfilms (Rollos) 23–6 contain records, several thousand to each roll, complementary to those in the AMAE, R 1047 and R 1048, and should be studied in conjunction with them. Together, the two sets reveal some very interesting stories.

Archivo del Ministerio del Aire, Villaviciosa de Odón
Expediente 196 contains the information collected in Paris by the Nationalist officer Captain Enrique del Castillo between March and May 1939. The papers had apparently been passed to him by a former member of the Comisión Técnica who had changed sides at the last minute. The *Expediente* includes a list of payments made to companies and intermediaries in Europe and the United States for aviation material between January 1937 and 24 January 1939, a list of aircraft and parts delivered, a report on SFTA and the contracts with Koolhoven and Fokker. The lists are not complete or always accurate.

Exp. 3,382 contains contracts for Potez 54s, Amiot 143s, Dewoitine D.510s and Blériot SPAD 510s signed by Félix Merodio of the Comisión Técnica and Rousso Nessim, July 1937. In the end, only four Potez 54s were bought (see Appendix I).

Exp. 8348/26 contains detailed lists of Republican aircraft and aviation material recovered in Spain by the Nationalists at the end of the war.

Fundación de Pablo Iglesias, Madrid (FPI)
The archive of the PSOE (Spanish Socialist Party). The most important documents for this book were in the Archivo de Luis Jiménez de Asúa, Embajada en Praga, 76 *informes* (dispatches) from ALJA 441–1 (15 Oct 1936) to ALJA 448–2 (11 Dec 1938, written in Geneva). *Informes* 7 to 10 are hand-written and my thanks are due to Rafael Varo for deciphering them and typing them out for me. Also used were files AH 70–44, a report on the finances of the Spanish embassy, Paris; 70–75, a report on finances and a contract for arms signed in Prague, April 1937, which came to nothing; 72–2, Socialist Party reports on the staffing of the Paris embassy and characters and shortcomings of individual persons, November 1937; AH 63–32, Exp. 2163, Asúa's letter to Antonin Hampl, the Czech Social Democrat leader, 21 July 1938 (see above, p. 161). There is an incomplete set of Asúa's dispatches in the AMAE, Archivo de Barcelona, RE 59 to RE 64 (twelve reports and most of the enclosures are missing). In Chapter 21 I suggest that a complete set of Asúa's 'Archivo secreto', with all the arms contracts and details of payments, bribes, etc., may still be in Moscow and that a search be made for it. Meanwhile, even as it stands, the Asúa archive is a mine of information for students of European history between the wars.

USA

Department of State Records (DOSR), National Archives, Washington DC
711.00111 series

Library of Congress, Washington DC
Cordell Hull Papers, 'The Morgan-Green report'

FBI Records Office, Washington DC
FBI Report SA File 54-31, on American aircraft that had been bought by Gordón Ordás and had reached Mexico.

Princeton University Library, Princeton
Joseph C. Green Papers

All copies and summaries of US documents were kindly sent to me by Richard Sanders Allen and Richard K. Smith.

PRINTED DOCUMENTS

Documents Diplomatiques Français (DDF), Series II, vols. 3 and 4.

Documents on German Foreign Policy, Series D, vol. 3.

Les événements survenus . . . (Rapport fait au nom de la commission parliamentaire chargé d'enquêter sur les événements survenus en France, 1933–1945: les témoignages), vol. 1, no. 2344, pp. 215–29, 'Audition de M. Léon Blum', 23 July 1947. Should anyone wishing to consult this work encounter difficulties, its shelf mark in the British Library is S.E. 5/4.

Foreign Relations of the United States, vols. 1936–8.

Hearings before the Special Committee of the United States Senate Investigating the Munitions Industry, US Senate, 74th Congress, 1934–5 [Nye Committee hearings]. There is a microfiche of the whole twelve volumes in the British Library, Official Publications Room, at SPR MIC c. 11.

Royal Commission on the Private Manufacture of and Trading in Arms (1935–6): pt 1, *The Report*; pt 2, *Minutes in Evidence.*

El informe del President Aguirre al gobierno de la República, with prologue and notes by Sancho de Beurko (1978).

Mexico y la república española: antólogía de documentos, 1931–1977 (Mexico, 1978).

Juan García Duran's *La guerra civil española: fuentes* (Barcelona, 1985) is a useful guide to Spanish Civil War archive materials all over the world, according to their accessibility in the early 1980s.

PUBLISHED WORKS

Since no one has seriously tackled the subject of this book before, there is little that can be done here to provide a bibliography of published works. Like everyone else, I have depended on the general and political histories of the Spanish Civil War – such as those by Hugh Thomas, Sir Raymond Carr, Gabriel Jackson, Broué and Timme, Paul Preston, David Mitchell, Ronald Fraser, Burnett Bolloten and many others (to mention only those in English) – that are well known and themselves contain admirable bibliographies. They are already cited in the notes, as are those of authors with whom I take issue (e.g., see above, Chapter 32, n. 10).

For information on the technicalities of armaments I have depended firstly on Ian V. Hogg, whose many reference books on the subject are available in most good libraries or are still in print. I am also indebted to him, as I have said elsewhere, for the copious data, corrections and identifications of weapons in photographs that he has sent to me by letter.

Books by other authors, past and present, that have been particularly valuable include: Col. H. A. Bethell's *Modern Guns and Gunnery* (1910); Professor Franz Kosar's *Light Field Guns* (1974) [unfortunately Professor Kosar's other handbooks have not been translated from the German]; W. W. Greener's *The Gun and its Development* (1910); H. B. C. Pollard's *A History of Firearms* (1926); David Nash's *German Artillery, 1914–1918* (1970); the several books by W. H. B. and J. E. Smith on rifles; and P. Chamberlain and T. Gander's *Machine-Guns* and *Anti-Tank Weapons* (both 1974).

In Spanish, especially useful have been: *Nomenclatura, servicio . . . de artillería pesada*, a manual published by the Spanish Dirección General de Campañas in 1930; various instruction booklets printed by the Republican Escuela Popular de Guerra (Valencia) in 1937; *Armas automáticas y fusiles de repetición*, a Nationalist army instruction manual published by the Jefatura de Movilización, Instrucción y Recuperación (Burgos, 1939) [published after the civil war, when the Spanish army took over large numbers of ex-Republican weapons]; B. Barceló Rubio's *El armamento portatil español, 1764–1939* (Madrid, 1976); *Armas de guerra: armas de repetición* (1910) by Lt.-Col. J. Génova é I [one of the Manuales Soler popular in Spain at that time and excellently concise]; *Armas del Museo del Aire*, by Rafael Varo Estacio and others; and, above all, the large illustrated catalogue of the exhibition of captured Republican war material held at the Gran Kursaal salon, San Sebastián, in 1938–9. My thanks to Rafael Varo for providing me with all these.

For France and Belgium I should mention: Stéphane Ferrard, *Les matériels de l'armée de terre à 1946* (2 vols., 1982–4); *L'industrie armurière liègeoise et le banc d'épreuves des armes à feu* (1940) by Lt.-Col. Joseph Fraikin [who examined and tested many captured Republican weapons for the Spanish Nationalists in order to ascertain where they might have come from]; and Michel Vincour, 'Les exportations belges des armes', in *Revue Belge d'Histoire Contemporaine*, vol. XIII, pt 1 (1987). In Czech, of value was *Prùvodce Výstavou – No Pasarán!*, an illustrated catalogue of an exhibition of International Brigade memorabilia and Republican weaponry held in Prague in 1986.

For the Republican army, weaponry and related matters I must mention: Michael Alpert, *El ejército republicano en la guerra civil* (1989); J.-L. Alcofar Nassaes, 'Armas de ambos bandos' in *La Guerra Civil* (no. 10), published by *Historia 16* in 1984; Manuel Tagüeña Lacorte, *Testimonios de dos guerras* (Mexico, 1973); General Vicente Rojo, *Así fue la defensa de Madrid* (1987 edn); Manuel Martínez Blázquez, *I Helped to Build an Army* (London, 1938); Jason Gurney, *Crusade in Spain* (1974); John Sommerfield, *Volunteer in Spain*; Tom Wintringham, *English Captain* (1941); Bill Alexander, *British Volunteers for Liberty* (1982); and, although I dispute a great deal that is in them, Ramón Salas Larrazábal, *La historia del ejército popular de la República* (4 vols., 1973), and *Datos exactos de la guerra civil* (1980).

For the shipping, I chiefly used Michael Alpert, *La guerra civil española en el mar* (1987); R. González Echegaray, *La marina mercante y el tráfico marítimo en la guerra civil* (1987) [strongly pro-Nationalist]; P. M. Heaton, *Welsh Blockade Runners in the Spanish Civil War* (1985); Dominique Grisoni and Gilles Hertzog, *Les brigades de la mer* (1979) [an account of France Navigation, though rather shaky on other aspects of the war]; *Lloyd's Shipping Registers, Shipping Index* and weekly shipping lists and various books on merchant ships and their design etc. published in the UK between *c.* 1900 and *c.* 1950.

With regard to the air war, as the author of *Aircraft of the Spanish Civil War, 1936–1939* (Putnam Aeronautical Books, 1990, in the UK and Smithsonian Institution Press, 1991, in the USA), I can hardly give a just bibliography of published sources, since it would run to several hundred titles, excluding magazines, trade journals and other ephemera. They include, however: many of the Putnam series of reference books; the books and articles of William Green; several of the excellent Docavia series of solid monographs published by Larivière in Paris, especially those by Jean Cuny and Raymond Danel; Jean Liron and Patrick Laureau's *L'aviation républicaine espagnole* (though he and I disagree on many details); in the USA, particularly the writings of Richard Sanders Allen, Richard K. Smith and Joseph P. Juptner; in Italian, Angelo Emiliani, *Italiani nell'aviazione repubblicana spagnola* (Florence, 1982) and, with Giuseppe F. Ghergo, *Nei cieli di Spagna* (1986).

Regarding Spanish books, the field has always been led by General Jesús Salas Larrazábal, to whose books and articles I have referred in note 10 of Chapter 32, and I regret to say, since our relationship has always been friendly, that I have to disagree strongly with almost everything he has written about the numbers, types and conditions of the aircraft imported by the Republicans, a fact of which I have already several times made him aware. With regard to memoirs by Republican airmen, by far the best and most valuable is Andrés García Lacalle's *Mitos y verdades* (Oasis, Mexico City, 1973). Despite many faults, for it badly needs editing to cut out repetitions etc., it is one of the most fascinating books on flying in any language and really ought to be translated into English.

The only published works that have referred to arms buying in any detail at all have been by Anarchists: *Negrín y Prieto: culpables de alta traición*, a pamphlet printed in Buenos Aires in June 1939 (there is a copy in the IISG Library, Amsterdam); José Peirats, *La CNT en la revolución española*, of which the first edition, published in Toulouse in 1951, contains allegations against various people that were deleted from the second (1974) edition, published by Ruedo Ibérico in Paris; Francisco Olaya, *La comedia de la no-intervención en la guerra civil española* (1976) and *El oro de Negrín* (1990). I have already commented on these (though Peirats's books are not foolish) in note 4 to Chapter 27 and note 19 to Chapter 28.

With regard to other aspects of the subject of this book, my sources are given in the notes.

Index

344